THE MARTYR AND THE TRAITOR

THE MARTYR AND THE TRAITOR

Nathan Hale, Moses Dunbar, and the
American Revolution

Virginia DeJohn Anderson

OXFORD
UNIVERSITY PRESS

OXFORD

UNIVERSITY PRESS

Oxford University Press is a department of the University of Oxford. It furthers
the University's objective of excellence in research, scholarship, and education
by publishing worldwide. Oxford is a registered trade mark of Oxford University
Press in the UK and certain other countries.

Published in the United States of America by Oxford University Press
198 Madison Avenue, New York, NY 10016, United States of America.

Library of Congress Cataloging-in-Publication Data
Names: Anderson, Virginia DeJohn, author.
Title: The martyr and the traitor : Nathan Hale, Moses Dunbar, and
the American Revolution / Virginia DeJohn Anderson.
Description: New York, NY : Oxford University Press, 2017. |
Includes bibliographical references and index.
Identifiers: LCCN 2016044452 (print) | LCCN 2016049884 (ebook) |
ISBN 9780199916863 (hardcover : alk. paper) | ISBN 9780199916870 (Updf) |
ISBN 9780190658335 (Epub)
Subjects: LCSH: Hale, Nathan, 1755-1776. | Dunbar, Moses, 1746–1777. |
United States—History—Revolution, 1775-1783—Biography. |
Spies—United States—Biography. | American loyalists—United States—Biography. |
Connecticut—History—Revolution, 1775-1783. |
New York (State)—History—Revolution, 1775-1783.
Classification: LCC E280.H2 A76 2017 (print) | LCC E280.H2 (ebook) |
DDC 973.3/850922 [B]—dc23
LC record available at https://lccn.loc.gov/2016044452

1 3 5 7 9 8 6 4 2
Printed by Edwards Brothers Malloy, United States of America

For Sam

CONTENTS

Acknowledgments ix

Prologue: Lives, Interrupted 1

1. Fathers and Sons 7

2. Moses and Phoebe 29

3. Son of Linonia 51

4. The Unhappy Misunderstanding 75

5. More Extensive Public Service 97

6. A Very Genteel Looking Fellow 121

7. The Terrible Crisis of My
    Earthly Fate 150

8. Post Mortem 181

Notes 213
Index 261

ACKNOWLEDGMENTS

EVERY TIME MY FATHER DROVE me from our home to my dormitory at the University of Connecticut, I knew we were getting close when we passed a highway sign marking the exit for the Nathan Hale Homestead. It was at UConn, during my undergraduate studies, where I first learned about Moses Dunbar. Little did I know then that, many years later, I would devote a decade to exploring what the experiences of these two men can tell us about living in the era of the American Revolution.

Along the way, I have received invaluable help from many individuals and organizations, which I am pleased to acknowledge at last. The National Endowment for the Humanities offered crucial financial support, in the forms of a summer stipend that allowed me to begin research and a yearlong fellowship during which I began writing. A Faculty Fellowship and College Scholar Award from the University of Colorado likewise provided the release from teaching essential to the completion of this project.

Staff members at numerous archives supplied timely and gracious assistance. I sincerely thank those who helped me at the Morgan Library, New York Public Library, Connecticut State Library (including Mel E. Smith, Bruce Stark, Allen Ramsey, and Lara Day), the Connecticut Historical Society (especially Barbara Austen and Karen DePauw), Yale University Libraries (Bill Landis, Susan Brady, Joan

Duffy, Martha Smalley, Danielle Reay, and Michael Frost), New London County Historical Society (Kayla Correll), and the William L. Clements Library (Brian Dunnigan, Kevin Graffagnino, Janet Bloom, and especially Barbara DeWolfe, who offered a delightful combination of research assistance, moral support, and jovial hospitality). Thanks also to Michael Dooling of the Mattatuck Historical Society in Waterbury, Beth Shults of the Hamden Historical Society, and Margaret Smith of the Episcopal Diocese of Hartford for help in locating elusive documents. I am also grateful to Mary Beth Baker for sharing her notes on Nathan Hale and Linda Smith for information about Moses Dunbar.

I presented portions of this work at the 2009 annual conference of the Omohundro Institute of Early American History and Culture and at talks sponsored by the Association for the Study of Connecticut History, the History Department at the University of Connecticut, and the McNeil Center for Early American Studies. Audience comments were much appreciated, especially those of Will Tatum and Mitch Fraas in Philadelphia, both of whom helped me sort out some documentary tangles connected to Dunbar.

Mary Cayton, John Grenier, and Jenny Pulsipher read portions of the manuscript and offered valuable and incisive comments. So too did Bruce Steiner, to whom I owe an enormous debt for saving me from error and helping me to understand the distinctive Anglican climate in eighteenth-century Connecticut and its impact on the Dunbar family. Toby Ditz, Bruce Mann, and Dennis Van Gerven readily answered a flurry of questions on all sorts of topics. Two of my graduate students also deserve thanks. Rachel Smith provided timely research assistance. Drew Detch offered a careful reading of one draft chapter, meticulous proofreading, and enjoyable scholarly exchange during our numerous discussions about early American history.

Three scholars read the entire draft with extraordinary care, for which I am extremely grateful. Ed Countryman and an anonymous reviewer provided thoughtful comments that encouraged me to rethink portions of the book. My colleague, Martha Hanna, deserves special recognition not only for reading the entire manuscript as well as countless grant proposals, but also for being in every way a model of scholarly integrity and a cherished friend. Other friends and colleagues—Lil Fenn, Peter Wood, Mark and Sharon Pittenger, Bob Hanna—make Boulder a remarkably congenial place to live and work, offering moral support and, when necessary, food and drink, to sustain our lively community. I am also grateful to Robin Saltonstall and Kathy Silbert for helping me to sustain the energy to complete this project, and to my indefatigable cheerleaders and coffee-drinking comrades, Helen Majzler and Michele Smith.

Lisa Adams, of the Garamond Agency, and my editor Susan Ferber demonstrated extraordinary patience in waiting for this book to reach completion. Both often expressed more faith in the project than I did, and readers should be grateful to Susan for expert editing that made the final product much better than it would otherwise have been. I have also had the good fortune to work with a wonderful team as the book made its way into print: Maya Bringe as production editor, Patterson Lamb as copy editor, and Katherine Ulrich as indexer. Sincere thanks to all.

I deeply regret that two people of crucial importance to this project did not live to see its completion. Gary Dunbar, who contacted me out of the blue when he learned of my research on his ancestor, offered genealogical material and warm encouragement. I wish I could have met him in person and presented him with a copy of the finished product. My debt to Drew Cayton is of much longer standing. A friend for more than thirty years, he supported this project from its inception, offering help in too many ways to count. If I ever grew dispirited about my progress, a conversation with Drew would invariably cheer me up. Although the book is dedicated to someone else dear to me, it is also for Drew.

Like Nathan Hale and Moses Dunbar, who both understood the importance of family ties, I happily acknowledge help supplied by my own kin. Particular thanks go to Tom DeJohn for accompanying me on a hike along the rugged "Mile of Ledges" to Tory Den, and to Marie DeJohn and Matt McKiernan for their unfailing hospitality during my frequent research trips to Connecticut. Many thanks to Suzanne DeJohn for her terrific work on the cover design. Closer to home, Fred Anderson offered love and unstinting encouragement as he has since we first embarked on our lives together. The book, however, is dedicated to a younger historian. Sam Anderson's imagination has been captivated by times and places far different from the ones depicted here, but he shares his mother's (and father's) devotion to understanding the past and its profound meaning for the present. It gives me immense pleasure to dedicate this book to the best of all possible sons.

THE MARTYR AND THE TRAITOR

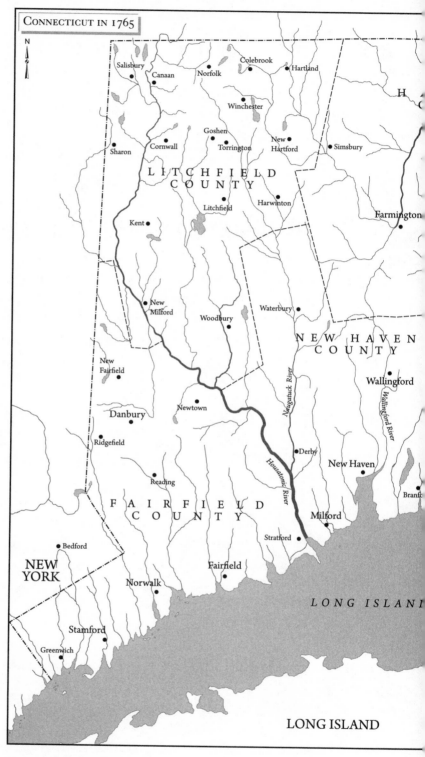

Connecticut in 1765

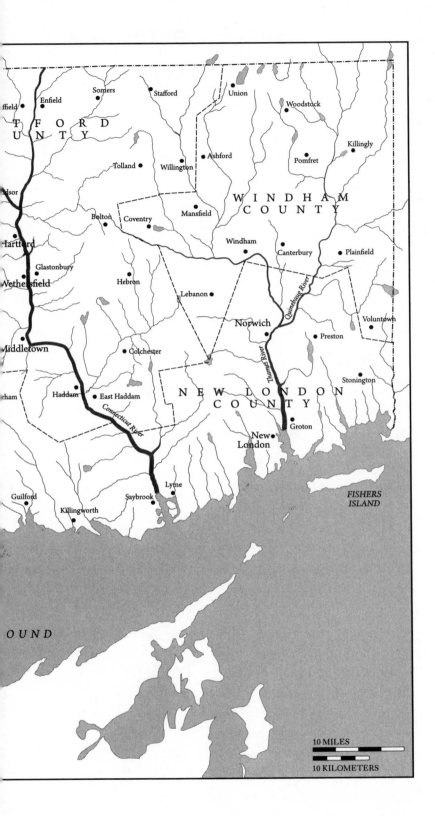

FISHERS
ISLAND

OUND

10 MILES

10 KILOMETERS

PROLOGUE

LIVES, INTERRUPTED

IN THE EIGHTEENTH CENTURY, EXECUTION by hanging was meant to terrify criminals and witnesses alike. Spectators watched with morbid fascination as the malefactor—often, but not always, a man—arrived in a horse-drawn cart. The conveyance stopped at the foot of the gallows, a wooden structure with one or two upright posts and a horizontal beam from which a noose ominously swayed. In his final moments, the doomed individual's arms were bound to prevent him from tugging at the rope around his neck. A hood was placed over his head and the noose was tightened. Then the cart on which he stood was driven away.

The criminal's body dropped, but rarely far enough or fast enough to break his neck and ensure instantaneous death. For up to several minutes, he writhed convulsively, sometimes soiling himself by urinating or defecating. He kicked his legs wildly in a manner often likened to a macabre dance. Witnesses hoped that during these final agonized spasms the condemned had one last chance to repent his evil deeds.[1]

Despite appearances, the dangling criminal had no more time for regret, for he often lost consciousness within seconds. Death generally resulted not from suffocation but from the blockage of blood vessels, which increased intracranial pressure and produced something like a catastrophic stroke. The convulsive movements that horrified witnesses were autonomic reflexes, not evidence of physical distress or spiritual turmoil.[2]

Those spectators and members of the public who read published accounts of executions were instead the ones with time to ponder the meaning of the state's exercise of its power to take life. In colonial Connecticut, such vivid demonstrations of governmental authority were all the more memorable for being fairly rare. Between 1636 and 1775, Connecticut courts sent a total of forty-eight people to the gallows, most of them before the turn of the eighteenth century. Just over three-fifths of the condemned were men; about a third were either Native Americans or African Americans. Their offenses included murder, rape, burglary, and (especially for women) witchcraft.[3] Officials intended these gruesome displays of judicial retribution to serve three purposes: punish the criminal, encourage penitence, and deter others from similar wrongdoing. Only the first goal was reliably achieved. Eliciting genuine contrition and discouraging other potential offenders were far more difficult to accomplish, and some hardened malefactors remained defiant to the end.[4]

But what if the defiant individual facing imminent death was not an incorrigible criminal but an honorable man? What if he admitted to the deed that led to his execution, but deemed it both honorable and necessary? And what if he committed that transgression in the midst of—indeed, because of—a war?

Such were the circumstances facing two young men from Connecticut hanged just six months apart, one of them on September 22, 1776, and the other on March 19, 1777. Caught up in the maelstrom of the American Revolution, each man died for what he believed to be a righteous act. Posterity, playing the role of vicarious witness with the benefit of time to consider the significance of these deaths, has drawn a distinction between them, identifying one as worthy of commemoration and consigning the other to oblivion. Nathan Hale, the American spy executed by the British, has been memorialized as a martyr to the cause of liberty. Moses Dunbar, the only loyalist convicted of treason in a Connecticut court and hanged for that offense, has been forgotten. Their stories, however, are not as different as the verdict of posterity suggests.

The American Revolution that extinguished the lives of Moses Dunbar and Nathan Hale was at once a national, a continental, and an imperial phenomenon. It produced a new American republic, rearranged power relations and territorial claims across North America, and altered Europeans' global empires. It inspired stirring statements about universal rights and liberties even as it exposed disturbing divisions rooted in distinctions of class, ethnicity, race, and gender. It affected—directly or indirectly, and often adversely—not only American colonists and Britons, but also French, Spanish, and even Russian colonists, Native Americans, and Africans and African Americans. The more we learn about it, the more complicated the Revolution appears.[5]

For people who lived through it, the Revolution was even more confusing. Political upheaval and warfare intruded upon their households and communities, causing unprecedented disruptions and forcing them to take actions with unpredictable consequences.[6] Driven by high-minded principles, self-interest, or a mixture of both, participants reacted to a multitude of factors—many of them local and highly personal—that loomed large for them but barely registered in subsequent grand narratives of the Revolution. This was as true for Indian peoples weighing the relative merits of neutrality versus alliance with one of the contending sides, African slaves pondering British invitations to seek their freedom, and French and Spanish officials along the Gulf Coast tracking developments on distant battlefields as it was for British Americans in the thirteen rebellious colonies.[7]

Anxiety led many of those Americans to look beyond their British adversaries and detect secret enemies closer to home, thereby transforming the War for Independence into a civil as well as an imperial conflict. Internecine strife erupted in such places as the southern backcountry and parts of Pennsylvania, New Jersey, New York, and Long Island, fracturing communities and even families.[8] It also broke out in Connecticut, perhaps the least likely setting for such internal discord. Yet even there, neighbors who shared similar backgrounds in terms of religion, race, ethnicity, and economic status found occasion during the revolutionary tumult to fear and hate one another.

The stories of Moses Dunbar and Nathan Hale were deeply rooted in that Connecticut countryside and those unsettled times. Both men started out in life as sons of striving farmers laboring in agrarian villages whose inhabitants took for granted their membership in Britain's empire. Although Hale and Dunbar never met, Connecticut was a small enough place that they had common acquaintances. Dunbar's pastor attended college with Hale, for instance, and Hale's cousin visited Dunbar in jail. Neither man's choice of allegiance during the Revolution was foreordained; rather, it developed fitfully in the context of preexisting social relationships that initially had nothing to do with politics. Those personal connections became politicized as armed conflict neared, driving Dunbar to oppose American independence and Hale to support it. The challenge of balancing private responsibilities toward friends and family against the public demands of politics and war during such perilous times vexed many—if not most—colonists, no matter which side they were on. For very few of them, however, did engagement with that struggle lead to the gallows.

The deaths of Nathan Hale and Moses Dunbar might have been exceptional, but their lives were not. Their tragic stories offer a particularly dramatic demonstration of a common experience, showing how a welter of personal and political factors could confound people's efforts to exert control over their lives in the midst of the Revolution. Matters of timing were especially crucial to Hale and Dunbar and their posthumous reputations. Each man undertook the action that led to his death at a moment when nearly everyone believed that Britain stood poised to win the war. Had that happened, their respective roles as martyr and traitor would have been reversed. Posterity often takes America's victory for granted; neither of these men—nor others in their communities—dared to do so.

Nathan Hale was only twenty-one when he died, just on the threshold of adulthood. Even so, a trove of documents survives that is rich enough to permit a reconstruction of his brief life. His friends and family preserved letters, his army diary, and reminiscences that would likely have disappeared had he died, like so many other soldiers, of disease or battle wounds, or had he returned from war to an uneventful civilian career.[9] Because of these materials, Hale's voice often resonates within this narrative with greater force than Dunbar's. Yet Hale's words can be used to obscure as well as reveal.

To focus exclusively on his final speech—the source of his posthumous fame as a Revolutionary hero—is to miss the fact that he lived the vast majority of his life not as an enthusiastic patriot of a country that was barely two months old at the time of his execution but as an ardent admirer of Britain. Like other revolutionaries, he first had to shed his British identity before he could assume an American one. He accomplished this, as he did much else in his life, in the company of friends who similarly redirected ambitions nurtured in a very different context to take advantage of new opportunities presented by the Revolution.

Moses Dunbar is, for the most part, a quieter presence in this narrative but not because he was a more taciturn man than Nathan Hale. Indeed, Dunbar's propensity to proclaim his political opinions when greater discretion was called for turned out to be a key source of his troubles. Yet like many Connecticut farmers who scarcely ever left home, he had little reason to write letters or compose the kinds of documents that would preserve his thoughts for posterity. Most surviving records describe his actions, especially the buying and selling of land, and show his preoccupation with making a living and supporting his wife and children. Only as he sat in jail on the eve of his death did the thirty-year-old Dunbar compose both a moving letter to those children and a remarkable "last speech" defending his reputation. His eloquence, if not his political allegiance, fully matched that of Nathan Hale and revealed the profound influence of his Anglican faith on his loyalist convictions.[10]

The animosities generated by the Revolution gradually diminished as the event shifted from lived experience into the realm of memory. Demonstrations of public and private remembrance of the victors, as well as deliberate attempts to forget their opponents, helped over time to mend Connecticut's torn social fabric. The same social network that influenced Hale's responses to wartime opportunities initiated the postwar campaign to transform a hapless spy into the hero of a nation he could never have imagined. Conversely, efforts to repress memories of Dunbar tended to conceal the painful divisiveness that the Revolution had spawned. Most studies of loyalists focus on those who fled the United States, even though most loyalists—including Dunbar's friends and descendants—stayed, finding ways to adapt to a changed political reality.[11] Family and community ties, in the end, meant more to them than an abstract sense of allegiance to a new nation. The success of their reintegration into American society, however, can be measured by their absence from the story of the Revolution.

The War for Independence is often seen as a "good war" with righteous patriots pitted against misguided, if not evil-minded, Britons and loyalists. Such an oversimplified popular version of events distorts what was a far more tangled history and ignores the participation of a far larger cast of characters, many of them living well beyond the bounds of the thirteen original colonies. It does not even apply to the experiences of revolutionaries and loyalists in a small place like Connecticut, where no faction held a monopoly on principle. *The Martyr and the Traitor* shows how two equally honorable young men could follow their consciences and yet reach opposite conclusions about the merits of American independence. Each man met his death for acting in accordance with his beliefs. Nathan Hale and Moses Dunbar are both worth remembering because their tragic fates represent two sides of the same coin. They are equally part of America's Revolutionary story.

1

FATHERS AND SONS

IN 1763, FARM BOYS THROUGHOUT Connecticut looked forward to a mid-week holiday on the sixth of July. Most summer mornings, they awoke at dawn to face hours of hard work. Older boys sweltered in the hot sun alongside their fathers, cutting hay, harvesting winter wheat, or planting row upon row of turnips. Brothers too young for such physically demanding tasks fetched water and firewood or looked for wandering livestock. Whatever the job, farm boys knew that by nightfall they would be exhausted, with aching muscles ready for sleep. But Governor Thomas Fitch had declared July 6, 1763, a special day of thanksgiving during which his constituents, young and old, should avoid "servile Labour."[1]

Families still arose at dawn on July 6. Certain daily chores demanded attention even on holidays: milking cows, feeding livestock, gathering water for washing faces and firewood for cooking meals. But then Connecticut colonists devoted the rest of the day to celebrating in true New England fashion. Forsaking the heat of the bright sun for the shadows and stale air of a crowded meetinghouse, they went to church to hear a sermon. As the governor's proclamation noted, they had good reason to be thankful. A treaty signed in Paris had finally ended the long war between Great Britain and her French and Spanish adversaries—a war that had convulsed North America for nine years and, before it was over, touched nearly every continent around the world.

Connecticut's inhabitants took immense pride in their contribution to Britain's great victory. The cost, however, had been high in
both men and money. As many as six out of ten eligible men—about
12 percent of Connecticut's entire population—served in the army at
one time or another, a level of mobilization unmatched by any other
colony. More than 1,400 Connecticut soldiers perished during the
conflict, most from disease rather than combat, and many others suffered debilitating injuries that would plague them for the rest of their
lives. Meanwhile, property owners struggled to pay the high taxes
that waging war required. To be sure, the colonists' tax burden eased
considerably after 1758 when Britain began to reimburse most of the
wartime costs. Even so, given its scope and duration, the French and
Indian War affected every Connecticut town and family in one way or
another. Their sacrifices made victory all that much sweeter.[2]

Proud as they were of their colony's participation in the war,
Connecticut's inhabitants gathered in their churches on that July
day to acknowledge the true source of military triumph. They knew
that British and provincial forces had merely been the instruments of
divine power and their success evidence of a design not of their making. But what a design! The newly signed peace treaty redrew the
map of the world. By marking new swaths of territory as British possessions, the document signaled a historic and, as colonists saw it, a
divinely sanctioned shift in imperial history. Although the Reverend
James Lockwood's congregation in Wethersfield hardly needed to
be reminded of how momentous Britain's conquest of Canada was,
the minister devoted much of his sermon to that very theme. After
decades of "horrid and inhuman Butcheries" committed by "blood-
thirsty *Savages*, spirited and set on by the faithless *French*," he proclaimed, New England's northern frontier was at last secure. Those
same Indians, liberated from the grip of the papist French, could
now be tamed by "the pure Gospel" of Protestant Christianity and
encouraged to trade their precious furs to New England merchants.
Such a profound demonstration of God's favor, however, should not
lull colonists into complacency. Delivering a message that resounded
from pulpits all over New England, Lockwood reminded his congregation that the Lord had sent the scourge of war to chastise colonists for their sins but then allowed Britain to triumph as a gift of
divine mercy. The fruits of that victory would surely wither in the

absence of spiritual reformation and heartfelt gratitude for the Lord's deliverance.[3]

Moses Dunbar of Waterbury knew that his father was one of the many Connecticut men who had marched off to war. He may have regretted that the conflict ended before he got his own chance at military adventures, even though John Dunbar would likely have opposed his eldest son's enlistment. Moses had just turned seventeen, a bit young for soldiering, although many eighteen-year-olds served in provincial armies. During the previous year he had begun mustering with his town's militia, as was required of all able-bodied males between the ages of sixteen and sixty. Of medium height, with light brown curly hair, Moses may already have developed a habit of speaking his mind, whether or not his opinion had been sought.[4] On the sixth of July, he and his family went to the Congregationalist meetinghouse near their farm in the parish of Northbury. Seated on hard wooden pews for at least a couple of hours—no proper sermon was shorter than that—the Dunbars listened to a preacher whom few in the parish really liked. The Reverend Samuel Todd, like Lockwood in Wethersfield, would have tempered his message of celebration for Britain's victory with stern admonitions calling for individual and collective moral reformation. The war with France had been won, but the battle with Satan never ceased.[5]

Nathan Hale, who lived about fifty miles northeast of Waterbury in the town of Coventry, understood little about the French and Indian War or the meaning of Britain's victory. The conflict's opening shots had rung out in the Ohio Valley nearly a year before he was born. For as long as he could remember, the adults in his household anxiously discussed dreadful defeats and stunning victories, yet by war's end he was still too young to grasp the full significance of their remarks. Nathan overheard more of these mysterious conversations than his siblings did, for he was a sickly child whose parents kept him close to home. Yet Richard Hale would have wanted his eight-year-old son with blue eyes, light brown hair, and ruddy cheeks to join the rest of the family in whatever holiday celebrations Coventry had planned. The local minister, a Yale graduate, was certainly up to the challenge of composing a vigorous thanksgiving sermon, although delivering it before an audience of people he did not know very well might have given him pause. The Reverend Joseph Huntington had been ordained pastor of Coventry's Congregational Church only a week before.[6]

When the sermons ended, townspeople all over the colony gathered outside meetinghouses for a bit of fresh air and a chance to catch up on news with friends and neighbors. Conversations may have turned to the quality of the minister's preaching or to Britain's great victory and what it might mean for Connecticut. More likely, farmers discussed the weather, prospects for a good corn harvest, progress in haying, and the declining price of cattle. Women exchanged news of births and illnesses and complained about the difficulty of hiring reliable girls to help with household tasks. Children enjoyed a rare opportunity to play as their families drifted home. Everyone knew that on the seventh of July life would resume its ordinary rhythms. Moses Dunbar would be back at work, planting more turnips or doing whatever his father told him to do. Richard Hale would also expect Nathan to complete his chores. Britain's victory in the French and Indian War may have been a world-changing event, but as far as Moses Dunbar and Nathan Hale could tell, it had not changed their world at all.

Change was not in fact something that many of Connecticut's inhabitants wished for unless it brought relief from the economic difficulties that accompanied the end of the war and cessation of British military subsidies.[7] Ever since the seventeenth century, Connecticut stood out as arguably the most stable of Britain's North American colonies. Its population was overwhelmingly of English descent, its economy predominantly agricultural, its churches exclusively Protestant, and its society characterized by a comparatively greater degree of equality. At the heart of Connecticut's political culture lay a shared reverence for the colony's charter, granted by Charles II in 1662 and based on a plan of government drawn up by the first settlers back in 1639. This precious document preserved the people's rights as well as Connecticut's anomalous status as one of only two colonies where freemen elected their governor as well as members of the legislature (the other was Rhode Island). By the eighteenth century, some external authority—the Crown or a proprietor—appointed the executive everywhere else. When King James II tried to seize the charter during an ill-fated experiment with imperial centralization in 1687, colonists conspired to keep it out of royal officials' hands. A bulwark against tyranny, the charter protected Connecticut's self-government and deflected unwanted scrutiny into its affairs. Wartime demands emanating from Britain had intruded on the colony's preference to be left alone, but peace would presumably reinstate the prewar status quo.[8]

The end of hostilities with European enemies, however, did not necessarily usher in peace and quiet at home. The relative autonomy enjoyed by this intensely provincial society had, in recent decades, produced spurts of fierce political infighting, and there was no reason to think that the years after 1763 would be any different. Connecticut's very homogeneity made minor differences loom larger than they might have elsewhere and made major disagreements appear irreconcilable. With no external target to unite the populace—without, say, an imperious royal governor trying to make them do his bidding—political debate tended to spiral inward upon itself, arranging people who were very much like one another into opposing factions.[9]

Tempers flared on any number of contentious issues, with religion an especially combustible one. Beginning in the late 1730s and extending into the next decade, a tremendous religious revival known as the Great Awakening swept through parts of Britain and the colonies. In Connecticut, the religious upheaval left in its wake a volatile mix of people, some of whom had been converted by fervent evangelical preaching (New Lights) and others who scorned what they regarded as a giddy enthusiasm (Old Lights). Each side believed that it held the high ground and that its adversaries were on the road to damnation. Churches splintered, with factions going their separate ways, but that was not enough to restore calm. Well into the 1760s, the rancor between Old Lights and New Lights inflamed politics, with each group vying to elect its own adherents to the legislature, where they could use the power of the state to circumscribe the activities of their opponents.[10]

Economic concerns similarly set colonists against one another. Many Connecticut inhabitants worried that economic development in their colony was not keeping pace with population growth. Money was scarce, but proposals to issue paper money to compensate for the lack of hard currency divided the eastern half of the colony (generally in favor of such policies) against a more conservative western region. Good farmland was likewise in short supply; Connecticut was, after all, one of the smallest of the mainland colonies. Some inhabitants looked to the 1662 charter for a remedy. That document, written when the continent's geography was poorly understood, located Connecticut's western boundary at the Pacific Ocean (or "South Sea"). This inspired a group of colonists to create the Susquehannah Company to promote settlement in the Wyoming Valley along a branch of the Susquehannah River, which they claimed fell within Connecticut's jurisdiction. Unfortunately, a subsequent charter placed the valley within the bounds of Pennsylvania. Thus another controversy erupted, between those who wanted to settle there anyway, despite Pennsylvania's claim and the opposition of the territory's resident Indians, and those who rejected such a foolhardy enterprise.[11]

Connecticut's inhabitants agreed on the sanctity of their charter but argued about almost everything else. Factionalism increasingly characterized political life, fostered by an array of controversial religious and economic issues and invigorated by annual electoral competition at every level of government. In 1763, Moses Dunbar and Nathan Hale were as yet too young and inexperienced to know much about the world outside their households. Yet the concerns that vexed Connecticut during the middle years of the eighteenth century would shape their towns, their families, and their own futures.

Moses Dunbar lived in Waterbury in 1763, but that was not where he was born. Like his father before him, Moses first drew breath in the neighboring town of Wallingford. Temperance Dunbar gave birth to this second son on the third of June in 1746. She had produced five more children—three sons and two daughters—by the time her husband John announced that the family would be moving about fifteen miles northwest to Waterbury. Only five of the seven children she had borne would make the trip, for two little boys had died in infancy.[12]

John Dunbar's decision to uproot his family coincided with a general restlessness in Connecticut society. All over the colony fathers were taking the measure of their economic resources and their families' present and future needs. If the two were not aligned, migration offered a possible way to bring them into balance. Opportunities to move within Connecticut were diminishing; by 1760 the entire colony would be divided into townships. Thus some of the more intrepid families looked farther afield to western Massachusetts or, more dangerously, the Wyoming Valley in Pennsylvania. Other household heads preferred to take fewer risks. They warmed instead to the idea of exchanging an uncertain prosperity in one Connecticut town for hopes of greater security in another where cheap land might still be available.[13]

In Wallingford, John Dunbar and his brother Edward contemplated this very strategy as a way to improve their families' prospects. Edward, two years older than John, fixed his sights on Waterbury and began buying parcels of land there in the late 1740s, not long after their father died. By around 1750, he had moved with his wife and four children to the town. Several more years passed before John Dunbar and his family could follow him. To relocate, John Dunbar needed money, and that was hard to come by for a hardscrabble farmer raising a large family in a colony chronically short of cash. But in 1755, he saw a way to hasten the day when he could put his plans into action.[14]

That spring, Connecticut's government put out a call for volunteers to fight in the war that everyone hoped would finally eject the French from Canada. Within weeks, hundreds of men responded, among them thirty-year-old John Dunbar. Enthusiasm for military glory may have played a part in his decision, but an equally compelling motive stemmed from the knowledge of what he could earn for just a few months' service. The government offered each volunteer for the 1755 campaign a bounty of £1 and 10 shillings upon enlistment, plus an equal sum if he brought his own musket and blanket. Dunbar had inherited a gun from his father, so he could collect the extra money. Enlistees also received a month's advance wages, with the remainder to be paid at the end of the campaign. Serving in the rank of sergeant, Dunbar could earn over £10 from his stint in the army—not enough to buy a Waterbury farm, but an important contribution toward that goal.[15]

With a wife and children waiting for him at home, Sergeant Dunbar may have hoped that his army sojourn would provide more excitement than real danger. If so, he got more than he bargained for. In April 1755, he joined Major Isaac Foot's company, a unit in the second regiment of Connecticut's provincial forces. That summer, the troops headed for Albany, New York, the staging area for the Crown Point campaign. By early September, nearly 3,500 colonial soldiers and 400 Indian allies were finally ready to mount an assault on Fort Saint Frédéric on Lake Champlain. What they got instead was a battle at the head of Lake George.[16]

The enemy had discovered their maneuvers and launched a surprise counterattack. On September 8, French and Indian fighters ambushed several provincial units, including Dunbar's regiment, as they passed through a narrow ravine. With shots raining down on them from both sides of the road, frantic colonial troops scrambled for cover. Those who were not killed or severely wounded in the initial volleys turned around and ran for their lives with the enemy at their heels. After this initial skirmish—an engagement that New Englanders would remember as the "Bloody Morning Scout"—a day-long battle ensued. It was marked, in the vivid memory of one participant, by the "most violent [*sic*] Fire Perhaps that Ever was heard of in this country In any Battle." By the end of the day, provincial forces prevailed in what New Englanders celebrated as a great victory, even though they were too weak to follow up by pursuing the enemy back to Fort Saint Frédéric.[17]

Colonial troops spent the next three days engaged in the gruesome task of locating and burying the dead. Connecticut's losses were especially high: 45 of its 800 men had been killed, and another 25 were wounded or missing. Six men from Dunbar's company—some of them, perhaps, young men whom he had recruited in return for his sergeant's appointment—perished. Although many officers and soldiers reenlisted for subsequent campaigns after the battle of Lake George, Sergeant Dunbar had seen enough of war. On September 27, he received his discharge and headed home to be reunited with his relieved family and obtain the bulk of his army wages.[18]

John Dunbar was no longer a soldier, but he could still make money from a war that ended up lasting seven more years. Each of those years Connecticut raised somewhere between 1,300 and 4,300 troops and every one of those men required provisions for the duration of his enlistment. Commissaries could not always provide the prescribed daily allowance for every soldier, including a pound each of bread and meat, but their efforts to do so aroused the productive energies of the countryside. There was an unprecedented need for flour, pork, beef, peas, beans, corn, butter, and cheese—just the sorts of commodities farmers like Dunbar produced. High demand for these agricultural goods, as well as for horses and oxen to transport military supplies, created new markets and drove up prices. Farmers took advantage of wartime conditions to sell surplus farm products that, in ordinary times, they would have consumed at home or exchanged locally. Every pig or cow or bushel of rye that John Dunbar could sell to the army added to the stake he needed for his next gamble: abandoning the town where his family had lived for at least two generations.[19]

By December 1758, he at last had enough. Army wages and earnings from his farm augmented his principal source of revenue: the sale of his Wallingford house and land for £205. For £200 in "lawful money," a combination of hard currency and paper money (most of it bills of credit issued by the colony government to help pay for the war), he bought his older brother's Waterbury farm, while Edward moved elsewhere in town. John Dunbar's Wallingford landholdings had amounted to about twenty-five acres; his new farm comprised fifty-six acres, including a house and outbuildings. Over the next year or so, he purchased several more acres, mostly undeveloped land that he managed to acquire quite cheaply, some of it for as little as eight shillings an acre.[20]

Dunbar obtained cheaper land because he chose to move to a community that was less populous and less prosperous than the one he left.[21] The colony's best agricultural land lay in the flat and fertile Connecticut River valley; to the east and west, upland towns spread across uneven ground and stonier soil. Waterbury, founded in 1686, was one of these upland villages, with a population of about 1,800 when the Dunbar family arrived. The town was studded with hills and veined with brooks and streams that flowed into the Naugatuck River running through its center. The Naugatuck valley would thrive in the nineteenth century from brass works and other water-powered manufacturing enterprises, but that prosperity occurred well after John Dunbar's day. In the mid-eighteenth century, the Naugatuck and its tributaries were more of a nuisance, hampering local transportation and requiring the building—and often, after spring floods, rebuilding—of numerous wooden bridges. A proposal put forward by several Waterbury men in 1761 to clear the river for shipping testified to their commercial aspirations, but nothing came of the plan.[22]

John Dunbar made his money go even further by moving to one of the poorer sections of town, about as far away from Waterbury's center as one could get and still be counted a resident. The bulk of his property lay in the parish of Northbury, a tract of about five square miles in the town's northeast corner on the border with Farmington. As early as the turn of the eighteenth century, families who wanted to move to Waterbury discovered that good land near the village center was limited in availability and high in price. Affordable property, however, could still be had as late as the 1750s on the town's margins, in places such as Northbury. Thus latecomers, like the Dunbars, ended up there. Northbury's first settlers arrived around 1730, and as its population increased, the neighborhood developed a sense of communal identity separate from Waterbury proper.[23]

That sense of identity reflected the neighborhood's isolation and often manifested itself in disputes with town officials. Northbury worshippers had to travel farther than many other townspeople to attend Waterbury's church, located in the southern part of town, and its children walked greater distances to attend school. Winter conditions frequently made such treks impossible, but Northbury inhabitants still had to pay taxes to support town institutions they could not always use. In the late 1730s, Northbury property holders urged town officials to create multiple school districts to accommodate outliers like themselves and to allocate to each one its proportion of financial resources. The first district schools were organized by about 1740, but disputes about school monies persisted into the 1750s and would reemerge as late as 1770.[24]

Northbury's request for its own Congregational church, or at least a reduction in church taxes if the neighborhood hired its own part-time minister, proved equally contentious. It took a Northbury petition to the colony legislature to make Waterbury officials agree to create a separate parish in October 1739. Within a month, parish members invited Samuel Todd, a twenty-two-year-old Yale graduate, to be their minister. His appointment generated yet another controversy, this time within the parish itself. Reverend Todd's May 1740 ordination coincided with the first stirrings of the Great Awakening in western Connecticut. Initially scornful of the revival, he experienced a change of heart. In addition to assisting at the ordination of a New Light clergyman—an act that led to his own ten-month suspension from the conservative New Haven ministerial association—Todd preached fiery sermons and held "conference meetings" to arouse the spiritual fervor of his flock. Many parishioners reacted angrily, and a slim majority of them eventually abandoned the congregation. They promptly joined the Church of England, appropriating the building that had been used for public worship for their Anglican services.

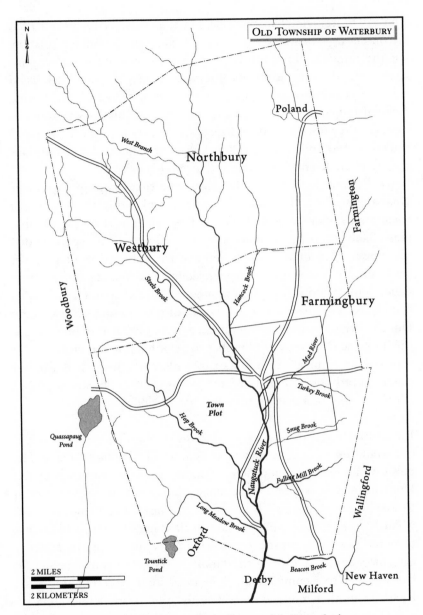

Figure 1.1 Town of Waterbury, including parish boundaries.

Those who remained in the Congregational parish registered their discontent by refusing to adjust Todd's salary to account for inflation, but the minister clung to his position for two more decades, most likely by curbing his evangelical fervor. Finally, in April 1764, Todd met with a committee to discuss his future with the parish. Noting "several Dificulties" between the minister and his congregation, as well as "Prevailing bodily Indispositions [that] for som Time past" had prevented Todd from fulfilling his pastoral duties, the contentious shepherd and his flock agreed to terms for his exit.[25]

By the time John Dunbar bought his brother's farm in December 1758, the worst of Northbury's troubles had diminished, although resentments over religion continued to smolder. Edward Dunbar presumably apprised his brother of the neighborhood's sporadic disagreements, but John would have been hard-pressed to find a town anywhere in Connecticut where residents did not fight over some issue. Wallingford was hardly immune to internal conflict; in fact, its church fractured over the appointment of a new minister just as the Dunbars were leaving.[26] Divisiveness was simply a part of life in these small towns. Besides, John Dunbar was not looking for harmony. He was looking to make a fresh start in a place where he had a better chance at prosperity, and Waterbury, whatever its problems, appeared to offer a more promising setting for such an endeavor.

Richard Hale was just as certain that his chances for economic security would improve if he moved away from his childhood home. His quest would require a much longer journey than the one taken by the Dunbars, and he would make it alone. Hale was born in Newbury in Massachusetts, a colony his ancestors had helped to found. In 1724, when he was seven years old, fate dealt Richard a sharp blow that rendered his future prospects uncertain. His father died that year at age thirty-seven, depriving the family of its breadwinner before he had a chance to accumulate much of an estate to pass on to his heirs. Richard's mother remained a widow for nine years before remarrying, raising three sons and two daughters whose inheritances would be limited when they finally came of age.[27]

Once he reached adulthood, Richard Hale realized that whatever financial stake he could accumulate through inheritance, his own labors, and the help of relatives would go much further in a place where land was cheaper than it was in Newbury, a long-settled town with growing commercial aspirations focused on trade with the West Indies. The northeastern corner of Connecticut, about a hundred miles away, beckoned. The area that would be carved into Tolland and Windham counties was still very much a frontier zone, dotted with sparsely populated towns scarcely older than Richard Hale himself. His uncle James Hale had moved to the region not long after Richard was born, becoming Ashford's minister and one of its earliest settlers. Richard may have visited him there and used the opportunity to look around for a potential home for himself. However it was that he learned about the region, by the spring of 1745, the twenty-eight-year-old Hale had decided to make a life for himself in Coventry, Connecticut.[28]

Incorporated in 1712, Coventry was another upland town, in this case located east of the Connecticut River.[29] For years, the quiet beauty of its rolling hills and patchwork of woodlands offered few attractions to prospective farmers who cared less about the aesthetic virtues of this landscape than about the practical difficulties it posed for agriculture. They knew that cultivating Connecticut uplands, at least at first, produced more plentiful harvests of fieldstones than crops to reward their labors. Thus they avoided areas like northeastern Connecticut until virtually all of the more easily farmed lands elsewhere in the colony had been taken up. Only then did prospective settlers reconsider Coventry's advantages. Even so, the town's founders were dismayed to discover how difficult it was to attract people to the new village. It took a generous land policy, which called for carving out large dispersed farms, to lure greater numbers of inhabitants. By the 1750s, Coventry's population numbered about 1,600, nearly as many people as lived in Waterbury at that time.[30]

As was the case in so many other Connecticut towns, Coventry's inhabitants proved ingenious at finding ways to disagree with one another and sometimes with the colony government. Disputes over land, stemming in part from property claims based on questionable Indian deeds, erupted in the 1720s. At one point, when the Superior Court tried to intervene, a mob of men from Coventry and nearby towns marched to Hartford, threatening violence in defense of their property rights. That disturbance had barely subsided when, in the 1730s, the failure of residents in one part of town to build roads stirred up more contention. Those inhabitants who were doing their civic duty to improve transportation resented shiftless neighbors who shirked their responsibilities.[31]

Religious matters, predictably, offered yet another opportunity for strife. In 1736, a group of Coventry residents petitioned the colonial legislature for permission to create a second Congregationalist parish in town, most likely because they lived too far from the existing church. The original boundaries of the town encompassed more than thirty-nine square miles, more than enough space to make it difficult for those who lived in Coventry's distant corners to travel to the meetinghouse. For some reason, the legislature dithered for four years before deciding in the petitioners' favor. Its action only set the stage for a new round of disagreements as members of the new parish began to quarrel over where their meetinghouse ought to be built and how to pay for it.[32]

Richard Hale knew that such disputes could be found in any New England town, but that cheap land was not similarly ubiquitous. Coventry was where he could find a farm at a price he could afford. In June 1745, Hale ventured what must have been nearly all of his available capital, £750 "Old Tenor" (a depreciated form of colonial currency worth about £100 Lawful Money), and purchased 240 acres of land. This transaction immediately launched him into the top tier of Connecticut landholders; only about 4 percent of colony farmers as young as Hale owned as much as a hundred acres. The purchase alone, of course, did not guarantee his success, for a lot of hard work lay ahead. Nevertheless, Richard Hale's future looked brighter than ever before.[33]

Nothing signified Hale's improving prospects more clearly than his May 1746 wedding to Elizabeth Strong. The bride's father, Captain Joseph Strong, belonged to one of Coventry's founding families and owned a farm near where Hale settled. Connecticut law did not require Captain Strong to consent to the match, but nothing prevented him from offering his opinion of his daughter's prospective husband. New Englanders agreed that romantic attraction contributed to a strong marriage, but no father wanted to see his daughter wed to a man who could not support her, no matter how fond of him she might be. Richard Hale's task of impressing the Strongs was unusually difficult, for he was a newcomer to Coventry and had no father or other relative in town to vouch for his character. Yet his new farm testified to his promising economic future, and he perhaps enlisted his minister uncle in Ashford to speak on his behalf. Whatever reservations, if any, the Strongs might have had about Richard Hale were not sufficient to prevent his marriage to eighteen-year-old Elizabeth.[34]

A year later, almost to the day, Elizabeth gave birth to her first child, a son named Samuel. Had the Hales followed typical New England practice, they would have named the infant after his father, not his grandfather. But Richard welcomed this birth as an opportunity to commemorate the long-dead father whom he could scarcely remember. In so doing, he established a link, however symbolic, with his past and with the family he had left behind in Massachusetts. But this first birth also pointed to the Hales' future. More children followed in regular succession, at the usual colonial New England pace of a newborn about every other year. Nathan, born on June 6, 1755, was the sixth child and fifth son in a family that eventually included a dozen children. If a brood of sturdy offspring could be interpreted as a sign of divine favor, the Hale family could consider itself blessed. Richard had become a New England patriarch, the status that his own father had had so little time to enjoy.[35]

From the vantage point of 1763, it might have seemed that the risks taken by John Dunbar and Richard Hale in moving to new communities had paid off handsomely and their futures were equally bright. Each man could gaze from the threshold of his front door at more hard-won acres than he would have possessed had he remained in his birthplace. This land allowed the men to support their families with greater peace of mind than would otherwise have been possible. And both Dunbar and Hale had unusually large families for whom to provide. By 1763, Temperance Dunbar and Elizabeth Hale had each given birth to ten children, with more to come. The Dunbars had already buried two infants, and the Hales had lost one baby son, a twin who lived for only a week. Such losses struck many, if not most, New England families with depressing regularity, but that did not make them any easier to bear. At least the abundance of sons among the surviving children—five for the Dunbars and eight for the Hales— guaranteed each family the labor force so essential to eighteenth-century Connecticut farmers.[36]

The similarities between these two families may have been striking, but they were also deceptive. The fortunes of the Hales and Dunbars did not proceed along equivalent paths. The families' respective futures were shaped not by one or two important decisions but by many factors, not all of which were under their control. It mattered, for instance, that one of the men (Richard Hale) was seven years older than the other, that they lived in different parts of the colony, and that they had markedly different personalities. And what was true for Richard Hale and John Dunbar would later apply with equal force to Nathan Hale and Moses Dunbar.

People who knew Richard Hale well described him as a sober, industrious, God-fearing man. Acquaintances recalled that he would often rush through his midday meal to resume work before the rest of his family had finished eating. His local reputation testified to an impressive sense of self-discipline. His father's early death surely contributed to this facet of Hale's character; he knew from a young age that he would have to make his own way in the world. He came from quite a respectable family—his grandfather, uncle, and brother had all graduated from Harvard—but Richard would have to work hard to maintain that standing as he established himself in a town where people knew little or nothing about his forebears.[37]

Richard Hale approached major life decisions with caution and deliberation. He took time to figure out where to look for a farm and spent years accumulating the capital needed to buy it. Yet luck also played a part in his eventual success. During the 1740s, when he was ready to purchase land, there were still towns in Connecticut, such as Coventry, trying to recruit settlers with offers of large farms at affordable prices. Such opportunities diminished in the next decade or so, as pressure from Connecticut's growing population on a fixed supply of land drove prices up. Had Richard Hale been born around the same time as John Dunbar and tried to move in the 1750s, he would not have been able to negotiate quite as good a deal as he did for his Coventry farm.[38]

Hale was equally prudent and fortunate in his choice of a spouse. He deferred marriage until he was twenty-nine, several years older than the typical New England bridegroom.[39] His prospective in-laws were not the only people concerned about his economic standing; Hale likewise wanted to be able to support a wife before he wed. His selection of Elizabeth Strong undoubtedly reflected a powerful emotional attachment, but his marriage also produced connections of a more practical nature. Just a year after arriving in Coventry, Hale established a bond with one of the town's leading families and through them became acquainted with other members of Coventry's elite. Thus his father-in-law acted as the patron who, under other circumstances, Hale's father might have been.

The connection with the Strongs helped the young man gain the friendship and respect of his Coventry neighbors, but maintaining their goodwill was ultimately Hale's responsibility. He fulfilled their expectations through judicious management of his farm and a stern yet loving exercise of authority within his family. When the French and Indian War broke out, neither a desire for money nor a thirst for glory could tempt Richard Hale away from farm and family to volunteer in the army. His public service during and after the war focused on Coventry. Hale's church community, which grew less contentious under the calm guidance of the Reverend Joseph Huntington, called upon him repeatedly to serve as deacon, a position that often served as a gateway to town officeholding. Not long after the war ended, Coventry trusted him with a much more substantial duty, electing him to serve as one of its two representatives in the Connecticut General Assembly. Fittingly, his fellow representative was one of his Strong relatives.[40]

John Dunbar, however, was the sort of young man who might have benefited from the wise counsel of someone like Deacon Hale to save him from his own impulsiveness. In 1743, when he was nineteen years old and probably not thinking all that much about possible repercussions, Dunbar got Temperance Hall—who was only sixteen—pregnant. The couple married five months before the child was born, and were hardly unusual in welcoming the arrival of an "early" baby. In some New England towns during the eighteenth century, a third or more of all brides were already pregnant. At an earlier point in the colony's history, fornicators faced stern justice from local courts, in the form of whippings or fines for behavior that was deemed both a sin and a crime. By the 1740s, however, civil authorities had many other matters to resolve, and formal prosecutions for fornication—at least for men—sharply declined.[41]

John and Temperance may not have had to endure public shaming in court, but that does not necessarily mean they escaped censure from community members and, almost certainly, their families.

Sexual relations carried special risk for Temperance, as more than a few young men, with little fear of legal retribution, abandoned pregnant partners to their miserable fate as dishonored unwed mothers. John Dunbar did not do that, but whether he stood by Temperance of his own free will or succumbed to family pressure to marry her is unknown.[42]

Marriage preserved their reputations, but the young couple now had to face the consequences of their actions. John Dunbar had little choice but to turn to his father for help in supporting Temperance and the child. Ordinarily, New England fathers used their control of property to delay sons' marriages, monopolizing their labor as long as possible to improve lands that would eventually form the sons' patrimonies. By the mid-eighteenth century, fewer fathers could provide all of their sons with full-sized farms and so were compelled to loosen their parental control. They allowed sons to hire themselves out to work for others—or, if such an opportunity arose, to serve in the army—to increase their financial resources. Young men could thus marry a year or two earlier than once was the case, but even so, most were in their mid-twenties before they embarked on this new stage in their lives.[43]

John and Temperance Dunbar, however, were still in their teens, about six years younger than the average New England newlyweds. Scarcely out of their own childhoods, the couple encountered all the responsibilities of adulthood. Whatever frustration John Dunbar's father—also named John—might have felt toward his troublesome son was probably not offset by the knowledge that he and his own wife had their first child only three months after their wedding. At least they had waited until they were in their twenties.[44]

John Dunbar Sr. perhaps resented his son's rash behavior as a challenge to his paternal authority, but when presented with a fait accompli he did what he could to help the young couple. He allowed them to live in—but not own—a separate house on a corner of his property and John probably continued working for him. The elder Dunbar (like his own father before him) combined farming with tailoring, activities that provided a modest support. Given time, he might have augmented his estate, but he did not have much time. Fewer than three years after his son's marriage, in May 1746, the elder John Dunbar died at the age of fifty-four. He and his children seem to have anticipated this sad event and planned accordingly. Edward's decision to join provincial forces for the 1745 Louisbourg campaign during King George's War allowed him to supplement a meager inheritance with a cash bounty and decent wages. Two months before his death, the ailing father deeded land to each of his sons even though Samuel, the youngest, was only nineteen. As the eldest, Edward received the largest portion—just over twenty-five acres, a third of which was reserved for the use of his soon-to-be-widowed mother. John Jr. assumed ownership of the house in which he already lived and twelve and one-half acres with a barn and orchard. The elder John Dunbar's decision to forgo deeding this land to John Jr. at the time of his marriage may have signified a lingering mistrust of his son's good judgment, although Edward too had married and fathered a child before receiving his portion. More telling was the father's decision to name his widow as his executor at a time when many men chose adult sons for the task. Edward was still in the army, but John Jr. would have been available.[45]

The contrasting experiences of John Dunbar and Richard Hale, deriving as much from their personalities as anything else, inevitably shaped the lives of their sons. Fathers in eighteenth-century New England served as role models for their boys, ideally demonstrating the virtues of hard work, self-discipline, and sober judgment. They provided sons with practical training in the business of farming and moral instruction to promote their spiritual development. The relationship between fathers and sons was definitely hierarchical, and yet it was also a partnership. Fathers needed their sons' labor as much as sons required their fathers' economic assistance, especially when the time came to marry and establish their own farms. In the meantime, they worked together for the benefit of the family, the social unit that defined their place in the community. Residents of these small New England towns tended to judge a person's character less by individual achievement than by the family's local reputation. Even before sons reached maturity, neighbors had often formed opinions about them based on an evaluation of their fathers. Depending on the nature of that assessment, sons could find their own paths in life made smoother or more difficult.[46]

To be known as Deacon Hale's son in Coventry was to begin life with a distinct advantage. By the time Nathan was born, Richard Hale was a prosperous, well-respected New England patriarch and town leader. No one in Coventry doubted his probity or his ability to raise children who would become pious and productive members of society. Throughout his childhood, Nathan could bask in the reflected light of his father's sterling reputation; the only difficulty he may have faced was trying to live up to the paternal example. Nathan's kin ties to the Strong family reinforced local assumptions about his promising future. The Strongs counted several college graduates and local leaders among their number, and women in the family helped ensure that the boy had an excellent upbringing. Long after he left home, Nathan recalled how his "good Grand-mother Strong" had "repeatedly favoured" her grandsons "with her tender most important advice."[47]

The Dunbar name did not carry anything approaching the same weight in Waterbury. John Dunbar's local reputation was shaped as much by struggles as achievements, and he forged no kin connections with similarly prominent local notables. Few who knew him could doubt his ambition. His move into town, which allowed him to double the size of his estate, testified to his striving. Even so, his Waterbury acreage amounted to about a quarter of Richard Hale's Coventry landholdings, and to get it, John Dunbar had to pay twice as much as Hale did for his land and settle for a farm in a marginal neighborhood. Moreover, political preferment did not come his way. There was no chance John Dunbar would ever be elected to an important town office, let alone be chosen to represent Waterbury in the colonial legislature. His public service mainly consisted of periodic stints on his parish's school committee and on another committee tasked with repairing the meetinghouse.[48]

For Moses to be known in Waterbury as John Dunbar's boy was to share his father's relative insignificance. Neighbors likely saw him as resembling any number of local farm boys of no particular distinction. At least he belonged to a family that supported itself, paid its taxes, and regularly attended church. It was also a family that continued to grow. John and Temperance had begun producing children at an early age, and the arrival of each new infant stretched their limited resources ever more thinly. John Dunbar would be lucky if he could provide Moses with even the modest patrimony he had received from his own father. To do so, he would need to extract as much labor as possible from Moses and his brothers to build up the family estate.

More than any other child in the family, Moses felt the effects of his father's relentless striving for economic security. John Dunbar was just twenty-one years old when Moses was born. Temperance was nineteen, and the young couple had barely recovered from the loss of their first son in infancy. This new baby arrived only a few months after John Dunbar had at last received title to his small Wallingford farm. Moses's childhood thus coincided with his father's most intense struggles to find his bearings as an adult member of society. Moses was not quite nine years old when his father volunteered for the Crown Point campaign—leaving him, his mother, and three younger siblings for several months—and he was twelve when the family moved to Waterbury. As the eldest son, Moses bore the weight of his father's demands more directly than the other children during these moments of family stress. John Dunbar's actions all aimed to promote the family's welfare and thus his son's own fortunes, but young Moses may not have been able to see beyond the daily round of work expected of him. His mother offered what comfort she could but was not able to relieve all of the tensions generated by John Dunbar's heavy reliance on the help of his oldest child.[49]

In 1763, seventeen-year-old Moses Dunbar was close enough to adulthood to imagine what it would be like. His father would no doubt try to keep him at home and at work on the family farm for several more years, but sooner or later he would have to let him go. When that moment came, Moses Dunbar would be free—free, that is, to replicate his father's experience. There were few other options for young men in these small New England towns. Moses would obtain land from his father, marry, and have children whose labor he would employ to keep his own farm going. Since his share of the family property would likely not amount to much, Moses would have to work hard to augment it. If he engaged in any extended flights of imagination about his future, Moses might have envisioned collecting what financial resources he could and moving away from Waterbury to a place where he could get more land at a lower price. Western Massachusetts, which attracted other Connecticut farmers, was one possibility, or maybe a new town farther to the north, now that British colonists no longer had to worry about frontier attacks from the French or their Indian allies. Away from Waterbury, he would be known as his own man, not merely as John Dunbar's son.

As the celebrations for Britain's victory over the French ended, eight-year-old Nathan Hale was too young to contemplate his future in similar fashion. If he gave it any thought at all, he probably imagined serving as Deacon Hale for a new generation of Coventry inhabitants. He would be a farmer, just like his father, or perhaps—since there were so many Hale sons with claims on the paternal estate—he might be trained in a useful trade like blacksmithing or carpentry. He might even go to college, like so many of his Hale and Strong relations, and become a minister, if Richard Hale could afford the expense of such an education.

When these boys and their families looked ahead, the future they envisioned looked a great deal like the present. The rising generation, like its forebears, would remain preoccupied with the enduring concerns of farming, family relations, and community life. Much as they celebrated the signing of the peace treaty on the sixth of July in 1763, Connecticut's inhabitants could not see that it would have much tangible impact on their daily lives. Like all British colonists, they took pride in being members of what they regarded as the greatest empire in the world. Yet this status was at best an abstraction, of far greater significance to statesmen in London, and perhaps leaders in Hartford, than to farmers and their sons in places like Northbury or Coventry.

No British subject, on either side of the Atlantic, could have predicted that notions of imperial membership would so quickly assume a real and disconcerting importance. If Connecticut's inhabitants presumed that the postwar era would usher in a resumption of their relative isolation from outside interference, allowing them once again to indulge in internal squabbling over religious matters and money problems, they were mistaken. These and other issues would indeed occupy them, but in new and utterly unexpected ways. Before long, colonists learned that Britain's victory in the French and Indian War had reshaped its empire in more than a geographical sense. The ink on the peace treaty was scarcely dry when imperial officials in London embarked on a set of policies aimed at reconfiguring the relationship between Great Britain and its American colonies. In ways neither Moses Dunbar nor Nathan Hale could have imagined, policy decisions made in London set in motion a train of events that would impinge directly on their own lives.

2

MOSES AND PHOEBE

Weddings are typically happy occasions. This was true even in eighteenth-century New England, where such events could inspire more discussions about land, livestock, and linens than thoughts of love and romance. To help the young couple get off to a good start, fathers of the bride and groom negotiated about land transfers and gifts of such "moveable" property as cows, plows, chairs, and kettles. Mothers and sisters went to work counting out bedsheets, blankets, and quilts. If there were not enough for the new household, the women brought out the loom or purchased cloth and threaded their needles to make whatever was required.[1]

After the flurry of preparations, the actual wedding might have seemed anticlimactic. New Englanders defined marriage as a civil contract, not a sacrament steeped in ritual. By the eighteenth century, a clergyman could join the couple in matrimony if that was their wish, but many people simply went to a local justice of the peace and entered into the marriage contract in his presence. Afterward, family and friends might gather at the bride's family home for food and drink, but that was it. No lavish celebration, no wedding trip; the next day, everyone went back to work. Sometimes brides even continued to live with their parents for several weeks after the wedding before setting up a separate household with their husbands. Subdued occasions by modern standards, colonial New England weddings were celebrations nonetheless, marking an important rite of passage.[2]

John Dunbar, however, did not offer hearty congratulations when his son Moses announced his intention to marry. It was the spring of 1764, and the news could not have come at a worse time. Temperance was still nursing their youngest child as John struggled to support his large family. A postwar economic slump magnified their difficulties. Now that the colony no longer needed supplies for thousands of soldiers, demand for agricultural products dropped sharply and, as a consequence, prices for grain, meat, and other farm goods plummeted. With the return of peace, the flow of British military subsidies into the Connecticut economy ceased, adding a scarcity of currency to the colony's woes. Many farmers sank into debt. Declining land prices reduced the value of their main capital asset, making it harder to sell property and move elsewhere. "Merchants and farmers are breaking," reported the *Connecticut Courant* in December 1764, "and all things going into confusion." John Dunbar did not welcome the potential loss of his main farmhand in such perilous times, but his son evidently had other plans.[3]

Moses was following a family tradition that had not served the Dunbars very well. He was not quite eighteen years old; his intended bride, Phoebe Jerome of Farmington, was barely seventeen and almost certainly pregnant.[4] John Dunbar, like his own father under similar circumstances, had little choice but to consent to—or perhaps even insist on—the match. But once again the impulsive behavior of a teen-aged son threatened to strain a family economy dependent on children's labor and focused on accumulating—not disbursing—property. John Dunbar was not yet forty, and his crowded Northbury house contained seven more children ranging in age from one to sixteen. He surely expected to have more time to build up his estate before bringing a daughter-in-law into the family.[5]

It is impossible to know how Moses and Phoebe first met. They lived in different towns (albeit adjoining ones), attended different schools, and grew up worshipping in different churches. Phoebe's father, Zerubbabel Jerome, owned some Northbury land, but there is no evidence that he knew John Dunbar before their children married.[6] All over New England, however, young people managed to evade their elders' watchful gaze and mingle with other adolescents in the area.[7] In the case of Moses and Phoebe, friendship led to sex and, probably more quickly than they imagined, pregnancy. If Moses was taken aback at first, he perhaps decided that this was a fortuitous turn of events. Phoebe's pregnancy (so long as Moses stood by her) would force John Dunbar to accept his eldest son's yearning for independence. Surely he would provide Moses with enough property to support a wife and child. With marriage, moreover, Moses would no longer be known only as John Dunbar's son. His newly formed ties with the Jeromes extended his kin connections into another town. At last Moses appeared to have found a way to carve out some space between himself and his demanding father.

Moses might also have expected a generous dowry for Phoebe. The Jeromes were more prosperous than the Dunbars, in good part because Zerubbabel had the advantage of a wealthy father. Timothy Jerome had sailed from England to Salem, Massachusetts, when he was twenty-one and soon settled in Wallingford, Connecticut. During the next three decades, he accumulated an impressive estate, with lands in Wallingford and the New Cambridge parish of Farmington. Few New England farms approached self-sufficiency, but Jerome's property came close. In addition to a large assortment of livestock and fields of corn, wheat, and oats, Jerome owned an apple orchard and cider press, kept bees, processed hides for leather, and cut timber for boards. He extended his influence in town by supplying credit to his neighbors. Yet what truly distinguished Timothy Jerome was his ownership of four slaves. He must have attracted considerable attention whenever he strolled through town in his best pale blue coat, glossy black vest, and fine leather breeches, with Pomp or Prince following a few steps behind.[8]

Timothy Jerome supplied Zerubbabel and his brothers with sizable pieces of the family estate, distributing land to the three oldest sons by deeds of gift and promising to bequeath the home farm to the youngest boy. In July 1746, Zerubbabel received 115 acres in Farmington, far more than what John Dunbar obtained from his father. And when Timothy died in 1750, he left another hundred acres in Farmington to be shared by his three oldest sons, directing William to buy out his brothers' portions at a fair price so the property could remain intact. At the time of his father's death, Zerubbabel was thirty-five years old and already well into his second marriage. After his first wife, Sarah Cook, died in 1737, probably in childbirth, he married her sister Phoebe. Over the next dozen years or so, Phoebe gave birth to at least seven children. Her namesake and Moses Dunbar's future wife was born around 1747, not long after Zerubbabel gained control of his Farmington property.[9]

With nearly 4,000 inhabitants, Farmington was one of Connecticut's oldest and most populous towns. It boasted some of the colony's best agricultural land, much of it located in the fertile Tunxis and Farmington River valleys. Many of its farmers teamed up with local merchants to sell surplus grain, meat, and other products in the West Indies, where planters imported provisions so they could devote more of their own land to sugarcane. As was true in most New England towns, the descendants of original settlers monopolized the best land near the town center, leaving property on the margins to latecomers. This was where Timothy Jerome had obtained land and Zerubbabel settled, on Farmington's western border, adjacent to Waterbury's Northbury parish.[10]

Ownership of 115 acres placed Zerubbabel Jerome in the top ranks of young Connecticut farmers, but he wanted more. Intent on parlaying his generous patrimony into a larger estate, he waded into the local land market. Between 1755 and 1768, he entered into at least a dozen transactions with neighbors, buying or selling plots ranging from three to ninety acres. The amount of his Farmington property thus waxed and waned over the years, but never seemed to reach the point where Zerubbabel could finally rest content. He was not even certain that he wanted to stay in Farmington.[11]

Like hundreds of other Connecticut farmers, Zerubbabel Jerome was captivated by the Susquehannah Company's grand project of settling in Pennsylvania's Wyoming Valley. Public enthusiasm for that speculative venture gained momentum just as Jerome acquired the resources for a possible investment. Between 1750 and 1753, the Connecticut General Assembly received—and rejected—a dozen petitions from land-hungry farmers asking for town grants in the area west of the Delaware River. Appended to a May 1752 request were more than 400 signatures, including those of Zerubbabel Jerome and his brothers William and Timothy. The Connecticut government cautiously sanctioned the scheme at last in the spring of 1755, contingent on royal approval, but the outbreak of the French and Indian War fore-stalled settlement in this volatile frontier zone for years.[12]

Once that conflict subsided, Susquehannah Company leaders renewed their speculative efforts. The first migrants arrived in the autumn of 1760 as the vanguard of what was intended to be a much larger exodus. In May 1762, Company officials voted to pursue further settlement despite a stern warning from Governor Thomas Fitch, who worried that the scheme invited royal displeasure that might, among other consequences, endanger Connecticut's precious charter. Irate Pennsylvania officials opposed the intrusion onto their land, as did Delaware and Iroquois leaders, raising the specter of a new cycle of violence. Nevertheless, in April 1763 the Company announced plans to survey land for eight townships, recruit settlers, and hire "a head or Teacher to Carry on religious Instruction & Worship." By that point, Zerubbabel Jerome had acquired a half share in Susquehannah lands, likely financed by sales of his Farmington property.[13]

Jerome fortunately made no effort to occupy his Susquehannah land right away. In the summer of 1763, a massive Indian uprising later known as Pontiac's War erupted in the west, making settlement across the Delaware a perilous endeavor. But the thirty or forty Connecticut families who had already transplanted there were determined to stay, despite continued opposition from imperial officials, resident Indians, Pennsylvania authorities, and Governor Fitch. In October 1763 a Delaware war party forced the issue, attacking and killing ten settlers and capturing the rest. Pennsylvanian soldiers arriving at the grisly scene a few days later were horrified to find scalped and mutilated bodies—punctured by arrows, spears, and pitchforks, with awls thrust into their eyes—and a woman "roasted," with "two Hinges in her Hands, supposed to be put in red hot." With such reports filtering back to Connecticut, enthusiasm for the Susquehannah project evaporated, although only temporarily.[14]

By the spring of 1769, a revitalized Company, assuming that a recent treaty between British authorities and the Iroquois cleared the way for settlement, sent off a new contingent of about thirty emigrants, one of whom was Zerubbabel Jerome. The men were busily hacking down trees and erecting log houses when several Northampton County officials appeared on the scene and charged them with "riotously" disturbing the peace and stealing timber that rightfully belonged to the

Penn family. Although the Connecticut men were armed and vowed to "put to Death any persons that attempted to dispossess them," they fought back with blows and not musket balls, and ultimately were forced to surrender. Some of the men escaped as they were being led to jail, others posted bail, and most—if not all—ended up back on the contested lands, where they met up with more than a hundred newly arrived emigrants from Connecticut. Thus the long-running battle for Susquehannah lands was joined, with engagements fought on paper—in petitions, proclamations, newspapers, and pamphlets—and in the flesh, with a steady stream of settlers occupying land and daring the authorities to try to drive them away.[15]

Zerubbabel Jerome was in the thick of it, at least for a time. But by the winter of 1769–1770, chances for real bloodshed escalated. Company leaders formed an alliance of convenience with the notorious Paxton Boys, who offered to dislodge Pennsylvania claimants on Wyoming lands in return for a large tract for themselves. This truculent group of Scots-Irish backcountry men had a well-deserved reputation for savagery. In December 1763 they had descended on a small village of Christian Indians, slaughtering several of them and subsequently attacking others who had been taken into protective custody. Hearing that Moravian Indian converts had sought refuge in Philadelphia, the Paxton gang marched on the city. Only the timely mustering of a combined force of royal troops and civilian volunteers prevented another massacre.[16]

The arrival of the Paxton gang in the Wyoming Valley escalated existing antagonisms between Pennsylvanians and New Englanders into outright war, complete with gunfights, besieged settlements, and widespread destruction of property. Zerubbabel Jerome's enthusiasm for the Susquehannah project ebbed as the violence intensified; in July 1770, Company leaders granted another settler rights to a portion of his claim. Dreams die hard, however, and as late as the autumn of 1772, Jerome joined his beleaguered neighbors in petitioning the Connecticut legislature to quell the disorder plaguing their settlements. Yet two months later, he was back in Farmington, apparently for good.[17]

Whatever advantages Moses Dunbar expected to gain from his connection to the Jeromes were confounded by his father-in-law's Susquehannah adventures. Zerubbabel was too preoccupied with his own business to act as the young man's patron and was frequently absent from Farmington. He provided Phoebe with only a modest marriage portion—a little more than £11—and it soon became clear that no other assistance would be forthcoming. In 1768, he sold three acres of land in Northbury to Moses for £3—the first land that Moses owned—but this probably had less to do with Jerome's desire to help the young couple than with his preparations to head out for the Wyoming Valley.[18]

Marriage, therefore, had not significantly reduced Moses's economic dependence on his father or provided a counterweight to John Dunbar's paternal authority. The elder Dunbar mimicked his own father's behavior toward him, setting Moses and Phoebe up in a separate house but refusing to transfer ownership so that a frustrated Moses likely continued working for him. Not until November 1769 did John Dunbar convey a portion of his estate to Moses: two pieces of land totaling about six acres, including the house where the couple already lived. Why he chose this particular moment, five years into his son's marriage, to make the gift is unclear, but once again his decision bore an uncanny resemblance to his own father's action. Moses was twenty-three, nearly the same age as John Dunbar had been when he received his own modest patrimony.[19]

Combined with the three acres he had recently purchased from his father-in-law, Moses Dunbar owned a grand total of nine acres, enough to place him squarely in the bottom rank of Connecticut landowners.[20] Quite likely, the only way he made ends meet was to work for wages or rent additional land and pay with a share of the harvest. Moses resented his father's parsimony, recalling some years later that he "never Assisted me but very little in gaining a Livelihood."[21] Such complaints ignored the very real challenges John Dunbar faced in supporting the rest of his family. Yet Moses was right to attribute his father's behavior, at least in part, to hostility and not just a scarcity of means. That hostility, however, had less to do with Moses's early marriage than with another factor related to his connection with Phoebe.

Soon after they married, Moses and Phoebe joined the Church of England. Moses insisted that they had "Sufficient & rational Motives" for doing so, but John Dunbar was nonetheless outraged. The conversion opened a "sorrowful breach" between father and son that would never be fully repaired. Although he might have suspected that his father would object, Moses was surely astonished by the intensity of his opposition. Anglicans had lived more or less peacefully alongside Congregationalists in Waterbury for years, and other families had accommodated themselves to religious differences without permanent rifts. Why could the Dunbars not do the same?[22]

John Dunbar's New Light beliefs, however, fostered a deep animosity toward Anglicans that few of his neighbors seemed to share. His marriage to Temperance Hall possibly intensified his intolerance by connecting him to a fervent New Light faction in her large kinship network. While the Dunbars still lived in Wallingford, the town suffered through a protracted religious controversy that began with a fight over the choice of a new minister. Dunbar's father-in-law, Jonathan Hall, along with other Hall relatives, rejected one candidate as insufficiently orthodox and demanded the appointment of a New Light clergyman. Before the crisis was resolved, the Dunbars had moved to Waterbury, but the experience might have had lasting effects that later poisoned John's relationship with his son. Temperance either did not share her husband's rigid beliefs or allowed maternal feelings to override them, for she never withheld her affection from Moses. Even so, none of his siblings ever followed him into the Anglican Church.[23]

This angry paternal reaction to Moses's announcement contrasted with recent religious developments in the colony. By the mid-eighteenth century, Connecticut had distanced itself from the fierce Puritanism of its founders, many of whom had fled to the New World to escape Anglican persecution. To be sure, suspicions about the Church of England lingered. In 1722, the Anglican conversions of Timothy Cutler, then rector of Yale College, and several recent graduates became something of a cause célèbre, and Cutler was dismissed. Yet he, Samuel Johnson, and a few other apostates were able to sail to England for ordination and return home to officiate as Anglican clergymen. By the time Moses and Phoebe converted, there were Anglican congregations in forty-five Connecticut towns.[24]

The appearance of such congregations did not represent a break with the past so much as a continuation of the religious divisiveness that had always plagued New England. The same kinds of disputes—over the location of a meetinghouse or choice of a minister—might produce either a new Congregationalist parish or an Anglican one, depending on the predilections of an outvoted faction unwilling to acquiesce in the victory of its opponents. Northbury's Congregationalists had already separated from Waterbury's parish due to distance from the meetinghouse, and not long thereafter, these same Northbury parishioners divided over the inflammatory preaching of Samuel Todd. This time, disgruntled members withdrew to form an Anglican society. In nearby Farmington, the choice of a New Light minister for the New Cambridge parish similarly sparked an exodus of the discontented into the Church of England. Indeed, there was no more effective source of Anglican recruitment in Connecticut, one observer later noted, than the Congregationalists' tendency to "bite & devour one another."[25]

The relative ease with which Anglican parishes proliferated in the colony reflected their homegrown character. Many members had been raised as Congregationalists, and this religious upbringing influenced their Anglican churches. As fond of good preaching as were Congregationalists, they retained a belief in the covenant and the necessity of grace for salvation. Anglicans shared with the more conservative Old Lights a reduced emphasis on predestination. They were slow to adopt the prescribed Church of England liturgy, in part because of a scarcity of copies of the Book of Common Prayer but also due to a habitual discomfort with rote prayer. If the New Cambridge church was typical, even Anglicans' sacramental vessels—beakers, tankard, and platter for the communion service and the basin for baptism—resembled those used in Congregationalist meetinghouses. Perhaps most important, Congregationalists who feared that the Church of England might send bishops to Connecticut as instruments of its authority were mollified when the local Anglican laity seemed to show little interest in seeing this happen.[26]

Furthermore, virtually all of Connecticut's Anglican ministers were native sons, not English immigrants as was the case in many other colonies. The Reverend James Scovil, who helped Moses and Phoebe on their spiritual journey into the Church of England, was born and raised in Waterbury. His father, William Scovil, was one of the town's first Anglicans. He had intended for his son to be trained as a weaver, but young James's lively intelligence attracted the attention of the town's retired Congregationalist minister. The Reverend John Southmayd urged William to let his son prepare for admission to college. A few years later, in 1753, twenty-year-old James Scovil found himself at Yale, studying alongside dozens of other young men destined for Congregationalist pulpits. William did not live to see him graduate, but he left a bequest of £200 to ensure that James could complete his education with the class of 1757.[27]

By the time of Scovil's graduation, Waterbury's Anglican church had existed for nearly two decades but still lacked its own minister. The Reverend Richard Mansfield of Derby visited occasionally to conduct services, but parish members wanted a resident clergyman. Here they encountered a problem that slowed Anglican expansion in the colonies: Church of England ministers, unlike Congregationalist clergy, required ordination and licensing by a bishop before they could assume their full clerical duties. That, in turn, entailed a trip to England, since no Anglican bishops lived in the colonies. James Scovil could scarcely afford a transatlantic voyage. In 1758, therefore, Waterbury's Anglicans offered to pay his £22 fare and promised him a salary if he returned to serve as their minister.[28]

Accompanied by his Yale classmate and fellow Anglican Samuel Peters, Scovil left home in early October and traveled to New York, where the young men obtained letters of recommendation from Samuel Johnson, president of King's College. After a month-long voyage, the travelers disembarked at Gravesend and took a chaise into London. The administrative and commercial heart of the mighty British empire was home to half a million people—more than twice the entire population of Connecticut. The sights, smells, and sounds of the great city astonished young men accustomed to the quiet lanes of their hometowns. With England and France at war, substantial numbers of red-coated soldiers and rough-looking sailors jostled with merchants, porters, peddlers, flower-sellers, beggars, and pickpockets in the city's labyrinthine streets and dark alleys.[29]

Scovil and Peters explored the great metropolis, likely visiting such landmarks as St. Paul's Cathedral, the British Museum, Tower Hill, and Kensington Gardens. A trip to St. James's Palace might have rewarded them with a glimpse of the king. Perhaps they devoted an evening or two to strolling along the circuitous paths of Vauxhall Gardens, marveling at the bizarre candle-lit follies and pavilions lining the walkways. The chance to see a play at Sadler's Wells or Drury Lane Theater enticed these rustic visitors from a colony where dramatic performances were forbidden by law. London's many shops likewise beckoned with an inconceivably diverse array of goods. Here Scovil could be fitted for his clerical garb but also pick up a fashionable new hat or waistcoat. He might succumb to the temptation to buy a watch as a mark of his new status or purchase books from London's countless shops and stalls. Afterward, he could brave the noise and tobacco smoke of the New England Coffee House, treating himself to the twin stimulations of caffeine and gossip. Scovil and his companion might even have joined with other tourists in a macabre form of amusement by visiting Bedlam, as London's hospital for the insane was known, or witnessing one of the many public hangings that drew throngs to the execution site at Tyburn just outside the city.[30]

Such diversions, however, would not have distracted the young men from the purpose of their trip. Not long after their arrival, Scovil probably accompanied Peters in calling on Thomas Secker, the Archbishop of Canterbury—an encounter that so overwhelmed Peters that he became speechless. Both men also paid their respects to officials of the Society for the Propagation of the Gospel in Foreign Parts. Created in 1701 as the evangelical offshoot of the Church of England, the SPG subsidized the salaries of Anglican ministers in Britain's colonies and helped to defray the costs of their travels for ordination. The bishop of London, or more likely one of his chaplains, examined the young men's letters of recommendation and college diplomas, and tested their scriptural knowledge before ordaining them as deacons. A bout of smallpox delayed Peters's clerical ordination for several months, but Scovil went ahead and on April 1, 1759, was ordained by Zachary Pearce, bishop of Rochester, in a quiet ceremony in Westminster Abbey. Three days later, Scovil obtained a commission from the SPG designating him as Waterbury's minister and guaranteeing him an annual stipend of £30, in addition to whatever salary his congregation could provide. After settling accounts at his lodgings, paying the requisite fees for his ordination and ministerial license, and perhaps indulging in a quick flurry of final sightseeing, the Reverend James Scovil was ready to head home.[31]

Back in Waterbury, Scovil quickly discovered how busy the life of a rural minister could be. His commission made him responsible for two parishes in town, the First and Northbury Anglican societies, as well as the New Cambridge parish in Farmington, whose members had agreed to pay a quarter of his salary. In all, his pastoral charge included more than a hundred families spread over a wide area. As he reported to the SPG in June 1760, he was compelled "to officiate alternately in my several parishes" instead of preaching every Sunday in each location. His Sabbath duties "afford Labour Enough," he noted the following year, but during the week he also had to visit the sick and baptize children. In addition, he was often summoned to preach in towns that lacked a settled minister, making trips that took him away from home for days at a stretch.[32]

Scovil found himself hard-pressed for money as well as time. His promised annual salary of £35 sterling, even when combined with his SPG stipend, barely covered his expenses, especially after he married in 1762 and children began to arrive. Moreover, many of his parishioners, especially in New Cambridge, were delinquent in their payments. As a consequence, Scovil repeatedly begged his SPG sponsors to increase his stipend and send much-needed supplies. New Cambridge parishioners had neither a Bible nor a Common Prayer Book for their church; the poorest among them could not even afford their own individual prayer books. Could the Society send those volumes, along with copies of Peter Barclay's *A Persuasive to the People of Scotland in Order to Remove their Prejudice to the Book of Common Prayer*? Scovil would distribute Barclay's book to his flock to "cultivate their good Disposition" and remove any stubborn objections these former Congregationalists harbored against the prescribed Anglican liturgy.[33]

To justify such impositions on the Society's generosity, the harried minister cited his progress in attracting converts. Membership in the western part of Waterbury grew with particular robustness, so much so that in 1765 the neighborhood's Anglicans formed a separate parish at Westbury, increasing Scovil's responsibilities from three to four such jurisdictions. All of these developments, Scovil reassured his SPG sponsors, occurred in an atmosphere of goodwill. Waterbury's burgeoning Anglican population lived "in Peace & unity among themselves, and in Friendship with the Dissenters." Northbury Congregationalists (probably in an effort to lure former Old Lights back into the fold) even voted to admit "any Member of Regular Standing in the Church of England ... to occasional Communion with us in this Church for the time to come." During this relatively harmonious interlude, Scovil's flock grew to include 172 families, with 244 communicants. Two of the new worshippers were Moses and Phoebe Dunbar.[34]

It was surely no accident that the couple waited until after their wedding to convert. Moses's status as a married man living under a separate roof—albeit one still owned by his father—gave him a little more freedom to assert himself. Zerubbabel Jerome was unlikely to have objected to Phoebe's conversion—or at least not as vehemently as John Dunbar—since she had connections on her mother's side to the Church of England. Her maternal grandfather, Henry Cook, had helped to found Northbury's Anglican parish, to which other Cook relatives belonged. Several of her siblings (though not her father) eventually joined the New Cambridge parish. Phoebe might even have begun attending Anglican services in New Cambridge as a non-member before her wedding; this could explain why the couple joined that parish rather than the Northbury one closer to their home.[35]

Phoebe's family ties, however, hardly sufficed to explain the Dunbars' conversion. No doubt a more decisive factor was the inability of Congregationalist churches in Northbury and New Cambridge to address the couple's spiritual needs, especially when those parishes' quarrelsome histories weakened members' sense of fellowship. Right when Moses and Phoebe decided to marry, for instance, Northbury Congregationalists were wrangling over the dismissal of their contentious minister, Samuel Todd. Like frustrated Old Lights during the Great Awakening, Moses and Phoebe perhaps also sought refuge from New Lights' hellfire-and-brimstone preaching, with its emphasis on human depravity and a fearsome divine sovereignty. Anglicanism provided a more congenial version of the Christian message, and in James Scovil the Dunbars found a kind and conscientious pastor who sought to welcome inquisitive people like them into a more peaceful congregation. A warm reception doubtless helped Moses to cope with John Dunbar's angry reaction. Eager as the teenaged husband was to establish his own independence, he had not intended to alienate his father altogether.[36]

But given John Dunbar's response, Moses and Phoebe treasured all the more the fellowship of New Cambridge parish. With just thirty-two member families when the Dunbars joined, it resembled an extended kinship network as much as a congregation. Many members were young and, like the Dunbars, striving to make their livings and pay the parish's share of Scovil's salary. Offering some compensation for his unhappy estrangement from his father, these families provided

Moses with friendship and spiritual support as his faith deepened over time. He and Phoebe, in turn, added to their numbers when, on a warm summer's day in 1765, they asked Scovil to baptize their first-born child, a daughter named Bede.[37]

Not long before Bede's baptism, the *Connecticut Courant* reported that Britain's Parliament had passed a Stamp Act for the colonies. The news aroused "the most alarming Apprehensions" in Connecticut leaders, who declared the measure an unprecedented infringement on liberty but carefully balanced their expressions of outrage with professions of loyalty to the empire. They reassured themselves that Parliament would soon recognize the righteousness of the colonists' protest and repeal the detested statute. If Moses Dunbar perused that issue of the *Courant,* he would have had no reason to suspect that this news would impinge in any way on his hardscrabble life. In the short run, he was correct.[38]

Parliament viewed the Stamp Act as a partial remedy for a grave problem. Great Britain emerged from the French and Indian War with an enormous public debt of £146 million. George Grenville, first lord of the Treasury, could not squeeze more money from heavily taxed British subjects without sparking serious protests. But the pockets of American colonists—major beneficiaries of England's triumph over France and lightly taxed by their own governments—presented an inviting alternative. The Stamp Act was in fact the second postwar effort to raise revenue from the colonists. Grenville's first venture, the American Duties Act of 1764 (known in the colonies as the Sugar Act), had—among other provisions—adjusted the duty on West Indian molasses in order to reduce smuggling. Merchants heavily involved in the Caribbean trade and expert at evading customs duties complained, but the Sugar Act failed to energize the colonial populace as a whole. Grenville assumed that he had established a precedent for extracting even more money from Britain's American subjects. And that he would need to do soon, since the Sugar Act only produced about £70,000 in revenue per year.[39]

The Stamp Act, however, incited nearly universal colonial alarm. It imposed duties on legal documents, playing cards, pamphlets, and newspapers. The first such parliamentary measure to apply to all colonies equally, it touched the lives of urban and rural dwellers alike.

Anyone who deeded land, wrote a will, or bought an almanac had to pay the tax. Up and down the Atlantic seaboard, outraged colonists objected that they were being taxed without representation since they elected no members to Parliament. They composed fiery pamphlets for local consumption and more temperate petitions for London officials. Merchants and consumers agreed to boycott British imports until the act was repealed. In October, nine colonies sent representatives to a Stamp Act Congress in New York to collaborate on a "general and united, dutiful, loyal and humble" statement of opposition to the measure. One of Connecticut's three delegates was William Samuel Johnson, son of the prominent Anglican minister and now former president of King's College, Samuel Johnson.[40]

As Johnson's appointment demonstrated, Anglicans and Congregationalists cooperated in opposing the detested act. But cracks in that unity surfaced as protests turned increasingly rowdy. Connecticut crowds never matched the extreme behavior of Boston mobs, which rampaged through the streets and pillaged the homes of Andrew Oliver, who had been appointed stamp distributor, and Lieutenant Governor Thomas Hutchinson. Yet in several towns colonists resorted to bullying and threats of violence. No one came in for more abuse than Jared Ingersoll. He had agreed to become a stamp distributor under the sorely mistaken assumption that the act's opponents would calm down if a native son took the job. In New London, a radical group calling itself the Sons of Liberty stirred up an angry crowd by erecting a gallows and stringing up an effigy of Ingersoll. The *Connecticut Courant* reported that "even the Children were crying, THERE HANGS A TRAYTOR, THERE's AN ENEMY TO HIS COUNTRY." Similarly boisterous street demonstrations erupted in Lebanon, Windham, and Norwich. When Ingersoll tried to make his way to a legislative session in Hartford in September, a mob of men armed with clubs blocked his path. Several leaders in the group who had served as officers in the French and Indian War felt profoundly betrayed by the empire for which they had so recently risked their lives. After a prolonged exchange, they forced Ingersoll to resign his position twice—once in their presence and again before the General Assembly, doubling his public humiliation. As tensions increased that autumn, Wallingford's Sons of Liberty announced that if necessary they would "take the field" to preserve their liberty.[41]

Such displays disturbed Anglicans and Old Lights, who objected to the virulent anti-British rhetoric and feared that violent resistance would give the monarch an excuse to revoke the charter. They suspected, moreover, that many New Lights were taking political advantage of the uproar in order to manipulate an angry electorate into choosing officials sympathetic to their religious views and the controversial Susquehannah Company. And, indeed, this was the case: New Lights triumphed in the 1766 elections, ousting Thomas Fitch (an Old Light long suspicious of the Susquehannah venture) from the governorship. Advertising their highly visible opposition to the Stamp Act, they portrayed themselves as true patriots and their more cautious and conservative opponents as insufficiently solicitous of colonial liberties.[42]

Old Lights and Anglicans were equally dismayed by these results, but Anglicans were in an especially awkward position because of their tie to England's established church. Anglican clergy pledged loyalty to the monarchy at their ordinations and worried about losing SPG support if the crisis continued. They warned parishioners against "taking the least part in any tumult or opposition to his Majesty's acts." Connecticut's clergymen later informed the SPG that their congregations behaved as they were told, but noted that this obedience came at a price. James Scovil claimed that his parishioners' "quiet behaviour hath, unhappily, subjected them to the odium of the dissenters, who are the governing part here, and have the authority in their hands; and what will be the consequence of their enmity, God only knows." Some frightened ministers reported that protesters threatened to demolish Anglican churches and parsonages. Fortunately, no such violence occurred. The Reverend John Beach noted with considerable relief that the mobs "hurt us in no way but by the Lash of the Tongue."[43]

These troubling internal divisions began to heal when colonists learned in late May 1766 that Parliament had voted to repeal the Stamp Act. The Connecticut Assembly proclaimed a day of "general Rejoicing," accompanied by the ringing of church bells and discharge of cannon. In Hartford, alas, the "Height of Joy" swiftly turned to "extreme Sorrow" when gunpowder intended for a fireworks display exploded prematurely, killing three men and wounding twenty-one others. Celebrations in other towns proceeded without incident, marked by countless speeches, banquets, toasts, and bonfires. Yet the revelers were wrong to conclude that British officials had "discover[ed] their Error" in imposing unconstitutional taxes on America. Parliament had voted for repeal with great reluctance, largely in response to pleas from British merchants suffering from the colonists' trade boycott. To push repeal through the House of Commons, the new prime minister, Lord Rockingham, had to accompany it with the Declaratory Act, which affirmed Parliament's sovereignty over the colonies and its right to make laws for them "in all cases whatsoever." Rejoicing colonists, intoxicated with victory and rum, paid little attention to what they regarded as a face-saving gesture—if, indeed, they regarded it at all.[44]

With public order restored, Connecticut's Anglican clergy met to discuss how to prevent such tumults from erupting again. Led by Samuel Johnson, long an advocate of an American episcopate, James Scovil and several other ministers urged Church of England authorities to consider appointing colonial bishops. This would eliminate the need for clerical candidates to travel to England for ordination, stimulate the growth of new congregations, and, not least of all, buttress royal authority in the colonies. Year after year, individually and collectively, Anglican ministers pursued this private campaign. The "Well Being of the civil Polity in America," Abraham Jarvis wrote from Middletown in 1767, "depends in a great Measure, upon the Settlement of Episcopacy here." In 1771 alone, the colony's Anglican clergy sent eight petitions to London begging for bishops.[45]

Those requests might as well have drifted to the bottom of the Atlantic for all the good they did. British authorities knew that the establishment of an American episcopacy was a contentious subject, especially in New England, and had no desire to reignite public disturbances so soon after the Stamp Act furor. Boston had been riled up over the matter of bishops as recently as 1763, and newspaper essays there and in New York and Philadelphia periodically denounced them as agents of religious tyranny and threats to civil liberty. Few of these pieces appeared in Connecticut papers, however. There the clerical campaign for bishops mainly occurred behind the scenes rather than in any public forum. Had the laity known of their clergymen's efforts, they might have objected, not least of all because of possible damage to their delicate political alliance with Old Lights.[46]

Before long that alliance was tested once again. Far from teaching Parliament the error of its ways, the Stamp Act protests strengthened the ministry's determination to tax the colonists, now as much to punish them for their obstreperousness as to raise revenue. Charles Townshend, the chancellor of the exchequer, meant to show the Americans that the Declaratory Act had teeth and they would soon feel its bite. In 1767, he presented Parliament with a package of proposals, including one that placed new customs duties on goods colonists imported from England, including lead, paint, paper, glass, and tea. Some of the funds were intended to pay the salaries of royal officials in the colonies. This was a matter of much greater concern in places with royally appointed governors than in Connecticut, with its elected executive. Nevertheless, Connecticut joined other colonies in denouncing this newest example of oppression.[47]

Anglicans united with both Old and New Lights in protest. The coalition remained firm this time because the main form of resistance was a relatively peaceful boycott of British goods, to which most Connecticut merchants had subscribed by late 1769. There were isolated attacks on shopkeepers and consumers who failed to observe the trade embargo, but nothing like the street violence during the Stamp Act unrest. The prominent Anglican William Samuel Johnson served as Connecticut's special agent to London, leading its opposition to the acts. The colony's Anglican clergy largely remained silent in the face of this new imperial controversy, or even cautiously expressed support for the protesters' position. "We hope in God for better times," declared the Reverend Ebenezer Dibble of Stamford, and "that the Provinces will obtain redress of Just grievances." Ministers hastened to reassure SPG sponsors that their congregations were "in a flourishing way" despite renewed tensions with Britain.[48]

As the colonists had hoped, economic pressure on Britain proved painful enough to elicit a political response, though not one greeted with universal American approbation. In March 1770, Parliament repealed all the Townshend duties except the tax on tea. For many colonial merchants, also hurting from the boycott, this was enough of a compromise to call for an end to non-importation. By July, the movement had collapsed in New York and Rhode Island; it was then suspended in Philadelphia, Boston, and Charleston. Merchants in other cities had no choice but to follow suit if they wanted to remain competitive. In Hartford, die-hard opponents of British policy insisted on trade sanctions so long as the detested tax on tea remained. But most colonists returned to business as usual. Sticklers for their rights could salve their consciences by refusing to purchase or consume taxed tea.[49]

On March 5, 1770, the same day Parliament voted to repeal most of the Townshend duties, British soldiers in Boston fired into an angry crowd of colonists who had been taunting nervous sentinels and pelting them with snowballs and rocks. The episode marked the culmination of several days of tension between soldiers and civilians and resulted in the deaths of five Boston men. Though word of mouth carried the news to Connecticut within days, it was two weeks before the *Courant* printed an account of what would become known as the Boston Massacre. The shedding of American blood by British troops seemed to fulfill the dire predictions of colonial radicals who decried the most violent example to date of Britain's alleged scheme to suppress colonial liberties. Less willing to discern such an ominous pattern in recent events, many Anglicans and other more conservative colonists urged caution, lest Connecticut endanger its special charter privileges by alienating imperial authorities with yet more protest.[50]

Daily life in Connecticut gradually returned to normal. Trade with Britain skyrocketed as colonists desperate for imported goods celebrated the end of the boycott with a purchasing frenzy. Merchants in Hartford and other towns tempted consumers with an array of textiles—cambrics, oznabrigs, callimancoes, worsteds, and silks in a veritable rainbow of colors—fresh off the ships from London. Storekeepers' shelves sagged with the weight of china, delft, and glassware; cabinets bulged with silver buckles, snuffboxes, combs, and buttons. Since currency remained scarce in the colony, many shopkeepers accepted "country pay" in the form of agricultural products rather than demand cash. Yet only the most daring merchants, more interested in profits than politics, announced that they had tea—which still bore the hated Townshend duty—for sale.[51]

Even though Parliament refrained from levying new taxes, Boston radicals remained apprehensive. They pointed to a plan put forward in 1772 for the crown to pay the salaries—and thus buy the allegiance—of Massachusetts's governor and Superior Court judges. William Samuel Johnson, however, joined other Connecticut officials in detecting a distinct propensity for "mischief" among Boston radicals when it came to imperial relations. They tended to agree with the newspaper essayist who noted in February 1773 that at least in Connecticut "the ferment of politics" had "pretty much subsided." The colony's legislature did accede to the wishes of Boston radicals by voting that May to appoint a standing committee of nine men "to obtain all such Intelligence, and to keep up, and maintain a Correspondence and Communication, with our Sister Colonies" respecting potential threats to liberty. Few disputed the need for vigilance, but most Connecticut colonists hoped that the political firestorm of recent years had finally burned itself out.[52]

Moses Dunbar could hardly have ignored the political ferment swirling around Connecticut during the first years of his marriage, but economic difficulties and family responsibilities left him with little time or energy to devote to politics and little money to buy newspapers or imported goods. Like other members of New Cambridge parish, he doubtless heeded the Reverend Scovil's admonitions to avoid public demonstrations against parliamentary taxation. If he attended town meetings and dared to offer his political views, his youth and insignificance guaranteed that he would attract little serious notice. On only one known occasion did Moses sign a petition of protest, but the case involved the misbehavior of neighbors and not the actions of a distant Parliament. In the spring of 1769, Moses joined his uncle Edward and several other Waterbury men in complaining to the General Assembly that the captain of their militia company had held an election of officers without giving everyone due notice as the law required. This homegrown abuse of power made a more immediate impression on Dunbar than any aspect of the imperial controversy.[53]

Moses Dunbar was further distracted in 1770 by an intensely personal anguish. On May 26, his mother died. Only forty-three years old, the exhausted woman perished in childbirth, not long after delivering twin boys. Temperance had borne fourteen children in nearly twenty-seven years of marriage, but of all her progeny Moses felt her loss most keenly. She had always bestowed upon him "the Greatest Care and Affection," and for that he remembered her "with the most filial Honour & Gratitude" and sorely missed her moderating presence. In the wake of her untimely death, mutual sorrow may have temporarily eased the tensions between Moses and his father. Other men in his position wasted little time seeking a new wife to undertake the burdens of childcare and housekeeping, but although John

Dunbar lived for another sixteen years after Temperance's death, he never remarried.[54]

Moses could not escape the sound of wailing infants by retreating to his own home. Phoebe bore seven children in a dozen years, and this growing family struggled to survive on a shrinking estate. In February 1773, with Phoebe pregnant with one of those children, Moses made the seemingly foolish decision to sell the three acres of land he bought five years earlier from Zerubbabel Jerome. The purchaser was Ebenezer Cook, Phoebe's maternal uncle, and Moses received £6 for the property—twice what he had paid for it. But now he had only six acres to his name in a colony where forty acres was considered the minimum holding for a viable farm. He evidently judged the money more useful to him at that moment than the land, but the sale pushed the family closer to the edge of poverty. It also prolonged his dependence on others, whether for land to rent or wages in return for his labor.[55]

It seemed that for every step forward, Moses Dunbar took one step back. The only—tiny—measure of recognition he received from his neighbors came in 1770. Colony law allowed towns with multiple parishes to decide whether the whole town, or each parish, would serve as the unit to manage church and school. Waterbury chose the latter option, which meant that the First and Northbury societies each handled these responsibilities for their respective districts. When the Northbury Congregational Society named the members of their district's school committee in December 1770, one of the seven men chosen was Moses Dunbar—an Anglican, but also a Northbury resident. Such practices offered further evidence of local cooperation between Congregationalists and Anglicans. But if Moses Dunbar thought that this modest gesture of trust would bring other opportunities for public service, he was disappointed. More important duties typically fell to men of more substantial means, and the trajectory of Dunbar's economic fortunes appeared to be sliding downward.[56]

On Sunday, May 30, 1773, nine years to the day after their wedding, Moses and Phoebe brought another infant to James Scovil for baptism. This time it was a son whom they named Zina. Whatever joy they felt on this happy occasion was tempered with concern. Marriage and parenthood, important hallmarks of adult status, had brought few improvements to Moses's life as he acquired new responsibilities but no additional resources with which to deal with them. He could only do what New England farmers had always done: work hard, tend to his family, and keep a sharp eye out for unexpected opportunities that might come his way. The returns on his investment of labor and energy had so far been meager, but Moses Dunbar could nevertheless hope, now that the political ferment had calmed down, that his future might one day be brighter.

3

SON OF LINONIA

ONE OF THE BOYS BROKE the wax seal and eagerly unfolded the letter. He and his brother had written home three weeks earlier and had been awaiting this reply. "I Rec[eive]d your Letter of the 7th instant and am glad to hear that you are well suited with Living in College," Richard Hale informed his sons. Enoch and Nathan could hear their father's voice in their heads as they read his admonitions to study hard, obey college rules, and "forget not to Learne Christ while you are busy in other studies." The familiar handwriting, as well as the letter's contents, comforted them on that chilly late-December day in 1769. It was good to know that their family and friends were well. It was also good to learn that their father planned to send them some money.[1]

The boys had only been away for a few months. The previous September, fifteen-year-old Enoch and fourteen-year-old Nathan made the sixty-mile journey from Coventry to New Haven with their father. Richard Hale may have timed the journey in order to attend the commencement ceremony on September 12. The boys' cousin, Nathan Strong, was graduating with the class of 1769 and would deliver a Latin oration that attendees later praised as "very elegant." Cousin Strong remained at Yale first as college butler and then as a tutor during the Hale boys' time in New Haven. His familiar presence helped them adjust to their first extended stay away from home.[2]

The Hale and Strong clans stood out at a time when very few colonists attended college. Nathan Strong's father had graduated from Yale, and several of Richard Hale's relatives went to Harvard. Deacon Hale had not followed in their footsteps, which perhaps intensified his desire to provide his sons with an experience he lacked. Elizabeth Hale particularly wanted Nathan to go to Yale. His uncertain health in childhood may have prompted her concern that he be trained for a less strenuous career than farming. It was perhaps no coincidence that the boys' preparation for college commenced around the time of Elizabeth's death in April 1767, a sad event that may have hastened Richard Hale's efforts to fulfill her wish.[3]

Although some college graduates did end up as farmers, the goal of a liberal education was to open up a wider array of possibilities. Many graduates entered the ministry—which was likely the intended goal for the Hale boys—but they could also choose among prestigious and often lucrative careers in commerce, medicine, or the law. A college education, however, did more than prepare a man to work with his head rather than his hands. The course of study also aimed to refine behavior and build character. Ideally, each entering class of anxious and unformed lads emerged four years later as knowledgeable, competent gentlemen capable of serving as town and colony leaders. A college education was meant to be a life-changing experience.[4]

That was precisely what Yale accomplished for Nathan Hale, even more than for Enoch. Yet the college's learned professors and formal curriculum were not solely responsible for Nathan's transformation. Equally influential was the informal education he obtained by associating with other inquisitive and ambitious youths, exploring books and ideas that lay outside the prescribed coursework, and experimenting with new patterns of conduct. At Yale Nathan acquired more than knowledge and polish to take back to Coventry. By the time of his graduation in 1773, he had crafted a new sense of himself, what he might do, and where he might go.

Coventry, not New Haven, was where the change began. Connecticut law required all towns with more than seventy families to keep a school, and the Hale boys probably attended their local one for a few years. But its curriculum—focused on reading, writing, and ciphering—was better suited to the needs of farmers, craftsmen, and shopkeepers, than young men (or parents) with higher aspirations. Admission to Yale obliged the brothers to be trained as "Latin scholars," thoroughly drilled in ancient languages and classical texts. One man in Coventry was particularly well qualified to teach them.[5]

The Reverend Joseph Huntington had graduated from Yale just five years earlier. He welcomed the extra income earned from tutoring Richard Hale's sons and relished the intellectually challenging diversion from his usual round of writing sermons, visiting parishioners, and preaching. The minister also recognized the benefits of ingratiating himself with two of Coventry's leading families, whose patronage could enhance his influence in town. What he might not have anticipated were the emotional rewards of the job. Huntington grew quite fond of his charges, becoming a friend and mentor as well as teacher. For years after they left his tutelage, the Hale brothers kept in touch through visits and letters. And in 1779, in what must have been one of the proudest moments of his career, Huntington delivered the sermon at Enoch's ordination as minister of Westhampton, Massachusetts.[6]

Known for delivering lively extemporaneous sermons, Huntington charmed the members of his congregation with his pleasing manners, keen wit, and love of conversation. He incorporated the same vibrant style into his teaching to enliven the lessons that prepared his pupils for their entrance examinations. He knew that each boy would have to appear before Yale's president and tutors and demonstrate that he could "read accurately, construe and parse Tully, Virgil, and the Greek Testament, and ... write true Latin in Prose." The boys also had to master "the Rules of Prosody and vulgar Arithmetic." After two years of assiduous instruction, Enoch and Nathan passed their exams and Huntington happily provided them with the "suitable Testimony of a blameless Life and Conversation" they had to bring along to New Haven.[7]

While his sons pored over books and memorized rules of grammar, Richard Hale jotted down numbers and totaled up sums. Tuition at Yale cost twelve shillings a quarter. Add in extra fees, multiply the sum by sixteen (four quarters for four years), and then double the result to account for two students: Hale needed roughly £25 to cover expenses for his boys, the equivalent of about a year's wages for a New England farm laborer. No wonder that Yale required the parents or guardians of prospective students to post "sufficient Bond" that they could afford a college education. Richard Hale regarded this outlay less as an expense than an investment. To divide his property among all eight of his sons would consign each heir to a reduced standard of living on a small farm of dubious viability. It made more sense to provide some of the boys with an education or training in a craft and concentrate transfers of land on the others. Enoch and Nathan, in effect, received their legacies while still in their teens. It would be up to them to make the most of their Yale educations.[8]

On their initial journey to New Haven, Richard Hale and his sons probably took the main road in from the northeast and crossed a broad sandy plain just before arriving in town, passing scattered farms with grazing livestock and rows of rail fences. New Haven's entire population numbered around 6,000, but only 1,500 or so clustered in the densely settled neighborhood near the college. This part of town was handsome indeed, dominated by a central green surrounded by three churches and an imposing new brick statehouse, where the legislature met for its autumn sessions (spring meetings were held in Hartford). More than 200 trees—elms and sycamores—shaded the green. New Haven's lanes were lined with stores and artisans' shops purveying all sorts of goods that were far harder to come by in Coventry. Wandering down by the shore and along the narrow pier that jutted into the harbor, the Hale boys had their first glimpse of the sea, with Long Island shimmering on the horizon.[9]

Then there was Yale College itself. Four buildings stood on the campus, the most impressive of which was Connecticut Hall. Modeled on Harvard's Massachusetts Hall and requiring nearly a quarter of a million bricks for its construction, the edifice was completed in 1753 and judged to be one of the colony's finest buildings. Like many imposing structures, however, it was more pleasing to look at than comfortable to live in. Students complained that their rooms were too cold in the winter and too hot in the summer. The windows in their studies were poorly arranged, never admitting enough sunlight for easy reading. Whatever the building's design flaws, Enoch and Nathan would have to learn to live with them. Connecticut Hall would be their home for the next four years.[10]

The Hales' entering class of thirty-six students was the largest Yale had admitted in years—large enough to spark discussion about the need for another college building. Fourteen-year-old Nathan was

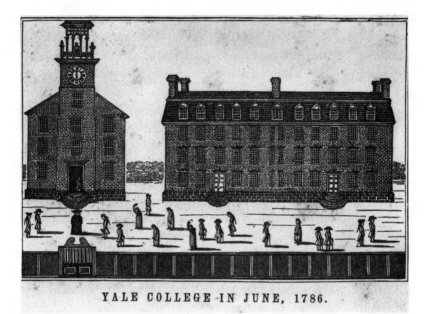

YALE COLLEGE IN JUNE, 1786.

Figure 3.1 1786 woodcut of "A Front View of Yale-College, and the College Chapel, New Haven," with Connecticut Hall on the right. Courtesy of Yale University Buildings and Grounds Photographs (RU 703). Manuscripts and Archives, Yale University Library.

not the youngest to matriculate; that distinction belonged to William Chandler, aged eleven. Most students ranged in age between fourteen and twenty, an awkward combination of boys and men who would sit together in the same classes, perform the same scholastic exercises, submit to the same rules, and live in close quarters. Twenty-four-year-old Samuel Dwight, older than his classmates and his tutors, must have felt most out of place.[11]

Four students usually roomed together. Tradition has it that fifteen-year-old Isaac Gridley, born in Farmington but raised in New Haven, was one of the Hale brothers' roommates. Two freshmen in the class were New Haven natives, with most others coming from towns dispersed around the colony, from Danbury on the western border to Killingly in the east. Six classmates hailed from Massachusetts, some from the Connecticut River valley, and others from communities in what had once been Plymouth Colony. Long Island supplied one freshman. This was a decidedly New England cohort, yet it probably struck its members—few of whom would have known anyone from outside of their hometowns except relatives—as rather cosmopolitan.[12]

Before 1766, each student's introduction to Yale meant quite literally being put in his place. College policy then required the president to arrange members of each entering class according to their families' social positions. This ranking shaped virtually every aspect of students' lives, from how they were listed on the class roll to where they sat in class, at meals, and during chapel services. In rare instances, a misbehaving classmate could be "degraded," subjected to the very public punishment of being dropped several places in the class roster and shuffled to a back seat. Sons or grandsons of high government officials—or a president of Yale—ranked first, followed by sons of alumni and preachers. Below them were arrayed the offspring of merchants, farmers, and artisans in an order whose logic was mainly discernible to the president himself. Had this system been in place when Enoch and Nathan arrived, James Hillhouse, son of a judge and related on his mother's side to a former Connecticut governor, would have ranked at the top. With their connections to the Strong family, which included several Yale alumni, the Hales would likely have been placed somewhere near the middle of their class.[13]

Enoch and Nathan appeared midway through the roster anyway, but not because of their social standing. By 1769, Yale had adopted a less subjective alphabetical ordering system, probably because President Naphtali Daggett disliked having to deal with angry parents offended by their sons' assigned places. Though purely practical in intent, this change struck a small but significant blow against the hierarchical assumptions of colonial society. As one of the first beneficiaries of the new policy gloated, "It is not he that has got the finest coat or largest ruffles that is esteemed here at present."[14]

President Daggett was busy enough restoring calm to an institution left in disarray by his predecessor. To his credit, Thomas Clap, who served as Yale's president from 1739 to 1766, had improved the college enormously. He broadened the curriculum by including instruction in science and mathematics, added tutors to the teaching staff, raised funds (some from his own pocket) to cover new construction, wrote a charter for the college, and codified its laws. Yet his distinctive combination of energy and rigidity invariably caused problems.

Clap held students to a rigorous disciplinary standard and resisted efforts by anyone—whether members of Yale's Corporation or colony legislators—to interfere with college administration, or even inquire into its workings. A major dispute erupted when he took the unprecedented step of allowing students to withdraw from New Haven's First Congregational Church, which they had customarily attended, ostensibly because of their discontent with the minister's lackluster preaching. In a move that accorded with his persistent campaign to enlarge his beloved Yale—and thus raised suspicions about his real motives—Clap arranged for students to worship at what became the first collegiate church in the colonies. Daggett's initial position as professor of divinity grew out of this discord, which became so bitter that in 1755 the Assembly refused to pass its customary grant of support to the college. During Clap's reign, episodes of student unrest broke out as well, sometimes over food—in one instance, rumor had it that students were being poisoned—and sometimes over the president's peremptory ways. After Clap resigned in 1766, the Corporation offered the Reverend James Lockwood the presidency. When he politely declined, it passed to Professor Daggett.[15]

With this stout, clumsy, and decidedly less confrontational leader at the helm, a measure of calm returned to the New Haven campus. For the first time in eleven years, the legislature voted to renew its subsidy to the college. Student unrest subsided, albeit temporarily. In March 1771, complaints about food blossomed into a direct challenge to college authorities. Students groused about paltry rations, especially in the winter—only ten pounds of butter to spread on ninety servings of toast! When they failed to gain redress through proper channels, a near-rebellion ensued. James Nichols and John Brown, members of that year's graduating class and ringleaders of the protest, urged fellow students not to return from their vacations until the quality of the commons was improved. Brown went so far as to publish an anonymous essay in a newspaper describing the students' plight and excoriating the college steward, tutors, president, and Yale's Corporation itself for ignoring it. This audacious breach of college laws provoked an immediate response, though not the one the rebels hoped for. Charged with gross insubordination, Brown and Nichols were ordered to apologize to college authorities and beg for forgiveness or face expulsion.[16]

It is hardly surprising that upperclassmen instigated this revolt, since they had the most time on their hands. Theoretically, the scholars' day was highly regimented. They awoke at 6 A.M. to the sound of a bell and, after attending prayers, had their first class and then sat down to their disappointing breakfasts. After a half-hour of free time, it was back to the books. Dinner at noon—meat, bread, fruit or vegetables, all washed down with beer—was followed by a short break, another class, and evening prayers at four. Supper came at five, and then another respite from work until nine o'clock, when the last study period of the day occupied the interval until bedtime, no later than eleven. This regimentation diminished, however, as students advanced in their studies. Juniors attended only one morning class, starting at eleven, and another in the late afternoon; seniors just had the morning class. The assumption was that at all other times upperclassmen were at work in their chambers preparing for exams. Tutors supposedly checked up on them regularly, but mischief-makers had little difficulty evading supervision. James Nichols had actually convened a "private meeting" of his class to plot insurrection without attracting notice.[17]

Although Yale had discarded its social ranking system, students sorted themselves into their own hierarchies. For years—probably since the college's beginnings—freshmen stood at the bottom of the pecking order, forced to comply with a ridiculous set of rules set by upperclassmen whose only purpose was harassment. First-year students were forbidden to wear gowns or carry canes. They had to doff their hats (except in bad weather) if they came near the president, professors, or tutors. They could not enter a gate if an upperclassman was nearby and had not given them permission to do so. They had to perform any "reasonable" errand an upperclassman requested of them; in one instance, "reasonable" meant bringing a pitcher of water to a sophomore's room and waiting there for him to return—however long that took. Exasperated freshmen surely found some consolation in the knowledge that they would eventually lord it over others, but that first year was a long one.[18]

By the time the Hale brothers arrived, a new sort of student hierarchy had begun to emerge. Each class included some members who were more intelligent, more eager, or simply more diligent than their fellows. Everyone knew who these strivers were, but before 1766 their achievements brought them limited credit within the Yale community unless their fathers were prominent men. The abolition of social ranking, however, helped to level the playing field, allowing students to compete for recognition based on their own merits. No one understood the implications of this change better than David Avery. Initially apprenticed to a house-carpenter, Avery later enrolled as a charity student at the Reverend Eleazar Wheelock's school to prepare for college. Suddenly, new vistas opened up for him. He was still poor, but he was determined to show his Yale classmates that a former carpenter's apprentice could rise above the sons of governors if he worked hard enough. Writing to Wheelock in 1767, Avery observed that some fellow students had begun to exhibit "a laudable ambition to excel in knowledge." The "best scholars and speakers" could earn "marks of distinction" for their own accomplishments, and Avery intended to be among their number. Yale was hardly a hotbed of egalitarianism, but a window of opportunity had opened for students with more intelligence and determination than money or social status.[19]

Achieving academic distinction, however, required spending countless hours with tedious texts and obscure languages. Despite President Clap's reforms, the curriculum still reflected the hidebound legacy of English scholastic tradition. The first year focused on "the Tongues"—mainly Latin and Greek, and perhaps some Hebrew—and Logic. Training in classical languages continued for at least two more years. Sophomores added rhetoric, geometry, and geography; juniors concentrated on natural philosophy (or science), astronomy, and mathematics. Students spent their final year mastering metaphysics and ethics. Every Saturday, every year, was devoted to the study of theology. The expectation that "the respective Classes shall recite the usual Books, and in the accustomed Manner" summed up the goal of such an education. A heavy emphasis on memorization, recitation, and declamation aimed to discipline rather than free the mind, to encourage emulation and not creativity.[20]

Few students possessed either the nerve or the imagination to question the wisdom of this course of study. Yet some did chafe under its restrictions, claiming that the stodgy curriculum perpetuated New England's provincial status and cultural inferiority. One of Yale's sons launched an attack on the college's suffocating intellectual traditions just when the Hale brothers arrived. John Trumbull, born in 1750, was by any measure a child prodigy. By the age of four he had read the entire Bible and by six he could speak Latin. At seven he passed Yale's entrance examination, though his parents wisely waited six more years before sending him to college. Once he got there, this son of a Yale-educated minister excelled in his studies even as he deplored the deficiencies of a curriculum little changed from his father's day. Trumbull remained at the college as a Berkeley Scholar (recipient of a post-graduate fellowship) for three years after his graduation in 1767, during which time he embarked on a quest to move Yale out of the shadows of medieval scholasticism into the light of the modern world.[21]

By age four, Trumbull had not only worked his way through the Bible but he had also composed poetry. By the time he was nine, he had transformed half of the psalms into verse. During the six years between passing its entrance examination and arriving at Yale, Trumbull immersed himself in the works of such writers as John Milton and James Thomson and pored over copies of the popular English literary journal *The Spectator*. This private reading exposed him to the delights of polite literature—a subject not just absent from Yale's curriculum but reviled by college officials as "folly, nonsense, and an idle waste of time." Trumbull was determined to convince them otherwise. His opening salvo took the form of a commencement address he delivered in 1770 proclaiming the "Use and Advantages of the Fine Arts." Shaping his message to appeal to his stern and pious audience, he insisted that the arts, like religion, "ennoble the soul, purify the passions, and give the thoughts a better turn." A few years later, Trumbull composed a scathing three-part satirical poem, *The Progress of Dulness*. Yale's supporters took particular offense at the first part, which narrated the "rare adventures" of Tom Brainless. It begins with young Tom going off to college to avoid the rigors of farm work. While there he musters every excuse to evade his schoolwork and learn as little as possible. After four years, he has acquired "the dullness of a letter'd brain," able—just barely—to read the classics, but incapable of appreciating their refined literary qualities. Tom then embarks on the usual career of a New England college graduate, finding "some unsettled town" where he can eke out a living as a soporific preacher who "does no good, and little harm."[22]

Trumbull had an equally precocious comrade in the campaign to introduce Yale to belles-lettres. Timothy Dwight, two years Trumbull's junior, had as a toddler memorized the alphabet in a single lesson, and at age four tried to instruct local Indians in the catechism. He too postponed entering Yale until age thirteen, though he was ready to go when he was eight. While in college, during what time remained after a self-imposed fourteen-hour daily regimen of study, Dwight composed poems. He chose his 1772 commencement address to extol the virtues of literature in an oration on the "History, Eloquence, and Poetry of the Bible." Following Trumbull's example, Dwight catered to the religious predilections of the audience. Scripture, he insisted, ought to stimulate the literary imagination as well as nurture faith. Students would not endanger their salvation by cultivating an aesthetic sense.[23]

This energetic duo sought to widen a small breach that had recently opened in Yale's wall of tradition when, in 1767, President Daggett added English grammar to the curriculum. Trumbull and Dwight, appointed as tutors in 1771, lobbied in favor of offering instruction in literature as well. When the conservative governing Corporation balked, Dwight went ahead and delivered lectures on composition and style outside of regular class hours. Not until 1776—and at the fervent request of the senior class—was Dwight allowed to teach history and belles-lettres. Even then these courses were optional, open only to students whose parents had given them permission to dabble in such frivolities.[24]

The tutors' enthusiasm proved highly contagious. Students expressed strong interest in belles-lettres, aware of the social value of such knowledge. Conversancy with polite literature added extra cachet to their educations, allowing them to engage with a broader Anglo-American elite culture. More affluent colonists increasingly strove to cultivate the genteel qualities they took to be the common currency of polite society. For some, this meant considerable investment in material goods—the houses, gardens, clothing, furniture, and other possessions that displayed their refined taste. For others, especially college students not yet able to indulge in conspicuous consumption, the quest for gentility focused on mind and manners. Developing enough familiarity with literary essays, poetry, and plays to discuss them in polite conversation was an accomplishment that many Yale students thought was within their reach—or ought to be.[25]

The college's dilatory response, however, forced students to take the initiative. Many turned to the Linonia Society, one of Yale's first literary clubs. Founded in 1753, its popularity soared in the 1760s and 1770s, fueled by the cultural aspirations of a new generation of students. In 1767, perhaps in a nod to the new sense of egalitarianism percolating within the college, the club dropped the requirement that members be upperclassmen and invited some lucky freshmen to join. Unsuccessful candidates, complaining that Linonia was still too exclusive, formed a rival organization in 1768, the Brothers in Unity. Exclusivity, of course, was precisely what attracted students to such clubs. And Linonia was not so very exclusive: twenty of the thirty-six members of the class of 1773 eventually joined, including Enoch and Nathan Hale. By then, it seemed that everyone belonged to either one society or the other.[26]

The clubs provided an ideal venue for these aspiring gentlemen to cultivate polite behavior. At society meetings they practiced the kinds of genteel social interactions taking place in the drawing rooms, coffeehouses, and salons of Europe and the colonies. Yale's foot-dragging on the subject of belles-lettres may even have been a blessing in disguise. Linonians could express themselves more freely in a private setting than in a mandatory class where students skeptical of the whole enterprise might ridicule them.[27]

Books were essential to this pursuit of refinement, serving as sources of knowledge and models of style and exposition. Yale's college library contained many literary works Linonians admired—including volumes by Shakespeare, Milton, Shaftesbury, Pope, Addison, and Steele, along with issues of the London magazines *The Spectator* and *The Tatler*—on shelves that otherwise groaned with weighty leather-bound tomes on ancient languages and theology. Students interested in taking such works back to their rooms to peruse in their free time were out of luck. Under most circumstances, only seniors could withdraw books of any kind from the college library, and they had to pay for the privilege of doing so—the bigger the volume, the higher the borrowing fee. With their belletristic ambitions thus frustrated by college policy, Linonians proposed to start their own library.[28]

At a meeting on July 16, 1770, they agreed to acquire "a number of usefull Books," which members could borrow without charge and keep for up to a week. With the library dependent on donations, however, the collection grew slowly. Not until November 1771 did the first two volumes arrive, supplied by alumni working in New Haven as booksellers. James Lockwood, a 1766 graduate, donated a copy of Jonas Hanway's *Travels*, an account of the author's peregrinations through Russia and Persia. William Sherman, class of 1770, supplied Charles Rollin's *The Method of Teaching and Studying the Belles Lettres*. Voting thanks to both men for their generosity—together these books cost a hefty £3 and ten shillings—Linonians decided to keep a record of future donations, including the title, cost, and name of the benefactor.[29]

The two inaugural volumes in Linonia's library gave a good indication of the direction in which club members' tastes ran. The initial catalogue of its holdings, recorded by Nathan Hale in his capacity as club scribe, included twenty-six titles, none of which was a work of theology or written in an ancient language. Histories, travel accounts, manuals of style in speech and writing, and works of polite literature predominated. Students often pooled their scanty resources to build the collection. Enoch and Nathan joined four classmates contributing six shillings each to purchase copies of *The Spectator*. Nathan helped with the cost of Lord Kames's *Elements of Criticism* and on his own donated a copy of Andrew Ramsay's best-selling *The Travels of Cyrus*. Tutor Timothy Dwight, who, if he did not plant the idea of a library in members' minds certainly supported it, added a copy of Charles Johnstone's *Chrystal; or the Adventures of a Guinea*, a bizarre novel narrated by the spirit of the gold in a guinea coin. In subsequent decades, the overwhelmingly secular emphasis in the collection persisted. By 1796, less than 10 percent of the more than 200 titles in the library dealt with theology.[30]

Linonians met weekly, gathering after dinner in a different member's room each time. On the November day in 1770 when Nathan Hale was admitted, it was Aaron Hall's turn to act as host; the following week everyone crowded into the Hale brothers' room. Five or six students—and sometimes tutors "Sir Dwight" or "Sir [Solomon] Williams"—would be in the spotlight each session. Someone opened the proceedings with a "narration" on a topic of his choice, such as "the first peopleing of America." A "dialogue," or scripted conversation between two students, might follow. Then someone posed a question on virtually any subject, hoping to stump his assembled comrades and display his own brilliance with the answer. "Why is the Weather coldest when the Sun is the nearest to us?" asked Samuel Barker one December evening near the winter solstice. Roger Alden piped up with the correct answer that time. A few months later, when no one knew "What thing is the most delightful to Man in the World?" Moses Cobb gleefully announced that "what is most delightfull to most Men, is getting Money." Linonians exhibited their powers of wit and eloquence most dramatically in "forensic disputes" on such questions as "Whether the Knowledge of Mathematicks is equally or more Advantageous than that of the Languages?" and "Whether an Idiot or wise man Enjoys himself best In the present Life?" Such debates generally focused on topics related to members' reading rather than to current events, although on one notable occasion four members held an "Extemporary Disputation" on "Whether it is right to enslave the Affricans?"[31]

Society meetings thus combined features of a boys' club, classroom, and literary salon, with youthful shenanigans breaking out whenever Linonians discovered any Brothers in Unity—mocked as "Plutonians"—spying on them. Yet beneath the friendly banter and juvenile rivalry lay a genuine interest in creating self-images as true literati. Linonians proofread meeting minutes for spelling and grammar to ensure that "nothing unworthy" of the club was recorded for posterity to see. In the privacy of their meetings, they "criticize[d] upon each other's Language," correcting bad grammar heard in conversation. Every member of the "Honourable Society" ought to represent a shining example of the salutary effects of exposure to polite literature.[32]

Club practices suggested an egalitarian ethos, with meeting places rotated weekly and leadership positions (chancellor, secretary, and scribe) monthly so that no clique would dominate. Yet just as in the college at large, members sorted themselves into a hierarchy, in this case one that reflected members' respective mastery of the kinds of performances featured in their meetings. Since the goal was amusement as well as edification, the wittiest and most dynamic members would be asked—or would volunteer—most frequently to give a speech or join a debate. For these individuals, Linonia served as an incubator in which they could develop a talent for oratory that would serve them well in later life, whether in the pulpit or public affairs.[33]

Enoch joined Linonia a week before Nathan, but in every other respect the younger Hale outpaced his brother. The methodical style that later characterized Enoch's preaching may already have been evident in his contributions to the club's proceedings. Only once did the earnest lad deliver a solo performance, with what could hardly have been a scintillating "Discertation upon the study of the Mathematicks." Otherwise, Enoch was content to participate in a dialogue or debate with others (including his brother) rather than hold center stage. Even these modest efforts tapered off over time, with just one performance recorded during his entire senior year.[34]

Nathan, however, reveled in the limelight. Between his election in November 1770 and his final Linonia meeting in April 1773, he performed at least twenty times, frequently on his own. The terse meeting minutes failed to record the subject matter of his narrations, dialogues, and debates but regularly noted Nathan's wit and talent. His colleagues often praised him as "entertaining" or "very entertaining"—compliments reserved for the best performances (and never, alas, directed at Enoch's efforts.)[35]

One wonders if Richard Hale knew about his sons' extracurricular activities. None of his letters mentioned Linonia. Instead they contained a familiar litany of fatherly advice to his sons: to mind their studies, obey college rules, pray frequently, read a Bible chapter every morning and night. He warned them that after suffering from measles during the summer of 1771 they should rest before resuming their schoolwork. Yet even as they received such letters, Enoch and Nathan were spending their evenings rehearsing for plays or laughing at colleagues' witticisms. It is hard to believe that Richard Hale would have condoned such goings-on. Surely a man who denounced card-playing as a "vice" would have regarded playacting as an even bigger waste of time.[36]

Richard Hale would nevertheless have approved of one benefit of club membership: the fostering of tight-knit friendships among the youths. Nathan formed especially close ties with Linonians Thomas Mead, Roger Alden, and James Hillhouse, along with a renegade Plutonian, John Palsgrave Wyllys, who jocularly called themselves the "Quintumveri." Familiar with the workings of patronage, Richard Hale could appreciate how connections with sons of judges, physicians, and colony secretaries could be of use to his own boys as they embarked on their post-graduate careers.[37]

Many colonists understood friendship in this utilitarian way, as an unequal relationship in which one person acted as another's benefactor. Such connections could still offer emotional rewards and in fact were often compared to kinship ties. But by the mid-eighteenth century, this practical definition was joined by a more egalitarian notion of friendship as a private sense of affinity between like-minded individuals. Sympathy, not self-interest, united equals in a powerful emotional bond similar to that shared by brothers. It was this understanding of friendship, as a sentimental attachment promoting personal happiness, that flourished among the sons of Linonia.[38]

Nowhere else in Connecticut but at Yale could one find a similarly large aggregation of young males—a hundred or more during the academic term—living in such close quarters. Here was fertile ground for the cultivation of friendships among boys away from home for the first time. Unlike brothers working on farms or in shops under paternal supervision, college youths lived relatively carefree lives. Out of shared classroom experiences, conversations in dormitory rooms, and mischievous pranks, students formed lasting bonds and powerful memories that would have been far more difficult to create in any other setting.[39]

The conclusion of their college years therefore saddened students even as their parents welcomed the end of quarterly payments. Graduation meant separation, and no group of youths lamented this prospect more than Linonians. Each spring, in anticipation of the bittersweet event, members organized a gala anniversary affair to commemorate the club's founding and bid a fond farewell to the seniors. The celebrations occurred off-campus in a private home, public hall, or—in at least one instance—a tavern. Often lasting from mid-morning to late afternoon, the events required weeks of preparation. Arrangements had to be made for food, including a midday dinner, and enough drink for everyone to lift a "Chearful Glass" or two (or maybe more). With opening and closing processions, numerous speeches, and ample refreshments, the anniversary celebration mimicked the actual commencement ceremony that would follow in September. Linonia's grand party gave club members one more opportunity to strut in front of an audience and poke good-natured fun at the educational institution that had brought them together.[40]

On the appointed day, New Haven residents were treated to the spectacle of club members promenading under the pale green of springtime trees to their chosen venue. Opening ceremonies resembled a typical weekly meeting, with several orations and dialogues. In this case, however, speakers made the delights of club membership their principal theme. At the 1772 celebration, Roger Alden struck a characteristically nostalgic pose, urging his audience to remember "the many agreeable hours we have spent together ... in qualifying ourselves in every part of knowledge & literature, that we may not appear unworthy the name of Linonia's Sons." Orators thanked and praised seniors while commanding underclassmen to uphold their predecessors' high standards. There was a place for humor as well. In one poem deemed by the audience to be "elegant indeed," Noah Atwater gently mocked the ambitious Linonian who "greatly seeks & strives to know/As much or more than others do," insistently reaching "For Honour, that enchanting prize/on which he always keeps his eyes." Speakers also admonished fellow members to defend their club's honor against "the despicable intrigues of Plutos hauty sons."[41]

Two additional activities differentiated the anniversary celebration from an ordinary meeting. First, Linonians staged a play, complete with scenery, costumes, and bravura performances. More than any other endeavor, this epitomized the club's raison d'être by giving members free rein to display their oratorical prowess, sociability, and wit. They usually selected a British comedy, demonstrating their familiarity with metropolitan taste and culture. In 1771, they chose Robert Dodsley's popular farce *The Toy Shop* (in which both Hale brothers acted); the following year, they staged the even more celebrated *Beaux Stratagem* by George Farquhar. In 1773, during an anniversary celebration that Nathan helped to plan, Linonians performed Richard Cumberland's *The West Indian*, a new comedy that had opened in London just two years earlier. Club members congratulated themselves that this time "the scenery & Action were on all hands allowed to be superiour to any thing of the kind heretofore exhibited on the like Occasion." The costumes provoked special delight. Youths playing the roles of military officers appeared "dress'd in Regimentals" and the "actresses" (who included Henry Daggett, the son of Yale's

president) strode onstage in "full & elegant suits of Lady's apparel."
At the close of the play, Nathan Hale delivered an epilogue that was
received by all with hearty "approbation."[42]

What filled students with particular glee was the knowledge that
they should not have been doing any of this. New Haven authorities frowned on theatrical productions; not until 1785 would the first
professional troupe be allowed to perform in town. Moreover, college
rules specifically forbade students from acting in plays or even attending them. Violators were subject to fines of one to three shillings, and
anyone who had the effrontery to don "Women's Apparel" during a
performance would be "publickly admonished." President Daggett
was evidently less assiduous than his predecessors in enforcing these
rules, but the threat of punishment nevertheless loomed over the
heads of the wayward thespians. Knowing that they risked possible
disciplinary action only made the Linonians' collective act of defiance
all the more enjoyable.[43]

The second distinctive element of these celebrations plunged
club members from the heights of jolly camaraderie to the depths
of mutual commiseration. As in a regular commencement ceremony,
each anniversary event closed with a valedictory address. Linonian
valedictories, however, differed sharply from the usual orations in content, delivery, and reception. College presidents or tutors—and only
rarely students—gave such commencement speeches and, as suited
an audience composed of local dignitaries and parents, they almost
invariably addressed topics of general public interest. Only in formu-
laic introductions and brief conclusions did these orations touch on
the theme that dominated Linonia's version of the genre: the imminent dispersal of the graduating class.[44]

Linonia's valedictorians addressed fellow members, who appreciated the effort that went into crafting speeches with a lugubrious
tone. Elisha Billings opened his April 1772 valedictory lamenting that
the "disagreable period" had finally come, when he and his fellow
seniors "with wa[tery] eyes" had to "bid a long, a lasting, adieu to
fair Linonia and her worthy Sons." Each year a member of the rising
senior class was chosen to compose an "answer" to the first oration. In
his response to Billings's speech, Nathan Hale echoed its mournful
style: "This day has brought about the unwelcome period, the melancholy prospect of which has so long sadden'd our Hearts." Both speakers identified a balm, however, that could ease the pain of separation.[45]

"Friendship," Elisha Billings proclaimed, "is the very foundation on which civil society is built, but most especially the amiable society of fair Linonia, in which it has ever reigned triumphant." Club members would go their separate ways, but their special ties of friendship would endure. "We have lived together, not as fellow-students, and members of the same college," Nathan Hale declared, "but as brothers & children of the same family, not as superior & inferior, but rather as equals & companions." And just as brothers remained close for life, so too would Linonia's offspring. In his 1773 speech, David Tullar implored fellow members to "cultivate a near and lasting friendship among us," for "by this we shall all go on hand in hand, as one body." Once a Linonian, always a Linonian, no matter what the future might hold.[46]

These orators infused their speeches with a stylized yet heartfelt sentimentality. Frank descriptions of their fluctuating emotions—"cordial affection," "sadness," "grief," "passion," and even "love"—may have drawn nervous titters from young men unaccustomed to discussing feelings so openly. Speakers doubtless accompanied their pronouncements with exaggerated flourishes, with hand over heart, so as to diminish some of the intensity. But, deep down, everyone shared the same feelings. Each Linonian, asserted David Tullar, was "possessed of a tender & sympathizing heart, that could share in his brothers troubles." Being able to acknowledge emotional ties in the company of equals, and yet keep those emotions in check, demonstrated that the Linonians had at last learned how to behave as gentlemen.[47]

Shortly after the Hale brothers first arrived in New Haven, the Assembly met there to discuss whether Connecticut should join the non-importation movement against the Townshend Acts. Enoch and Nathan could not have been entirely ignorant of political matters, since their father had served several terms as Coventry's delegate to the legislature. Yet by the time they began their studies in the autumn of 1769, the waves of unrest that first surged with the Stamp Act and reemerged with the Townshend Acts had begun to recede. When Parliament repealed all duties except the tax on tea in March 1770, protests against British policy subsided even further. The college careers of Yale's class of 1773, therefore, happened to coincide with a period of relative calm in Anglo-American relations.[48]

This was not true for the classes matriculating immediately before and after the Hales' cohort. In 1764, Yale students responded to the Sugar Act's tax on imported wines with a vow "not to Drink any foreign spirituous Liquors any more." The following year they protested against the Stamp Act, which would have taxed their diplomas as well as other documents. When Joseph Lyman delivered a speech in December 1765 containing "unjustifiable Reflections on that August Body the British Parliament," however, he was chastised by Yale officials who suspected that he really meant to cast aspersions on the "Laws and Authority of this College." There may have been other instances when mischievous students took advantage of current events to camouflage acts of resistance against President Thomas Clap. But that was not the case in January 1769, with Clap long gone and the Townshend Acts still in place. Members of that year's senior class unanimously agreed to abide by non-importation measures and appear "wholly dressed in the manufacture of our own country" at commencement. They publicized this decision well in advance, giving their families time to buy or make "homespun cloaths" for the big event.[49]

Yale officials often gave tacit approval to such actions, revealing to students where their political sympathies lay. Naphtali Daggett made little effort to disguise his views. In 1765, he submitted a vituperative essay against the Stamp Act to the *Connecticut Gazette*. Lambasting men who accepted stamp distributorships as "mercenary Publicans," Daggett directed his most impassioned abuse at Jared Ingersoll (a 1742 Yale graduate), denouncing him as a "vile miscreant" motivated by a "rapacious and base spirit." Although he composed this screed under the pseudonym "Cato," Daggett's identity as the author appears to have been common knowledge, and he had the satisfaction of seeing his essay reprinted in newspapers from New Hampshire to Pennsylvania.[50]

President Daggett would not have let these political opinions influence his academic duties, which included leading daily prayers and instructing seniors in moral philosophy. Whether tutors, who interacted far more frequently and informally with students, exercised the same restraint is less clear. Both Timothy Dwight and John Trumbull harbored deep concerns about British policy. They were responsible for assigning topics for debate, a task that had the potential to spark political discussions. If they did touch on contemporary events, tutors did so carefully, aware that their primary responsibility was preparing students to pass their final examinations.[51]

On one public occasion—his 1770 commencement address lauding the benefits of the fine arts—John Trumbull ventured cautiously onto political territory. Any society that promoted literature, painting, and music, he argued, strengthened the aesthetic and moral sensibilities of its people and magnified its national glory. "Look into the annals of antiquity," he proclaimed. First Greece and then Rome exemplified societies where "Arts and Arms" flourished together before each polity in turn sank into decline. In the modern age, only Britain could "claim the glory of an equality with Greece and Rome," as measured by its impressive artistic and imperial achievements. Yet after two centuries of "almost unabated luster," Britain too had passed its cultural apogee. Eventually it would be America's turn, but only so long as colonists steadfastly defended the "heroic love of Liberty" essential to the flowering of artistic genius. By placing America's cultural—and presumably imperial—efflorescence well into the future, however, Trumbull avoided even a whiff of rebelliousness. "America," he predicted, "hath a fair prospect in a few centuries of ruling both in arts and arms." And as the colonies proceeded toward the fulfillment of their destiny, he added with a nod to the students and alumni in the audience, "fair Yalensia" would naturally lead the way.[52]

Trumbull's stirring words raised neither eyebrows nor especially enthusiastic applause. In its account of the commencement proceedings, the *Connecticut Journal* merely reported that the "usual Exercises of Orations and Disputations, were performed to good Acceptance." The tutor, who received his master of arts degree at the ceremony, had fashioned his speech around a notion familiar to many in his audience. Eighteenth-century Europeans took for granted the idea that empires' political and artistic fortunes rose and fell together, and that political freedom promoted economic prosperity and cultural progress. In Great Britain, Whigs had been making this point for years, urging countrymen to safeguard their precious rights from the depredations of the party's political opponents. Few Englishmen would have blanched at Trumbull's forecast of America's glorious destiny. That eventuality lay so far into the future that no eighteenth-century Briton needed to take it seriously.[53]

Trumbull's caution reflected the character of the academic institution that had shaped him and its relative isolation from the centers of protest. Harvard's faculty and students could scarcely ignore events in Boston, especially after British troops arrived there in 1768. Yale, however, was probably the least politicized of all colonial colleges at the time. Its library, unlike those at Harvard and Princeton, contained comparatively few works by the English Commonwealth writers and eighteenth-century Whigs who inspired colonial pamphleteers. At Harvard commencement ceremonies during the 1760s and 1770s, graduates debated topics closely related to the Stamp Act and popular rights and liberties. Yale seniors at the same time defended "ethical theses" on less overtly political subjects such as "The prince endowed with wisdom cannot be a tyrant" [1770] and "The stability of the state rests on the virtue of the people" [1772]. Nearly all of the "quaestiones" presented by master's degree candidates at Yale commencements addressed theological topics that would not have seemed out of place at graduation ceremonies during the 1720s.[54]

Members of the Linonia Society were evidently no more inclined than other Yale students to engage with political matters. As of 1773, the only work in Linonia's library by a prominent English Whig was Joseph Addison's *Evidences of the Christian Religion*, an attack on atheism and not one of his better-known political tracts. There were copies of *The Spectator*, but like aspiring gentlemen elsewhere in the colonies (including Benjamin Franklin), Linonians mainly pored over its pages for lessons in literary style. For their anniversary plays, Linonians chose comedies that best suited the lighthearted mood of the event. One of them—*The West Indian*—addressed themes of liberty and tyranny by following the misadventures of a Jamaican planter in search of a wife, but the "tyranny" that costumed performers and audience probably contemplated on this occasion was that of the college rules they were happily defying.[55]

Yale's commencement ceremony on September 8, 1773, when the Hale brothers received their diplomas, reflected this apolitical atmosphere. As professors garbed in black robes, white wigs, and cocked hats took their seats, the graduating class—also clad in black gowns—prepared for the public display of their erudition. Most of their efforts directed the audience's attention to matters of local interest. During the morning exercises, four students debated "Whether a large Metropolis would be of public advantage to this Colony?" Roger Alden, Stephen Keyes, and Elihu Marvin then presented a dialogue on the learned professions, followed by Ebenezer Williams with an oration on the subject of prejudice. The afternoon exercises focused on the topic of education. Tutor John Davenport led off with a speech on "the State of private Schools in this Colony." As the final student performance of the day, Nathan Hale, Ezra Sampson, William Robinson, and Benjamin Tallmadge debated "Whether the Education of Daughters be not, without any just reason, more neglected than that of Sons?"[56]

These three Linonians and sole Plutonian (Tallmadge) perhaps drew on their extracurricular reading to formulate their arguments. The pair taking the negative position could have cited any number of European writers to buttress New Englanders' long-standing preference for limiting women's education. The two proponents of greater opportunities for daughters (one of whom was likely Hale) might have had their own futures in mind as they made their case. For four years they had cultivated genteel aspirations in the company of young men. Now they were about to reenter a society with young women. That prospect would be especially attractive if they encountered young ladies who, within what were thought to be the natural limits of the female intellect, had enough learning to appreciate the delights of polite literature and carry on an entertaining conversation. As audience, perhaps, more than participants, educated women could help the newly minted graduates continue the self-improvement projects launched during those evening meetings in Connecticut Hall.[57]

Members of the class of 1773 took final examinations in the late spring and summer before the commencement ceremony. During that period, Enoch and Nathan frequently traveled between New Haven and Coventry, all the while keeping in touch with classmates. Nathan and Benjamin Tallmadge exchanged several letters, signing them as "Damon" (Tallmadge) and "Pythias" (Hale) to invoke the famous friendship of Greek legend. William Robinson, who lived in nearby Lebanon, visited the Hales in Coventry in early August, and Gershom Lyman, a Coventry neighbor, also stopped by the Hale homestead. If Enoch and Nathan took time away from their studies to help with haying and other agricultural activities, they perhaps felt a secret relief that their futures were unlikely to require such unremitting physical labor.[58]

Enoch, perhaps from the moment he began studying with Joseph Huntington, had his sights set on a career in the pulpit. For a year or so after graduation, he taught school in Windsor while reading theology in preparation for receiving a license to preach. Only then could he serve as a visiting clergyman, honing his sermon-writing skills and speaking style while waiting for some congregation to offer him a permanent position.[59]

Nathan loved his family but did not love the prospect of staying in Coventry. If he had ever entertained the idea of becoming a preacher, the notion vanished by graduation. A pulpit was too small a stage for his ambitions. Nathan had grown too fond of striving for just the right gesture, tone of voice, spark of wit, and turn of phrase to give up the enterprise, especially when his efforts had earned him such accolades from his friends. He could not disappoint them, or himself, by taming that ambition, submerging his talents, and forgoing the opportunity to play to its fullest the role of colonial man of letters that he had been practicing for the past four years.[60]

The question that bedeviled Nathan Hale was how to fulfill his aspirations. He could pursue a career in the law, a profession that rewarded effective public speaking.[61] That, in turn, might lead to political office. In the meantime, perhaps he could sharpen his literary talents by submitting the occasional essay to a newspaper and waiting for friends to tell him what they thought of it. Nathan had some important decisions to make, but his first one was to leave Coventry soon after graduation and head for the small town of East Haddam. There he would teach school while he contemplated his next step.

4

THE UNHAPPY MISUNDERSTANDING

EVEN A CAREFUL READER OF the December 21, 1773, issue of the *Connecticut Courant* could have missed the news. It was buried on page 3 beneath an account of Widow Emmins's death at her son-in-law's home and a report that Mr. Wells's just-completed house in Newington had mysteriously burned to the ground. The inconspicuous notice read:

> We hear from Boston that last Thursday Evening, between 300 And 400 Boxes of the celebrated East-India TEA, by some ACCIDENT! which happened in an attempt to get it on Shore, Fell overboard—That the Boxes burst open and the Tea was Swallowed up by the vast Abyss!

But the Boston Tea Party was no accident, and this flippant account gave no indication of the grave consequences to come. Britain's angry reaction to the dumping of the tea fanned whatever embers of imperial discord still smoldered back into a roaring blaze.[1]

An urgent fiscal crisis sparked this new controversy. The East India Company, which owed the British government more than £1 million in loans and customs duties, teetered on the brink of bankruptcy.

To rescue it and its influential shareholders from financial disaster, Parliament passed the Tea Act in May 1773. The measure allowed the Company to ship to the colonies half a million pounds of tea sitting unsold in its warehouses, reimbursing it for a tax normally paid when the tea arrived in England from India. Because this rebate reduced the price of the Company product below that of smuggled Dutch tea, Parliament assumed that frugal colonists would buy it and help bail the Company out.

But the despised Townshend tea duty remained in force, and colonists regarded the Tea Act as a ruse to trick them into paying it. Many merchants objected to another of the act's provisions, which allowed the Company to select its own agents to receive the tea in America and sell it directly to customers, excluding other colonial traders with long experience in the tea trade. In Philadelphia, New York, and Charleston, mass meetings of outraged colonists forced the Company agents to resign. Boston's agents, however, included two sons of Governor Thomas Hutchinson, who had never forgiven protesters for demolishing his home during the Stamp Act crisis. When Hutchinson refused to be intimidated by popular meetings and threats of violence, the stage was set for a showdown.

The *Connecticut Courant*'s description of what happened on the night of December 16, 1773, had one detail right: 340 chests of East India Company tea were indeed destroyed. But the containers did not simply fall overboard. Instead, a hundred or more Bostonians dabbed on face paint, pretending to disguise themselves as Indians, and made their way to the harbor. They boarded the ships carrying the tea, hauled the chests onto the decks, hacked them open, and dumped the containers and their contents into the sea. Reports circulated around Boston that gentlemen stood alongside workingmen and apprentices in carrying out the dramatic protest. As the perpetrators and the large crowd of observers returned to their homes that night, they congratulated themselves on striking a clever and effective blow in defense of liberty.[2]

Had the *Courant* provided a more elaborate account of the episode, its readers still might not have paid much attention. Boston's crowds were known for orchestrating this kind of political theater, and while Connecticut inhabitants opposed the Tea Act, its dangers initially appeared no more threatening than the original Townshend duty.

What really engaged Connecticut colonists at this time were local concerns, especially the Susquehannah Company and the status of its claims in the Wyoming Valley. Governor Jonathan Trumbull and the legislature finally endorsed the Company's project, raising the hopes of hard-pressed farmers ready to move. But the Assembly's action also energized conservatives to launch one last fight against a speculative enterprise they feared would endanger Connecticut's charter. During the winter of 1773–1774, the colony's inhabitants expended far more energy debating western expansion than worrying about tea.[3]

Moses Dunbar was too preoccupied by other matters to pay much attention to either tea or western territory. Family concerns as always loomed large, but so too did the future of his religious community. In his annual reports to the SPG, an overworked James Scovil repeatedly bemoaned the fact that his pastoral responsibilities were "too great to be discharged by me in such a manner as I could wish." Members of the New Cambridge and Northbury parishes were searching for some-one to assist him, and if they found a suitable candidate, Scovil hoped the SPG would offer support. Waterbury's Anglican community had doubled in size since he began his ministry, but to build upon this success would require additional help from London.[4]

Early in the summer of 1773, SPG officials received an uncharacter-istically optimistic message from James Scovil. Northbury and New Cambridge parishes had at last found a "promising young Gentleman" willing to serve as their minister. The candidate had his Yale degree and had begun to lead the two congregations in prayers. Members of all four of Scovil's parishes were scraping together the money to send the young man to London for ordination. Pleased as he was to send this news, Scovil nevertheless appended his usual lament that "it will be almost beyond their Power to support an other Clergyman" unless they could count on "some small assistance" from abroad.[5]

The "promising young Gentleman" upon whom Scovil pinned his hopes was none other than James Nichols, the feisty fellow who, just two years earlier, had led his Yale classmates in a revolt against the deplorable quality of college food. Now nearly twenty-five years old, he had matured, or had at least learned when good behavior was called for. Scovil described him as "Mild and Amiable in his Temper prudent and discreet in his behaviour, sober and pious in his conversation."

The vestrymen and churchwardens of Nichols's prospective parishes echoed Scovil's commendation, remarking on the young man's "known Exemplary Sober Life."[6]

It took Waterbury's Anglicans longer than expected to arrange for Nichols's passage to England, forcing him to endure a rough winter voyage. He returned to Connecticut in late April 1774 with proof of his ordination and an SPG stipend. There was no way for him to have known that he would be the last Connecticut Anglican to travel to England for ordination. What he did know—or perhaps learned only after taking up his responsibilities—was that he had agreed to serve two parishes in crisis. Doing so would require all the amiability, sobriety, piety, and discretion the untested young clergyman could muster.[7]

Most of James Scovil's proselytizing success occurred in Waterbury and Westbury, the two congregations he retained for his own pastorate. The parishes of Northbury and New Cambridge, by contrast, were struggling. During the decade before Nichols arrived, church membership in Northbury had stagnated; New Cambridge experienced a sharp decline and was only beginning to show signs of recovery. The 120 families in Scovil's two parishes shared the cost of his salary, but the burden of paying Nichols fell to just 84 families in Northbury and New Cambridge. At least their new minister was as yet unmarried and therefore cheaper to support.[8]

The exodus from New Cambridge had commenced in 1767. About a dozen families—more than one-third of the parish—trekked over 150 miles northward and across the Connecticut River to the tiny settlement of Claremont in New Hampshire. These weary travelers could be forgiven for imagining themselves as latter-day Israelites seeking refuge in the midst of a "wild uncultivated Desert." Claremont's first English settlers, many of them Connecticut Anglicans, had arrived in the thickly forested area only in 1762 and had made little progress clearing land and constructing cabins by the time the New Cambridge contingent showed up. As soon as Anglicans comprised about half of the town's population of nearly 400, they launched a campaign for an SPG-funded minister, for the only Anglican cleric in the colony lived 100 miles away in Portsmouth. Claremont Anglicans feared that without a resident pastor, their children would fall "Prey to [Congregationalist] Enthusiasts carried about with every wind of Doctrine." At the very least, they requested permission to hire the elderly Samuel Cole as catechist and schoolmaster—a short-term expedient that James Scovil and other Connecticut ministers, who had once counted these families among their own parishioners, readily endorsed.[9]

Thus by 1767, just three years after the Dunbars joined, only twenty families remained in the New Cambridge Anglican parish, many of them as young and poor as Moses and Phoebe.[10] If the couple entertained a notion to join the Claremont migration, however, they soon realized they could not afford to do so. Moses, Phoebe, and little Bede still lived in a house John Dunbar owned, and Moses tilled acres belonging to his father. Such circumstances appeared to guarantee that Moses would remain as firmly rooted to the paternal estate as any of the ancient trees that shaded its stony soil.

Yet seven years later, Moses Dunbar was ready to move to Claremont. All he needed was his father's agreement to buy back the six acres of Northbury land that John Dunbar had given him in 1769 as his share of the family property. On February 12, 1774, Moses signed the deed that returned the land to John Dunbar and gave the son £40 and his freedom. The road to Claremont might still be blanketed in winter's snow, but it beckoned nonetheless.[11]

In choosing this particular moment to leave, Moses must have assumed that it was now or never. Nearly twenty-eight years old, with a wife and several children to support, he was making no economic headway in Northbury. Perhaps he heard reports that Claremont offered both cheap land and a friendlier environment for Anglicans. Benning Wentworth, New Hampshire's former governor, had belonged to the Church of England and required new townships like Claremont to reserve tracts of land specifically for the support of Anglican churches, lessening the financial burden on parishioners. A persistent sense of frustration likely goaded Dunbar into action, but he could reassure himself that this move would improve his family's welfare as well as his own peace of mind.[12]

Dunbar left Phoebe—who was pregnant yet again—and the children behind while he traveled to Claremont to see what sort of farm he could get for forty pounds. As she awaited her husband's return, Phoebe looked forward to their move with a mixture of anticipation and dread. It would be no easier for her to make the journey later that summer in a state of advanced pregnancy than to wait until the following spring and travel with a babe in arms. If she put the journey itself out of her thoughts and concentrated on the new life the family would lead in Claremont, she could keep her hopes up about the wisdom of Moses's decision.[13]

Happy as she was to greet Moses on his return, Phoebe must have been astonished when he told her that he had arranged to spend his £40 on a farm not in Claremont but in Waterbury. He negotiated the purchase with Ebenezer Judd, another Waterbury Anglican who had already transplanted his family to New Hampshire. Moses eased the shock of his announcement by explaining what a good deal he had made buying land from a man very eager to sell it. In this roundabout way he had transformed his six-acre patrimony into a thirty-acre farm, bringing him closer than ever to the independence that he longed for. Phoebe no longer had to worry about a lengthy journey and the Dunbars were better off than ever before.[14]

Two days before Ebenezer Judd signed the deed transferring his property to Moses Dunbar, fifty-six men gathered in Philadelphia's Carpenters' Hall as delegates to the Continental Congress. Their task was to coordinate an American response to the unprecedentedly harsh legislation Parliament had enacted to punish Boston, and Massachusetts generally, for the destruction of East India Company tea. While Dunbar had been busy imagining himself with a Claremont homestead and then revising those dreams to fit a Waterbury setting, the relationship between Britain and the colonies had rapidly deteriorated. The Connecticut neighborhood to which he returned in September 1774 was nowhere near as quiet as the one he had left just months before.

When news of the Tea Party reached London, members of the ministry and Parliament were outraged. Even George III admitted to feeling "much hurt" by the colonists' wanton attack on private property and defiance of British authority. Many officials assumed that a cabal of insolent radicals had incited the protest, but they chose to punish a much larger group. From the end of March to early June, Parliament deliberated on a set of measures that would teach Massachusetts colonists a lesson they would never forget. The result of their efforts was four laws that came to be known as the Coercive (or, to the colonists, Intolerable) Acts. The first measure closed the port of Boston until the East India Company received compensation for the loss of the tea and the British treasury was paid the tax due on it. Another act allowed any civil or military official accused of a capital crime in Massachusetts, including soldiers and customs agents, to have his trial transferred to London or another colony to avoid facing a biased local jury. Bay colonists were especially shocked by the Massachusetts Government Act, which essentially nullified their charter. Members of the Council would no longer be elected by the other legislative chamber but would henceforth be royal appointees. A new royal governor was empowered to appoint judges and sheriffs. To curtail the meetings that radical Whigs had used to stir up the populace, the act provided for only one town meeting per year to elect local officials; additional gatherings required the governor's written approval. Finally, a new Quartering Act applied to all colonies, allowing troops to be billeted not just in deserted buildings but also in occupied dwellings.[15]

Connecticut joined other colonies in a collective gasp of horror at these measures. News of the Boston Port Act reached Connecticut in mid-May, just as Lieutenant-General Thomas Gage disembarked in Boston to take over the Massachusetts governorship. Connecticut's Assembly swiftly endorsed a set of resolves that simultaneously acknowledged loyalty to George III, declared the recent parliamentary measures unconstitutional, and proclaimed the colonists' intention to use any "lawful ways and means" at their disposal to preserve their rights and liberties. Vigorous as these pronouncements were, they were no match for the protests that once again erupted on the streets.[16]

Farmington's radicals proved especially boisterous. On May 19, "a very large and respectable Body" of residents—estimates ranged as high as a thousand—gathered at the behest of the local Sons of Liberty near the town's "place of execution." After a rowdy parade, a group of men erected a forty-five-foot-tall pole dedicated to the Goddess of Liberty. Sons of Liberty staged a mock trial of the Port Act, summarily condemning it to death. The crowd shouted its agreement to several "spirited Resolves," accusing the British ministry—labeled "pimps and parasites"—of conniving to "take away our liberties and properties, and to enslave us for ever." Then someone produced an effigy of the detested Thomas Hutchinson. This was carted around town, tarred and feathered, and finally set ablaze with a burning copy of the Port Act.[17]

Raucous protests as rich with symbolism as Farmington's display flared up in other Connecticut towns—New London, Lebanon, Windham—but it soon became clear that more practical measures were necessary. Not long after the closure of their port on June 1, Bostonians began to suffer from shortages of provisions and fuel. All across the colonies, communities organized for Boston's relief. Connecticut responded with special generosity as town committees collected livestock, grain, firewood, and money to send northward. Farmington provided more than 500 bushels of rye and Indian corn along with reassurance that the town was as "resolute in the common cause of liberty" as Boston. The Port Act was "an invasion of the Rights and Privileges of every American," the townsmen declared, and it ought therefore to inspire "unremitted Vigilance and Resolution" in each and every one of them. Connecticut already had a colony-level committee of correspondence keeping track of the political situation. Now individual towns like Farmington created local committees to do the same.[18]

Connecticut inhabitants were especially alarmed about the safety of their charter, since it was clear from Massachusetts's experience that Parliament would not hesitate to nullify the document if doing so tightened Britain's control. Thomas Gage believed that many of the "commotions" in Connecticut stemmed from precisely this anxiety and predicted that Britain would eventually have to exert as much force there as in the Bay Colony. Rhode Island promised to be just as troublesome. Parliament's effort to rein in one belligerent colony had, Gage feared, created a regional insurgency that would likely require more troops to suppress.[19]

By midsummer, as tempers flared and no one could foretell how the crisis might end, Governor Jonathan Trumbull sought to provide a moment of reflection by proclaiming August 31, 1774, a day of public fasting and prayer. Clergy should conduct special services and inhabitants should "humble themselves deeply before GOD," contemplate their sinfulness, and offer sincere repentance. The governor went on, however, to inject partisan sentiments into his instructions, urging his constituents to ask God to unite the colonies "in such just, righteous, wise and good Measures, as will have the best Tendency to secure and continue our Privileges." He directed colonists to implore the Lord to strengthen the king's resolve to "prevent the mischievous Operation of the Misrepresentations made by ambitious, designing and evil Men." If the governor intended this day of prayer to bring his constituents together, his proclamation had precisely the opposite effect.[20]

Anglicans in particular faced a quandary. The revival of street protests reanimated their deepest fears of social disorder and harassment by Whigs. Their clergy had no desire to deliver sermons that followed Trumbull's instructions and offered tacit approval of colonial resistance to British authority. Yet only the boldest chose outright confrontation. That number included Samuel Peters, James Scovil's erstwhile companion to London and now minister of Hebron. The cantankerous clergyman sent a lengthy defense of the Tea Act to several newspapers, specifically denouncing the Sons of Liberty. On August 15, a crowd of some 300 men confronted Peters, calling him a traitor and accusing him of sending "unfriendly" messages to England. Peters denied the charge, but the suspicions of radical colonists were hardly allayed. Though accounts of what happened in Hebron on September 6 varied, by the end of the day the minister's stately house and its contents had been severely damaged by a mob. Peters fled to Boston, seeking protection from royal troops; a mob from as far away as Farmington allegedly threatened to "visit" him should he dare to return.[21]

Just months into his ministry, James Nichols decided to ignore the proclamation, refusing to hold a prayer service on the designated day "on account of some scruples of conscience." Other Anglican clergy, including Samuel Andrews of Wallingford, did the same. Unlike them, however, Nichols was responsible for New Cambridge, the sole Anglican parish in Farmington, a town that had emerged as a hotbed of radicalism. The *Connecticut Courant* reported that 200 "patriotic gentlemen" descended upon the minister and, after "some considerable conversation," convinced him "freely" to sign a confession of error. In it, Nichols begged forgiveness for actions stemming from his "criminal ignorance" and promised never to repeat his mistake. He vowed to "obtain a competency of political knowledge" and treat the 200 benefactors who had shown him the error of his ways "with the utmost tenderness." The crowd claimed to have carried out its mission "without noise or tumult" and "with great decorum and unanimity," but the cornered minister was painfully aware of the potential for violence as he signed the confession in front of them.[22]

Farmington radicals then marched into Waterbury to confront James Scovil. Their search lasted eight days before they located the beleaguered minister in a house surrounded outside by more than a hundred of his supporters. This time the radicals dispersed. Although Farmington mobs mainly targeted Anglican clergy, they bullied anyone rumored to be a defender of Britain. They went after John Smalley, the Congregationalist pastor in New Britain (then one of Farmington's outlying parishes), after he reportedly uttered opinions "dangerous to the Liberties of America." By this point, Farmington's Sons of Liberty had acquired such a reputation for intimidation and abuse that they felt obliged to defend their proceedings against Smalley in the newspaper.[23]

As the weeks passed, Anglicans in general, not just clergy, became targets of attack if they did not announce their opposition to Britain. Whig animosity, fueled by anger at the Intolerable Acts, reached unprecedented levels. In East Haddam, a seventy-year-old Anglican parish clerk was yanked out of bed on a cold night, stripped, and beaten. When the clerk's nephew protested, he was likewise seized, stripped, slathered with hot tar and hog's dung, and had dung crammed down his throat. The crowd then attacked the clerk's property, smashing the windows of his house and damaging his gristmill. Rumors began circulating that Anglican clergy, in league with the detested Samuel Peters and with the approval of their congregations, were plotting to enslave the colony.[24]

Six senior Anglican clergymen, including James Scovil, hastened to defend themselves, publicly disavowing any knowledge of a plot against colonial liberties. Lamenting the "gloomy Aspect" of the times, the ministers asserted that all they desired was "a secure Enjoyment" of the same rights and privileges they shared with their fellow colonists. Several members of the Assembly agreed to try to dissuade popular throngs from making the clergymen's lives so miserable, though how they would go about accomplishing that difficult task remained unspecified.[25]

The approach of autumn brought cooler days and nights but did nothing to lower the political temperature. Among the colony's Whigs, the Intolerable Acts summoned up a nightmare vision of discarded charters, arbitrary government, unrestrained taxation, political corruption, economic distress, and military occupation. It seemed only a matter of time—and probably not much time—before Connecticut suffered the same fate as Massachusetts. Many, though hardly all, Whigs believed that defenders of Britain deserved whatever rough treatment they got at the hands of incensed lovers of liberty. Such attitudes, however, transformed some neighbors, especially Anglican ones, into dangerous foes. Those neighbors, many of whom were also uneasy about recent parliamentary actions, had their own nightmare visions of rampaging mobs, destroyed property, utter lawlessness, and continual threats to life and limb. The shouts of a raucous crowd, the acrid odor of pitch, and the glimpse of a sack of feathers emboldened one faction and terrified the other. This was the environment to which Moses Dunbar returned from his brief expedition into New Hampshire.

As late as the autumn of 1774, it still seemed possible that ties of kinship and community might restore some measure of peaceful coexistence. That September, Connecticut voters elected six Anglicans to the Assembly. Anglicans joined Congregationalists on many committees, including those sending relief to Boston. As the crisis persisted, however, harmony became harder to sustain. Even if Connecticut's Whig leaders disapproved of crowd actions, they had to respond to popular demands if they wanted to be reelected. Moreover, they had few ways of suppressing mobs once these were on the loose.[26]

During these same months, delegates to the Continental Congress in Philadelphia struggled to define their goals and agree on a course of action. By mid-October, they had completed both tasks. First, the Congress adopted a Declaration of Rights and Resolves that denounced as unconstitutional the Intolerable Acts and, indeed, all British tax measures imposed since 1763. The delegates likewise condemned the keeping of a standing army in the colonies in peacetime. They went on to assert the colonists' rights to life, liberty, and property, and insist that colonial legislatures had the exclusive power to tax their constituents. The delegates' second achievement would prove to have an enormous impact on the way radical Whigs in Connecticut and other colonies imposed local control. This was the Continental Association, a pledge taken by all delegates to see that their colonies ceased importing goods from Britain immediately, stopped all exports to Britain as of September 1, 1775, if the imperial crisis had not yet ended, and created local committees to ensure that these trade sanctions were enforced. Congress then voted to reconvene in May 1775 if Britain had not yet redressed colonial grievances.[27]

Within weeks of the Continental Congress's adjournment, towns all over Connecticut scrambled to appoint what were variously called committees of inspection or observation. More than 650 men—about 1 in 60 of the colony's adult white males—signed up to enforce the non-importation agreement and scrutinize their neighbors' political activities and speech. Together these committees constituted a grassroots radical movement ready to impose its will in every single community, ferreting out anyone who disagreed with them or even tried to remain neutral. Several leading inhabitants joined Waterbury's committee of fourteen men, including one Anglican. Farmington at first named forty-two members to its committee and then, two weeks later, in yet another demonstration of its radical zeal, added eleven more. The town assigned subcommittees of four to seven men to keep an eye on individual parishes, including New Cambridge, monitoring those whom they now called Tories. Farmington's voters then gave these committeemen free rein "to Determine Every Matter & thing Respecting Torys During the Town Pleasure." And away they went.[28]

During the winter of 1774–1775, Farmington radicals patrolled their neighborhoods like bloodhounds, sniffing for any trace of Toryism. Some of their prey made the job easy. Matthias Leaming and Nehemiah Royce (a New Cambridge Anglican) boldly announced in a town meeting that they opposed the proceedings of the Continental Congress and refused to accept its resolves. Their punishment was ostracism, a serious penalty in communities where residents interacted with one another all the time. Everyone in Farmington was enjoined to "withdraw all Connection" with Leaming and Royce until they retracted their opinions. Their wives and children, despite having no formal political role, suffered along with the men. Some townsmen even proposed that their children be barred from the public school. Yet after months of having their neighbors shun them, neither man gave in.[29]

Farmington committeemen often relied on rumor and gossip in their hunt for alleged enemies of liberty. Someone reported that the cost of goods in James Percival's store had suddenly shot up—a breach of the Association's prohibition against hiking prices to profit from the trade boycott. A vigilant neighbor saw Martha Cowles brew India tea and serve it to Seth Bird and Daniel Sheldon. She and her husband Solomon, who was warned to keep stricter control over his wife, were forced to confess. It did not matter that Seth Bird, who claimed to support the Association, had made just this one exception to the ban on tea to treat the symptoms of a cold. He ought to have known better and imbibed a patriotic potion made from sassafras or strawberry leaves instead.[30]

In Waterbury, much of the anti-Tory animosity focused on schools, with Congregationalist parents no longer wanting their children associating with Anglicans. One school district actually divided into separate denominational units. Whig mischief-makers also smashed all the windows in Westbury parish's Anglican church, much to the distress of members who had dug deeply into their pockets to find more than £300 to construct the building. A general suspicion of anyone who belonged to the Church of England overshadowed the fact that not all of them rejected the Whig cause even if they were uncomfortable with radicals' tactics. It was commonly believed that every Anglican in Northbury was a Tory, and right next door was New Cambridge, full of people "suspected to be unsound in their political sentiments."[31]

Moses Dunbar tried not to let this escalating political turmoil distract him from domestic responsibilities. In December 1774, he and Phoebe brought another infant daughter—this one named for her mother—to James Nichols for baptism. The following March, Moses had an opportunity to add to his property when Phoebe's aunt agreed to sell him a house on a half-acre lot in Northbury. Unfortunately, just at the time when circumspection was called for, Moses could not resist openly declaring his sympathy for Britain. Perhaps his tongue was loosened by a mug of hard cider after militia training or a glass of rum punch at the local tavern. The precise circumstances of Dunbar's outspokenness are unknown, although they were likely connected, at least in part, to his loyalty to England's established church. Yet he could surely have guessed what the consequences would be. His inflammatory words all but invited attack from radical Whigs.[32]

Dunbar called attention to himself at an exceedingly dangerous moment. New England Whigs had progressed from orchestrating protests to arming themselves in the expectation of a fight. There had been a scare in early September 1774, when rumors spread of a British bombardment of Boston. Several Anglican militiamen in Connecticut who refused to muster for Boston's relief suffered abuse for their stance. Although the rumors proved false, they steeled the Whigs' resolve to prepare for the worst. Thomas Gage warned the Earl of Dartmouth, the secretary of state in charge of colonial affairs, that in Massachusetts, Connecticut, and Rhode Island colonists were stock-piling arms and conducting military exercises. Dartmouth urged Gage to consider disarming them, acknowledging that such a mission might well prove impracticable. Among the communities making the kinds of preparations Gage and Dartmouth wanted to halt was Farmington. Yet on the same day when townsmen instructed their selectmen to procure 36 barrels of powder and 10,000 gunflints, they also voted to provide each constable with a large staff emblazoned with the King's Arms. The breach between England and the colonies gaped wider than ever before, but Farmington inhabitants still considered them-selves loyal British subjects. They were intent on resistance, not revolution.[33]

All that would change sooner than anyone expected. On April 19, 1775, colonial militiamen and British soldiers exchanged fire, first at dawn on Lexington Green and again hours later in Concord. General Gage tried to follow through on Lord Dartmouth's proposal to seize colonial arms and ammunition, but Boston Whigs discovered his plans in time to alert the countryside. Nearly 4,000 militiamen from all over east-ern Massachusetts saw action that day, which ended with Americans attacking the British expeditionary force as it made its way back to Charlestown and the protection of British naval vessels in the harbor. That evening, a total of 93 Americans were dead, wounded, or miss-ing. With 73 men killed, 174 wounded, and 26 missing, the British casualties were three times higher.[34]

By the evening of April 20, messengers on horseback had brought the news to parts of Connecticut; within two more days virtually every-one in the colony had heard about the fighting. The following week, the Assembly held an emergency session and imposed an immediate embargo on food exports before turning to matters of military defense. Legislators organized one-quarter of Connecticut's militiamen into six regiments that would serve as a provincial force for up to seven months. They arranged to strengthen coastal defenses, responding to rumors that Gage planned to seize ships in New London and other Connecticut ports. To pay for all of this, the Assembly approved the issue of £50,000 in bills of credit, to be redeemed at a later date with tax revenue. Finally, knowing that all such preparations were for naught unless God was on their side, the lawmakers urged the colony's ministers to "dissuade their several Congregations, from all Excess and all Diversions" and lead them to "cry mightily unto GOD" for his protection and deliverance.[35]

Once blood had been spilled, colonists had to choose sides and do so publicly. Claims of neutrality satisfied no one: if you were not a vocal defender of colonial rights, you must be an enemy. The burden of choice fell with particular urgency on militiamen, who were being ordered to risk their lives in defense of the Whig cause. In Northbury, the call to arms exacerbated a quarrel that had already divided its militia into factions. Reports that one of the militia companies was infested with Tories had circulated for months, driving members of its Whig minority to petition the Assembly for reassignment to a new company so that "the friends & foes of the Libertys of America will be Intirely Seperated from one another." Although the Assembly endorsed this expedient, the controversy persisted and became a full-blown emergency after April 19.[36]

Whig members of Northbury's West Company warned the Assembly in late April that its officers were "wholly Disaffected to the American Cause." An investigating committee appointed by the legislature corroborated the report. Amos Bronson, the company's captain, had ignored an order to muster his men on a Saturday, waiting until the following Wednesday to do so. Instructed to gather his men at the Congregationalist meetinghouse, Bronson instead mustered them at the Anglican church a mile away. Samuel Scovil, the company's ensign (and James Scovil's younger brother), announced that Boston deserved to be punished for destroying the tea and the Continental Congress acted "Like a Pack of fools." A sergeant proclaimed his unwillingness to bear arms against royal troops and boasted "he would Shoot any Man if he see him going to help the People in Boston." When the Assembly ordered a new election of officers, a majority of the militiamen promptly reelected Bronson and Scovil. Legislators dissolved the defiant company, reassigning its men to Northbury's two remaining units in order to disperse Tories among Whig majorities who could monitor their behavior. The controversy dragged on for months, keeping everyone's nerves on edge from spring until autumn.[37]

Anxieties about Tories intensified as the conflict with Britain expanded. On May 25, 1775, General Gage declared Connecticut and Rhode Island to be in open rebellion, raising the frightening specter of imminent military retaliation. Following the Americans' victory at Bunker Hill in June, British forces were bottled up in Boston, but there was no telling when they might break free and attack Connecticut. Yet even though Tory militiamen might support redcoat invaders, colonial officials were reluctant to disarm them because doing so reduced the available manpower for self-defense. They preferred to identify British sympathizers and employ whatever means were necessary to "convince, convert, or confound them." If need be, Whigs might have to force recalcitrant Tories "to bow before [them], and lick the Dust."[38]

Whigs required no encouragement to be extra vigilant. Waterbury's committee of inspection warned neighbors that "reproachful, contumelious language" against the Continental Congress was as bad as any action taken against its directives and would be punished. Other towns moved to restrict freedom of speech. From the summer of 1775 on, newspapers regularly published confessions by Tories accused of casting aspersions against Congress or the Whig cause in general. Timothy Porter of Waterbury, for instance, had to beg forgiveness for saying he "wished that the Regulars were now firing on the Towns of New Haven and Milford" and that he "believ'd the damned Congress would undo the Country." Tories also invited censure when they disobeyed government directives to avoid labor on public fast days. And Wallingford's Anglican minister, the Reverend Samuel Andrews, surely knew he courted trouble on one fast day when he chose these lines from Amos 5:21 for his sermon: "I hate, I despise your feast days, and I will not smell in your solemn assemblies."[39]

For a while yet, Britain's supporters in Connecticut generally faced intimidating "conversations" with Whig mobs rather than physical harm. Local committees of inspection also resorted to ostracism. Once a townsman was publicly proclaimed "an ENEMY to his country," anyone who had dealings with him ran the risk of being declared an enemy as well. As the fighting continued, however, Connecticut's Whig majority was no longer satisfied that such measures adequately contained the Tory threat.[40]

During the final months of 1775 and into 1776, towns began urging the colony's government to increase the pressure on Tories. New Haven called for a colony-wide association—in effect, a Whig loyalty oath—which everyone would have to sign or expose himself as an enemy to liberty. Elsewhere, townsmen pressed for laws that prescribed severe penalties for anyone who aided the British. In so doing, they voiced demands that echoed a recommendation from the Continental Congress calling for the arrest of anyone who endangered the safety of the colonies. Several communities decided to disarm alleged British sympathizers, more fearful than ever of harboring a fifth column in their midst. As they searched for arms and ammunition to confiscate, Whig committees made little effort to protect Tories' property from damage.[41]

Despite mounting calls for government action, Governor Trumbull and the Assembly hesitated. In part, this reluctance to accede to popular demands reflected their preoccupation with an agenda already packed with items related to military recruitment and the procurement of supplies for the troops. Connecticut contributed heavily to the disastrous American attack on Quebec in the winter of 1775–1776, providing £15,000, more than 2,000 soldiers, and a large store of gunpowder. When spring brought new demands for men and matériel, lawmakers had to figure out how to meet these quotas and pay for them. Coastal areas needed to be fortified as well. Yet the lawmakers' unwillingness to crack down on Tories also reflected their prudence. To enact the harsh measures demanded by increasing numbers of Whigs threatened to transform the nature of the political struggle. Governor Trumbull regarded the conflict as a transatlantic civil war, pitting Britons on each side of the ocean against the other. Adopting unprecedentedly severe penalties against Tories raised the ugly specter of a civil war that would rage within Connecticut itself.[42]

In some communities it was already too late, as neighbors confronted one another with escalating levels of violence.[43] What made this turn of events especially tragic was the fact that Britain's supporters were not as conservative as the label "Tory" implied. So-called Tories and Whigs shared a reverence for Connecticut's charter rights, and many had joined forces in opposing parliamentary taxes and observing trade boycotts. The adversaries mainly differed in their approach to seeking a resolution to the imperial crisis. Moses Dunbar characterized colonial grievances against Britain as an "Unhappy Misunderstanding" that did not go so far as to undermine Parliament's legitimacy. His admission that "I never could reconcile my Opinion to the necessity or Lawfulness of taking up Arms against Great Britain" echoed the views of other loyalists who believed that all peaceful means of redress should be exhausted before more drastic measures were warranted. Until then, tyranny loomed in the forms of Congress, extralegal committees, and roaming mobs that sought to usurp control from properly constituted authority.[44]

Farmington radicals had no use for such arguments. During the winter of 1775–1776, they escalated attacks on perceived enemies, viewing New Cambridge Anglicans as especially inviting targets. One by one, parish members fell victim to violence. A mob of forty men attacked Moses Dunbar with such brutality that his life, he declared, was "nearly taken away." The crowd then forced him to "sign a Paper Containing many Falsehoods"—yet another "voluntary" Tory confession of error. A radical gang captured Joel Tuttle and hanged him from an oak tree; a Whig neighbor cut Tuttle down only after he had lost consciousness. Whigs pursued Chauncy Jerome, Dunbar's brother-in-law. After grabbing him, they pulled his shirt over his head, tied him by the shirttail to an apple tree so that his feet barely touched the ground, and began beating him with a stout hickory stick. Jerome escaped by wriggling out of his shirt and running to Jonathan Pond's house. Both men might have suffered additional injury had not Pond stood at his door and, gun in hand, warned the vigilantes not to enter. Another mob dragged Stephen Graves, married to Ruth Jerome, to the Waterbury border and there subjected him to a severe beating. There was no way James Nichols, seen as the parish's Tory ringleader, would evade painful punishment. He endured tarring and feathering, being tossed into a brook, and having shots fired at him.[45]

When New Cambridge women heard rumors of an imminent attack, they immediately warned their menfolk to flee. Descendants recalled that Ruth Graves blew into a conch shell to sound the alarm. Sometimes the marked men sought refuge in a small cave, situated in a rocky and inaccessible part of town, that became known as the Tory Den. Briars and woodland undergrowth obscured the entrance so well that Whig pursuers never found it. The cavern had a small space on one side just big enough to hold seven tightly packed men and a small

Figure 4.1 Tory Den, now in Burlington, Connecticut. Photo ©
Terry Foley.

rear exit from which they might escape by crawling on hands and
knees. There the men would hide until it was safe to emerge, subsist-
ing on food brought to them by their wives and daughters.[46]

For their pains, these women along with their children were also
subjected to Whig mistreatment. Although colonial women lacked any
formal political role, everyone assumed that Tory wives shared their
spouses' opinions. Women with property or prominent family connections might find ways to distance themselves from their husbands'
political identities, but that was not the case for these beleaguered
New Cambridge families. What made the wives' lot particularly hard
was the radicals' redefinition of everyday domestic duties as subver-
sive political actions. Even such innocuous activities as procuring and
storing foodstuffs provoked retaliation. Wives of suspected loyalists
could only stand by and tremble in fear as parties of Tory hunters
burst into their homes, raided their cellars, and destroyed provisions
lest they be used to nourish the enemy.[47]

Such incidents reinforced the loyalists' belief that all those fiery
radical speeches about preserving the rights of Englishmen and
defending the sanctity of property were nothing more than the
rankest hypocrisy. The Whigs seemed hell-bent on defying every

instrument of British authority that actually protected colonial rights. They concocted an array of makeshift substitutions—from an extra-legal Congress down to local posses that harassed defenseless families with impunity—that posed a far greater threat to liberty and property than any parliamentary tax. Whigs were manifestly the most dangerous element in society, not law-abiding British sympathizers.

At least one out of five inhabitants in the thirteen mainland colonies remained loyal to Britain, bewildered by the speed with which their world had turned upside down.[48] Just a dozen years before the crackle of gunfire echoed across Lexington Green, colonists from New Hampshire to Georgia had joyously celebrated their membership in a victorious British Empire. It did not matter which side of the Atlantic they lived on; as Britons they enjoyed the blessings of a prosperous trade, a vibrant Protestantism, and a mixed and balanced government uniquely designed to preserve freedom. Loyalists simply could not accept the proposition that imperial reforms had so thoroughly undermined the foundation of this common identity as to nullify Britain's claim to sovereignty over its colonies. Even if some of those policies were misguided—and many loyalists were willing to grant this point—the solution was to negotiate, not to grab one's musket. Whigs were not the only ones to harbor fears of conspiratorial agents working against them. Loyalists too could not help but conclude that everywhere Sons of Liberty and their collaborators plotted to destroy the very freedoms they claimed to defend.[49]

In Connecticut, alleged loyalists—including some who preferred neutrality to choosing either side—comprised no more than 5 or 6 percent of the population. Even in the western half of the colony, where their numbers were more concentrated, they constituted a vulnerable minority. Many, perhaps most, were Anglicans. Radical Whigs blamed Anglican ministers, whose SPG subsidies supposedly purchased their loyalty to Britain, for leading their flocks astray. No one was surprised to learn that every one of Connecticut's twenty-three Anglican clergymen held fast to his loyalist allegiance for the duration of the war. Ties to England's state church doubtless influenced Anglicans' political views, but so too did their treatment at the hands of Whig mobs.[50]

The intermingling of politics and religion in New England invited interpretations of the rebellion as a moral confrontation. "I am not so much afraid of the power of England," announced Wallingford's Anglican minister Samuel Andrews, "as I am of the sins of America." As the political situation deteriorated, the Reverend Roger Viets of Simsbury preached again and again from Jeremiah 5:29—"Shall I not visit for these Things? Saith the Lord: Shall not my Soul be avenged on such a Nation as this?" Rewording the verse to fit the times, Viets proclaimed, "shall not I visit great Britain and N. E. in particular for such Things as they practice?" Injustice and oppression overflowed the land, and its people were consumed with lying, hypocrisy, hatred, and revenge. Viets called upon his congregation to repent and reform, but his cry of sympathy for "the Poor, the helpless the Widow & the fatherless" shifted the burden of sin to those who oppressed them—in Anglican neighborhoods, that included the Sons of Liberty and their minions.[51]

The loyalists' plight was about to get worse. In December 1775, Governor Trumbull and the Assembly at last gave in to popular demand and mounting fears of direct British military intervention by passing "an Act for restraining and punishing Persons who are inimical to the Liberties of this and the Rest of the United Colonies." The statute made it a crime to aid British forces with supplies or intelligence, or to take up arms against the American side. Writing or speaking against the Continental Congress or the measures enacted by the colony's legislature would be treated as criminal libel. The law specified provisions for trial by civil authority and, as had been the case since the creation of the Continental Association, local committees were empowered to monitor their neighbors. Penalties for "inimical" transgressions went beyond threats and beatings, and included confiscation of property, imprisonment, fines, disfranchisement, and disarmament.[52]

On January 1, 1776, Governor Trumbull informed General George Washington of the Assembly's passage of this anti-Tory measure. Writing from his camp in Cambridge, Massachusetts, Washington expressed delight at the news, for the law demonstrated how firmly Connecticut supported "the Common Cause." Even so, the governor's report was but small compensation for the dreadful information that Washington had just received of the disastrous American defeat at Quebec, during which General Richard Montgomery was killed along with nearly 100 men, and another 300 soldiers taken prisoner. Washington was also preoccupied with transforming thousands of eager militiamen into an effective fighting force and replacing those troops whose terms of enlistment had expired at the end of 1775. The last thing the American commander wanted to worry about was the possibility that Connecticut's Tories might help the enemy infiltrate the countryside to the rear of the Continentals. Washington also counted on the colony for food and munitions and welcomed any effort that might prevent Tory-directed disruptions to his supply lines.[53]

Connecticut's statute was one of the earliest anti-Tory laws passed in the mainland colonies; only Rhode Island followed suit in the waning months of 1775.[54] It was no coincidence that these were also the only colonies with elective executives and legislatures. Their governmental structures, free from direct British oversight, allowed for unusually smooth transitions from colonial to revolutionary status. And nothing announced that new status more than laws identifying anyone who actively sided with Britain as a traitor. But a traitor to what? At the end of 1775, despite the torrent of eloquent speeches and pamphlets decrying the dangers of British tyranny—and after months of bloody conflict—Connecticut and all the other colonies still belonged to Britain's empire. There was no agreed-upon alternative that commanded the Americans' collective allegiance. Moderates in the Continental Congress continued to search desperately for a compromise that would acknowledge dependence on the king, if not on Parliament. The imperial tie had unraveled to a single thread, but it had not broken.[55]

Connecticut's law aimed to protect the "United Colonies," but few could have described precisely what that entity was or dared to declare the fragile alliance an independent state. In passing the anti-Tory measure, lawmakers also ignored the fact that it directly contravened a similar statute already on the books. The colony's existing Act against High Treason labeled as traitors those who gave aid to the King's enemies—in other words, every Connecticut inhabitant who took up arms against Britain or otherwise supported the Whig cause.[56] For a brief moment, everyone in the colony except those who were frantically trying to remain neutral qualified as a traitor. The irony of the situation could hardly have escaped Moses Dunbar or Connecticut's other disheartened loyalists, but they were in no position to call their adversaries' attention to it. Which definition would prevail in the months to come, no one knew.

5

MORE EXTENSIVE PUBLIC SERVICE

NOVEMBER 8, 1773, DAWNED BRIGHT and clear, a good omen for the start of an important journey. It was two months to the day since Nathan and Enoch Hale had marched with their classmates at Yale's commencement exercise and the younger brother was about to put his college education to use. His destination was a small red clapboard schoolhouse located nearly thirty miles from home in a hilly town nestled alongside the Connecticut River. Enoch accompanied his brother on the trip and then returned alone to Coventry. Nathan remained in East Haddam to take up his position as the town's new schoolmaster.[1]

Other Yale classmates likewise began teaching soon after graduation: Roger Alden and Samuel Dwight in New Haven, Isaac Gridley in Middletown, Elihu Marvin in Norwich, William Robinson in Windsor, Benjamin Tallmadge and Ebenezer Williams in Wethersfield. Enoch Hale taught briefly in Windsor, while continuing to prepare for a career in the ministry. By assuming such responsibilities, these youthful pedagogues—still in their late teens or early twenties—took their first steps toward adulthood.[2]

Before embarking on his journey to East Haddam, Nathan Hale sought advice and reassurance from a seasoned veteran. In late September, he made a pilgrimage to Portsmouth, New Hampshire, to visit his uncle Major Samuel Hale. A 1740 graduate of Harvard, the elder Hale had arrived at his vocational destination via a circuitous route. After experimenting with the law and preaching, he served as captain in a New Hampshire regiment during King George's War, participating in the 1745 Louisbourg campaign against the French. Only after this adventure, and his subsequent rise to the rank of major, did he settle at last on a career as headmaster of the Latin school in Portsmouth. More feared by his students than beloved, Major Hale maintained a perfect record of seeing every candidate he prepared for college successfully gain admission. He warmly encouraged his nephew in his plans to enter a profession both honorable and useful, where such a promising young man could continue to feed his hunger for knowledge as he animated students with his own love of learning.[3]

Nathan Hale arrived in East Haddam in a time of peace, yet booms sounding like cannon fire and crackles resembling gunshots periodically echoed through town, startling both residents and visitors. These were the eerie "Moodus noises," the causes of which had mystified local inhabitants for generations. The original Algonquian residents—who called the area Machemoodus, or "place of noises"—linked the sounds to powerful spiritual forces; early English settlers attributed them to the Indians' alleged devil worship. Because tremors often accompanied the noises, however, some people speculated that the rumblings resulted from a far less sinister cause—small earthquakes. Whatever their origin, these strange sounds and shakings constituted the most exciting features of an otherwise sleepy town.[4]

In moving to East Haddam, Nathan Hale exchanged residence in one small community for another. East Haddam, like Coventry, contained fewer than 3,000 inhabitants, limiting the young schoolmaster's opportunity to re-create the kinds of lively social circles he had known at Yale. For all he knew, he was the only college graduate in East Haddam besides the minister. A couple of ferries regularly crossed the Connecticut River to the west of town, yet the waterway seemed to Hale more like a barrier than an avenue of communication. To the east and south, a line of hills, including the imposing Mount Tom, rose steeply from the more level terrain near the river. Topping out at just over 1,300 feet above sea level, Mount Tom was not a particularly high peak, but viewed from the narrow window of a red schoolhouse it loomed above the neighboring hills, joining them to cordon off the

Figure 5.1 Nathan Hale's schoolhouse in East Haddam. Courtesy of State Archives, Connecticut State Library, PG 180, Mills Photograph Collection, 1895–1955.

community in yet another direction. East Haddam's stony soil posed a daily challenge to its hardworking farmers; the town's isolation presented a challenge of a different sort for its new schoolmaster.[5]

Hale's pupils delighted in their vigorous and handsome teacher. Their enthusiasm, however, could not compensate for his profound sense of loneliness. The thought of an extended sojourn in East Haddam filled him with dread, especially as the bleak winter months approached. Not long after he arrived in town, Hale began searching for an escape. He had by no means given up on teaching but was determined that if this was to be his calling, he would have to pursue it in a livelier town.[6]

Nathan Hale may not have known that his uncle's experience was the exception, not the rule: few men in eighteenth-century New England made schoolteaching their life's work. College graduates often undertook it as a short-term expedient, occupying them for a year or two until they decided on a permanent career. The attractions of the job were limited. Although they no longer lived with their parents, few young teachers were truly independent. Low initial salaries generally precluded matrimony or landholding, at least for some time. Unmarried schoolmasters typically boarded with a local family that monitored their activities to ensure good behavior. Young men accustomed to the comparative freedom of college life often found such scrutiny and the routine demands of the job to be oppressive. "I like it not at all," Ebenezer Williams bluntly announced to his friends. Summoning up the spirit of Linonia, he turned to verse, complaining about teaching school that

> 'Tis too dependent, if not too confin'd
> Dependance ever Galls the Generous mind.

Elihu Marvin's acquaintances likened a schoolhouse to a prison and marveled that he could tolerate such a suffocating environment. Roger Alden confessed that he dreaded class time at his New Haven school as much as he once did early-morning prayers and Saturday recitations at Yale.[7]

Prolonged dependence was one problem, inexperience another. None of these young men had received pedagogical training. For the most part, they adapted by recalling their own early educations, trying to emulate their teachers' good qualities and avoid their failings. The challenges of the colonial classroom could be formidable. Teachers typically faced a motley assortment of students, mostly boys, but occasionally girls too. Some were as young as six or seven, others nearly full-grown. Some pupils could not yet read; others could handle fairly advanced texts. Attendance was often sporadic, reflecting the rhythms of agricultural life and the fluctuating need for labor at home. Even when he did show up in class, an adolescent farm boy eager to start working his own piece of land often found it difficult to pay close attention to some youth barely older than himself droning on about rules of grammar or multiplication tables.[8]

College-educated teachers were expected to tackle a broader curriculum than were instructors without similar training. The youngest pupils needed exposure to basic spelling and arithmetic, while more advanced students learned complex mathematics, geography, and surveying. Prospective college applicants required training in Latin and

Greek. Juggling a variety of subjects and attending to class members with widely varying abilities drove the neophyte teachers in Hale's college cohort to write to one another for advice.

How to keep one group of students busy while teaching another? Elihu Marvin advocated "much spelling, as well as a good deal of reading." Part of the class could write out columns of words while the teacher listened to others read aloud. Marvin often dismissed his youngest pupils early and then helped older ones struggling through Virgil. The former classmates consulted about instructional materials. Marvin asked to borrow a useful grammar text from Nathan Hale. The two teachers exchanged a set of tables (probably used for teaching arithmetic) and even discussed forming a partnership to sell copies of them—not for the money, Marvin hastened to add, but to make them available to their pupils. Benjamin Tallmadge sent Hale some geography cards, requesting that they be returned once Hale's students had copied the information printed on them. The friends likewise debated the virtues of setting quarterly examinations. Ebenezer Williams thought they were a wonderful idea. Tallmadge and Williams held such exams in Wethersfield and Roger Alden planned to do so soon in New Haven. Williams urged Hale to follow suit. Offering regular examinations, he insisted, would "raise your reputation as a school-master"—presumably among parents—and "be of eminent service to your students."[9]

Maintaining discipline in the classroom posed another challenge for teachers as prone to youthful boisterousness as their pupils. Elihu Marvin admitted to spending a great deal of time reprimanding his students for their "nonsense," even as he indulged in it himself. Hale entertained his pupils, presumably outside of class time, with such athletic exploits as jumping straight from one large barrel into another "like a cat." Although some of his charges remembered him as a stern disciplinarian, others praised the "mildness" of his instruction. Hale clearly preferred the carrot to the stick, bestowing rewards on students to motivate them to work hard. This approach, however, led one of his fellow pedagogues to chide him for catering to students' "mercenary" impulses and trying to ingratiate himself with their parents. "Those persons that we go out of an ordinary way to gain the esteem of," William Little scolded, "will often look upon us with contempt, tho' they will professedly accept acts of benevolence with gratitude."

Earning the esteem of students and parents may have made life in East Haddam a bit more tolerable for a young man who missed the popularity he had enjoyed in college, but Hale's yearning to escape never diminished.[10]

He may have heard by word of mouth about the possibility of a teaching position in New London or seen the advertisement in the *New-London Gazette*. The Union School had just been established by twelve leading town citizens and would soon receive a charter of incorporation from the Connecticut legislature. The institution's proprietors only wanted applicants "whose Characters will bear the strictest Enquiry" and who could teach Latin, English, writing, and arithmetic. Excellent penmanship was also desirable. Nathan Hale fit the bill in every way and wasted no time in letting the proprietors know it. The advertisement first appeared on December 3, 1773, and within days Hale had contacted Timothy Green, the paper's printer and one of the school's proprietors, who informed his colleagues of the young man's interest.[11]

Phineas Tracy of Norwich, however, had already snagged the position for himself. The proprietors were nevertheless impressed with Hale's credentials, which included a character reference from the Reverend Joseph Huntington and a sample of the applicant's neat handwriting. Green suggested that Tracy was unlikely to stay beyond his three-month contract and it would be to Hale's advantage to visit New London and meet the proprietors. The young man did so and in early February 1774 received the welcome news that the position was his. By mid-March, Hale had exchanged the stifling environment of East Haddam for the bracing salt air of Connecticut's busiest port town.[12]

New London contained twice as many people as East Haddam—including more black residents than any other Connecticut town—and infinitely greater excitement. Seagoing commerce was its lifeblood, as befitted a community with the best natural harbor in the colony. Hundreds of townsmen, including many of the black inhabitants, labored at seafaring trades. Scores of ships carried livestock, lumber, and provisions to the West Indies, returning with holds packed with barrels of sugar and molasses. Vessels laden with flaxseed for Ireland or timber and potash for Gibraltar crossed paths in the Atlantic with ships sailing westward with British textiles, pottery, and other manufactured goods for Connecticut consumers. New London merchants also pursued a vigorous coastal trade in provisions. During his leisure hours, Hale could wander along the docks and observe the continual activity, listening to the distinctive patois of rugged seafarers who had seen parts of the Atlantic world that the young schoolteacher had only read about.[13]

At the Union School, Hale was responsible for teaching about thirty boys, half of whom were Latin scholars destined for college. During his first summer in New London, he also launched a school for about twenty girls, holding classes for them from five to seven o'clock in the morning. This venture may have reflected Hale's opinions about the importance of girls' education—he had, after all, debated the subject at his Yale commencement exercises—or simply a desire for more income. By charging the girls' families six shillings each for the summer, he added £6 to his salary of £70. Even with this extra responsibility, Hale preserved time for his own intellectual pursuits, including scientific study. He professed to be quite "happily situated" in his new home.[14]

What contributed further to New London's congenial environment were the opportunities the town offered for Hale to "find many friends among strangers." He boarded at the home of John Richards, one of the Union School proprietors, and through him became acquainted with the Christopherses, Hallams, and other prominent local families. Gilbert Saltonstall, the son of General Gurdon Saltonstall and a descendant of a Connecticut governor, soon became Hale's close friend. Three years older than Nathan, Gilbert had graduated from Harvard in 1770 and returned to New London to work in his father's mercantile business. Here at last—unlike in dreary East Haddam—there were interesting people with whom the gregarious Hale could exchange ideas, discuss books and plays, share witticisms, and act the sophisticated gentleman.[15]

And yet it was not quite enough. These new companions could never replace the dear friends Hale had met at Yale. Those classmates had deepened his sense of isolation in East Haddam when they cheerfully reported "tarrying" with this or that friend who happened to pass through the towns where they lived. East Haddam, Hale bitterly complained, was "inaccessible, either by friends, acquaintance or letters."

He joked that because its inhabitants could not read anything but the clearest penmanship, most letters went astray when locals failed to decipher the name scrawled on the outside. Opportunities for regular communication with old friends, Hale was certain, would improve dramatically after he moved to New London.[16]

Difficulties with the mail were hardly unique to East Haddam. The colonial postal system was notoriously expensive and erratic. Throughout Connecticut, bad roads littered with rocks, choked with dust, or mired in mud depending on the season tested the stamina of post riders. Many of them mingled private with public business, further delaying the mail so they could deliver packages, money, and even livestock to people living along their route. The official post road linking Rhode Island to New York ran right through New London, but mail service probably continued to disappoint an impatient correspondent like Hale. He, like most colonists, would come to rely on acquaintances, merchants, and other trustworthy travelers to carry letters to friends and bring back replies.[17]

The delights of such correspondence more than compensated for the frustrations of the mail, leading Hale to urge his friends to engage in "constant writing." A creased scrap of paper could never replace the witty repartee and back-slapping camaraderie of Linonia meetings, but each missive helped the dispersed youths to sustain their web of friendship. Their correspondence provided the youths with a semblance of continuity in a changing world.[18]

So they took up their quill pens whenever they had the chance, scratching out letters long and short, apologizing if their handwriting or stylistic flourishes did not quite measure up to Linonia's high standards. They kept track of letters received and used their own missives to thank diligent correspondents and chide negligent ones. Scarcely a month went by when Hale did not hear from at least one college friend and he sent as many letters as he received. The youths listened for news of anyone headed to Windsor, or Wethersfield, or New London, and implored travelers to deliver messages to dear friends and bring back accounts of how they fared and letters in return. If no new letter was forthcoming, they eased their disappointment by going through a cache of old correspondence and reading it again.[19]

The correspondents rarely discussed mundane activities beyond offering bits of pedagogical advice to fellow teachers. It may have seemed pointless to waste precious paper and ink describing experiences they had in common.[20] Far more interesting was news or gossip about others in their circle. William Robinson could not wait to tell Hale about a recent encounter with brother Enoch, who had heard from Gershom Lyman about Daniel Cooley's recent marriage. Roger Alden, John Wyllys, and other friends who stayed on in New Haven were doing well, James Hillhouse reported. Meanwhile he wrestled with his legal studies, ruefully wishing that "I had improved my time to better advantage when at Colledge." Now and then Linonians revived their literary aspirations by embedding information in doggerel verse. The poets would have preferred to declaim their masterpieces in their friends' presence and watch for a reaction; as it was, imagining how their witty productions were received would have to suffice. If they were lucky, a subsequent letter would satisfy their curiosity on the matter.[21]

Lurking beneath this surface exchange of gossip in their correspondence, however, lay a deeper purpose. The youths yearned to share not just news but also feelings with one another, sending messages from the heart. In so doing, they conformed to a sentimental style of letter writing that had become quite popular by the middle of the eighteenth century. Numerous printed manuals offered instruction on how to compose a "familiar" letter that reflected the writer's good manners and sympathetic nature. Contemporary fiction and even political tracts (such as John Dickinson's *Letters from a Farmer in Pennsylvania* protesting the Townshend Acts) adopted an epistolary model to create a sense of intimacy between author and reader, as if they were engaged in conversation. This was precisely the effect the young men in Hale's circle hoped to achieve, replicating in writing the easy familiarity they had cultivated in person at Yale. Just as Linonia meetings had provided a safe environment where friends could express genuine emotions without fear of ridicule, so too private letters meant only for the recipient's eyes could convey the depth of feeling that sustained their fellowship. It may, in fact, have been easier to accomplish this in writing than in person.[22]

More than anything else, these young men wanted to express how much they missed each other. William Robinson took time away from his teaching duties one cold January day in 1774 to write to Hale, lamenting his separation from Nathan and other "special Friends."

Hale worried about Thomas Mead when he had not heard from him for months. He begged Mead to write lest they lose touch altogether. "It would be a matter of real grief to me," Hale implored, "should our friendship cease." James Hillhouse feared that Hale's new companions in New London would "Root out old ones" like himself. "The Friendship which subsisted between us when at Colledge," Hillhouse scolded, "I should think sufficant to warrant a Correspondence." Writing allowed them to continue "enjoying each others Thoughts" despite physical separation. In closing their letters, the friends described themselves as "sincere," "constant," and "loving," employing terms that were no less meaningful for being stylized. Such expressions of sincerity were genuinely felt, the insistence on free and honest communication essential for preserving the special quality of their sympathetic brotherhood and distinguishing it from the connections they had begun to form with people who stood outside the charmed circle.[23]

When Ebenezer Williams admitted to Hale that "I have my melancholy times now & then," he revealed another important function of their correspondence. Williams noticed that he was "peculiarly subject to these turns when employed in writing Letters to absent Friends." Although writing seemed to bring these spells on, Williams may have derived some relief from the very act of exposing his fragile emotional state to a sympathetic confidant. Merely acknowledging such feelings of sadness reduced some of their intensity, so long as Williams could be certain of his friend's affection and discretion. Open expression of emotion could be risky in a society that valued careful management of the passions, but private communication among genteel friends offered an acceptable way to admit to powerful feelings and yet keep them under control. Like Williams, Roger Alden was often plagued with a "dull, sour, Melancholy Temper." Yet he too could disclose his troubled thoughts to "Friend Nathan" as "Proof of my Friendship," secure in the knowledge that Hale would maintain the confidentiality of their frank exchange and offer a consoling response when he had a chance to do so.[24]

Only one topic demanded the most delicate touch. For the friends to share thoughts on romantic love was to venture onto dangerous emotional terrain, even though the subject preoccupied all of them. The youths had, just at the point of reaching sexual maturity, exchanged Yale's all-male environment for a new social world populated by young women eager to make their acquaintance. This gave them plenty of opportunities to perform before new audiences the genteel roles they had been rehearsing at college. Elihu Marvin, for one, testified to the delights of taking tea in Norwich "with an agreeable circle of young Ladies" and indulging in the occasional evening of eating, drinking, and dancing.[25] Even so, entry into mixed society was also fraught with anxiety. The likely result of such social interactions was courtship and, eventually, marriage. Most colonial youths looked forward to this important rite of passage. Indeed, some—like Moses Dunbar—rushed precipitately into the wedded state. But the members of Hale's coterie approached marriage with trepidation, aware of what they might lose as well as gain by taking this step.

Moses Dunbar assumed that marriage to Phoebe Jerome would goad his father into providing him with land, liberate him from paternal authority, and mark his entry into full-fledged manhood—all by the age of eighteen. Although events had not turned out as planned, Dunbar understood the social and cultural significance of marriage as a marker of male independence in colonial society. But that transition to autonomy was less clear-cut for the young men in Hale's circle. Complain though they might about the dependent condition of schoolteachers, Hale and his friends enjoyed greater freedom than most single young men of their day. Having "weaned" themselves from home and family (as the nineteen-year-old Hale put it), they had already escaped direct parental supervision and could experiment with establishing new connections. They relished the comparative liberty of their bachelor status all the more for knowing it was almost certainly temporary. This was their last chance to cultivate the egalitarian bonds of friendship before turning to the inevitable responsibilities and distractions that matrimony would bring.[26]

Hale and his friends were still quite a bit younger than the typical New England bridegroom.[27] Even so, they regarded any news of a classmate's romantic relationship—or even the rumor of one—as an imminent threat to their fraternal bond. To enjoy female company in general was perfectly acceptable, but to form a "particular connection" with one woman was to set up a rival to one's friends. Hence the intense interest in Daniel Cooley's marriage. The erstwhile Linonian

was the first in their group to wed, barely two months after graduation. Gershom Lyman visited the newlyweds and, in his report to
friends, slyly insinuated that an untimely pregnancy left Cooley with
little alternative. "His Glory is departed from him," Lyman declared,
and—voicing the somber conclusion they would all reach—"he cannot
(as you may well guess) appear before his old intimates as he used to
do." Marriage, as far as the friends were concerned, constituted defection from their circle. "Cooley no doubt," Ebenezer Williams agreed,
"has made a sad mistake."[28]

There was even worse news to come. In the spring of 1774, rumors
began circulating that Nathan Hale had formed a "particular connection" with a young woman in New London. Hale had admitted as much
to a few friends, and the disconcerting information spread as rapidly as
the mail could carry it. The object of his affections was Betsey Adams,
who was also boarding at the home of John Richards, her uncle. Hale
cautiously broached the subject of romance with Benjamin Tallmadge,
making an ambiguous reference to "an ideal or expected Happiness."
Tallmadge may not have fully grasped his meaning, for he responded
with a playful admonition that Hale not "mention one word, nor ask
me one Question" in his next letter "about ideal happiness." By July,
however, Tallmadge had heard numerous accounts that his friend
"was all over (head and heels) in love" and demanded some "direct
news" about the matter.[29]

Ebenezer Williams groped for a way to dissuade Hale from pursuing Miss Adams. It did not matter to Williams if she possessed "every
charm which was in the power of Nature to bestow." He tried humor.
"What is there in your *London* air," he quipped, "that should make a
constant settled spark of you"? "At Yale," Williams continued, "your
Character was certainly that of a Scholar, & not of a Buck!" He also
tried reason. Hale had not yet settled on a permanent calling, and "a
Wife without Employment is not the most desirable acquisition." None
of this helped. On the contrary, all the probing and unsolicited advice
touched a raw nerve. Hale took particular offense at what he understood to be Williams's characterization of him as a "rake." Fearful of
seeing their friendship dissolve, in January 1775 a chastened Williams
proposed dropping the subject. Yet he could not resist enclosing with
this last missive on the topic a copy of a "Love Letter" containing
risqué puns constructed from Latin grammar terms. Williams hoped

that Hale would agree that the "humor of the piece" compensated for its "scurrility."[30]

His friends need not have worried so much; before the year was out, Betsey Adams had married Thomas Poole of New London.[31] But the intensity of their interest in this romance, and their general anxiety about any member of their coterie straying from the fold testified to the extraordinary value they placed on their mutual friendship. Even as they ventured out along separate paths into the world, they strove to remain tethered to one another. Their close relationships had blossomed in the hothouse environment of Yale at a time when only their studies distracted them from socializing. They now realized how hard it was to sustain their connections as they took up new responsibilities and met new people. Soon an even larger distraction intruded. The temporary lull in imperial tensions ended just at the point when the class of 1773 left Yale, presenting unexpected challenges that forced the young men to subordinate personal concerns to public affairs.

Nathan Hale may have been daydreaming about Betsey Adams, or grumbling to himself about the insensitivity of his friends, when he heard about the New London town meeting called for June 27, 1774. News had arrived of the Coercive Acts, Parliament's punitive response to the destruction of the tea in Boston, and New London joined other Connecticut communities in raising an immediate public outcry. Meetinghouses everywhere filled to capacity as townsmen debated what to do. At the New London gathering, which Hale may have attended, inhabitants dutifully acknowledged their loyalty to the British monarch, but then characterized the "alarming situation of the North American colonies" in ways that would not have pleased George III at all. They denounced what they saw as the British ministry's scheme to place the empire "under the nod of an absolute monarch—whereby property and liberty—civil and religious, will be annihilated" and its colonial subjects reduced to slavery. New Londoners adopted the cause of Boston, already suffering from the closure of its port, as their own. They called for a General Congress of Commissioners to coordinate intercolonial policy and advised it to adopt a strict embargo closing off all trade with Great Britain. Finally, they named five prominent townsmen to a committee of correspondence, instructing them to transmit the proceedings of New London's meeting to Boston and communicate with similar committees elsewhere as needed.[32]

Focused on personal crises—of romance, of melancholy, of preserving their fragile fraternity—as well as on their studies or teaching duties, the Yale coterie initially had little energy to spare for public matters. Hale did briefly discuss recent events with Elihu Marvin, who seems to have been more politically engaged than the others. Marvin was teaching in Norwich, a town dominated by radical Whigs pledged to defend colonial liberties by any means necessary. Virtually all of his acquaintances there, he told Hale in late May 1774, were "ready to condemn the proceedings of Parliament" and join Bostonians "in any effectual method that can be contrived to evade the intended destruction." Marvin hoped that "Liberty has as many fast Friends in N. London" as in Norwich, and went on to denounce Lord North, who he had heard was proposing a bill to prohibit colonists from discussing trade and politics altogether as subjects "they know nothing about." But then, for the last half of his unusually long letter, Marvin turned to pedagogy and closed with an extended argument about reading and spelling being more important skills for students to master than penmanship. Did Hale agree?[33]

Soon, however, politics began to absorb the attention of these friends. "Liberty is our reigning Topic," reported James Hillhouse from New Haven in July of 1774, and everyone was expected "to Exert his Tallants & abilities to the utmost in defending it."[34] Normally youths like themselves—unmarried, scarcely out of their teens, without permanent callings or property—had no real political role. But the deteriorating relationship with Britain changed that. It seemed as if every facet of colonists' lives had acquired political significance, and everyone regardless of age, gender, or status, was being drawn into the swirl of public affairs. People monitored one another's speech— as Moses Dunbar and other Anglicans in Farmington were painfully learning—to assess its political content. Purchasing imported British goods after the Continental Congress established a trade embargo in late 1774 invited Whig retaliation. Militia duty—required of all those in Hale's cohort who were not continuing their studies at Yale—no longer conjured up the conviviality of muster days but instead the very real possibility of taking up arms against agents of the same British Empire to which the colonists still claimed allegiance.

These were bewildering times, but for a while yet, Hale remained more an observer than a participant in the unfolding political drama. "No liberty-pole is erected or erecting here" in New London, he informed Enoch in early September 1774. Even so, "the people seem much more spirited" since being riled up by the false report of a British bombardment of Boston. Indeed, a particularly incendiary version of the rumor had swept through New London, alleging that British cannons had indiscriminately mowed down men, women, and children in Boston's streets. Nathan also told Enoch that he had heard about the recent encounter in Hebron between the Sons of Liberty and the Anglican minister Samuel Peters. Whether he believed that Peters had only gotten what he deserved, Nathan did not say.[35]

In his September letter to Enoch, Hale understated the level of Whig fervor in New London. The town's inhabitants loudly proclaimed their intention to aid Boston in its distress and strictly enforce the resolutions of the Continental Association. By the autumn of 1774, they prepared to resist with more than speeches and street demonstrations. The town's location on Long Island Sound rendered it vulnerable to naval assault, and New Londoners feared that they might become the unfortunate target of British aggression. So they set about repairing the decaying coastal battery and readying its cannons for a possible engagement.[36]

As the weeks went by, Hale was drawn into the political ferment. He read newspaper reports about resistance to British measures in New London, around Connecticut, and in other colonies. He heard fellow townsmen hold forth on the streets and in taverns about the perilous state of colonial liberties. In New London's bookshops he found cheap pamphlets and printed essays offering more elaborate versions of the arguments that leading Whigs made in their public meetings. Hale could not help but notice how urgent lessons about current affairs were being drawn from texts he had studied in college for their grammatical constructions and rhetorical forms. What he and his classmates knew of the dangers of tyranny, the fragility of liberty, the glories of virtuous republicanism, and the decline of empires derived from their readings of Plutarch, Cato, Aristotle, and other Ancients whose wisdom, as far as the students had been concerned, applied more to distant places and times than the present.

Demosthenes and Cicero had provided models of oratorical skill and effective disputation useful for class exercises and Linonia Society performances. More modern thinkers such as Pufendorf and Locke introduced the students to what at the time seemed fairly abstract ideas about natural law. Now Hale and his classmates saw how their educations illuminated the problems of their own time.[37]

Hale's political education was further advanced by the local context in which it occurred. The Union School proprietors, who were so pleased with Hale's teaching that they offered him a permanent position, were fervent Whigs. Timothy Green championed the colonists' cause in his weekly newspaper. Three of Hale's patrons—Guy Richards, Richard Law, and Gurdon Saltonstall—served on the town's committee of correspondence. These men dominated New London's social and political elite and had been protesting against imperial reforms since Hale was a young boy. Law, the son of a former Connecticut governor, represented New London in the General Assembly, where his fellow delegate was William Hillhouse, the father of Hale's classmate James Hillhouse. Gurdon Saltonstall, whose son Gilbert was Hale's best friend in town, was an equally eminent figure. Hale greatly admired these "gentlemen of sense and merit," and their ardent support of the Whig cause surely influenced his thinking about the imperial crisis.[38]

Moreover, on September 5, 1774, Hale's patrons invited their protégé to join one of New London's most exclusive clubs, the Independent Artillery Company. Founded in 1762 toward the end of the French and Indian War, the company aimed to "revive the too much neglected & declining exercise of the Firelock." Members conducted training exercises several times a year, substituting such meetings for regular militia service. The company's purpose, however, was as much social as military. Admission was by invitation only, and to participate, members had to acquire an elaborate uniform—short white broadcloth coat with gold buttons, white breeches with black straps, black leggings, hat with a black cockade, and ideally, a "handsome Wig"—along with arms (musket with bayonet, cartouche box). Such accoutrements were not cheap, which reinforced the elitism of the organization. Hale's patrons—several Union School proprietors belonged to the Company—thus made a generous gesture in inviting the nineteen-year-old schoolmaster to join them, and quite likely subsidized his purchase of the requisite clothing and gear. On June 5, 1775, Hale was chosen first sergeant, a minor position that nonetheless reflected his superiors' favorable impression of him.[39]

One by one, energized by the temper of their times and fervor of their communities, Hale and his friends moved from the sidelines toward active support of the Whig cause.[40] Accustomed to sharing thoughts and feelings with one another, they discovered not only that politics was a far less touchy subject to raise than romance, but also that aspects of the current imperial discord resonated closely with their personal experience. The escalating tensions with Britain caught these young men at a crucial moment in their lives. Having recently "weaned" themselves from parental authority, they were particularly receptive to Whig challenges to the hierarchical assumptions underlying monarchical rule. Elihu Marvin certainly did not hesitate—at least in private correspondence—to reject what he now saw as the oppressive dominion of "our Mother Country." Young men who assiduously cultivated sympathetic bonds with each other had little difficulty endorsing the Whigs' assertion that love, benevolence, and what was thought to be a natural human instinct for empathy could sustain civil society in the absence of monarchical constraints. What worked so well within their small circle of friends might indeed knit society as a whole.[41]

The first signs of spring in New England were usually cause for optimism, but in 1775 neither lengthening days nor the occasional warm breeze could dispel the sense of gloom. Everyone expected war. Hale must have been shocked to hear from Richard Sill in March that Yale students were training with firearms on the college green. This was unprecedented: college personnel had always before been exempt from military service. A few weeks later, Ebenezer Williams similarly reported that politics "engross so much of the attention of people of all ages & denominations among us that little else is heard or thought of." Indeed, Hale and his friends might themselves soon be called upon to lend more than moral support to the Whig cause.[42]

That day—April 19—arrived sooner than anyone anticipated, with the bloody skirmishes between colonial militia and British redcoats at Lexington and Concord. News of the battles spread like wildfire. Riders galloped frantically from town to town throughout a cold and rainy night to alert the countryside. By the following evening, New

Londoners—a hundred miles away from the scene of the action—
knew what had happened. Within a week, thousands of Connecticut
militiamen—including Nathan Hale's older brothers John and
Joseph—marched to the aid of Massachusetts.[43] It was now "hardly
proper," Benjamin Tallmadge declared, for the group of Yale friends
to indulge in "epistolary productions of mere Compliment & form."
America was in danger and the "Eyes of the world are now bent on
us." Tallmadge's generation had neither seen nor expected anything
like this. "The great wheel of the State & Constitution seem to have
grown old & crazy," he proclaimed, and "every thing bids fair for a
Change; every Machine needs to be refited or renewed." What such
a transformation might entail, no one knew. Tallmadge warned Hale
that "we ought by all means to prepare for the worst."[44]

Buried within the direst of threats, however, lay the greatest of
opportunities. Tallmadge sounded a note of caution, but he and his
friends recognized that the renewal of "every Machine" of society
and government offered an outlet for their considerable ambitions. If
the danger posed by British tyranny once seemed distant or abstract,
the outbreak of fighting made it suddenly quite real. Their very lives,
and those of other colonists, were now at stake. The adult world
they had just entered was crumbling about them, and they grasped
at the chance to help construct its replacement, whatever that would
be. Until now, even the most enthusiastic Whig in their cohort could
only applaud the speeches and actions of the older men who led the
resistance effort. But in wartime, youth became an advantage. Armies
needed strong bodies. Hale and his friends could demonstrate their
manhood on the battlefield in ways unavailable to them as bachelors
in civilian society and do so from positions of some authority. Their
college diplomas marked them as colonial gentlemen, eligible for
appointment as junior officers. Never could they have guessed that
such a noble cause would emerge so quickly, providing a stage upon
which they could perform in a new drama linking their own futures to
those of their colony and, indeed, the empire.[45]

Ezra Selden was one of the first to answer the call to arms. The smoke
had barely cleared from Lexington Green when he enlisted in Colonel
Samuel Parsons's regiment as an orderly sergeant and headed off to
join other New England soldiers besieging the British outside Boston.

Stephen Keyes followed soon thereafter, then Joshua Woodbridge. Ezra Sampson, recently ordained a Congregationalist minister, volunteered to serve as chaplain to the troops in Roxbury camp. Their decisions occurred so swiftly that it was difficult for everyone else to keep track of who had shouldered his musket and who—at least as yet—had not.[46]

In considering his options that spring, Nathan Hale struggled to reconcile two competing calls to duty. His yearlong contract with the Union School still had a few months to run, and he could not in good conscience abandon his employers, his students, and a job he professed to love. Neither could he imagine missing out on the excitement his soldier-friends experienced as they marched off toward Boston. The first volunteers engaged to serve just until the end of November 1775, at which point some solution to the imperial crisis would surely have been found.[47] Ezra Selden's vivid account of camp life quickened the pulse of his friend and intensified Hale's desire to undertake his own military adventures before the fighting ceased. British forces had fired on Roxbury just before he arrived, Selden reported, killing a few men and raining "bombs" (mortar shells) on the encampment that sent shingles flying but did little other damage. No one yet knew what the casualties had been at the recent battle of Bunker Hill, he went on, or what the relative strengths of the two armies might be. As for his immediate surroundings, Selden described the New Englanders' camp as consisting of a fort on a hill, a battery, and soldiers' quarters, with some troops assigned to houses, and others (including Selden) in tents. "I dont learn any thing worth mentioning," he concluded, but Hale was enthralled by every detail in his friend's report.[48]

By the time he received Selden's letter, dated June 25, 1775, Hale had made up his mind to serve. On July 1, the General Assembly offered him a commission as first lieutenant of the third company in the Seventh Regiment of Connecticut troops, under the command of Colonel Charles Webb. His Yale friend and fellow Linonian, William Hull, joined the same regiment, as first lieutenant of the second company.[49] Richard Law, one of the Union School proprietors, was clerk of the Assembly and perhaps recommended Hale for the commission. By this point, his contract had barely two weeks to run, and Hale hoped that his early departure would produce "no great inconvenience" to his employers. He had grown so fond of teaching, Hale assured them, that he had anticipated making it his life's work. The war, however, offered an "opportunity for more extensive public service" that Hale simply could not resist.[50]

Meanwhile, Benjamin Tallmadge traveled to Cambridge to see what a soldier's life was like. His "military friends" pressed him "to think of the oppression which was so abundantly exhibited by the British government towards the Colonies" and join them. Invigorated by their martial spirit, Tallmadge departed from camp determined to sign up.[51] His zeal, however, dissipated on the journey home. Then he learned from an impeccable source—Hale's landlord, John Richards—that Nathan had been offered a lieutenant's commission. Not knowing whether Hale had accepted, Tallmadge immediately composed a meandering letter that betrayed his own ambivalence as he suggested to his old friend how "I think I should act myself." The two schoolteachers already served "in a publick capacity," he reminded Hale, and since "liberty is closely connected with learning" their pedagogical efforts could rightly be construed as support for the Whig cause. Tallmadge hesitated to advise Hale to abandon his honorable vocation, along with "so agreeable a circle of connections & friends" as he had made in New London. Yet "our country" cried out for help in its "sore distress," and Hale no doubt had "some turn for the military art." "Was I in your condition," Tallmadge concluded, "I think the more extensive Service would be my choice." Hale appreciated the fact that this counsel was sent from "a heart ever devoted to your welfare," but it made no difference. By the time he received the letter, he had already accepted his commission. Despite earnest expressions of devotion to "the cause," Tallmadge postponed his own enlistment for nearly a year.[52]

Hale did not leave New London immediately. His regiment was one of two created by the Assembly in July 1775, each to consist of ten seventy-man companies. The task of recruiting common soldiers for these companies fell to the officers. Normally figures of some standing in their communities, officers used their influence with friends, family, and neighbors to fill the ranks. Since he was a relative newcomer to New London with few such ties, Hale relied on the company's second lieutenant, John Belcher, to help find suitable men. General Washington desperately needed this infusion of Connecticut troops and even suggested he would be happy to get undermanned units if those were all that were available. Yet officers doggedly endeavored to meet their quotas, virtually ensuring that the Seventh Regiment would not head for Boston before autumn.[53]

Governor Jonathan Trumbull was eager to come to the aid of Washington and the American cause, but not if doing so imperiled his own colony. That was the dilemma he faced as the summer wore on. In late July, four British vessels approached New London harbor, depositing men onshore who proceeded to spike several of the town's cannons by plugging their touchholes with "old Files." Other British sailors plundered livestock from nearby islands. With enemy ships cruising just off the coast and threatening colonial lives and property, Trumbull ordered Colonel Webb's regiment to remain in Connecticut and guard the shore from Stonington (which was bombarded by British naval guns on August 29) to New Haven.[54]

Trumbull's decision—justifiable as it seemed from his headquarters in Lebanon, Connecticut—added to the enormous challenges Washington faced as commander in chief. He had to answer to the authority of the disputatious members of the Continental Congress on matters of policy, if not military strategy. He also dealt with thirteen colonial assemblies who demonstrated mixed levels of success in raising the troops and supplies he needed and always had the interests of their own constituencies uppermost in their minds. Colonies that did send men into the field squabbled over having their own officers appointed as major generals and brigadiers. The citizen-soldiers who volunteered in 1775 had far more enthusiasm than military training, equipment, or even suitable clothing. Thus Washington struggled to forge an effective military force from a motley collection of provincial militiamen who, at this point in the conflict, fought for a cause—the defense of their liberties and communities—but not for a nation.[55]

On the first of September, in accordance with the terms of his original commission, Nathan Hale rose to the rank of captain, a promotion that likely rewarded his success in recruiting his quota of men.[56] A few weeks later, Governor Trumbull at last released the Seventh Regiment to join Washington outside of Boston. It took the unit just a week to make the hundred-mile march, covering more than sixteen miles on some days. The troops headed first to Providence, Rhode Island, then tramped through southeastern Massachusetts up to Roxbury camp on the southern outskirts of Boston. Just before sundown on September 26, the weary soldiers pitched their tents. Three days later, they were on the move again. The troops made a circle around the western side of the peninsula where Boston was situated, arriving at Winter Hill, not far from Washington's headquarters in Cambridge. Here Hale and his unit would stay through the winter and into the following spring.[57]

In his effort to advise Hale on whether or not to enlist, Benjamin Tallmadge had worried that his affable friend would sorely miss his "agreeable circle" of New London connections if he joined the army. Hale doubtless did regret leaving Gilbert Saltonstall, Betsey Adams, and other acquaintances. Yet the gregarious young soldier was hardly bereft of companions. Among the New Englanders participating in the siege of Boston, no fewer than sixteen men had attended Yale during the same years as Hale, and most of them had belonged to the Linonia Society. Five were from his own class of 1773: Stephen Keyes, Ezra Sampson, Ezra Selden, Joshua Woodbridge, and John Palsgrave Wyllys. Because Washington dispersed his forces around Boston's perimeter to keep the British bottled up, this Yale contingent was scattered from Winter Hill in the north to Roxbury in the south. The distance between encampments, however, posed no barrier to young officers eager to renew their friendships in person.[58]

The outbreak of war made possible something that the business of ordinary life had hindered: the reconstitution, albeit in partial form, of Hale's college cohort. If the fighting lasted long enough, their more cautious colleagues—Tallmadge, Alden, Hillhouse, Marvin, and others—might be convinced to join up as well.[59] The young men could not help but marvel at the sudden shift in their fortunes. Just two years after leaving Yale, they were fighting in a war against Britain, the most powerful nation on earth and home to the sophisticated literary culture that they, as Linonians, so admired. Reunited in their military camps, the young officers were acutely aware that their own martial performance affected the fates of nearby soldier-friends as well as distant homes and families. The personal dimensions of the conflict thus loomed as large as the political cause for which they were fighting.

The stakes were already high when Hale joined the army. Early fighting at Lexington, Concord, and Bunker Hill had produced more than 400 American casualties. Seeking to end the bloodshed, the Continental Congress adopted the Olive Branch Petition on July 5, imploring George III to halt British military actions while a resolution to the imperial crisis was negotiated. The following day, however, Congress issued a more bellicose declaration, denying that the colonists sought independence and yet insisting that they would sacrifice their lives rather than forfeit their liberty. Such statements revealed the inchoate nature of the colonists' political goals during the summer of 1775. If not independence, what did they want? A return to the pre-1763 status quo? A new imperial framework that eliminated Parliament's authority over the colonies altogether? Colonial Whigs had a far keener sense of what they were fighting against—unlawful taxation, British corruption, military aggression—than what they were fighting for.[60]

Those stakes rose even higher as Hale set off in early September with the Seventh Regiment for Boston. Colonists would not hear the news until later in the autumn, but the king had refused to receive the Olive Branch Petition, let alone read it. Infuriated by the Americans' insubordination, George III fed the flames of discord on August 23 by declaring the colonies to be in open rebellion. This royal pronouncement effectively transformed every member of Washington's army, from the general himself to the newest recruit—indeed, any supporter of the Whig cause—into a traitor. As members of Congress struggled to identify what a successful resolution of the crisis should look like, everyone could see that the costs of failure were incalculable.[61]

Matters of high politics, however, fell to the province of other men. Captain Hale attended to more immediate concerns, preparing for the unfamiliar duties of commanding soldiers in the field. To mark the opening of this new chapter in his young life, he purchased a small book with a red leather cover and some 300 blank pages, packing it along with pen and ink and other belongings. Hale had never before kept a journal. Now that his company was on the move at last, he suspected that army service would provide plenty of excitement. Such experiences deserved to be recorded, so that in the future he could reminisce about his participation in the great events of his day, sharing stories of his wartime adventures with friends, students, and perhaps his own children.[62]

What lingered in his mind as Hale penned his first entry on September 23 were the sounds of war. The echoing booms he and his men heard throughout much of the day were nothing like the strange

"Moodus noises" that plagued East Haddam. These came from real cannon—"40 or 50" of them, Hale guessed—mounted on the British vessels patrolling Narragansett Bay to cut off Rhode Island's trade. His company halted for the night at Benjamin Waterman's house in Johnston, Rhode Island, not far from Providence. The handsome dwelling offered comfortable lodging for officers and good food. The soldiers needed their rest, for they still had about fifty miles to go to Roxbury. As he rose early the next day, rousing his men to march by six o'clock, Captain Hale may have paused for a few moments to muse about what new experiences he would record that evening on the next page in his journal.[63]

6

A VERY GENTEEL
LOOKING FELLOW

THE DAYS GREW SHORTER AS the autumn of 1775 advanced, yet each seemed longer than the last. It had taken just a few weeks for the excitement of the march to give way to the tedium of camp life. Everywhere at Winter Hill, the din of sawing and hammering announced the frantic construction of barracks for thousands of soldiers. Now and then British troops bombarded the outlying camps from besieged Boston, offering a thrilling counterpoint to the usual dull routine. The cannonades generally produced little damage, although one unlucky soldier had his arm torn off by British fire on October 6. Even these sporadic interruptions diminished as the weeks wore on. Far more persistent were rumors that swirled like dry leaves caught up in the wind: General Thomas Gage had departed for England; the redcoats he left behind were succumbing to scurvy and smallpox; 25,000 British and Hanoverian troops were en route to Boston. Such talk still provided only momentary distraction from the daily frustrations of wretched provisions, cold and rainy weather, and, for Captain Nathan Hale, boredom.[1]

Whatever bright visions Hale had entertained of army life faded in the pale October light of Winter Hill. Sieges were waiting games, with little scope for displaying martial prowess. Hale had not planned on leaving home only to tarry in a ramshackle army encampment. "I once wanted to come here to see something extraordinary," he admitted in a letter to his New London friend Betsey Christophers, but after barely three weeks, "my curiosity is satisfied." "I would only observe," he continued, "that we often flatter ourselveves [*sic*] with great happiness could we see such & such things; but when we actually come to the sight of them, our solid satisfaction is really no more than when we only had them in expectation." For all the action he had seen, Hale might as well have been drilling with New London's Artillery Company.[2]

Regular stints of picket duty provided some excitement because of the greater exposure to enemy fire. So did intermittent alarms, such as the one on November 9 when Hale's company was sent to repel British troops who had landed at Lechmere Point to steal cattle. But such occasions offered Hale little opportunity to distinguish himself as an able officer. Furthermore, he was dismayed to learn that several subordinates in his regiment objected to his commission, insisting that neither he nor William Hull ought to have been appointed as captains. The officers' youth (aged twenty and twenty-two, respectively) likely irritated older men who had hoped for preferment. A common problem in these hastily formed units, this bickering irritated Washington. "In an Army so young as ours," the frustrated general complained, "the Claims arising from real Service are very few, & the accidental Circumstance of obtaining a Commission a Month or two sooner can with no reasonable Person claim any Superiour Regard or make such a Scrutiny of any Consequence." With the backing of Colonel Charles Webb and other officers, Hale and Hull continued in rank, but the dispute increased the pressure on them to gain their subordinates' respect.[3]

Whatever the disappointments of military life, Hale was not ready to give it up. He would not even accept a furlough, he declared to Betsey Christophers, were one offered to him. In fact, as the end of his five-month commitment drew near, Hale contemplated extending his term of service. The British could not stay in Boston forever; sooner or later the armies would have to move. Better to be a participant in this unpredictable drama than a passive observer reading about what others had accomplished.[4]

"It is of the utmost importance that an Officer should be anxious to know his duty," Hale scratched in his journal on November 6,

1775. It was equally crucial "that he should carefully perform what he does know: The present irregular state of the army is owing to a capital neglect in both of these." Painfully aware of his lack of real military experience, Hale wanted to be sure that none of his superiors could accuse him of negligence. In the neat penmanship that had so impressed the Union School proprietors, he kept meticulous accounts of his company's payroll and expenses for clothing, food, and equipment. Studying his manual of arms, he pored over the instructions for preparing a company for review and copied the "Directions for the Guards" into his diary as a guide to commanding men on picket duty. He was one of the few officers who followed Washington's orders to visit the sick men in his unit. Such attention to detail recalled the conscientious behavior of Hale the student and the schoolmaster.[5]

Hale's youth and genial nature, however, often made it difficult for him to maintain a proper distance from the men under his command. Eighteenth-century armies—American as well as European—presumed that martial discipline required a strict separation between officers, who should be gentlemen, and ordinary soldiers. This distinction, though harder to maintain in an army drawn from a comparatively egalitarian American society, pervaded military life. Officers earned higher pay, wore uniforms that displayed their ranks, and received better food and housing. They risked punishment—even to the point of court-martial—for fraternizing with their men. Yet Captain Hale, who once entertained students with schoolyard capers, played football in camp and engaged in wrestling matches, on one occasion skipping evening prayers for a competition. The former teacher who had been scolded by a colleague for ingratiating himself with students and parents could not repress a similar desire to be liked by his men. Catching some soldiers playing cards, he made them surrender the deck, which he "chop[pe]d" to pieces, but "in such a manner," one observer recalled, "that the men were rather pleased than otherwise." In late November 1775, responding to Washington's request that officers urge their men to extend their service to the first of January, Captain Hale promised his unit that "they should have my wages for that time" if they did so. Most of his company stayed on, though probably not because of this financial incentive. Despite three months in rank, the earnest young officer still had a lot to learn.[6]

Hale also found time to engage in the leisure activities that affirmed his genteel credentials. Known in camp as someone who could "make a pen the quickest & the best of any man," Hale sharpened his quills not only to keep army accounts but also to compose poetry. One unfinished verse described the sights along his march to Winter Hill. As for the camp itself: "The hills with tents their whiteness show/Resembling much Midwinter's snow." Hale probably meant to enclose this piece in a letter to some friend who would appreciate his literary exertions.[7] Indeed, he devoted much of his spare time to writing letters, producing a dozen in the month of October alone. Military service had done nothing to stanch the flow of his correspondence. Some letters made their way to family members (especially Enoch), but most went to friends in New London. In return, Betsey Christophers and Betsy Hallam supplied him with local gossip, including notice of Betsey Adams's wedding to Thomas Poole. Gilbert Saltonstall and John Hallam described the town's defensive preparations and recounted inhabitants' frenzied responses to false alarms of invading redcoats. They provided what news they had of the war's progress, sometimes enclosing newspapers with their missives. Saltonstall begged for details of camp life, eager to experience the war vicariously through his friend's letters. He ached to join the fledgling American navy, but his father objected and the dutiful son could not "leave him in the Eve of Life against his consent."[8]

Hale received plaintive letters from college friends as well, who accused their classmate of neglect. From his New Haven schoolhouse, Roger Alden worried that "the Life & Business of a Soldier has worn off all that Friendship & Tenderness" that Hale had once bestowed on him. Alden wanted "to be in the Army very much," but was waiting for "a Lieutenancy" or even "an Adjutancy"—commissions he thought suited to his social position. Elihu Marvin, teaching in Norwich, similarly complained in December 1775: "Three month at Cambridge and not one line ... well I can't help it, if a Captain's Commission has all this effect." A letter, he noted in a postscript, "would not be disagreeable." Hale's former tutor Timothy Dwight was less censorious, probably because he needed a favor—help in finding subscribers to underwrite publication costs for his new poem, "The Conquest of

Canaan." As a "Gentleman," Dwight hinted, Hale surely knew other officers in "the circle with which you are connected" who would gladly support the poet's literary endeavors.[9]

Hale had not in fact forsaken his Yale ties but rather focused his attention on college friends he could greet in the flesh. William Hull was his constant companion; the two captains often took walks and dined together. Royal Flint showed up in camp one day, perhaps to see if he might want to seek a commission. While on a day trip to Cambridge, Hale sought out Joshua Woodbridge, stationed there in a regiment commanded by a cousin. During rainy days at Winter Hill, Hale and other officers visited one another in their tents, passing the time in reading, conversation, and games of checkers. Taking advantage of what leisure moments army life allowed, these men endeavored to re-create as best they could the sociable interactions of their college days.[10]

Hale knew how to behave as a gentleman; what he lacked was a thorough education in army ways. He needed to learn to think and act like an officer, to develop habits of discipline and command. But he could not teach himself every skill from books. Like other young officers, Hale carefully observed more seasoned warriors. He was regularly invited to wine and dine with generals who had earned their reputations during the French and Indian War. There was Israel Putnam— "Old Put"—whose vast reserves of energy belied his fifty-seven years. He had distinguished himself as a ranger during the Battle of Lake George in 1755 and later saw action in the expeditions to Montreal and Havana. In 1775, Putnam's aggressive counterattack against British raiders near Boston earned him an appointment as major general, fourth in seniority to Washington. Charles Lee, besides serving with distinction in the French and Indian War, fought as a soldier of fortune with the Polish army during the 1760s. When the war with Britain began, he too was poised to accept an American generalship. Another veteran officer, Joseph Spencer, upset that Putnam had received the appointment he thought he deserved, had to be persuaded to serve with the Connecticut troops outside Boston. Lowly captains like Hale doubtless said little at these dinners, but they could see how officers behaved among themselves, learn the latest news about the war, and if drawn into conversation with their superiors, try to impress a possible

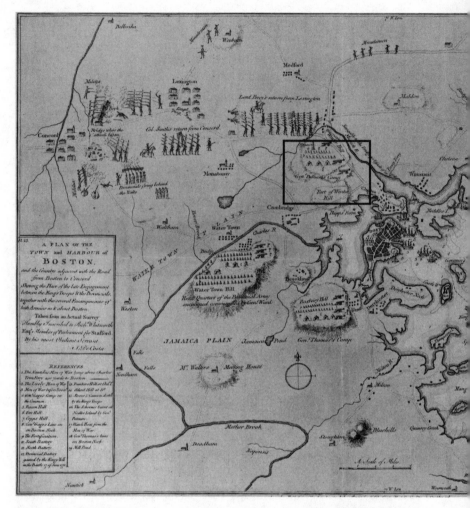

Figure 6.1 Map of Boston area at the outbreak of the Revolution. Detail on right shows Winter Hill camp where Nathan Hale initially served. J. De Costa and Charles Hall, *A plan of the town and harbor of Boston and the country adjacent with the road from Boston to Concord, shewing the place of the late engagement between the King's troops & the provincials, together with the several encampments of both armies in & about Boston. Taken from an actual survey.* London, 1775. Courtesy of the Library of Congress, Geography and Map Division.

patron. Until the war gave them a chance to exhibit their own valor, the young men had to be satisfied with paying close attention to duty and proper protocols of army life, and demonstrating steadiness and good character.[11]

In late autumn, Hale asked to be commissioned for another year. His company, still under the command of Colonel Charles Webb, was to be reorganized as of January 1, 1776, from a Connecticut unit to part of the 19th Regiment in the Continental Army. William Hull also requested reappointment, which would allow the two captains to stay together. For much of December, Hale negotiated with the army's overburdened quartermasters, trying with considerable difficulty to obtain provisions, clothing, and other supplies for his company. He arranged furloughs for soldiers in his unit who had agreed to serve another year. Hale, too, was eligible for a month's furlough, and despite his earlier claim that he would not accept one, he did. His new commission required him to recruit more men back in Connecticut, and this might be his last chance to see his family for some time.[12]

Indulging in a bit of vanity, Hale had his hair dressed and hat refurbished before setting off for Coventry. How well this primping withstood the rigors of his three-day journey is unclear. He traveled the eighty-odd miles mostly on foot, occasionally losing his way and having to retrace his steps in "ancle deep" snow. Each night, he recorded his progress in his diary, commenting on the quality of accommodations at the various taverns he stopped at along the way. Arriving at the paternal homestead just after sunset on December 26, he basked in his family's attention as he nursed a sore foot. Despite his injury, the ever-sociable captain managed to visit married siblings, Strong relatives, nearby Yale friends, and the Reverend Huntington.[13]

By early January 1776, Hale was in New London seeking to replace men who had left his company. Because the initial war fever had subsided, it was harder to fill the ranks. Army leaders had recently endorsed a shift from short-term to annual enlistments, but many potential recruits proved unwilling to sign up for so long. Even twelve-month terms of service did little to address the problem of frequent turnover in personnel, encouraging some generals to argue for enlistments lasting for the duration of the war. At this point in the conflict, however, colonists wary of the dangers of a standing army demurred. Compounding their difficulties, recruiting officers could not simply sign up anyone who came forward. While Hale was away from camp, one soldier in his company attempted to stab another "through the Heart" with a bayonet, prompting Ensign George Hurlbut to warn Hale "To be Careful who you Inlist."[14]

Hale had found one trustworthy recruit in Coventry. Asher Wright, born the same year as the captain, was a childhood friend and neighbor. Hale asked Wright to serve as his waiter, or personal servant, replacing a New London man who left the army because of illness. Waiters performed a number of tasks, such as looking after baggage, carrying food to officers on duty, and erecting and disassembling tents. The physical embodiment of officers' gentlemanly status, waiters occupied a relatively safe berth, protected from the dangers of the battlefield. Thus Hale could at once enjoy Wright's companionship and shield him from harm. Ever the conscientious friend, Hale periodically wrote to Wright's family to assure them that he was well.[15]

His recruiting stint completed, Hale stopped off to see his father and other kin in Coventry before heading back to camp on January 24, 1776. He borrowed a horse for the first few miles, leaving it in Ashford, probably with relatives who lived there. The remainder of the three-day trek, in the company of eleven recruits, took place on foot along snow-packed roads. On January 27, Hale left the new recruits with General Spencer at Roxbury, where his own unit soon relocated. If the captain, anxious for more adventure than his service had so far provided, anticipated that this change of venue presaged some more significant movement in the near future, he was disappointed. Hale's company remained in Roxbury as winter slowly gave way to spring.[16]

Late-winter days in camp were colder than those of autumn but just as dull. Soldiers drilled under leaden skies, performed picket duty, and waited for something to happen. There was a brief commotion on February 14, when "a very considerable body" of British troops tried and failed to take Dorchester, leaving a couple of houses in ashes. Otherwise, Hale continued to fill empty hours socializing with officers and nearby college friends—among them Andrew Hillyer, Isaac Sherman, Stephen Keyes, Ezra Sampson, Ezra Selden, John Palsgrave Wyllys, and, of course, William Hull—who shared his impatience with the army's inaction.[17]

Hale also kept up with his correspondence. He assured William Robinson in New Haven that despite the tedium of camp life, he was "pleas'd with [his] conditions & companions" and thus "happy." Robinson, in turn, admitted to "Dear Nathan" that "the society only of a few *old* Friends is wanting to render my situation here perfectly agreeable." Elihu Marvin renewed his gentle mockery of Hale's romantic life with a poem mentioning a mysterious young woman described as "Nathan's other self": "Poor Girl she's left almost alone, / Since Neighbour Hale's been gone from home." The captain evidently found it easier than before to ignore such comments; at least he did not respond to Marvin's provocation with the same display of pique.[18]

Less easy to dismiss was a disturbing letter from Gilbert Saltonstall, whose envy of his friend's military experience was tempered by a growing realization of what warfare actually entailed. An unusually introspective Saltonstall wrote on March 18, prompted by a report that Hale's company had recently attempted to take Nook Hill south of Boston and that Hale had "there left them expos'd to the Fire of the Enemy." Saltonstall begged to know the outcome of the engagement and went on to ponder the ethics of military discipline. Must a general's orders always be obeyed, or can an inferior officer "Judge of their expediency, or inexpediency?" Pushing his query further, he asked if orders must be followed even if compliance meant certain death. "I have been inform'd," he noted, that Oliver Cromwell personally executed two officers during the siege of Drogheda for refusing to follow orders they regarded as suicidal. Saltonstall found "something unaccountable in the personal Bravery of some Characters that I have met with in History" who faced "instant Death," and he seemed unnerved by their predicaments. For such a doomed individual, "there must be something shocking in the thought that he is to quit existence, that he is to pass to a state of nonentity." Saltonstall described another episode from the siege of Tortona, when a commander deliberately ordered "one Carew," an Irish officer, to march his men into a deadly enemy trap. Carew obediently "led on his Men in silence to the dreadful Post," but just before they arrived, the city capitulated, allowing his detachment to escape with their lives. Despite that happy ending, Saltonstall admitted, "It makes my Blood crawl, in realizing Carews feelings."[19]

Hale could scarcely have missed Saltonstall's choice of sieges as the settings for suicidal missions, but his reaction to such macabre musings is unknown. The captain would hardly have regarded his recent orders as "inexpedient," if his friend meant to imply that. Moreover, by the time he received the letter, Hale knew that the Nook Hill engagement had been part of a spectacularly successful set of maneuvers that placed American batteries on Dorchester Heights, overlooking the British army in Boston.[20] This achievement diverted Hale's attention from his friend's unsettling letter, for it meant that his unit's seemingly interminable wait for something to happen had come to an end.

Events in the first months of 1776 were moving at a faster pace than at any time since the conflict began. General William Howe replaced Thomas Gage as the British army's commander in chief. He and his brother Admiral Richard Howe were also appointed peace commissioners, tasked with simultaneously prosecuting the war and seeking its negotiated end. Throughout the colonies, Americans debated the powerful argument for independence found in Thomas Paine's wildly popular pamphlet *Common Sense*. Hale's classmates were among the tract's avid readers. Enoch read it. William Robinson proclaimed that "Upon my word 'tis well done." "I confess," he wrote to Nathan, "a perusal of it has much reform'd my notions upon several points.... I own myself a *staunch independent*." American independence was hardly a foregone conclusion that spring, but increasing numbers of influential colonists thought it a justifiable response to Britain's waging of war against its own subjects.[21]

The most important development, as far as American troops were concerned, was the British army's decision to evacuate Boston. The cannons aimed down at them from the American fortifications on Dorchester Heights made the redcoats' continued occupation of the city too dangerous. By March 17, after a final round of plundering houses and shops, about 8,000 British soldiers and another 1,000 loyalists finished boarding naval transports in the harbor. Nine days later, they sailed for Halifax, Nova Scotia. Washington cautioned his elated troops not to celebrate by flooding into Boston lest they succumb to smallpox, which, he alleged, the British had "with a malicious assiduity" spread throughout the town. The general also issued orders to begin moving American forces. No one expected the

British army to remain in Halifax for long; everyone assumed that its next target would be New York, with its excellent harbor. British occupation of that city would cut troublesome New England off from the rest of the colonies, a strategy designed to stop the Revolution in its tracks.[22]

Washington aimed to get there first. On March 14, even before the British had left Boston, Hale's company was one of several units ordered to New York. Given five days' worth of provisions (which they were advised to cook before departure since there would be no time to do so en route), the men set off on a trek through springtime mud for Norwich, Connecticut. From there, they marched to New London and boarded the vessels that would carry them to New York. During his brief stay in town, Hale settled accounts with local merchants and may have visited Saltonstall and other friends. But his duties kept him very busy—so busy that he had no time to write in his diary. It would be July before he made another entry. Enoch, a more assiduous diarist, noted in his own journal on March 29: "5 Reg[imen]t gone by water from N London. Brother Captain gone."[23]

By April 5, Hale's regiment reached New York, a city whose complicated topography of rivers and islands confounded the Americans' plans for defense. Washington had earlier dispatched Charles Lee with a body of troops to begin the laborious process of constructing forts, digging trenches, and erecting barricades. Desperate for reinforcements, the American commander in chief begged the Continental Congress for more men. In the end he had to settle mainly for militiamen provided by reluctant colonial governments, including many who had only signed up for short terms of service. These unseasoned troops dispersed across the region to prepare for any number of possible avenues of British invasion—along the Hudson River, on Manhattan, over to Long Island, and especially on Brooklyn Heights. In late May, Colonel Webb's regiment, including Hale's company, briefly occupied tiny Governor's Island at the mouth of the East River. Compounding Washington's frustrations, ammunition was in short supply. On June 1, the general requested that eight men "that understand making Cartridges" be collected from each of five regiments—including Webb's—either to produce more ammunition themselves or to teach other soldiers how to do so.[24]

Despite these frenzied preparations, Hale still found time now and then in the evening to light a candle and under its flickering glow write yet more letters. Throughout the war, people, goods, and correspondence flowed in and out of New York City with comparatively little difficulty, allowing officers like Hale to maintain contact with the home front. In one letter, "P.H.," a female correspondent in Norwich, chided Hale for having "drolly described" a group of women in a recent missive. "[H]ow easy it is for your sex even in the most trivial matters to ridicule ours to a great length," she complained. Despite her disapproval, however, she admitted to "the most tender & friendly consern" for Hale's safety. The captain also wrote frequently to Enoch, begging him to pass on greetings to family and friends in Coventry.[25]

In early June, Hale could at last entertain correspondents with an account of a genuinely exciting military adventure. For some weeks, American soldiers gazing out at the East River from Manhattan or Long Island beheld the menacing silhouette of the massive sixty-four-gun British warship *Asia*. Around May 31, a small contingent of New England troops, including Captain Hale, made a daring nighttime raid from shore under a mere sliver of moonlight, capturing a small sloop that had been transporting men and goods to the enemy vessel. Seven of the British sailors aboard the sloop managed to escape, but the Americans brought three others to General Putnam for questioning. This was just the kind of bold action Hale had longed for.[26]

He could also boast about his exploit in person to officer friends who had relocated to New York and to a welcome newcomer. Benjamin Tallmadge finally accepted a lieutenant's commission on June 20 and reached the city shortly thereafter.[27] He and Hale had little opportunity to socialize, however, for the first contingent of British transports carrying some 10,000 troops appeared off Sandy Hook on June 29. In early July, British forces set up operations on Staten Island. With an invading army of some 32,000 men—a quarter of whom were Hessian mercenaries—General William Howe intended to overwhelm the recalcitrant American rebels.[28]

On July 9, as they prepared for an imminent British attack, American forces in the city learned that the ultimate purpose of their military exertions had been transformed. Ordering the troops to assemble in regimental formation at six o'clock that evening, Washington announced that the Continental Congress, "impelled by the dictates of duty, policy and necessity," had declared "the United Colonies of North America, free and independent STATES." The general reminded each soldier "that now the peace and safety of his Country depends (under God) solely on the success of our arms." This pronouncement likely confirmed what many soldiers had anticipated, that reconciliation with Britain was neither possible nor desirable after more than a year of bloody conflict. An observer at the camp reported that the "highly pleased" troops greeted the news with three hearty "Huzzas." Yet the wording of this declaration—simultaneously proclaiming both the birth of one country and thirteen "free and independent STATES"—bore witness to a crucial structural ambiguity that would long plague the new nation.[29]

The "Country" to which Washington referred on that July day was at best a hazy abstraction to most soldiers. Far more vivid in their minds were the villages they had left behind when they marched off to war.[30] Officers, especially those who were well educated, could better grasp the revolutionary implications of creating a new nation; common soldiers gained a similar appreciation only as the conflict progressed. Yet even Hale likely conjured up visions of the clapboard houses and quiet lanes of Coventry, the brick façade of Connecticut Hall, and the tangle of ship masts in New London harbor, along with the faces of beloved family and friends, when he contemplated what he was fighting for. Whether these familiar places and the new state and nation to which they now belonged would survive the coming British onslaught was anyone's guess. As July gave way to August, shrewd gamblers would have placed their money on Great Britain.

"I have only time for a hasty letter," scribbled Nathan to brother Enoch on August 20. "For about 6 or 8 days the enemy have been expected hourly," he explained, keeping American forces at a fever-pitch of excitement and anxiety. A few days earlier, four members of Hale's company had tried to maneuver fire vessels close enough to two British warships, the *Phoenix* and the *Rose*, to set them ablaze. The "wind [was] too slack for the attempt," however, and the effort produced little damage. As for the Americans' readiness to fend off the British, Hale wrote, "We hope, under God, to give a good account of the Enemy" when the battle was finally under way.[31]

The following evening, August 21, a spectacular thunderstorm, lasting two or three hours, alarmed both armies, especially soldiers who were inclined to see the Lord's hand at work in such remarkable natural events. The "perpetual Lightening," Hale noted in his diary, was "the sharpest I ever knew." The thunder, another witness declared, "did not come in successive peals, but in one long and continuous crash, as if the very frame work of the skies was falling to pieces." Morning light revealed the extent of the havoc the storm had wrought. Three men in one regiment had been struck dead by lightning, "the points of their swords melted off, and the coin melted in their pockets." Their bodies appeared "roasted, so black and crisp was the skin." Ten more men from a Connecticut regiment, cowering in a single tent, were similarly electrocuted. Still other soldiers were injured, and buildings damaged. As one observer mused, "there seems a hidden meaning, some secret purpose, when the bolt is launched, by an invisible arm, and from the mysterious depths of space." Was this a sign of the Lord's disapproval of the Americans or the British—or both contending armies?[32]

Within days, as the roar of cannons and crack of musket fire replaced the crash of thunder, American troops had every reason to think that the divine chastisement was meant for them. On August 22, British forces began landing on Long Island, and within three days there were 15,000 redcoats in place. Expecting Howe to attack lower Manhattan, Washington had fortified Brooklyn Heights overlooking the island's southern tip, just as he had secured Dorchester Heights looming over Boston. He initially assumed that the redcoats' appearance on western Long Island was a diversionary tactic, but when he realized his mistake, Washington rushed ten regiments to the area. Even with these reinforcements, the Americans were outnumbered more than two to one by the enemy. During the night of August 26, Howe's troops marched virtually unnoticed around the vulnerable left flank of General Israel Putnam's American line. On the morning of the twenty-seventh, the redcoats launched their deadly assault.[33]

"This was the first time in my life that I had witnessed the awful scene of a battle," Benjamin Tallmadge later recalled, "when man was engaged to destroy his fellow-man." Many years later, another eyewitness still trembled at the recollection. "It is impossible for me to describe the confusion and horror of the scene that ensued," the Pennsylvania volunteer Michael Graham remembered, "the artillery flying with the chains over the horses' backs, our men running in almost every direction, and run which way they would, they were almost sure to meet the British or Hessians." Several terrified Americans who sought refuge in a millpond drowned. Gruesome as such a watery death might be, the victims might have thought it preferable to staring up at a redcoat brandishing a bayonet. British soldiers were encouraged to use this fearsome weapon, "charging the Rebels" in face-to-face combat, as one officer instructed, "even in Woods where they thought themselves invincible." Washington, observing the chaos from a distance, allegedly exclaimed, "Good God, what brave fellows I must this day lose!" Indeed, the American losses were grievous—somewhere between 1,100 and 1,500 killed or taken prisoner, compared to fewer than 400 British and Hessian casualties.[34]

Days of rain that followed intensified the gloom of dispirited American troops. Swarms of mosquitoes added to their misery. On August 29, Washington convened a Council of War to discuss what few military options remained for his army. The attending officers unanimously advocated removing American forces from Long Island to Manhattan before the British cut off every avenue of escape. That very night, and continuing into the early hours of the next morning, Massachusetts soldiers familiar with watercraft ferried some 9,500 troops, plus equipment and provisions, under cover of fog across the East River to New York City. Washington had preserved his army, but he despaired for their fate and the cause for which they fought. On September 2, the general unburdened himself to John Hancock, president of the Continental Congress. "Our situation is truly distressing," Washington lamented. The army was disintegrating before his very eyes. The militiamen under his command were "dismayed, Intractable, and Impatient" to go home. Many of the men were ill; many others had deserted. Without a "permanent, Standing Army I mean One to exist during the War"—and the money to pay for it—the general lacked the necessary tools to fight with any realistic chance of success.[35]

Howe did not immediately press his advantage after the British victory, but the exhausted American troops knew that he would eventually make a move toward Manhattan. Washington wondered if the city should be destroyed to prevent the British from using it as their winter quarters. Major General Nathanael Greene strongly urged him to do so, predicting that the British Navy's overwhelming superiority would prevent the Americans from retaking the city once it fell into British hands. Besides, Greene argued, "Two thirds of the Property of the City of Newyork and the Subburbs belongs to the Tories." However, knowing that the city's destruction would deliver a catastrophic blow to American morale and under extreme pressure from New York delegates to prohibit it, the Continental Congress insisted that "no damage be done to the said City." As military and civilian authorities debated New York's fate, news of the shattering American defeat spread from town to town and colony to colony, raising citizens' fears of a swift and ignominious end to their infant republic. Within a matter of days, Coventry's inhabitants had learned of the "melancholly disaster at N York," Enoch Hale noted in his diary, and "our army obliged to leave Long Island & soon NY."[36]

In early September, Congress sent Benjamin Franklin, John Adams, and Edward Rutledge to confer with Lord Richard Howe about prospects for reconciliation. The admiral cordially greeted the emissaries on Staten Island. He treated them to a hearty meal of cold meats and bread, accompanied by excellent claret. But he refused to recognize them as congressional representatives, for doing so would acknowledge American independence. He would, however, happily meet with them as influential colonial gentlemen to discuss the logistics of an American surrender, which he considered a necessary precondition for negotiating an end to the conflict. The three emissaries just as cordially rejected the admiral's peremptory demand and returned to Philadelphia. Their report to Congress of the unsatisfactory proceedings discouraged many delegates but energized radicals who cited Howe's intransigence to contradict loyalist claims that Britain was serious about ending the war.[37]

The failed negotiations intensified the already immense pressure on Washington and the army. Edward Rutledge made that clear when he informed the general that "Our Reliance continues therefore to be (under God) on your Wisdom & Fortitude & that of your Forces." Moreover, even as Richard Howe discussed peace, his brother William pursued war. On September 10, the day before Admiral Lord Howe met with the congressional emissaries, General Howe began moving troops to tiny Montresor's Island near the mouth of the Harlem River. British warships also headed up the East River, sparking American fears that the Continental Army would once again be outflanked. Although Washington's officers had urged him to hold the city, British maneuvers made them reconsider that advice. They "not only determined a removal of the Army prudent but absolutely necessary." Thus Washington saw no alternative but to transfer men and supplies to the northern end of Manhattan as he wondered what the redcoats' next move would be.[38]

On September 15, when British forces landed at Kip's Bay, a few miles south of the Harlem River, the American retreat northward very nearly became a rout. The deafening sound of cannon fire from British vessels in the East River was so "terrible and so incessant" that "few even in the Army & Navy" had ever heard such a din. Connecticut militia fled in wild disarray from the coastal fortifications they were supposed to guard and were joined in their panicked withdrawal by two Continental brigades sent in as reinforcements. Washington raced to the tumultuous scene, exposing himself to enemy fire, in a futile attempt to "rally and get them into some order." At dawn on the following day, he dispatched men from Lieutenant Colonel Thomas Knowlton's company of rangers—soldiers specially selected for reconnaissance and light infantry operations—to report on the location of British troops. Enemy pickets caught sight of them, forcing the rangers to retreat under fire to American lines. Washington took advantage of their return to draw British forces into a larger engagement, later known as the Battle of Harlem Heights. The overconfident redcoats pursued the Americans "without proper precautions or support," a British officer subsequently complained, and had to retreat once they fell dangerously low on ammunition. Although the Americans hailed this encounter as a victory, neither side gained any ground and the Americans lost two talented officers in the fighting—Major Andrew Leitch of Virginia and the rangers' leader, Thomas Knowlton.[39]

Washington especially regretted the loss of Knowlton, whom he regarded as "a Most Valuable & Gallant Officer." Only thirty-six years old at the time of his death, Knowlton had as much military experience as any American general. He had joined Connecticut's provincial army as a teenager during the French and Indian War, seeing action at Wood Creek on the New York frontier—where he attracted Israel

Putnam's attention—and later at the capture of Ticonderoga. In 1762, he sailed with a contingent of Connecticut troops to aid in the reduction of Havana. After the war, he returned to his farm in Ashford, Connecticut, until the outbreak of hostilities with Britain compelled him once again to don a military uniform and shoulder his musket. Reunited with Putnam at the Battle of Bunker Hill, Knowlton spent the winter of 1775–1776 with Connecticut troops in Cambridge and relocated with them to New York after the British evacuation of Boston.[40]

Not long before the dreadful American defeat in late August, Knowlton began recruiting volunteers from Connecticut units for his provisional force of rangers. During the previous winter, perhaps at the dinner parties hosted by Israel Putnam and other generals, Knowlton had time to observe junior officers, discuss their qualities with their superiors, and identify likely candidates for the difficult operations that rangers undertook. Many young officers, eager for action and the chance to burnish their military reputations, would have volunteered for such duty despite its dangers. But enthusiasm was not enough; the ideal ranger combined boldness and initiative with sufficient discretion to carry out sensitive intelligence gathering and reconnaissance operations with a reasonable chance of success.[41]

On September 16, most of the men in Knowlton's unit were with him in the thick of the fighting at Harlem Heights. When the colonel fell, his skull shattered by a musket ball, they mourned the loss of their "gallant" leader as keenly as did General Washington.[42] But one of Knowlton's men was not with him on the battlefield and at day's end had no idea that his commander had perished. This ranger had just embarked on a solitary mission that required him to travel to Long Island as the remainder of his unit marched up Manhattan with the rest of Washington's army.

The Americans' crushing defeat in the Battle of Long Island made Washington more desperate than ever for reliable intelligence about British troop movements, supply lines, and armaments. He instructed two of his generals, William Heath and James Clinton, to try to discover the enemy's intentions, exhorting them "to exert yourselves to accomplish this most desireable end, leave no stone unturn'd, nor . . . stick at expense" in their endeavors. There was talk of trying to bribe or even kidnap loyalists who might have valuable information. Some informers came forward voluntarily, but their motives demanded careful scrutiny lest the Continental Army be led into a trap. Because none of these expedients was wholly satisfactory, Washington decided to find a trustworthy man willing to go behind British lines and spy on the enemy.[43]

Washington may have approached Knowlton directly, or used Heath or Clinton as an intermediary, to see if one of his rangers would undertake this exceedingly hazardous mission. Because of the danger and the taint of dishonor associated with espionage, no soldier could be ordered to do it. Washington needed a volunteer. Knowlton discussed the plan with his junior officers—the scheme was far too risky to employ a higher-ranking individual—and one of the newest members of his unit agreed. Though his record of military accomplishments was admittedly thin, Captain Nathan Hale was young, intelligent, and energetic. From Knowlton's perspective, these characteristics gave Hale at least a modest chance at success. If he failed, the army would be no worse off than it already was, and there were plenty of young officers who would happily join the rangers as Hale's replacement.[44]

William Hull was horrified when his friend—who ought to have kept the matter secret—told him of the plan. Years later, Hull recalled with genuine anguish his failure to dissuade Hale from accepting a mission of "doubtful" propriety that "was not in keeping with his character." Hale's nature was "too frank and open for deceit and disguise," Hull insisted, "and he was incapable of acting a part equally foreign to his feelings and habits." He would almost surely fail, but even if successful he would "stain [his] honour by the sacrifice of integrity." Hale conceded that the enterprise was fraught with peril but, according to Hull, countered that this was his chance, after more than a year in the army, to render "material service" to his country. He longed to be "useful" and argued that "every kind of service, necessary to the public good, becomes honourable by being necessary."[45]

Moreover, despite Hull's misgivings, Hale was certain that he could "act a part." Just a few years earlier—though it must have seemed a lifetime ago—he had taken the stage during the Linonia Club's boisterous anniversary celebrations and he had not forgotten the accolades his performances received. Collegiate experiences meant to establish Hale's credentials as a British gentleman could now be put to a very different use. His ambition to excel, to earn the approbation of others, had not diminished. He designed for himself a role that he knew he could play, for he had already performed it. A plain brown suit and broad-brimmed hat would comprise his costume. He would travel to Long Island in the guise of a schoolmaster, carrying his Yale diploma as evidence of his qualifications. He could record any information he gathered in Latin, a language incomprehensible to all but the educated few. This would be the grandest performance of his young life. The stakes were dangerously high, but if successful, he would contribute immeasurably to the nation's cause. Hale told Hull that such an outcome would be reward enough; he did not expect money or military preferment upon his safe return. But he surely hoped to impress Colonel Knowlton—and General Washington—with his ingenuity and devotion to his country. Once the mission was completed, he could entertain Hull and other soldier-friends with tales of his adventures, and fill letter after letter with details to thrill distant correspondents.[46]

Leaving camp in his uniform so as not to attract attention, Hale explained to Asher Wright only that he would be gone for a while. The waiter was to take care of Hale's possessions and move them if the army relocated during his absence. Just a few trustworthy men, whose help Hale needed, knew of the captain's real mission. One confidant was Stephen Hempstead, a sergeant in Hale's company, who joined him on a circuitous journey from Harlem Heights to the coastal Connecticut town of Norwalk. Another was Captain Charles Pond, whose armed sloop carried Hale over to Long Island, leaving him ashore somewhere around Huntington. Before his departure from Norwalk, Hale changed into his brown suit and deposited his uniform, commission, other papers, and silver shoe buckles (too grand for an ordinary schoolmaster) with Hempstead. The sergeant was to wait in Norwalk for Hale's return and accompany him back to camp to deliver his precious information to his superiors.[47]

Hale had no desire to stay on Long Island any longer than necessary. He had to pass through Queens County, a place crawling with loyalists ready to ingratiate themselves with British authorities and avenge festering grievances against local Whigs. Loyalist refugees from Connecticut also poured onto Long Island, increasing the chances that Hale might encounter someone who recognized him. With Britain seemingly poised to win the war, some discouraged revolutionaries in the area had accepted Howe's offer to pardon those who swore allegiance to the Crown; such men might be induced to betray their erstwhile compatriots. Throughout the countryside, disaffected neutrals upset by abuses perpetrated by both sides in the conflict mistrusted everyone. Any stranger wandering from town to town would arouse suspicion.[48]

To his dismay, by the time Hale reached Long Island much of the British army had relocated to Manhattan. Unwilling to abandon his mission and disappoint his superiors, he decided to follow the redcoats across the East River, prolonging his risky subterfuge. He got to Manhattan during a spell of warm and sunny weather during which he strolled around the British encampments, furtively taking notes and making sketches. Deployed around the lower part of the island were three battalions of light infantry, four of British grenadiers and three more of Hessians, along with several artillery units. Guards had been posted at the five-mile marker up from the island's southernmost tip. Hale watched men set up tents and survey the extensive fortifications the Americans had so recently abandoned. British troops were also busy making thousands of fascines—long bundles of brushwood used for filling in ditches and constructing roads and earthworks. Droves of deserters from the American army reportedly arrived daily. After a few days of observation, Hale chose not to tempt fate any longer. He carefully folded the papers with his information and tucked them in the inner soles of his shoes. Then he headed back to Long Island for his rendezvous with Captain Pond.[49]

Not long after Hale left Manhattan, the western part of the island erupted in flames. The fire began in the early-morning hours of September 21, roaring along broad avenues and narrow alleys, consuming scores of wooden dwellings, shops, and warehouses in its path. Swirls of sparks flew from one shingled roof to ignite another. The conflagration transformed the wooden spire of Trinity Church into a "lofty Pyramid of fire," leading some observers to suspect that incendiaries had specifically targeted the Anglican place of worship. Frantic inhabitants, many half-dressed, thronged the smoke-choked streets screaming for help. British soldiers and sailors rushed to their assistance but could not obtain enough water, buckets, or functioning fire engines to make a difference. Some nine or ten hours after the inferno began, a shift in the wind and a light rain finally extinguished it. Between 500 and 600 buildings had been reduced to ashes, perhaps a fifth to a quarter of the city destroyed.[50]

Few people thought the fire was an accident. Some witnesses reported that the flames had broken out in several places simultaneously; others claimed to have seen piles of combustible materials stashed in empty houses. Those who tried to extinguish the blaze later testified that numerous pumps were either broken or in disrepair and the handles of many fire buckets had been cut. The British were unlikely culprits, having no reason to incinerate the city they planned to use as their winter quarters. The weight of suspicion thus fell on rebel arsonists. Frederick Mackenzie, a British officer, remarked that prior to the redcoats' arrival, various inhabitants "were heard to say they would burn" the city, so that it would not "become a nest for Tories." Other residents reportedly declared that "they would set fire to their own houses sooner than they should be occupied by The King's troops." Some persons allegedly caught in the act of kindling the flames were killed on the spot, and eventually more than 200 suspects were jailed. In the chaotic aftermath of the disaster, however, no definitive proof of arson could be found. Washington, who had refrained from ordering New York City destroyed in compliance with Congress's directive, was nonetheless pleased. "Providence—or some good honest Fellow, has done more for us than we were disposed to do for ourselves," he later declared. Even so, he grumbled, the British army would find that despite the damage to the city "enough of it remains to answer their purposes."[51]

Captain Hale was already too far from Manhattan to see the columns of smoke rising into the sky on September 21. He was on Long Island, somewhere near Flushing, with Huntington and Captain Pond's vessel still a long day's walk away. What happened next has long been a matter of speculation. From the fragmentary evidence that survives, it appears that Hale somehow attracted the attention of one of the most notorious men in New England. Robert Rogers's fame derived from his command of a daring group of rangers (one of whom was Israel Putnam) who carried out numerous reconnaissance patrols and bloody raids during the French and Indian War. Many people celebrated Major Rogers as a hero; others scorned him as a scoundrel. After the war, in 1765, he fled to England to avoid prosecution for debt and unlawful trading with Indians. Not long after returning to the colonies in 1766 to serve with the British at Fort Michilimackinac, he faced a court-martial on trumped-up charges of treason for supposedly planning to deliver the fort to the Spanish in Louisiana. His acquittal for lack of evidence hardly signaled an improvement in his fortunes; he soon fled again to England, where he ended up jailed for debt. When Rogers reappeared in America in 1775, it was unclear whose side in the revolutionary conflict he would take.[52]

The rascally major kept everyone guessing for as long as possible. First he promised American authorities that he would not aid the British. Then, in November 1775, he offered his help to General Gage in Boston. A month later, he tried to meet with Washington in Cambridge. The American commander, highly suspicious of Rogers's every move, arranged instead for him to see Brigadier General John Sullivan at Winter Hill. A couple of brief conversations with the duplicitous ranger did little to allay Sullivan's equally strong concerns, and he warned Washington to keep his distance from the man. Rogers, however, was relentless. In late June 1776, he finally met with Washington in New York, slyly hinting that he was on his way to Philadelphia to make "a secret Offer of his Services" to the Continental Congress. Washington, not so easily fooled, sent Rogers there with an escort who carried a letter to Congress stating that "under all Circumstances" the major was "not to be sufficiently relied on." Congressional leaders accordingly placed Rogers under guard once he reached Philadelphia. Yet on July 9 the wily ranger escaped, making his way to a British ship in New York harbor. From this point on, there was no doubt where his political sympathies lay—or, at least, from which side he thought he could gain the most advantage.[53]

General Howe had been hoping to lure the famous ranger over to the British side and turn him loose against the American rebels. He swiftly promoted Rogers to lieutenant colonel and authorized his prize catch to raise a ranger battalion from among New York's loyalists. This was what brought Rogers to Long Island in September. It was there, as Rogers mingled with local residents trying to find men for his Queen's American Rangers, that Nathan Hale somehow caught his eye. There was a remote possibility that Rogers had seen Hale before, during either his visits with Sullivan at Winter Hill in December 1775 or with Washington in New York in late June 1776. But Hale's physical features—light brown hair, blue eyes, a bit taller than average, with a few scars from powder burns on his face—were not especially noteworthy. More likely, Hale said or did something that piqued Rogers's interest.[54]

Perhaps Rogers or one of his loyalist officers eavesdropped on a tavern conversation and overheard Hale probe a little too conspicuously to discover a local resident's political sympathies. Long Island, a prime recruiting ground for both loyalist and revolutionary soldiers, teemed with would-be spies and informers cautiously exploring an uncertain political terrain that neither contending side controlled. Or maybe Rogers simply caught a glimpse of this intelligent and physically vigorous youth and wondered why he was not in uniform. Whatever the exact circumstances, Rogers was determined to find out more about Hale.[55]

According to one story, recorded years later, Rogers arranged to meet Hale on September 20 for a casual conversation. The novice spy was no match for the cunning ranger. Having somehow guessed Hale's true sympathies, Rogers allegedly declared his own allegiance to the American cause and insinuated that he was spying on its behalf. Hale, whose character William Hull had accurately judged as "too frank and open for deceit and disguise," readily took the bait. After Rogers proposed a toast to the health of the Congress, Hale divulged to his newfound friend the nature of his own secret mission. Rogers toyed with his prey a bit longer, inviting Hale to dine with him the following day and meet other men engaged in their shared clandestine business. When the hapless captain disclosed his mission yet again before additional witnesses, Rogers immediately had him seized.[56]

Unnerved by this shocking turn of events, Hale at first tried to deny "his name, and the business he came upon."[57] Yet as he was conveyed to Howe's headquarters on Manhattan, people along the way claimed to recognize him. Hale's company had been stationed in the area for months before the Battle of Long Island, and the captain had dined in local establishments and made purchases from inhabitants who perhaps recalled their encounters with him. Rogers had also been recruiting loyalist rangers from coastal Connecticut, and some of them possibly knew Hale. Deserters from the American army could also have identified him.[58] Right after his capture, a rumor began circulating that his cousin Samuel Hale had betrayed him. This cousin, a known loyalist, was serving in New York as Howe's Deputy Commissary of Prisoners and could have been called upon to confirm Nathan's identity once he was in custody. The report of the cousin's involvement spread first by word of mouth and later made its way into print, in an article in the *Essex Journal* in February 1777. Samuel Hale always denied his complicity, asserting that "there was never the least truth" in the allegation. But many people at the time believed it, and the very possibility that the story might be true later brought great pain to the Hale family.[59]

In the end, Nathan Hale's fate was sealed not by the testimony of others, but by hard evidence of espionage—those papers containing incriminating information—found on his person.[60] The city still smoldered from the morning's fire as his captors brought the doomed captain to British headquarters. There was no longer any point in denying his true identity, so he admitted to his name, rank, and mission. Everyone present knew the penalty for spying, and no one doubted that Howe would impose it. Given the evidence, there was no need for a court-martial. With the acrid stench of smoke lingering in the air as a pungent reminder of the city's vulnerability to subversives, Howe ordered the rebel spy to be hanged at eleven o'clock in the morning on the following day, September 22, the Sabbath.[61]

The reversal in Hale's fortunes had occurred with stunning swiftness. He was immediately turned over to Provost Marshal William Cunningham, a bitter man with a powerful grudge against the rebels. Cunningham still seethed over an incident that had occurred in March 1775, when a New York mob of some 200 men assailed him for being a "Tory." When he refused to kneel at the city's liberty pole and "damn his Popish King George," the enraged throng beat him, ripping the clothes from his back. Cunningham subsequently fled to Boston, seeking refuge with General Gage's troops in the occupied city. Returning with British forces to New York, the scene of his public humiliation, the provost marshal had little sympathy for the rebel spy. He summarily refused Hale's request to meet with a clergyman or be given a Bible to provide him some solace during his final night.[62]

The frightened youth knew his Scripture well enough to summon up familiar passages and try to calm his roiling thoughts during the hours of darkness. But peace of mind was elusive, and sleep impossible. William Hull had been right. Hale had failed to perform his designated role to the finish—had failed Colonel Knowlton, General Washington, his comrades-in-arms, the American cause itself. His would not be a valiant death on the battlefield but an ignominious demise at the end of a hangman's rope. The prospect that his family and friends would be embarrassed, even ashamed, at what many would regard as a dishonorable fate was unbearable, but so too was the possibility that they might never know what happened to him. The young man who so enjoyed the company of others spent his last night "alone, without sympathy or support, save that from above."[63] In the morning, the brief speech he would be allowed to make at the gallows would be his final performance, his last chance to make a good impression. What could he possibly say?

Never before had the first light of dawn been so unwelcome a sight. But as the British soldiers in camp awakened to face the new day, one of their officers, Captain John Montresor, took pity on the rebel prisoner. Montresor had served as a military engineer and surveyor since the French and Indian War, displaying considerable artistic flair in his meticulously drawn maps. A gentleman himself, he recognized Hale's genteel bearing, despite the young man's obvious distress. Montresor convinced the provost marshal to allow Hale to spend his last hours with the engineer in his private field tent. A grateful Hale, having composed himself, asked for pen and paper to write two final letters— one to his beloved brother Enoch and the other to his commanding officer. Neither missive reached its intended recipient, but Hale was mercifully spared that knowledge.[64]

Hale's last audience, at the gallows, was small but attentive— probably some officers and a contingent of enlisted men. Witnesses commented on the condemned man's remarkable composure in the face of death and on his dignified delivery of a final speech. If Hale appealed to Scripture for solace and vindication, no one remembered that. Instead, the officers in attendance recalled passages that spoke to their shared genteel status. Frederick Mackenzie, in his diary entry for that day, noted that Hale defended his actions by saying "he thought it the duty of every good Officer, to obey any orders given him by his Commander in Chief." This remark echoed passages in the military manuals that Hale had assiduously studied at Winter Hill and that were familiar to all officers. Another of the doomed man's comments reflected a common theme of last speeches—his warning to "the Spectators to be at all times prepared to meet death in whatever shape it might appear." For his most memorable line, at least as recalled by Captain Montresor and later told to William Hull, Hale chose "I only regret, that I have but one life to lose for my country."[65]

If Hale indeed spoke these words—a paraphrased line from Joseph Addison's wildly popular play *Cato*—he could not have selected a more fitting peroration. Seeing the body of his son Marcus, who had just died in battle, Cato—the last of the Roman republicans fighting against Caesar's tyranny—exclaims, "What pity is it that we can die but once to serve our country."[66] Addison's play attracted enthusiastic audiences from the moment of its premiere in 1713, in good part because it portrayed the dramatic tension between liberty and tyranny in broad enough strokes to appeal to all political factions. Anglo-Americans keen to display their own genteel taste followed their British brethren in flocking to performances and memorizing the most stirring lines. Hale knew the play, and *Cato* was one of Washington's favorites. But as the revolutionary crisis intensified, Americans appropriated the play's generic republican message for their own political purposes, relegating Britain to the role of the tyrannical Caesar. Hale knew that the British officers in his audience—gentlemen all—would instantly recognize the line. By uttering it, the rebel spy at once invoked the genteel status they shared and the distinctively American republican principles that divided them and for which he was about to die. Hale had every reason to assume that his audience had little sympathy to spare for him and would quickly forget his final speech. But if he chose his words carefully, they might resonate after he was gone in the memories of redcoat officers who grasped in full their double significance.[67]

On the day of Hale's execution, Loftus Cliffe, an Irish-born lieutenant serving with General Howe's 46th Regiment of Foot, was slowly recovering from a bout of dysentery—a malady the redcoats laughingly called "the Yanky." Thin and still a bit weak, he wandered the streets of New York to gaze at the devastation wrought by the recent fire. Cliffe presumed that the rebels had set the blaze in an effort to destroy the whole city along with the many ships moored at its wharves. "Oh Washington what have you to answer for!" the lieutenant later scribbled in a letter to his brother back in Ireland. Cliffe's sense of outrage at the destruction mingled with sympathy for its victims, especially women and poorer folk whose homes were incinerated and whose few salvaged possessions had been stolen. "I can not paint the Misery" of the city's inhabitants, he admitted to his brother.

What struck Cliffe most forcefully during his sojourn in New York were the awful consequences of this war—"a beautiful Country layd waste one part ravaged by Rebels the other by their opponents." "The Horrours of a Civil War," he lamented, "are every Day before my Eyes." Perusing a list of American soldiers, Cliffe saw "almost every Name thats amongst us" (even a "Captain Van Clift"), stark evidence of the internecine nature of the conflict. Cliffe—like any true gentleman—was a man of feeling as well as action, and he freely revealed his emotions in this private missive to his brother.

Among the unforgettable sights that caught his eye on his walk through the city was "a Spy hanging up, a Captain of the Rebels," alongside whom someone had suspended a crude wooden effigy of General Washington. There was something about this unfortunate rebel that moved Cliffe to pronounce him "a very genteel looking fellow." Was it the fabric and cut of Hale's brown suit, his fine linen, or some other aspect of his apparel—even without the silver shoe buckles? Did the Irish officer glimpse the hands tied behind Hale's back, too smooth to belong to someone accustomed to manual labor? Nothing in Cliffe's letter indicated that he made this comment in jest. It hinted instead at a pang of sympathy and perhaps a wish to know how the youth had come to such a tragic end.[68]

Meanwhile, on that same day, some 130 miles away in Coventry, Connecticut, Enoch Hale sat at a table in his father's house and scratched out another entry in his diary. The Sabbath had dawned warm and sunny, a "pleasant" September day that marked the transition from summer to autumn. As he put away his pen, Enoch told himself that tomorrow he would find some time to write to Brother Captain and ask how he fared.[69]

7

THE TERRIBLE CRISIS OF MY EARTHLY FATE

She was not yet thirty, but Phoebe Dunbar could easily have been mistaken for an older woman. The strain of bearing seven children in a dozen years of marriage had taken its toll. Keeping house with a couple of toddlers underfoot taxed her strength more than ever. Her ten-year-old daughter Bede helped as much as she could, but the domestic burdens mainly settled on Phoebe's weary shoulders. It did not help that her mind was as restless as her hands were busy. Moses's purchase of Ebenezer Judd's Northbury farm in 1774 was not the stroke of good fortune they had hoped it would be, for it kept them in a place whose residents had turned against them. The outbreak of war in April 1775 transformed her family, friends, and fellow Anglicans into pariahs. She could never have dreamed that neighbors would descend upon her husband with fists and cudgels, inflicting painful injuries that she would later try to soothe. Perhaps they should have gone to Claremont after all. By the spring of 1776, the future looked bleaker than ever.

Fate spared Phoebe Dunbar from seeing how that future would turn out. On May 26, after months of illness, she died. Moses and one of their children had scarcely recovered from their own bouts of sickness; another child hobbled about the house with a slowly mending broken leg. The grief-stricken husband hoped that Phoebe could at last enjoy the peace and happiness that earthly life had denied her. But her death increased Moses Dunbar's already ample portion of misery. Rejected by his father and brothers and reviled by neighbors, he was now bereft of his helpmeet, with five young children depending on him.

Under the circumstances, Dunbar saw no alternative but to withdraw from the revolutionary turmoil. Those motherless children required his attention, as did his farm. Dunbar therefore approached Waterbury's committee of inspection with a proposition. He promised that henceforth he would "give no Offence by word or deed" that might arouse their concerns. Indeed, he would go so far as to "Enter into a Voluntary Confinement" on his farm, tending to his children, his livestock, and his crops, keeping his head down and his mouth shut. Moses knew that the committeemen would still keep an eye on him, but surely they would leave a bereaved man in peace.[1]

Unfortunately, Dunbar extended this olive branch to local Whigs at a most inauspicious time. Connecticut was awash with rumors that spring, its inhabitants consumed with anxiety. The British army had left Boston for Halifax, but no one thought that it would remain there. At any moment, colonists expected to hear reports that vessels bristling with cannon and laden with redcoats had sailed into New York harbor. Should the King's forces take that city, Whigs predicted that Connecticut's loyalists would rise up to help the soldiers wreak havoc on New York's rebellious neighbor. Panicky members of Fairfield's committee of inspection already proclaimed "that a horrid plot is laid by the Tories to destroy the people of the country, to co-operate with our enemies in every measure to reduce us, and that *Long-Island* is appointed for headquarters."[2] Given this public frenzy, Waterbury's Whig leaders were unlikely to put much faith in Dunbar's pledge of good behavior.

Like Dunbar, most of the colony's Anglican clergy wished to remain as inconspicuous as possible. Ministers avoided political pronouncements and quietly went about their business conducting Sabbath services, administering sacraments, catechizing the young, and comforting the sick and dying. In Waterbury that June, James Scovil hosted the annual Trinity Week convention for New Haven–area Anglican clergy. Keeping a low profile, the churchmen delivered sermons to one another and focused their discussions on such unobjectionable matters as assessing the merits of a clerical candidate's application for ordination. At the meeting's close, the attendees chose New Cambridge parish as the venue for their 1777 gathering.[3]

The clergymen had barely returned home from Waterbury when an urgent call went out for them to reconvene in New Haven. Only five pastors had arrived by July 23, so the meeting was adjourned for a day to let stragglers—including James Scovil—get there. What brought them together was the distressing news that the Continental Congress had declared the colonies independent of Great Britain. The same announcement that caused Washington's troops to erupt in cheers struck fear in the hearts of these nervous clergymen pacing the floor in the Reverend Bela Hubbard's New Haven home. Their overriding concern was whether, under the radically altered political circumstances, "we can go on as usual in the performance of Divine Service in our Churches consistently with the general benefit of the Church and our own personal security." The assembled clergymen unanimously agreed: "we cannot." At their ordinations, they had sworn allegiance to the monarchy and they dared not violate those solemn oaths. The Anglican Prayer Book included invocations on behalf of the king and his family. To "go on as usual" would incite the wrath of Whigs and invite charges of treason. Yet the ministers could not alter official liturgical practices to suit the times; to do so would be "a sacrilegious invasion" of the authority of the bishops in England.[4]

The distraught clergymen decided that their only option was to suspend formal services. On the Sabbath they would not preach, but merely read passages from Scripture and politically innocuous published commentaries and sermons. They would still teach children their catechism but strictly limit the administration of sacraments. Celebration of the Eucharist would only occur in sickrooms, private spaces where reciting the requisite prayers for the king could be hidden from public view. These expedients, in addition to encouraging parishioners to conduct family devotions at home, might suffice to preserve the colony's Anglican churches during the current crisis.[5]

Reverend Scovil hurried back to Waterbury to inform his congregation, as well as James Nichols, who had missed the emergency meeting, of these decisions. The Anglican laity could see the wisdom of the new policies but were disheartened nonetheless, especially when some timid clergymen decided to suspend public worship altogether.[6]

Congress's declaration of independence rendered their insecure positions in their communities even more precarious. Already the targets of Whig attacks, they worried that American independence would further embolden their adversaries to destroy churches and arrest clergy and laymen on the pretext of ferreting out traitors to the new nation. Although Connecticut's Anglicans were sure that the massive disparity between British and American military power made it virtually impossible for the rebels to win the war, they could certainly make loyalists' lives miserable in the short run. At the very least, Anglicans would be deprived of the familiar liturgy that sustained their spiritual community. Though it was cold comfort to him, Moses Dunbar was grateful that Phoebe did not live to see this grim turn of events. What it meant for him, his children, and his friends, however, was a matter of deep concern.

Passage of the Declaration of Independence was the last in a series of legal steps that dislodged Connecticut from the British Empire. The first occurred in December 1775, when the colony's government enacted its initial anti-loyalist measure punishing those who helped British forces or opposed the actions of the Continental Congress. Six months later, the Assembly repealed the Act against High Treason directed at the king's enemies, eliminating the legal paradox created by that law's coexistence with the newer statute prosecuting the king's friends. The Assembly further declared that henceforth all legal documents would be issued in the name of the "Governor and Company of the Colony of Connecticut" and not the king; officeholders would swear allegiance to the local rather than royal authority. Thus by May 1776, Connecticut was effectively, if not officially, independent, its transition from colony to state eased by its lack of an appointed governor with English ties who would have blocked the legislature's actions. Within weeks, the Assembly authorized local officials to confiscate the personal as well as real estate of any loyalists who joined Britain's forces.[7]

On June 24, 1776, the Continental Congress branded as traitors all those who persisted in their loyalty to the British monarch. It also announced that persons who levied war against any one of the United Colonies committed treason against that colony. The delegates urged all colonial assemblies to pass laws punishing traitors within their jurisdictions, if they had not (like Connecticut) done so already. Congress's subsequent vote for American independence, historic though it was, merely severed the imperial tie that these measures had already unraveled to the breaking point. Moreover, by defining treason as an offense against individual colonies—now states—Congress acknowledged that political sovereignty lay with those constituent units, not the newly independent nation.[8]

With Congress sanctioning the efforts of state and local committees, the campaign against loyalists intensified. Jonathan Trumbull—Connecticut's last colonial and first state governor—abandoned his usual caution and encouraged a volatile populace to go after Tory "Malignants."[9] He urged local officials to require travelers passing through town to produce "a certificate from some congress, committee of safety or inspection, some magistrate, justice of the peace, or General, or Field Officer" attesting to their adherence to the American cause. Simsbury's committeemen cast particular suspicion on peddlers whose wares included "*indigo, feathers, wooden dishes, teas,* and many other goods," fearing that such wandering strangers might join other itinerants to form "inimical *combinations*" against the "*United American States.*" The luckier victims of Whig interrogations endured public humiliation, with front-page newspaper announcements identifying them as "ENEMIES to their COUNTRY." Less fortunate men suffered imprisonment, some in county jails and others in the infamous Newgate prison—an old copper mine where despairing loyalists shivered alongside convicted criminals in the chill, dank darkness for weeks and even months at a time, unsure of when they might see daylight again.[10]

In town after town, relentless Tory hunters scrutinized the speech, actions, and even the mysterious silences of their neighbors, straining to identify friends and isolate enemies—especially enemies who might pretend to be friends. Waterbury Whigs suspected that Moses Dunbar's earnest promise to mind his own business was a ruse, intended to obscure sinister activities. Committeemen scoffed at the very idea of his "Voluntary Confinement" and sought instead a mandatory one. Members of Waterbury's committee of safety seized Dunbar at his home and marched him to the New Haven county jail. Once there, they discovered that neither the sheriff nor the jailer would take Dunbar, presumably because there were no specific charges lodged against him. Undaunted, the committeemen tried again just a few days after Dunbar's release, insisting that he be imprisoned "during their Pleasure, not exceeding 5 Months 14 days." Once more, however, New Haven authorities sent him home.[11]

Dunbar knew that he would find no peace if he stayed in Waterbury. Local Whigs were determined at the very least to incarcerate him and might be hatching plans for something worse. "Finding my life uneasy & as I had reason to Apprehend in great Danger," Dunbar concluded that he and his family had to leave town. During a sweltering heat wave, as temperatures climbed into the eighties and nineties, he disposed of most of his movable property—livestock, tools, household items—perhaps deriving some small satisfaction from reducing the store of possessions that vengeful Whigs might try to confiscate before he made his escape. Seeking buyers for his land, Dunbar approached members of his late wife's family and fellow Anglicans whose property lay near his own. On June 17, Ebenezer Cook, Phoebe's uncle, paid £5 for Dunbar's half-acre house lot; only a year earlier, Dunbar had bought the plot for that same price from Ebenezer's sister Thankful Cook Batchelor. Eight days later, David Shelton, a Northbury Anglican, offered £40 for the thirty acres Dunbar had purchased with such great optimism from Ebenezer Judd in 1774. His business nearly finished, Moses Dunbar could not resist making one final gesture that expressed his powerful resentment at being run out of town. He boldly crossed out the phrase "in the year of our Lord" printed at the bottom of each deed of sale for his land and scrawled "16 year of the reign of our Sovereign Lord George the 3d of Great Britain & King Anno Dom 1776" in its place.[12]

Scarcely a month had passed since Phoebe's death. In that brief time, Moses divested himself of his house, goods, and land—the very components of family independence he had struggled so hard to obtain. All the defiance in the world would not compensate for the fact that he was now homeless, with £45 in his pocket and five motherless children. He had to make plans quickly. First, with his family needing shelter, he turned to a fellow New Cambridge parishioner. Lemuel Carrington, a farmer and tavern keeper, could commiserate with his friend. Like Dunbar, he was a thirty-year-old father with young children; he too had felt the sting of his Whig neighbors' enmity. In addition to his homestead, Carrington owned a small clapboard house in the Chippeny Hill neighborhood of Farmington. He arranged to rent it to Dunbar while the anxious widower contemplated his next move.[13]

Dunbar also needed to find a wife. In seeking to remarry so soon, Moses meant no disrespect to Phoebe's memory. She may even have beseeched him from her deathbed to do so, if only for the children's sake. Many New England widowers—especially those with young children—remarried within a year of their spouse's death. Under normal circumstances, men carefully assessed compatibility and domestic competence in a prospective new mate, as well as the property she would bring to the marriage.[14] These, however, were hardly normal times. Moses Dunbar was painfully aware that no sensible woman or potential father-in-law would consider him an attractive marital prospect. He could hope for compatibility, but not much in the way of property.

Dunbar cautiously made inquiries, confining his tentative overtures to the small coterie of Chippeny Hill families who understood his predicament. Discussions with Samuel Adams bore fruit. Adams's son John was known to be "much inclined to toryism," and Samuel's willingness to negotiate with Dunbar strongly suggests that he too harbored loyalist sympathies. Practical considerations likely influenced the decision as well, for Adams—the father of four daughters—knew that Dunbar was in no position to demand a generous dowry. Whether seventeen-year-old Esther Adams had much to say in the matter of her marriage to Moses Dunbar is unknown.[15]

There was no chance that Moses, Esther, and the children would remain in Farmington. That town's Whigs were even more assiduous in their pursuit of loyalists than were Waterbury's committeemen. Anxious to identify a place of refuge for his family before the wedding took place, Dunbar was weighing his limited options when a fortuitous turn in the war's progress made his choice clear. Once he heard news of the spectacular British victory in New York in late August, he resolved that his "safest method" of action was "to fly to Long Island."[16]

Dunbar's plan took shape at a time when swarms of people were fleeing both to and from Long Island. The arrival of a massive British fleet in New York harbor in July launched an exodus of terrified Whig civilians, who frantically sought safety elsewhere in

New York, New Jersey, or Connecticut. By early September, after the redcoats and Hessian mercenaries sent Washington's army fleeing up Manhattan, stranded Continental soldiers who remained on Long Island hurried to get away. Meanwhile, many Connecticut loyalists, celebrating Britain's victory as their salvation and hailing its troops as their protectors, sought sanctuary in the very same place that others abandoned.[17]

The waters of Long Island Sound churned with the traffic of vessels large and small, guided by men intimately familiar with the region's irregular coastlines, hidden coves, capricious winds, and treacherous currents. Often under cover of darkness or fog, boatmen aligned with either the Whig or loyalist cause—and some who claimed whatever allegiance suited the highest bidder for their services—crept along the shore or charted a direct course across the narrow passage between Norwalk or Stamford and Long Island's Huntington Bay. Whaleboats and other small craft teetered precariously as frantic refugee families struggling with children, baggage, and even livestock, climbed aboard. Sailboats slipped in and out of sheltered bays, collecting provisions to sell to whichever army would submit to paying inflated prices. Privateers prowled these same waters, even as furtive scouts sought enemy victims to kidnap and hold as hostages. Strong-armed mariners rowed passengers in either direction to their desired destinations. Around the middle of September in 1776, Nathan Hale departed on one of the boats crossing from Connecticut to Long Island. At about the same time, Moses Dunbar embarked on another.[18]

Hale tried to avoid British sympathizers while he was on Long Island. Dunbar sought them out, and they were not difficult to find. Relieved loyalists welcomed the triumphant British and Hessian troops, offering to work for them and supply food and other provisions. On September 19, Admiral Richard Howe and General William Howe jointly issued a proclamation offering protection for inhabitants who accepted British sovereignty, and for months thereafter droves of loyalists came forward to take oaths of allegiance. Many of them expected the mighty British army to deliver the coup de grâce to the overmatched Continentals within months, if not weeks. A few British military leaders shared their optimism. In a letter dated September 23, 1776, General Henry Clinton, second in command to William Howe, confided to his sisters that he expected the Americans would soon "wish for terms," adding that "I do not despair of eating my Christmas dinner at Weybridge" with his family in England.[19]

Hundreds of enthusiastic loyalists volunteered to take up arms, eager to hasten the Revolution's demise and, during the conflict's final throes, exact revenge against the despised rebels.[20] General Howe, less sanguine than many others about the war's speedy conclusion, greeted the loyalists' martial fervor with ambivalence. Since late 1775, Howe had employed them only on an ad hoc basis for small-scale operations, insisting that it would take a thorough trouncing by a professional army to convince the obstinate colonists to surrender. The general was dismayed, however, to see Washington and his battered troops slip away after their disastrous defeat in New York and to find American officials still unwilling to sue for peace. Therefore, as Howe planned for a 1777 campaign, he reconsidered his reluctance to mobilize loyalist support. In September 1776, he began issuing warrants for the creation of several loyalist units to supplement his army's efforts. Robert Rogers received one of the earliest commissions for his Queen's Rangers and immediately began skulking around Long Island in search of recruits.[21]

Edmund Fanning, a Long Island native and 1757 graduate of Yale (thus a classmate of James Scovil), sought another of these commissions for himself. Fanning's political career began in North Carolina, where he wasted no time ingratiating himself with William Tryon, the province's royal governor, and, with equal briskness, antagonizing frustrated backcountry settlers protesting against oppressive taxes and political corruption. When Tryon was reassigned to New York's governorship in 1771 after a violent clash with those angry farmers, Fanning followed his patron north. Serving first as Tryon's private secretary, he soon accumulated other lucrative positions that strengthened his imperial ties and guaranteed his loyalty to Britain once the Revolution began. After Howe's army occupied New York, Fanning petitioned the general for a colonel's commission to organize a loyalist unit. Howe finally granted that request on December 11, 1776, creating the King's American Regiment.[22]

Loyalist officers, like those in Whig forces, received commissions on the condition that they raise a certain number of soldiers within a designated period of time. Fanning began seeking commitments of men and money as early as September, presuming that Howe would eventually provide his commission. Drawing on his social and political connections, he collected over £3,000 from loyalist friends on Staten Island, Long Island, and in New York City. He used some of this money to offer what were in effect enlistment bounties to attract prospective regimental and company officers. These men, whose own appointments required them to sign up recruits, received additional funds with which to secure their quotas. In this way, the actual task of recruitment fell not to Fanning directly but to an array of subordinates who sought enlistees among family members and neighbors, as well as from the large pool of loyalist refugees on Long Island. Fanning and his would-be officers, however, faced considerable competition in their quest for soldiers. Recruiters for as many as six prospective loyalist units were combing the area for able-bodied men.[23]

When Dunbar left for Long Island, did he know about these loyalist regiments? If so, such news must have traveled at lightning speed to reach Farmington so swiftly. Had he already made up his mind to join one? Or did he simply go to Long Island to reassure himself that it would be a "Place of Greater safety" for his family, but then crossed paths with a persuasive recruiter?[24] Surviving evidence about his activities during the final months of 1776 is both fragmentary and chronologically confusing. In January 1777, for example, Dunbar allegedly claimed that "in the month of September last he then being at East-Chester with the Minesterial Army and in Company with General Howe & Lord Howe . . . he then took a Cap[tai]n Warrant to serve in the s[ai]d Army." But the Howe brothers were in Eastchester in October, not September, and the captain's warrant Dunbar eventually obtained placed him in the King's American Regiment, which did not yet exist in September. Dunbar's testimony—or the version recorded by Farmington's justice of the peace—appears to conflate a series of events that occurred over several months. What follows is an attempt to untangle the meager and sometimes contradictory documentary strands and propose a likely sequence for Dunbar's actions between September 1776 and the beginning of January 1777.[25]

Since he stated quite specifically that he first traveled to Long Island in September, Dunbar probably did so. There he likely encountered one of Fanning's recruiters and agreed that when the regiment was officially mobilized (thus becoming an auxiliary to the "Minesterial Army"), he would serve as a captain. He could not then be granted a formal warrant; that would have to wait until Fanning received his own commission in December. Dunbar may have procured some sort of provisional warrant certifying his agreement to serve, however, along with money to use for recruitment.

Why Fanning's regiment and not another one? Dunbar's choice may have resulted from a chance encounter on Long Island, but it is tempting to speculate about another possibility—that he learned about this unit from James Scovil or another Anglican clergyman. The evidence is circumstantial but nonetheless intriguing. In late 1775, Richard Mansfield, Derby's Anglican minister, informed New York governor William Tryon that thousands of western Connecticut loyalists were eager to fight on behalf of Britain.[26] Tryon might have passed this information along to his protégé Fanning, who attended Yale at the same time as seven Anglican clergymen—not just Scovil, but also Abraham Beach, Bela Hubbard, Roger Viets, Samuel Andrews, Abraham Jarvis, and Ebenezer Kneeland. Getting word to the ministers about his plans would have allowed Fanning to tap into a reservoir of potential recruits in the Connecticut towns where they resided, including Waterbury, New Haven, Simsbury, Middletown, and Stratford, as well as in New Brunswick, New Jersey. Despite his fervent loyalism, Fanning harbored considerable affection for his alma mater and later took credit for protecting the college from destruction during the British invasion of New Haven in 1779. It is not inconceivable that he might have maintained contact with some Yale alumni even after the war started or renewed those ties when doing so could help with recruitment.[27]

Why Moses Dunbar would accept the substantial risks of military service poses less of a mystery. Joining a loyalist regiment affirmed his political convictions and also gave him the means to support his soon-to-be-refugee family. The financial inducement was fairly generous. Dunbar later stated that his wages amounted to two dollars—or roughly ten shillings—a day at a time when farm laborers earned less than a third of that sum. This salary provided the kind of steady income that would otherwise have been much more difficult for him to secure in a place where he knew no one. There were rumors, moreover, that at war's end (which everyone seemed to think was imminent), a grateful king would reward loyalist soldiers with land grants. With a little luck—a scarce commodity in Dunbar's life thus far—he would have a brief and uneventful military career. His family could then make a new start as Britain reasserted its sovereignty over the colonies.[28]

Dunbar perhaps spent a week or two on Long Island making these arrangements. He had rarely been away from home for so long and sorely missed his children and friends, who were more important than ever to him in those troubled times. The banns for his marriage to Esther Adams had already been announced, and he was keen to make good on his promise to wed her.[29] So Dunbar prepared for his passage back across the Sound. If he had received some sort of provisional captain's warrant, he probably placed it in his pocket along with the recruitment money he had been given. Once he reached home, Dunbar would use these funds to entice loyalist neighbors to join his regiment, as his commission obliged him to do.

Moses Dunbar realized that he courted arrest by embarking on this recruiting mission, but he had no way to know that it placed his life in jeopardy. On October 10, Connecticut's General Assembly convened in New Haven for the autumn session. As one of the first items of business, members passed yet another law punishing loyalist traitors. This time, alarmed by the relentless advance of the king's forces in neighboring New York, legislators strengthened the penalty for aiding the enemy, going well beyond the existing sanctions of property confiscation, disarmament, and incarceration. Now, any state resident found guilty of joining the British army or persuading others to do so would "suffer death." After several adjournments, the legislative session ended on November 7, and it took another week or so for newspapers to inform the populace about this new statute. By then, Dunbar's recruitment efforts had taken him past the point of no return.[30]

Moses Dunbar probably returned to Farmington shortly before the legislature began its deliberations. Happily reunited with his children and friends, he discharged the first of two pressing obligations by marrying Esther Adams. He then attended to his other sworn duty. Dunbar's commission did not reflect his military experience—he had none, beyond the usual militia training—but rather his age; captains in provincial armies were typically about thirty. This rank also testified to his powers of persuasion, for he had to convince Fanning or his agent that he could meet a captain's recruitment quota of twenty-five men. Dunbar doubtless emphasized his loyalist ties in his neighbor-hood and congregation. He may even have mentioned the names of some of the men he would contact as soon as he reached home.[31]

Among the first was his new brother-in-law, John Adams, aged twenty. This robust youth, with a "stout, hardy, black look" and well-known loyalist sympathies, readily agreed to enlist. Dunbar then approached other Farmington men. John Clark and Daniel Tuttle (a fellow New Cambridge parishioner) also signed up, in Tuttle's case at the risk of having his farm confiscated by Whig authorities. Waterbury's loyalist community supplied four more men: Titus Way, Ashbel Stiles, and the cousins John and Asa Blakeslee. Ties of kinship as well as political allegiance linked Dunbar to the Blakeslees. Asa's mother was Moses's aunt Hannah, and John's brother Enos had mar-ried Moses's sister Temperance two years earlier.[32]

The most surprising of Dunbar's recruits was David Smith of New Cambridge parish. Despite his youth, Smith had more military expe-rience than Dunbar or his other enlistees, but it involved fighting against the British and not for them. In May 1775, at age seventeen, Smith had joined (perhaps without his father's permission) one of the Connecticut units sent to capture Fort Ticonderoga. While there, he became seriously ill, lingering at the fort until August. When Joseph Smith received word that his son's condition was "very low & Poor," he traveled 200 miles to Ticonderoga to retrieve the boy. David even-tually recovered his health, but at considerable emotional and finan-cial cost to his father. Joseph Smith lost a "good Likly Mare" while on his rescue mission; he suspected that the horse, worth £12, was stolen. Once back in Farmington, he also had to pay more than £2 in doctor's bills on behalf of his son. Reasoning that these costs had been incurred because of David's service to the state, Smith petitioned the General Assembly—unsuccessfully—for reimbursement. Why, only a few months later, David would switch sides in the war is not known.[33]

That Dunbar could harvest eight recruits in just a few weeks was no small achievement for he had plenty of competitors. During the final months of 1776, about eighty Waterbury men left to join the British, some responding to rival recruiters' efforts and others simply taking off on their own initiative.[34] Dunbar promised Daniel Tuttle an ensign's appointment in return for help in finding recruits, and he per-haps made a similar offer to others.[35] Recruitment could thus proceed while Dunbar went back to Long Island in October to prepare for moving his family there.

Suspecting that he would be away from home longer this time, Dunbar brought all his clothes with him, probably leaving Esther and the children in the care of her family.[36] He had to travel about sixty miles to get to the Sound, passing through towns full of vigilant inhabitants on the lookout for suspicious strangers. He probably traveled at night, perhaps departing around October 12 to take advantage of the darkness of a new moon. He almost certainly knew of safe houses along the way, where he could stop during daylight hours for food and sleep without fear of betrayal. A night crossing of the Sound further reduced his chances of capture. When he got to Long Island, Dunbar discovered that the main body of the British forces had moved to Westchester County, so he followed them there.[37]

This second New York sojourn probably lasted from mid-October 1776 until the beginning of January 1777.[38] If Dunbar joined the Howes and the British army in Eastchester as he later declared, he must have arrived there before October 19, when General Howe began moving his troops to New Rochelle.[39] Dunbar might have caught a glimpse of the general and his admiral brother, marveling at their impressive uniforms adorned with glittering buttons and the elaborate insignia of their exalted ranks. Yet he almost certainly was not directly "in company" with them. The haughty British commanders would have had no reason to come into contact with a lowly loyalist captain; moreover, they were busily making plans to entrap Washington's army at White Plains.[40]

While in Eastchester, Dunbar doubtless sought news about Fanning's regiment. He would have learned that the unit's headquarters had been established back on Long Island, near the town of Flatbush.[41] Dunbar headed there with two goals in mind. First, he had to find suitable housing nearby for his family. Second, he wanted a receipt certifying his initial recruitment of eight men for his company.

One of those recruits was already on his way to camp. Around the seventh of November, Asahel Barns, Farmington's constable, arrested Dunbar's brother-in-law, John Adams, "in a matter of delinquency"— a vague charge that perhaps referred to his flight to join the redcoats. But the young man wriggled out of the constable's grip and escaped. Barns immediately placed a notice in the *Connecticut Courant* offering a reward to anyone who captured "the Villain," whose "toryism" was well known and who was presumed to be headed for New York. The notice first appeared on November 11 and reappeared in two subsequent issues of the weekly paper, suggesting that Adams made good in his getaway. What he left behind in Farmington, however, were hyper-vigilant town authorities more determined than ever to crush the loyalist menace in their midst.[42]

Back on Long Island, Edmund Fanning resolved to transform the motley crew of men drifting into camp into an effective fighting force, thereby impressing British commanders with his competent leadership. He urged recruiters to be expeditious in signing up soldiers, for "we cannot be too Ardent in our desires and too Industrious in our endeavours to compleat our Battallion." Any "Negroes, Mollatoes, and other Improper Persons" whom they enlisted to fulfill their quotas, however, would be discharged so that the unit remained "on the most Respectable Footing." But as recruits arrived in Flatbush, the enormity of Fanning's task became apparent. Troops had to be scolded repeatedly about the importance of punctuality. They required explicit instructions on keeping their shirts clean, hats "brush'd and trim'd up," and hair cut short. Some enlistees showed up with dilapidated shoes that had to be replaced. Others, who changed their allegiance after fighting on the American side, appeared in camp wearing Continental Army uniforms and had to be reminded that "all Remnants or badges of the Rebel Service" on those garments should be "Carefully taken off and conceal'd."[43]

To deal with the formidable challenge of whipping the regiment into shape, at least one captain or commissioned officer was supposed to remain in quarters with each company to supervise the men.[44] Captain Moses Dunbar, as unfamiliar with military discipline as most of the enlistees under his command, may have prolonged his stay in camp in order to address his lack of experience. Financial considerations also dictated that he remain until Howe's formal approval of the regiment on December 11. Once Fanning received his commission, any funds disbursed for soldiers' wages and recruitment would come from British coffers, not the loyalist colonel's rapidly dwindling resources. Only then—presumably after the men he enlisted had shown up in camp—could Dunbar obtain his official captain's warrant and a receipt acknowledging the partial success of his recruitment efforts. And only at this point, at year's end, did he receive permission to go home and fetch his family. If all went well, he might accomplish the round-trip journey in a couple of weeks. Dunbar did not bother to bring a change of clothes and left his captain's commission with his belongings in camp. But before he departed, he tucked the recruitment receipt into his pocket.[45]

That folded scrap of paper became Moses Dunbar's death warrant. He had scarcely set foot in town when Farmington authorities—one of whom may have been the constable Asahel Barns, still seething over John Adams's escape—seized him. They frisked the hapless Dunbar and in his pocket found the incriminating receipt, listing recruits' names and amounts paid for expenses and travel. On the reverse side of the paper, someone scrawled "Forcys [Forces] Kings" and "A Papper found in Dunbars Pocket" to identify the only piece of evidence a jury would need for a conviction. The arrest occurred so swiftly that Esther might not even have known Moses was back in town, much less have had a chance to tell him that she was with child.[46]

The arresting party transported Dunbar to Waterbury, but since he no longer owned land nor lived there, town officials refused "to have any Concern in the Affair." So the doomed man was hustled before Farmington's selectmen and committee of inspection. Solomon Whitman and John Strong, justices of the peace and pillars of Farmington's Whig establishment, recorded Dunbar's testimony. He admitted to signing up to serve with the British, but as for the charge that he had recruited others "he would not say any thing about them as he was under a Solemn oath." Whitman then ordered Dunbar sent to Hartford jail. The Hartford Superior Court, already in session, would hear his case right away.[47]

Grand jury members swiftly delivered a bill of indictment, accusing Dunbar of treason. The trial took place on January 23, 1777. The defendant entered a plea of "not guilty," but the jury found otherwise. Moses Dunbar, "not haveing the Fear of God before his Eyes & being seduced by the instigation of the Devil," was convicted of "Wittingly & feloniously wickedly & Traiterously" going to New York to join the British. He was charged with recruiting "one John Addams" and "Divers Other Persons" to enlist in his loyalist regiment and levy war against the state. The jury also declared Dunbar guilty of providing

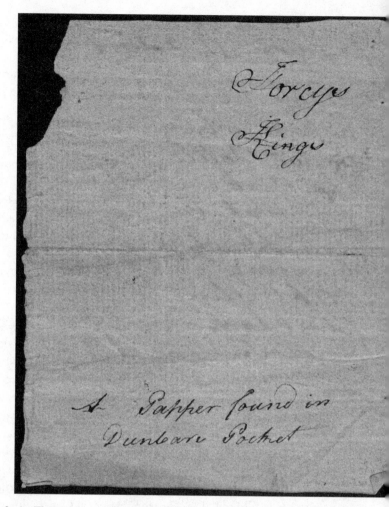

Figures 7.1a & b Two sides of the incriminating receipt for loyalist recruits found in Moses Dunbar's pocket. Courtesy of State Archives, Connecticut State Library, RG 3, Hartford County Superior Court Records, Papers by Subject, 1711–1886, Box 128.

for pasage 14 Dollers

Expence £5:10:4

Moses Dunbar
Daniel Tuttle
Asa Blakeslee
John Blakeslee
John Adams
Titus way
Ashbel Stiles
John Clark
David Smith

intelligence to the British about the "Situation" of Connecticut, with intent to betray it and "the rest of the united States of America." Two days later, on January 25, the court sentenced Moses Dunbar to "be hanged up by the Neck between the heavens and the Earth until he shall be Dead." The date of execution was set for March 19.[48]

With this verdict, Moses Dunbar became the first and only Connecticut loyalist convicted in a civil court of treason against the state and executed for that crime. The jury's finding of guilty was hardly surprising, given Dunbar's confession and the incriminating evidence found in his pocket. But no trial—especially a treason trial conducted in the midst of a war—occurs in a vacuum. Despite Washington's stunning successes just a few weeks earlier in the battles of Trenton and Princeton, few people in Connecticut or anywhere else in the United States would have dared to predict an American victory in the war.[49] That the British army could recover quickly from recent setbacks and still crush the rebellion was never far from the minds of Americans, including those charged with deciding Dunbar's fate.

The trial occurred at a moment of profound anxiety in Connecticut about loyalist subversives. Three days before it began, Governor Jonathan Trumbull publicly denounced these "Enemies yet more unnatural" who had "arisen from among ourselves, making use of all their wicked Policy and Power, to help on and aggravate the Cruelties of our more open and foreign Foes." Stanching the flow of loyalists into British-held New York was vital to the state's defense and its support of the American cause. Success in this endeavor would deprive the enemy of men and intelligence. It would also undermine British attempts to portray the Revolution as the work of a disaffected rebel minority acting against the desires of a loyal majority. In true New England fashion, Trumbull assumed that human effort alone would not suffice to meet the multiplicity of wartime challenges. He thus proclaimed January 29, 1777, a day of fasting and prayer, requiring inhabitants to suspend their "servile" labors, repent their sins, and implore the Lord to bestow his protection and mercy upon them.[50]

Mercy, at least from earthly authorities, would not be granted to Moses Dunbar. Making an example of him delivered a potent warning to other loyalists and asserted an independent Connecticut's claim to sovereign status. During the colonial era, treason was defined as an act—such as rebelling or levying war—directed against the monarch. After July 1776, the Continental Congress in partnership with the states redefined the objects of treasonable actions as the United States or any one of its thirteen constituent units. Connecticut's Assembly, with the October passage of its "Act for the Punishment of High Treason," reiterated this point and for the first time identified traitors as deserving of capital punishment. Dunbar's sentence offered incontrovertible evidence that neither the legislature nor the judiciary intended this statute merely to pose a paper threat. His execution would provide a grisly yet necessary demonstration of the sovereign state's power to take life in order to protect the citizenry and preserve their government.[51]

After the sentencing on January 25, Sheriff Ezekiel Williams escorted Dunbar back to jail. In recent months, escapes from the building had become so embarrassingly frequent that the Assembly ordered guards to be stationed around its perimeter to prevent prisoners from contacting "inimical persons" outside who could abet attempts at flight.[52] Aware of Dunbar's desperate state of mind, Williams had him locked in irons lest he too try to flee. The condemned man was left to count down his remaining days in a cold, damp room overrun with mice. He would have to cope as best he could with the overpowering stench produced by too many prisoners—many of them ill—crammed into a jail too small to accommodate them.[53]

At least four other prisoners shared Dunbar's room.[54] Elisha Wadsworth of Hartford, the eldest of them at nearly sixty, had been arrested on January 17 and awaited trial. Employed as a guard to help conduct a group of British prisoners to Saybrook, Wadsworth came under suspicion for "carrying on a Correspondence with said Prisoners, unfriendly to the American States." When he was found wandering around Saybrook without a pass, local authorities decided that he was "upon no good Design" and so arrested him and sent him to Hartford.[55] Wadsworth later asserted that his reputation for being "unfriendly to the Caus of Liberty" had no "Just foundation," but stemmed from prejudice linked to an earlier accusation about tea-drinking. He hoped that the court proceedings would clear his name, but his legal difficulties were just beginning.[56]

Fifty-year-old Solomon Bill of Middletown, tall, gaunt, and gray-haired, notable for his "droll way of speaking," had already made one escape attempt. One night the previous November, while awaiting trial on a charge of counterfeiting, Bill put on his blue greatcoat and slipped past the guards and out of jail. Recaptured after a few sweet weeks of freedom, he was tried at the same Superior Court session as Dunbar. The jury declared Bill guilty as charged, despite his insistence that the evidence against him was "insufficient in the law." Although sentenced to serve four years in the infamous Newgate Prison, he remained incarcerated in Hartford for another year.[57]

The Reverend Roger Viets, Anglican minister of Simsbury, had also been tried at that same January Superior Court session. Thirty-eight years old, the feisty clergyman had never kept his loyalist sympathies a secret and had occasionally conducted worship services for Anglican prisoners in the same jail where he now sat. He had been arrested in November 1776 on suspicion of harboring two British prisoners, Major Christopher French and Ensign Joseph Moland, after their first attempt at escape from Hartford jail. The grand jury hesitated to indict Viets, judging the facts of the case uncertain, especially the dates on which his alleged actions occurred. The case went to trial anyway. Viets pleaded not guilty, but was convicted of helping the officers and having a "traitorous correspondence" with the enemy. The court sentenced him to a year's imprisonment at Hartford and fined him £20. Several months later, in May 1777, the minister successfully petitioned the Assembly for permission to serve out his term confined to his Simsbury home, so long as he paid his fine, posted a £1,000 bond, and agreed to say nothing detrimental to the interests of the United States.[58]

Then there was twenty-seven-year-old Gurdon Whitmore of Middletown. Short in stature but "well made," he epitomized exactly the sort of "unnatural enemy" whose nefarious activities terrified Connecticut officials. Whitmore first landed in jail in late April 1776 after he was arrested for helping two British officers escape from American custody in Northampton, Massachusetts. He had guided them, probably via the Connecticut River, to his hometown, where he hid them in a cave and brought them food. The plan was for them to escape on a sloop (of which Whitmore was part owner) all the way to the Mississippi River. Whitmore later claimed that his actions had nothing to do with politics, but rather that he had been "seduced" by offers of money and the officers' promise to protect his vessel from capture by British cruisers.[59]

However, according to Whitmore's self-serving version of events, while he was in jail his mind was poisoned by the evil influence of fellow prisoners, most notably the British-born officer Philip Skene. A valiant veteran of the French and Indian War, for which service he received huge land grants near Lake Champlain, Skene remained loyal to Britain when the Revolution erupted. American authorities arrested him in June 1775 and confined him to Hartford jail for more than a year. Before his release in a prisoner exchange in October 1776, Skene allegedly convinced the impressionable young Whitmore that resistance against Britain was "unjustifiable and wrong."[60]

Skene was not the only British officer incarcerated with Whitmore. Christopher French and Joseph Moland—the men whom Roger Viets may have helped—were also there. When those two officers first attempted escape on November 16, Whitmore went along. The men crawled out a hole they had made in the wall of their room, climbed over the palisade surrounding the jail yard, and sneaked past the sentries. The officers remained at large for four days, part of the time poorly disguised in women's clothing (the stubble on French's chin was a dead giveaway), and made it to the coastal town of Branford before they were apprehended and returned to Hartford.[61] Whitmore, who had separated from them, eluded capture for a longer period. By November 28, he had allegedly made it to the British in New York, where he supplied the enemy with information and, having received a sum of money, persuaded several New York men to fight on the king's behalf. He then returned to Connecticut, perhaps to find more recruits. If so, it was a fateful decision. On December 17, Whitmore was back in Hartford jail, "accus'd of High Treason."[62]

Undeterred by their previous failure, the reunited prisoners hatched another escape plan. This time the officers obtained a saw and cut through the iron bars on their room's window. On the frigid night of December 27, having received word that accomplices were stationed outside, French, Moland, and Whitmore clambered through the window, went over the palisade once more, and ran. French and Moland did not stop to rest until they had covered thirty-seven miles; by January 6 they reached the coast and freedom aboard a British transport. Two days earlier, however, Whitmore—who again had separated from the others—was recaptured. He returned to the dismal confines of Hartford jail, locked in a room with a disconsolate Dunbar awaiting trial for the same crime with which Whitmore was charged.[63]

Both Moses Dunbar and Gurdon Whitmore were convicted of high treason, but only one of them was hanged. To explain why their fates diverged so dramatically is to understand how vitally important local connections could be in mediating an individual's encounter with the divisive forces of the Revolution. Despite his manifest misbehavior, Whitmore's ties to family and community remained intact and ultimately served as lifelines pulling him to safety.

Daniel Whitmore, Gurdon's father, may have been enraged by his son's behavior, but he was not prepared to cut him adrift. He hired a lawyer, a Mr. Ellsworth, to defend Gurdon, and that made all the difference in the resolution of his case. At the same court session that saw Dunbar condemned, a jury likewise declared Whitmore guilty of treason. Ellsworth, however, requested an arrest of judgment on his client's behalf, on the grounds that there were legal defects in the trial record. The case was postponed to March, at which time Ellsworth successfully challenged several features of the original indictment, suggesting that if the guilty verdict stood it could be overturned on appeal. He did not dispute all the facts of the case but questioned whether they were legally sufficient for conviction. Some of the charges, he argued, were "breaches of no Law," and the indictment failed to specify which alleged acts violated which statutes at which point in time. This introduced an unacceptable ambiguity; the Assembly had over time passed different treason laws with varying penalties. The court granted Ellsworth's motion and reduced the charges from treason to "high handed Misdemeanours." When the adjourned court reconvened in September 1777, Whitmore was found guilty only of aiding the two British officers who escaped from Massachusetts. That action had occurred in April 1776, when the December 1775 Connecticut law then in force specified penalties such as property confiscation and imprisonment for those convicted of aiding the enemy, but not death. Whitmore was thus sentenced to serve two years in Hartford jail and forfeit all his real and personal estate.[64]

He actually served fewer than four months. In January 1778, Whitmore submitted a petition for mercy to the Assembly that bore clear signs of advice of counsel, though Ellsworth's name appears nowhere. Whitmore pleaded that he had been a "young man, raw & unexperienced in the world" when he first got into trouble. His foolish loyalist phase alienated him from his father, causing Daniel no end of grief, but now Gurdon had "forsaken his inimical principles & practices." Months of incarceration had left "his Health impaired, & his Constitution failing"; his life depended on being released to the custody of his father and he would happily take an oath of fidelity to the United States if he could go home.[65]

Daniel Whitmore stood by his son and—no doubt on Ellsworth's recommendation—presented his own petition, promising to post bail and ensure that Gurdon would "give no Occasion of Complaint or Censure" again. Daniel also rounded up scores of Middletown neighbors to sign a document certifying that he was "a true steady & Zealous Friend" of the United States and—invoking the patriarchal values that infused New England society—that Daniel could be trusted to monitor his son's behavior. The two houses of the Assembly tossed the matter back and forth for days until a conference committee finally agreed to grant Gurdon's request.[66]

Gurdon Whitmore's neck escaped the noose because family and neighbors—the bedrock of local society—rallied to his support. No one came to Moses Dunbar's defense, even though aspects of his case also prompted questions about the timing of events. That incriminating receipt in his pocket bore no date. Dunbar's confession before Farmington's committee of inspection specified that he first went to New York in September—a month before the Assembly made aiding the enemy a capital offense. The indictment, however, dated his New York trips to "on or about the 10th day of November" and "on or about the 1st day of January"—language as imprecise as that in Whitmore's indictment. If the source of information for this approximate timing is unknown, the effect is not: these dates made Dunbar eligible for the death penalty prescribed in the October 1776 treason statute.[67]

A lawyer might have raised objections, but Dunbar could not afford legal counsel. Nor could he expect paternal help. Dunbar, unlike Whitmore, was a married man, no longer the dependent of a father who could guarantee his son's good behavior. Even if he had been, it is highly unlikely that John Dunbar would have come to his aid. Moses's loyalism intensified the alienation between father and son that had begun with Moses's conversion to Anglicanism. Indeed, according to local tradition, far from bearing any goodwill toward his oldest son, John Dunbar offered to supply the rope with which to hang him.[68]

Neither could Moses expect friends or neighbors to speak up for him. His pastor certainly could not do so. James Nichols had been tried for treason at the same court session as Dunbar, accused of encouraging loyalists to join British forces. Acquitted because of insufficient evidence, the clergyman dared not tempt fate by attracting the authorities' attention once again.[69] While some fellow parishioners surely wished they could help Dunbar, the New Cambridge community would not unite on his behalf. War-induced tensions and fears of Whig retaliation ruptured communal bonds that could no longer bear the strain. In fact, Farmington authorities were alerted to Dunbar's return to town by a New Cambridge Anglican. The informer was none other than Joseph Smith, the father of Dunbar's youngest recruit. A potent mixture of emotions compelled the elder Smith to act: anguish over eighteen-year-old David's foolish decision to change his allegiance, anger at the man who enticed the boy to do so, and fear of the consequences of David's action for the family's reputation and welfare. The Smiths, like all New Cambridge parishioners, were already under surveillance by Farmington's committee of inspection. David's defection stripped the family of whatever protection it enjoyed from the boy's previous service on the American side, and his father was determined to limit the damage. In seeking to protect his family, however, Joseph Smith betrayed a man who had come back to town to fetch his own wife and children and carry them to safety.[70]

On March 1, 1777, just eighteen days before his scheduled execution, a desperate Moses Dunbar concocted an escape plan with virtually no chance of success. Somehow he procured a large jackknife with which he broke off his leg irons. When guards came into the room to conduct their usual search of the premises, Dunbar and Elisha Wadsworth knocked them down and ran. They did not make it far, thanks to a vigilant jailer and sentry. Wadsworth, accused of supplying the knife and otherwise aiding Dunbar, insisted that he was "wholly guiltless"; he never provided the knife and "only followed the s[ai]d Dunbar out of the Goal [gaol, or jail], after he had cleared the way."

The authorities, unconvinced by such a feeble excuse, added abetting escape to the charges against him.[71]

The newspaper notice alerting the public to the swift recapture of "the notorious Moses Dunbar" supplied a description of him, to aid in his apprehension should he try again to flee. Its details exposed the physical and psychological toll that his ordeal had exacted. Dunbar was estimated to be "about 40 years of age"—ten years older than he really was. With despair etched into every line on his face, he was "hollow eye'd," his chin roughened by a sandy-colored beard. The weight of his troubles gave him "a down look." He could not bear to meet anyone's gaze, since virtually everyone seemed to be against him. He would make no further attempt to free himself.[72]

Struggling to come to terms with "the Terrible Crisis of my earthly Fate," Dunbar knew that he had to convey a final message to his children. What could he possibly say? In a brief letter, he chose to focus not on paternal love but on religious duty. He began with the "good advice" that Phoebe had "groaned out" as she lay "on her death bed."

> MY CHILDREN: Remember your Creator in the days of
> your youth. Learn your Creed, the Lord's prayer, and the
> ten commandments and Catechism, and go to church as
> often as you can, and prepare yourselves as soon as you are
> of proper age to worthily partake of the Lord's supper.

Such words exhorted the children not just to be good Christians, but good Anglicans. The imminence of death compelled Dunbar to go even further in trying to ensure an outcome that he would not live to see. "I charge you all," he commanded, "never to leave the church." His children constituted his only legacy, and with this order he bequeathed them to the Anglican Church that had shaped his personal life and, ultimately, his political fate. Reminding them to read the Bible and "Love the Saviour wherever you may be," Dunbar interjected a terse statement about his current situation:

> I am now in Hartford jail, condemned to death for high
> treason against the state of Connecticut. I was thirty years
> last June, the 14th.

After asking God to bless his offspring, Dunbar added one final, poignant instruction: "Remember your Father and Mother and be dutiful to your present mother." Even as he composed these words, it surely pained the condemned man to know that of his five surviving children, only eleven-year-old Bede would likely retain any lasting memory of him and Phoebe. The others were simply too young.[73]

One more task remained. It was customary for those facing execution to produce a "dying statement" that explained how they ended up at the gallows. By the late eighteenth century, such compositions followed a familiar pattern, typically including a confession of sin, a declaration exonerating worthy parents of any responsibility for their wayward offspring's bad decisions, and a warning to others not to follow a similarly evil path. Ministers and civil authorities frequently intervened to ensure that the accounts adhered to the proper narrative formula, and street vendors then hawked printed versions to the spectators gathered to witness the execution. A literary genre that focused on the repentance of criminals, however, did not suit a man unwilling to renounce the political beliefs that led him to the noose. Thus Moses Dunbar's statement diverged from the prescribed form. It also failed to find a publisher.[74]

No copy of the statement survives in Dunbar's hand. Perhaps he dictated it to the Reverend Roger Viets, his fellow prisoner. Like other such compositions, it began with a biographical sketch. But instead of identifying each step on a path to crime, Dunbar simply narrated basic facts—when and where he was born, when the family moved to Waterbury, when he married, and so on. He praised his mother, but not the father who treated him "very harshly" after he became an Anglican. Nevertheless, Moses declared that he "heartily" forgave his father and his equally hostile brothers. He admitted to his unwillingness to take up arms against Britain and his outspokenness on political matters, but instead of expressing remorse, he described his mistreatment by mobs and Whig authorities. Dunbar made it clear that he had been forced to seek safety with the British and would have succeeded had he not been "betrayed by Jos. Smith."

Far from concluding with an admission of guilt, Dunbar was "fully persuaded that I depart in a State of peace with God & my own Conscience." He "sincerely repented" his sins, but did not regard treason as one of them. He forgave his enemies, even Joseph Smith, despite the fact that "Some part" of his "Evidence was false." Dunbar thanked the "worthy Ministers of the Gospel" who came to the jail to comfort him, including two Congregationalists, John Marsh of Wethersfield and Nathan Strong of Hartford, and also Roger Viets, who administered the Eucharist to him the Sunday before the execution date. He wound up with a peroration that was at once eloquent and defiant.

> I die in the Possession and Communion of the Church
> of England. Of my Political sentiments I leave the Readers
> of these lines to Judge—perhaps it is neither Necessary nor
> proper that I should declare them, in my Present situation.
>
> I Cannot take my last farewell of my Country-men
> without desiring them to shew Kindness to my poor Widow
> & Children, not reflecting upon them Concerning the
> Method of my Death.
>
> Now I have given you a Narrative of all things Material
> Concerning my Life, with that Veracity which you are to
> Expect from a Man going immediately to Appear before
> the God of Truth.
>
> My last Advice to you is, that you Above all other
> Concerns, prepare yourselves (with Gods Assistance)
> for y[ou]r future Eternal State, you will all shortly be as
> near Eternity as I <u>now</u> am & will then view both worldly
> and Spiritual things in the same Light in which I do <u>now</u>
> view them. You will then see all worldly Things to be
> but Shadows, but Vapours, but Vanity of Vanities, & the
> Things of the Spiritual World to be of importance beyond
> all Description. You will then be sensible that the Pleasures
> of a Good Conscience, & the Happiness of a near Prospect
> of Heaven infinitely outweigh all the Riches, Pleasure &
> Honor of this Mean, sinful World.
>
> God the Father, God the Son, God the Holy Ghost, have
> Mercy upon me & receive my Spirit. Amen! Amen![75]

March 19 dawned clear and unseasonably warm. Winter's snow had begun to melt into puddles of mud and piles of slush.[76] Sheriff Ezekiel Williams had arranged for workers to build the gallows and make a coffin. He hired a hangman and gravedigger, along with a contingent of guards to escort the prisoner. He bought more than three gallons of rum to distribute among those guards once the hanging was over. In all, Williams disbursed about £23 to cover the state's expenses related to the execution—more than half of which he paid himself for his "time, trouble and expense preparing and attending execution and cash paid Jack Ketch" (an alias used to preserve the anonymity of the hangman).[77]

By midday a "prodigious concourse of people" had gathered on Hartford's Gallows Hill to witness the lurid spectacle; there had not been a hanging in town since 1743. Before making their way to the execution site, many in the crowd first heard a sermon delivered in the North Meeting House. The Reverend Nathan Strong, pastor of Hartford's First Congregational Church (and Nathan Hale's cousin), had been chosen to explicate the moral lessons to be learned on such a solemn occasion. Normally, the doomed criminal attended the execution sermon, impressing upon the audience the consequences of sin and the possibility of redemption. Yet just as Moses Dunbar refused to compose a contrite final statement, so too did he decline to perform the role of repentant sinner. Dunbar preferred to have the last sermon he would ever hear preached by an Anglican. The sheriff asked the Reverend Abraham Jarvis of Middletown to come to the jail and do so.[78]

Had he been at the meetinghouse, Dunbar would have derived scant comfort from a sermon that expounded upon the righteousness of the state's assertion of its sovereignty. Nathan Strong's text, "Them that sin rebuke before all, that others also may fear" (1 Timothy 5:20), reinforced the civil authorities' decision to make an example of Dunbar so as to terrify other loyalists into submission. The minister reminded his hearers that although government was divinely ordained, its preservation required obedience and vigilance, especially in such perilous times. Invoking the Whig ideology central to the Revolutionary movement, Strong emphasized that only selflessness and a concern for the public good would safeguard precious liberties. The state's enemies, however, were governed by passion and avarice rather than reason and virtue. Loyalists preferred "a *sordid gain* to the salvation of their *country, and would damn an empire to share a penny.*" Sinners like the man about to be hanged "must be cut off from the earth that others may be safe."[79]

The execution took place at three in the afternoon. The sounds of tramping feet and a steady drumbeat heralded the passage of a lengthy procession through the crowd. There were 100 guards, one eyewitness reported, who "marched the Slowstep with the Musick Playing." These were probably local militiamen, who appeared in such great numbers more to impress the crowd with the state's power than to prevent Dunbar from escaping or being rescued at the last minute. In their midst, the hangman led a horse-drawn cart carrying Dunbar and a coffin. The doomed man had a rope around his neck and a Bible tightly clasped in his hand. When the cart reached the gallows, Dunbar climbed atop the coffin, from which vantage point he could see Esther, her belly swollen with his child. Allowed to deliver some final words, he "Prayed that his men that he had Listed would Not seek Revenge for his Blood." Dunbar then "mad[e] a Short Prayer & Read Part of a Chapter in Job," a scriptural choice signifying his identification with the righteous man whose faith, despite being tested by unspeakable trials, had endured. Which chapter he selected is unknown, though many would have suited his purpose.[80] Perhaps it was from chapter 27, verses 3 to 6:

> All the while my breath is in me,
> and the spirit of God is in my nostrils;
> My lips shall not speak wickedness,
> nor my tongue utter deceit.
> God forbid that I should justify you:
> Till I die
> I will not remove mine integrity from me.
> My righteousness I hold fast,
> and will not let it go:
> my heart shall not reproach me
> so long as I live.

After Dunbar fell silent, the hangman covered his face with a cloth and tightened the noose, looping the other end of the rope over the crossbar of the gallows. Then the horse and cart were quickly led away, removing the support from under Dunbar's feet. Because the tiny Anglican community in Hartford had yet to build a church in town, Moses Dunbar's body was buried in the cemetery at the Congregationalist Center Church.[81]

On the day after Dunbar's execution, Governor Jonathan Trumbull and the Council of Safety met, as they did most weekdays, to deal with matters related to the conduct of the war. General Washington had recently asked Connecticut to supply 2,000 additional soldiers, and the councilors debated how to do so at a time when men were needed at home to begin spring planting. Toward the end of their meeting, the councilors briefly considered a letter they had received from "a large number in Farmington." The townsmen were worried about "their tories" and wanted the state government to take action against these internal enemies. Rather than provide an immediate response, the councilors chose to ponder the matter further and have a "long answer prepared."[82]

Twelve days after Moses Dunbar's execution, his nineteen-year-old brother Miles enlisted for three years' service as a Fife Major with the Eighth Connecticut Regiment of the Continental Army. His brother Joel had served as a drummer with the First Connecticut Regiment for several months in 1775, and again with Colonel Samuel Elmore's Regiment for ten months from April 1776 to February 1777.[83] The timing of Miles's enlistment hardly seems accidental. Having at least one member of the family serving with the Continental Army helped to fend off worries that the Dunbars were all politically suspect. Perhaps further to reassure neighbors of his Whig sympathies, John Dunbar attended a town meeting the day after Miles's enlistment and agreed to serve on a committee charged with arranging for the payment of bounties to soldiers from Waterbury.[84]

Several months after Moses Dunbar's execution, his eighteen-year-old widow Esther cried out with the sharp pains of childbirth. When her ordeal was over, she held a squirming baby boy in her arms. Now she was responsible for six children. James Nichols baptized the infant on December 21, 1777. The name Esther chose for him was Moses.[85]

8

POST MORTEM

THE JUDICIAL PROCEEDINGS AGAINST MOSES Dunbar had advanced with stunning swiftness and, given the temper of the times, left his young wife and friends with little reason to hope for a last-minute reprieve. Although they surely derived no comfort from the fact, at least they did not endure prolonged suspense about his fate. That was not the case for the Hale family. Nathan had been dead for more than a week before anyone in Coventry knew that something dreadful had happened to him, and even then the first news arrived as hearsay. On September 30, 1776, while visiting his uncle Joseph Strong in Granby, Enoch Hale heard that "a Capt Hale . . . who was educated at College was seed to hang on the enemies lines at N York being taken as a spy." Enoch's terse diary entry for that day, an admission that he was "somewhat troubled" by the news, belied his turbulent emotions. That night he would "sleep not very well."[1]

Back in Coventry on October 2, Enoch's hopes rose when another uncle, Elnathan Strong, reported on "some further rumors . . . not altogether agreeing with the former!" About two weeks later, however, a letter from Dr. John Waldo, a surgeon in a Connecticut regiment stationed in New York, confirmed the family's worst fears. This missive compounded their misery by reporting that Nathan's cousin, Samuel Hale, had betrayed him to the British. As Gershom Lyman, a Yale classmate and former Linonian from Coventry, rode ahead to

New York to see what he could learn, Enoch arranged for his own journey to meet with the leaders of Colonel Webb's regiment on behalf of the heartbroken Hale family.

Hale's fellow officers learned of his execution the day after it occurred. Captain John Montresor appeared in their Harlem Heights camp under a flag of truce to negotiate a prisoner exchange, and before departing he informed Alexander Hamilton, General Washington's aide, of Hale's death. A distraught William Hull confronted Montresor, pleading to hear "the melancholy particulars" about the dear friend whom he had tried to dissuade from undertaking his fatal mission. The news about Hale sped so rapidly along channels of military communication that the British officer Christopher French, sitting in Hartford jail, "heard that a Captain of Provincials . . . had been hanged at [New] York . . . for being a spy" four days before the first rumors reached Enoch. Arriving at Colonel Webb's camp on October 21, Enoch spent the next few days discussing his brother's fate with the officers. Most of Nathan's effects had been saved and would be shipped home, but the family would never recover his body or discover where he was buried.[2]

The Hale family slowly absorbed the traumatic news and tried to fill in details as best they could. In late January 1777, Enoch heard that his college classmate John Palsgrave Wyllys, captured by the British during the Americans' retreat from New York, had been released from custody and was back in Connecticut. Enoch visited him in Wethersfield and asked if he had seen Nathan while in the British camp. Wyllys had not, but he had encountered William Cunningham, the provost marshal who had treated Hale so roughly. Cunningham had taunted Wyllys by showing him the Yale diploma that Nathan carried as part of his schoolmaster disguise and the two letters Hale wrote on his last day, which the provost marshal later destroyed. Wyllys was thus the first of Nathan's friends to learn of his death, but he had not been in a position to let anyone else know.[3]

"A Child I sot much by," Richard Hale lamented, "but he is gone." The grieving father inserted this sorrowful declaration into a March 1777 letter to his brother Samuel, the schoolmaster uncle in Portsmouth, New Hampshire, whom Nathan had visited shortly after his Yale graduation. The knowledge that his son had not died in battle or from disease, but was hanged as a spy magnified Richard Hale's anguish. Nathan had been caught in an act that, however essential it might have been to the military effort, carried the taint of dishonor.

What made matters worse was the way newspapers capitalized on the Hales' suffering. "You have doutless seen the Newbery Port paper," Richard wrote to his brother, with its assertion that "our kinsman Sam[ue]ll Hale" had betrayed Nathan to the British. Richard suspected that his son "doutless wass [betrayed] by somebody," but was not convinced that a cousin was responsible. The account reappeared in other papers, further publicizing painful family political divisions. Meanwhile, as the war dragged on with no end in sight, Richard Hale worried about another son, Joseph, serving with the army in New Jersey. Joseph "wass well the last we heard from him," he noted, but the family's loss might all too easily be doubled.[4]

On June 3, Hale's army trunk finally arrived in Coventry. The sturdy box, measuring thirty inches long, twenty inches wide, and just over twenty inches high, was in remarkably good condition. Asher Wright, Hale's grief-stricken waiter and boyhood friend, had carefully preserved it until it could be returned to the family. Inside were Hale's captain's commission, army diary and receipt book, other official papers, and most likely his cache of letters from friends. The trunk also contained clothing, though not Hale's uniform. Enoch probably took some of the clothes for his own use, much as he had once hired a seamstress to make him two shirts from fabric Nathan had left in Coventry. Given the wartime shortage of textiles, Enoch was only being practical. Yet every time he slipped on one of those shirts, feeling the linen against his skin, Enoch must have thought of the brother who should have been wearing it instead. Perhaps he wore one of the shirts when, a few days after the trunk's arrival, he decided to "busy myself a little looking over some paper &c of brother N." It was June 6, 1777—what would have been Nathan's twenty-second birthday.[5]

As weeks and then months passed, the families and friends of Nathan Hale and Moses Dunbar grieved in private and struggled to understand how the grim politics of war had propelled their loved ones toward ignominious deaths. Until the conflict ended and the victor was known, it was impossible to predict how contemporaries would assess the significance of the men's respective sacrifices. It was equally unclear how—or if—posterity would remember either Hale or Dunbar or the tragic circumstances that shortened their lives.

On November 18, 1776, three weeks after Enoch's return from Colonel Webb's camp, his sister Elizabeth gave birth to her second son. She and her husband, Dr. Samuel Rose, named the infant Nathan Hale Rose. In so doing, the couple initiated a family tradition of naming sons to commemorate an ancestor who had no chance to produce his own descendants. Joseph Hale, safely returned from the war at last in 1782, would surely have followed Elizabeth's example had he not been the father of four daughters but no sons.[6]

Not surprisingly, Enoch, who married in 1781, named his eldest son Nathan. By the time of the child's birth, Enoch had begun what turned out to be a fifty-year career as pastor of the Congregational Church in Westhampton, Massachusetts. The Reverend Joseph Huntington, the Hale brothers' beloved tutor, had journeyed to Westhampton in late September 1779 to deliver the sermon at his former pupil's ordination. Toward its conclusion, Huntington recalled that his friendship with Enoch "began in your early days." He gently admonished the new minister to remember that "God has favoured you with a pious education from your infancy; you have had liberal advantages in rising youth, you have precious talents" that ought to be devoted to "the peculiar service of that God of whom you have received them all freely." As he spoke these words, Huntington, along with Enoch and other Hale family members in attendance, could not help but think about the pious and talented younger brother who had once been Enoch's constant companion and who would have loved to have been with them in the meetinghouse that day. Poignant as the moment was, however, everyone knew that despite their grief they had to get on with their lives.[7]

This was also true for Nathan's friends. Hale was the second member of his Yale class to die, but the first (and, in the end, only) one to perish during the course of his military service.[8] Former classmates in the army, although stunned by the news of their friend's death, could not let sorrow interfere with the performance of martial duties that affected the lives of the men under their command. Two officers—William Hull and Benjamin Tallmadge—may have channeled their grief and an urge to avenge Hale's death into expanded military ambition and a greater willingness to take risks on behalf of the American cause. The exploits of both men attracted Washington's attention, and their activities may give some sense of the direction Hale's military career might have followed had he safely returned from New York.

William Hull served with distinction in the Continental Army for the duration of the war. Like Hale—who once offered to donate his own wages to encourage soldiers in his unit to reenlist—Hull looked out for the best interests of his men. In 1779, for example, he joined other officers in petitioning government officials to address the currency depreciation that made soldiers' pay virtually worthless. He also fought gallantly in numerous battles, including Trenton, Princeton, and Saratoga, repeatedly displaying courage under fire. As a result, he steadily rose in rank, and by late 1779, his skillful command of Continental troops during an attack on Stony Point in New York led to a recommendation that he be promoted to lieutenant-colonel. When the Massachusetts legislature tried to thwart that appointment by advancing the claim of another man, Washington intervened. Praising Hull as "an Officer of great merit . . . whose services have been honourable to himself—and honourable and profitable to his Country," the commander in chief proclaimed him fully deserving of the promotion. Washington was so impressed with Hull's talents that in 1780 he offered to bring him into his military "family" as an aide-de-camp. A grateful Hull declined. He had recently become a deputy inspector working with the Prussian-born officer Friedrich von Steuben to professionalize the Continental Army and believed "that I could do more for my country in the discharge of my present duties."[9]

Benjamin Tallmadge more than compensated for his initial reluctance to join the army by compiling a distinguished military record during service that likewise lasted until the war's end. Following a stint in the infantry during the New York campaign in 1776, Tallmadge eagerly accepted a captain's commission with a newly formed regiment of dragoons. Soon promoted to major, he took part in the disheartening American defeats at Brandywine and Germantown in the autumn of 1777 before Washington discerned a more fruitful way to employ the young officer's talents. As Tallmadge later, and rather coyly, recalled, in 1778 he "opened a private correspondence with some persons in New York (for General Washington) which lasted through the war." He had in fact become a central figure coordinating Washington's intelligence-gathering efforts in Westchester County and the lower Hudson Valley. A far more elaborate and effective spying enterprise than the ill-planned scheme that doomed Nathan Hale, this secret service employed a network of men who adopted code names and used ciphers and invisible ink to convey information about redcoat maneuvers and loyalist activities. Tallmadge never mentioned Hale's death as a reason for his own decision to engage in espionage, but it is difficult to believe that there was no connection. He did, however, admit to summoning up memories of his friend during one of the most vivid episodes of his own military career.[10]

In late September 1780, Tallmadge escorted a captured British spy, Major John André, to Continental Army headquarters. André had been plotting with the turncoat American general Benedict Arnold to deliver the West Point garrison into British hands. When their plan was discovered, Arnold managed to escape behind enemy lines, but André did not. There was little doubt about his guilt. André had exchanged his uniform for civilian clothes, used an alias, and carried incriminating documents tucked into his boots. Thus there was little doubt about his fate. He would be executed. Far less predictable was the reaction of many American officers to the plight of the charismatic captive. Alexander Hamilton was among those who admired André's elegant manners, refined sensibility, and bravery in the face of death. Benjamin Tallmadge openly expressed sympathy for the doomed British spy, much as John Montresor had for Nathan Hale, and for a similar reason: both men looked beyond political differences to identify with the gentility of their respective captives. In their short time together, Tallmadge struck up a friendship with the "genteel, handsome, polite" André, who displayed precisely those social graces that Tallmadge and his college friends had once assiduously cultivated as expressions of their Englishness. After independence, of course, officers like Hamilton and Tallmadge rejected any necessary link between gentility and English identity. Americans too could be gentlemen, and for Tallmadge there was no better example of this than his friend Hale. Responding to an anxious question from André about the method of his execution (he wished to be shot rather than hanged), Tallmadge reminded him about Hale's experience at the hands of his British captors. In so doing, he implied that the manner of their deaths would be the same, despite being equally incompatible with their genteel characters.[11]

Shortly after André's death, an item appeared in a London newspaper likewise equating the sad fortunes of the two spies. The unnamed source, claiming to be a former soldier who served under Howe in

1776, wished to acquaint a British public decrying André's cruel treatment with the very similar story of Nathan Hale. Some details were incorrect—Hale, for instance, was identified as a major—but the account was generally accurate. Once again the assertion that "a near relation" of Hale had betrayed him appeared, with the source adding that this individual currently received a pension from the British government—as Samuel Hale, who had fled to England, in fact did. The gist of the piece was that although the two men's fates were lamentable, their executions were "consistent with the laws of war." That may have been true, but it offered little consolation to those who mourned their passing.[12]

Those whom Moses Dunbar left behind faced even greater challenges as they tried to return to a semblance of normal life while the fighting continued. Anyone with the slightest connection to the notorious loyalist attracted malicious gossip, heightened surveillance, and, sometimes, outright harassment. Such circumstances made Dunbar's father and brothers all the more anxious to distance themselves from him. Miles Dunbar demonstrated his American allegiance by joining the Continental Army shortly after his brother's execution, participating in the defense of Philadelphia and the battles at Germantown and Monmouth.[13] Although Joel Dunbar had been discharged from his army regiment in February 1777, he marched again with the Waterbury militia on several brief expeditions. His military service ended for good, however, when he, like so many soldiers, caught smallpox. In addition to bearing the telltale scars on his face and body, he went blind in one eye and lost partial sight in the other.[14] John Dunbar and his eldest surviving son, Aaron, made every effort to support the American cause from the safer grounds of the home front. Local officials trusted the father and son enough to let them serve on ad hoc committees charged with collecting supplies and bounty money for Waterbury soldiers and gathering provisions to aid families whose menfolk were off fighting.[15]

In Farmington, Moses Dunbar's execution did little to allay inhabitants' anxieties about loyalists. Barely a month after the hanging, such worries sharply escalated. On April 26, 1777, a combined force of more than 2,000 British and loyalist troops led by New York's last royal governor, William Tryon, attacked Danbury, about fifty miles southwest of Farmington. Continental Army commissioners had stockpiled a large quantity of military stores there, making the place a tempting target for just such a raid. Tryon's forces encountered little opposition as they marched toward the virtually undefended town. Only fifty Continental soldiers and a hundred militiamen were stationed there, and they scrambled to save supplies rather than try to fend off their far more numerous enemies. The invaders ransacked the town, setting fires that destroyed more than forty buildings and most of the army supplies, including desperately needed food, clothing, and tents. Even as the first flames ignited, couriers raced across western Connecticut with news of the assault and pleas for help. Militia officers in several communities speedily mustered their companies to go to Danbury's rescue.[16] When the call went out for Farmington's militia to respond to the alarm, however, seventeen men refused to go.

Among the seventeen were Lemuel Carrington—Moses Dunbar's onetime landlord—and his brother Riverus. So too were Chauncy Jerome and Zerubbabel Jerome Jr., brothers of Phoebe Dunbar, along with Simon and Joel Tuttle, the father and brother of Daniel Tuttle, one of Dunbar's recruits. Another delinquent was Nathaniel Jones, whose son was also suspected of running off to fight with the British. All of the men belonged to the New Cambridge Anglican parish, and most had endured abuse at the hands of local Whigs. Town officials promptly rounded them up and transported them to Hartford jail.[17]

Dunbar's gruesome fate surely loomed large in the minds of the imprisoned men. Although their actions did not warrant the death penalty as prescribed by law, in the wake of the Danbury attack, who knew what panicked authorities might do? The men were also deeply concerned about their families and farms, which were "lying waste & Suffering" during planting season while they remained jailed indefinitely. Rather than waiting to see what might happen, on May 16 the men petitioned the General Assembly asking for an investigation of their predicament. The "only Crime they can possibly conceive themselves to have Commited" was that "they did not hastily & without proper order run for the Relief of Danbury." But, the petitioners reminded authorities, they had previously been disarmed and confined to their farms because of suspicions that "they were not in favor of American measures." Mustering with the militia would have meant violating these restrictions and getting themselves into a different sort of trouble.[18]

The Assembly immediately appointed a five-man committee, including two of its own members, to look into the situation.[19] They convened on May 22 at David Bull's tavern in Hartford, first meeting with Farmington's selectmen and committee of inspection, and then separately interrogating each of the petitioners. Their report, delivered to the Assembly on the following day, strongly implied that Farmington authorities had grossly exaggerated the threat when they charged the petitioners with "being highly enemical" to the United States and "secretly plotting the destruction thereof." The men had indeed failed to turn out for the alarm, but the investigating committee found them to be "very Ignorant of the true grounds of the present war with great britain" and "at a loss about the Justice of it." Far from aiding the enemy, these men—some "Considerably advanced in years," and others "infirm"—simply wished to be "Neuters." They might have been "Cold, indifferent & lukewarm in the Cause" (allegedly because of the malevolent influence of James Nichols), but they posed no real danger to the country.[20]

The attack on Danbury, the report continued, actually had the salutary effect of convincing all but one of the petitioners that "there is no such thing as remaining Neuters." (The lone holdout was Nehemiah Royce.) They were particularly appalled by the fact that several Connecticut loyalists had joined redcoats in wreaking havoc in the town. Having "thought more Seriously of the Matter," the jailed men now "believe the States to be Right & that it is their duty to Submit to their authority." It would be easy to dismiss this political conversion as a matter of expediency rather than conviction. Yet the General Assembly was sufficiently convinced of the men's sincerity— or at least their harmlessness—to order them freed after they took oaths of fidelity to the state and paid jail costs. Some of the younger men had even indicated a willingness to take up arms in America's defense. Only nineteen-year-old Levi Frisbie subsequently enlisted in a Continental regiment, but other petitioners might have joined militia expeditions.[21]

The Danbury raid—the first significant British incursion into Connecticut—brought the violence of war home as no previous military engagement had done. Such a brutal assault directed at a town very much like Farmington aroused a powerful response among townspeople who suddenly imagined how they too might fall victim to British atrocities. That dreadful possibility horrified both avid supporters of the American side and those who were "lukewarm" to the cause. The attack might not have transformed Farmington's jailed petitioners overnight into enthusiastic Whigs, but it encouraged them to consider "the Justice" of the fight against Britain. Submission to the state seemed a small price to pay if it helped to protect their families and friends, those to whom they really owed allegiance.[22]

Assembly members were equally shocked by the British raid and devoted considerable time and effort to assessing its costs and providing relief to victims.[23] Yet they refused to follow Farmington officials' lead by giving way to panic and instead intervened to prevent volatile local animosities from spawning a frenzy of retribution. After Moses Dunbar's execution, state authorities no longer had to convince the populace that they took genuine loyalist threats seriously. It was equally important, however, to show that they could distinguish between active loyalist subversives and "indifferent" men who might yet be won over to the American cause. Showing mercy was as much an attribute of sovereign power as dispensing justice and under certain circumstances could be just as effective in protecting the state from harm.

Connecticut officials' ability to maintain order improved as the fighting moved away from New England, lessening the sense of imminent threat. By May 1779, the Assembly deemed conditions safe enough to suggest that the governor offer amnesty to repentant loyalist refugees willing to return home, so long as they had not engaged in any treasonous activities.[24] Yet legislators' confidence evaporated only two months later, when British forces once again launched destructive attacks, this time against civilian property in New Haven, Fairfield, Norwalk, and other coastal towns. Governor Trumbull, preoccupied with state business, had never issued the amnesty proclamation, and in late July the Council of Safety strongly advised him not to do so. Two years would pass before the next British strike against Connecticut, an attack on New London followed by a vicious assault on nearby Fort Griswold that included the killing of scores of Continental soldiers after their surrender. Anxieties about loyalists ebbed and flowed in synchrony with these military events and with fluctuating concerns that Tories were trading with the enemy. This made it virtually impossible for anyone still ambivalent about the war to let down his guard.[25]

Grateful for the Assembly's intervention on their behalf, Moses Dunbar's friends and fellow Anglicans still had to carry on with their lives in a town that did not want them. Farmington officials ought to have been relieved when Chauncy Jerome married Esther Adams Dunbar and assumed responsibility for supporting her and the six children. Yet animosities persisted, driving James Nichols to seek refuge in Salisbury and Litchfield until tempers cooled in New Cambridge. The minister had returned by January 1780, however, for he once again baptized parish children. In August of that year, Chauncy and Esther Jerome asked Nichols to perform the sacrament for four young children—a son and three daughters—born during his absence. Before the war was over, Nichols baptized another Jerome daughter. No one knew as yet what kind of world these children would inherit, but their births testified to their parents' faith that the painful trials of revolution and war would someday end.[26]

Peace arrived at last in 1783. Twenty tumultuous years had passed since Governor Thomas Fitch instructed colonists to thank the Lord for preserving them during the French and Indian War. Back then, Connecticut and British soldiers had fought alongside one another, and everyone assumed that Britain's victory portended a strengthening of bonds between colonies and mother country. After another long war in which former comrades fought as enemies, those imperial ties were permanently severed and a new nation made its first tentative steps onto the world stage. This signified momentous change, to be sure, but there was one familiar feature to the altered political circumstances that Connecticut's inhabitants now faced. Once again their governor—this time Jonathan Trumbull, executive authority of an independent state—decreed that his constituents should commemorate a military victory by observing a day of public thanksgiving. Peace, liberty, and prosperity, he reminded them, all derived from divine "beneficence," and maintaining the "stability of our Republic" in the face of the many challenges that lay ahead depended on the Lord's continuing favor. The governor initially chose November 20 for the state's observance, but shifted the date to December 11 after the Continental Congress designated it as a national day of thanksgiving.

For Connecticut residents, as for many of the new nation's citizens, relief and excitement that the war had finally ended with an American triumph mingled with concern about whether the wounds inflicted on families and communities could ever be healed. It might indeed take divine intervention, as the governor suggested, to "conciliate and harmonize the citizens" in the months, and even years, to come.[27]

In accordance with the proclamation, clergymen all over the state dutifully mounted their pulpits to explicate the significance of victory to their congregations. Some ministers preached more exuberantly than others, emphasizing the enormous odds that citizen-soldiers had faced in their epic confrontation with a battle-hardened professional army. "Never had we occasion of thanksgiving like this!" enthused the Reverend John Marsh of Wethersfield, who was old enough to remember the 1763 commemorations. He attributed the Americans' upset victory to God's blessing, of course, and urged his audience to express profound gratitude and improve "the singular advantages Heaven is putting into our hands for national glory and happiness." In this and other sermons, General Washington—"that prodigy of a man," as the Reverend Benjamin Trumbull put it—figured prominently as further evidence of divine favor. Heading into the future, the nation's strength and prosperity would require its citizens to devote themselves both to the principles of true religion, as these Congregationalist clergy defined them, and to republican ideals of liberty and virtue.[28]

For the most part, focused as they were on the spectacular defeat of an external foe, the ministers devoted few words to internal threats. One exception was Thomas Brockway of Lebanon, who likened "the lukewarm, the timorous, the secretly designing and the openly malicious" opponents of the Revolution—and especially the "Judas like" Benedict Arnold—to Israel's enemies in biblical times. Denouncing loyalists as "united against God" as well as the American republic, he reveled in the fact that they had been "troden down," their suppression adding "much to the joy and triumph of the day." Benjamin Trumbull, however, barely mentioned anything about loyalism in his sermon. Even John Marsh, who had visited Moses Dunbar in jail, simply thanked Heaven for protecting the states from "every insidious, artful and base attempt of enemies without and enemies within, to divide and weaken them." Basking in the glow of victory, these ministers consigned civil discord to the murky shadows of the past now that the war was over.[29]

The transition to peacetime in Connecticut was not quite as smooth as such silences suggested, although not nearly as difficult as in states with much larger loyalist populations. For all the heated rhetoric during the war about Tory subversives, there were at most 2,000 or so active loyalists in Connecticut.[30] At war's end, those who had not already gone into exile and could not reconcile themselves to the new political reality joined a diaspora of loyalists from other states moving to Britain or one of its remaining colonies in Canada or Jamaica. Yet many British sympathizers, or neutrals misidentified as such, were willing to accept the American victory and had no desire to leave. Some refugees who had fled during the conflict now longed to come home. How to incorporate such individuals into the political community, and into society more generally, loomed as key challenges in the immediate postwar period.[31]

On the whole, state officials were more forgiving than many of their constituents. Some assemblymen opposed the return of refugees and wanted to prohibit ex-loyalists from voting or holding office, but more moderate voices prevailed. Conciliatory policies, they argued, abided by the spirit of the peace treaty and could encourage former adversaries to become good citizens. Moreover, the return of prosperous loyalist refugees would bring an infusion of capital into the state economy. By late 1783, Assembly moderates had succeeded in repealing nearly all wartime anti-loyalist legislation. Temperate actions at the state level, however, did not necessarily restrain the strong localist impulses that had always been part of Connecticut's political culture. Many towns, still in the grip of radical committees, expelled returning loyalists, and their inhabitants continued to harbor rancor against those who had never left.[32]

Yet those same localist tendencies also provided a means of easing tensions in the postwar world. It had long been the practice in Connecticut for inhabitants of outlying parishes in large towns, once their populations reached sufficient size, to ask the legislature for permission to split off and form new communities. Petitioners typically complained about the time and trouble it took for them to travel from their distant dwellings to the town center for worship and public meetings. So long as the original town was not left with a dangerously depleted tax base, the Assembly usually granted these requests. But in the Revolutionary era, the number of petitions skyrocketed, with twenty-nine new towns carved out of older communities between 1767 and 1790, compared to just six in all of Connecticut's previous history. While some of this growth reflected demographic pressures, it mainly attested to inhabitants' insistence on access to political participation at a time when town meetings—and taxes—proliferated in response to the revolutionary crisis and war.[33]

In 1785, one of those new towns—Bristol—was formed out of two Farmington parishes, New Cambridge and West Britain. Petitioners employed the familiar justification: living at a distance from Farmington center effectively disfranchised them, forcing them "to give up their rights in several important respects." Political considerations inspired the townsmen's desire to re-draw the map, yet their successful request also had religious ramifications. New Cambridge Anglicans thereby left the jurisdiction of a town that had long harassed them. There is no evidence that they actively promoted Bristol's creation, and they remained a minority in a town dominated by Congregationalists. But this development enabled New Cambridge Anglicans to undertake the work of revitalizing their spiritual community in a less hostile environment without having to move.[34]

Aiding their efforts, the animus against Anglicans, which owed much of its fervor to wartime conditions, had begun to diminish during the waning years of the conflict. Those willing to accept American nationality as the prerequisite for staying in their neighborhoods tacitly renounced allegiance to the British monarch or Parliament. This removed the main source of friction that had inflamed relations between Anglicans and other Protestants. Congregationalist candidates for public office even began competing for Anglican votes, signaling an attempt to renew political alliances that had existed before the revolutionary crisis began.[35]

Ironically, it was neither the Connecticut political establishment nor local tensions but rather the Church of England that posed the greatest obstacle to Anglican recovery from the war. Because the charter of the Society for the Propagation of the Gospel in Foreign Parts specified that the organization could only support missions within Britain's empire, Anglican ministers in an independent America lost crucial financial assistance. Connecticut clergymen, writing to London in May 1783, begged for an exemption, pleading that their "greatly impoverished and distressed" churches would surely fail "without the Continuation and indeed in some Instances the farther Extention of the venerable Society's Bounty." They mentioned the ordeals of three ministers as especially deserving of recognition, including those of James Nichols, who had endured physical assaults and a stint in jail because of his loyalty to Britain and the Anglican Church. Officials of the SPG were not inclined to look kindly on Nichols, who may have been soliciting excessive financial support for pastoral services rendered in New Cambridge and Litchfield toward the end of the war. Their refusal to entertain the clergymen's plea for help, however, had less to do with individual cases than the general rule. If the parishes were not under English dominion, they would get no funding from the English national church.[36]

The only way Anglican clergy could retain SPG stipends was to move to Canada; in fact, they could expect larger salaries and land grants if they did so. For pastors who had stood by their long-suffering parishes during revolution and war, this represented a heartbreaking ultimatum. James Scovil postponed the wrenching decision for as long as possible. His roots in Waterbury ran deep; he was born there and had served as its Anglican pastor for a quarter of a century. But his congregation lacked the means to support him, his wife, and their nine children. After enduring so many hardships alongside his parishioners, Scovil was "very unwilling to leave them to go astray like sheep having no shepherd." In the end, financial necessity compelled him to do just that. In the spring of 1786, Scovil, feeling profoundly betrayed by the Anglican Church to which he had devoted his life, reluctantly accepted a position in an enormous and sparsely settled parish in Kingston, New Brunswick. One of the first tasks facing the fifty-three-year-old clergyman upon his arrival in the wind-swept hamlet was building his own house.[37]

New Cambridge Anglicans lacked a pastor after James Nichols departed for good in 1784, first to Litchfield and eventually to Vermont, forcing them to make do with visiting clergy. Members' morale rose when the Assembly passed an act in 1784 allowing Anglicans to organize as Episcopal societies, yet the parish struggled. Its church building, which "had lain desolate for some time on account of the persecution of the times," badly needed repair. Raising the requisite funds for its renovation and for hiring a new minister proved impossible. Finally, in 1790, the congregation joined with Episcopalians in nearby Harwinton and Watertown (part of which, carved earlier from Waterbury's Northbury parish, became the town of Plymouth in 1795) to form a single parish. Members erected a new church accessible to all three communities. A local farmer purchased the old church building, using it as a barn until it burned down.[38]

The creation of this new parish was part of the general transformation of colonial Anglicans into members of an American Protestant Episcopal Church. In July 1783, the Reverend Samuel Seabury arrived in London, hoping that English prelates would consecrate him as America's first bishop. They declined on several counts. A self-appointed group of clergymen had nominated him without any authorization to do so. Moreover, he could not take the oath of loyalty to George III that formed part of the consecration ritual. Finally, in November 1784, Seabury convinced Scots bishops in Aberdeen to perform the ceremony. Back in the United States, Episcopalians had already begun to organize their church, eventually adopting a constitution and a revised prayer book that, among other changes, eliminated references to the English monarch. As they became just one of several dissenting religious groups in a state with a Congregationalist establishment, residual concerns in Connecticut about Episcopalians' political allegiance evaporated.[39]

But time and the return of peace did not heal the wounds festering within the Dunbar family. The only known contact with Moses's descendants occurred when Aaron Dunbar, now the oldest of John Dunbar's sons, twice had to serve as the administrator of a deceased relative's estate. First, when his twenty-two-year-old brother, John Jr., died unmarried, childless, and intestate in the spring of 1782, Aaron had to arrange for the meager estate to be divided equally among his siblings. Moses's share (just under £3 in state notes, payable over four years) went to his heirs, as the law required. Then, in early October 1786, John Dunbar died at the age of sixty-two. He left behind a modest estate, having already distributed property to his older sons. According to his will, the two youngest twin sons Jonathan and David would share the house, barn, and forty-two acres of land, while everyone else received varying amounts of personal property. Even with his own death looming, John Dunbar clung bitterly to his animosity against

Moses. In his will, Dunbar described each of his ten surviving children as "beloved." That adjective was conspicuously absent when he mentioned "my Gran Son Moses Dunbar," who received a small bequest most likely for legal reasons, to prevent him from making a subsequent claim against the estate as his dead father's representative.[40]

It was up to Aaron Dunbar to distribute John Dunbar's personal property to his heirs. One can imagine him accompanying his bereaved siblings as they roamed around the house, identifying items they wanted. For their five-shillings-worth portions, Dinah received a bedstead, mat, and one old pair of pale blue stockings; Temperance—probably at her husband Eliakim Potter's request—took an ax and some horse gear; Aaron appropriated his father's shaving knife and a handsaw. Young Moses Dunbar almost certainly did not join his aunts and uncles at the house to choose his five-shilling bequest. Aaron Dunbar made the selection for him. He gave his nine-year-old nephew a dungfork.[41]

America's victory in the War for Independence confirmed Moses Dunbar's status as a traitor, strengthening the resolve of his siblings to expunge him from family memory. Townspeople, according to one local historian, tried not to remember him either, "other than as one that should not be remembered." The reintegration of loyalists into Connecticut society required this historical amnesia, allowing those who had taken opposite sides in the war or who had desperately tried to remain neutral to continue living alongside one another.[42]

After the war, the Hale family treasured private memories of Nathan but preferred to keep his fate out of the public eye as well, in their case not from shame but from grief. For the remainder of his long life, Enoch refrained from discussing his brother's death. Other relatives broke down in tears whenever Nathan was mentioned.[43] But some of his friends were determined to publicize the story of Hale's sacrifice of his life for his country. America's triumph over Britain sealed his reputation as a Revolutionary martyr who deserved not merely to be remembered but to be celebrated. To his friends, Hale represented the ideal republican citizen who had, in the most profound way, put the public good before his private welfare. Sincere regard for their unfortunate comrade largely drove these commemorative efforts, but so too did a sense of injustice stemming from all the attention given to a different victim of the Revolutionary War.[44]

That figure was the British spy Major John André. It was hardly surprising that Britain would honor the officer's memory. Only three days after news of his execution reached London, members of the House of Commons began discussing the placement of a monument to him in Westminster Abbey, a move that George III heartily endorsed. But sympathy for André persisted in America too, prompting one writer to submit an essay that appeared on the front page of a Boston newspaper in 1781 chiding readers that "while we pay the debt of humanity to our enemies, let us not forget what we owe to our friends." Captain Hale "exhibited all the firmness of *André* without the aid of a single countenance around him that spoke either respect or compassion." The essay concluded with a plea that "justice be done to the character both of the Briton and American," who faced execution with equal fortitude.[45]

Once the war ended, Hale's friends took up this challenge, hoping to translate their private bereavement into public acknowledgment of the significance of Hale's death. First there was Aeneas Munson, a New Haven physician who had grown close to the much younger Hale during his college years. Munson complained that "while the English Magazines, news, &c. were filled with the praises of Major Andre, it gave me no small degree of regret, that Capt. Hale's virtues should be so little celebrated in the country, where, and for which, he died." The physician may have been particularly upset by the warm reception accorded on both sides of the Atlantic to the English poet Anna Seward's *Monody*, which she "consecrated" to André's memory. So Munson took up his pen to produce a companion poem for America's hero, "To the Memory of Capt. Nathan Hale." Composed around 1784 but not published until 1836, it began by scolding:

> Shall haughty Britons in heroic lays,
> And tuneful numbers, chant their ANDRÉ's praise;
> And shall Columbia,—where blest freedom reigns
> With gentle sway, to bless her happy plains,—
> Where friendship, truth, and simple manners shine,
> And noblest science lifts her head divine;
> Shall she forget a son's—a patriot's name,
> A hero's glory, and a martyr's fame?

Thereafter followed a lengthy paean to Hale's noble sacrifice in the cause of liberty.[46]

At about the same time, Timothy Dwight—fervent defender of the arts, Hale's former tutor, and now minister at Greenfield Hill parish in Fairfield—paid equal homage to his friend and to André in *The Conquest of Canaan*, the first American epic poem. Appearing in 1785, it took far longer than expected to complete; Dwight had solicited Hale's help as early as February 1776 to find subscribers to cover projected publication costs. A reworking in verse of the story of the Israelites' battles against the inhabitants of Ai and Gibeon as described in the Book of Joshua, it struck most readers as an allegory of America's victory over Britain, an impression reinforced by the poem's adulatory dedication to George Washington. Near the beginning, Dwight inserted a passage lamenting Hale's and André's premature deaths. The section on Hale, however, reflected Dwight's personal connection, with a poignant reference to friendship that would have resonated with particular force among members of the Linonia Society.

> Thus, while fond Virtue wish'd in vain to save,
> Hale, bright and generous, found a hapless grave.
> With genius' living flame his bosom glow'd,
> And science charm'd him to her sweet abode:
> In worth's fair path his feet adventur'd far;
> The pride of peace, the rising grace of war;
> In duty firm, in danger calm as even,
> To friends unchanging, and sincere to heaven.
> How short his course, the prize how early won!
> While weeping friendship mourns her favourite gone.
> With soul too noble for so base a cause,
> Thus Andre bow'd to war's barbarian laws.
> In morn's fair light the opening blossom warm'd,
> Its beauty smil'd, its growing fragrance charm'd;
> Fierce roar'd th' untimely blast around its head;
> The beauty vanish'd, and the fragrance fled;
> Soon sunk his graces in the wintry tomb,
> And sad Columbia wept his hapless doom.

Acknowledging in a footnote that these lines digressed from his main topic, Dwight admitted that they had been "annexed to the poem to indulge the Author's own emotions of regard to the persons named in them."[47]

Yet elegiac poems, especially unpublished ones, failed to attract the kind of public attention to Hale that his friends craved. Historians of the Revolution might have advanced the cause of his commemoration, but of those writing in the first postwar decades, all but one ignored him. The exception was Hannah Adams, whose *A Summary History of New England* was published in 1799. Adams had taken up writing in order to help support her impoverished family, and after producing two well-received works on religious topics, she embarked on a history of New England from Plymouth's founding to the ratification of the Constitution. Modestly describing herself as a "compiler" who wielded a "female pen," she acknowledged her reliance on numerous published and manuscript sources. It was surely no coincidence that this sole historical account to mention Hale drew upon William Hull's unpublished memoir, which included a tribute to his fallen friend and a complaint about the disparity between Hale's obscurity and André's fame. Adams devoted four pages to Hale's story, with a reference to the British spy that echoed Hull's memoir: "To the memory of Andre, his country have erected the most magnificent monuments, and bestowed on his family the highest honors, and most liberal rewards. To the memory of Hale not a stone has been erected, not an inscription to preserve his ashes from insult."[48]

Unfortunately, the friends' commemorative project, motivated by sentimental attachments to Hale, was all but doomed to fail. Americans had not reached consensus about how best to remember the war, and none of the few points on which they agreed furthered the friends' cause. When the Fourth of July emerged as the national day of celebration, for instance, it took precedence over a ritual calendar linked to local events or local heroes. Indeed, focusing on individuals and erecting monuments to them conjured up images of an elitism better suited to a monarchical society than a republican one. Many Americans, long suspicious of the dangers of a standing army, preferred to conceive of their Revolution as a "people's war," won by all citizens working together. Just a very few officers deserved special consideration, George Washington preeminent among them. Others,

such as Joseph Warren and Richard Montgomery, achieved heroic status for dying on the field of battle early in the war, earning fame by the
shedding of their blood. Nathan Hale also died early in the war, but
not in a valiant fight on the battlefield.[49]

Moreover, Munson, Dwight, and others muddled their message by
tying Hale's posthumous fate so closely to commemorations of André.
It was awkward, to say the least, in the aftermath of a hard-fought war
to pair sympathetic portraits of an American and an enemy officer. Not
all Americans succumbed to the attractions of the charismatic André;
some preferred instead to see the three militiamen who captured him
as patriots worthy of honor. Fellow gentlemen familiar with the culture of sensibility recognized the rhetorical strategy of Hale's college-
educated friends, who believed that sentimental ties could strengthen
political bonds. Others might regard their enterprise more as a celebration of gentility than patriotism. Thus, despite their efforts, the
eighteenth century closed with just one small private monument to
Hale's memory. In 1794, Richard Hale arranged for the erection of
a stone cenotaph in Coventry's old burying ground, dedicating it to
Nathan and other family members who had died far from home.[50]

Decades would pass before there were renewed attempts to rescue Hale from obscurity and secure him a place in the pantheon of
Revolutionary heroes. This time, Coventry residents, family members, and other admirers led the campaign. Their collective efforts
eventually achieved success, although for reasons that had less to do
with the promoters' exertions than with changing times. Americans
were finally prepared to celebrate Revolutionary soldiers just as aging
veterans were disappearing from the scene.

The conclusion of the War of 1812—America's "second war for
independence"—produced a burst of patriotism that stimulated
expressions of gratitude for the military service of Revolutionary soldiers and more recent combatants, crediting them with creating and
then preserving the nation. Less inclined to subordinate the army's
contributions to a vision of the Revolution as a "people's war," the
American public paid greater attention to common soldiers—even to
Deborah Sampson, a Massachusetts woman who had disguised herself as a man in order to serve. Americans also became aware that
many Revolutionary-era soldiers, now in the twilight of their years,

suffered from illness, injury, and economic distress that could, in part, be attributed to their sacrifices on behalf of the nation. Sympathetic members of Congress accordingly passed a general pension act in 1818, providing funds to indigent veterans. In 1832, a revised pension statute eliminated the requirement that the few surviving veterans document their descent into poverty in order to receive compensation.[51]

Pension applicants had to provide sworn affidavits describing their military service in enough detail for the War Department to verify their truthfulness. When Joseph Church of Montville, David Canada of Windham, and four other Connecticut soldiers produced such statements under the terms of the 1818 law, they specifically mentioned that they had served with "Capt Nathan Hale afterwards executed by the British." It was not strictly necessary for them to refer to Hale's death, which they had not witnessed. That they did so anyway indicated that, more than forty years after the event, Hale's execution lingered in their memories and they regarded their long-ago association with him as an important feature of their military experience. Elisha Bostwick of New Milford, who first enlisted as a sergeant in Colonel Charles Webb's regiment in 1775 and later rose to captain, reminisced at greater length, scratching out a narrative of his military service on the reverse of his army commission and enclosing it with his pension application. The seventy-eight-year-old Bostwick treasured his vivid memories of Hale. "I can now in imagination see his person & hear his voice," he recalled, describing the blue-eyed, flaxen-haired captain with "strait & very plump" limbs, "regular features" and a "rather sharp or piercing" voice. At the end of his narrative, Bostwick added one final reflection: "why is it that the delicious Capt Hale should be left & lost in an unknown grave & forgotten[?]"[52]

These were not college graduates but ordinary men, poor enough to be asking for public assistance. Their comments suggested that the potential constituency for Hale's memorialization was larger and more diverse than Aeneas Munson or Timothy Dwight realized. Moreover, the veterans offered their testimony just as a powerful wave of Revolutionary nostalgia engulfed the nation. During the 1820s, Americans gathered for fiftieth-anniversary commemorations of various battles and the signing of the Declaration of Independence. Other events, such as Lafayette's visit to America in 1824–1825 and the remarkable coincidence of both John Adams's and Thomas Jefferson's deaths on July 4, 1826, reminded everyone that the number of eyewitnesses to the Revolution was rapidly dwindling.[53]

Time's passage lent renewed urgency to the task of recording personal memories of Nathan Hale before it was too late. One man who did so in 1827 was Stephen Hempstead, the devoted sergeant who had waited in vain in Connecticut for Hale to return from Long Island. Now in his seventies and a resident of St. Louis, Hempstead published a detailed account of Hale's capture and execution in the *Missouri Republican*. He concluded his narrative with what had become a familiar refrain. "But I do think it hard," he scolded, "that HALE—who was equally brave, learned, young, accomplished, and honorable—should be forgotten on the very threshold of his fame, even by his countrymen; that while our own historians have done honor to the memory of André, HALE should be unknown; that while the *remains of the former* have been honored, even by our own country, those of the latter should rest among the clods of the valley, undistinguished, unsought and unhonored." Hempstead's lament struck a chord with at least a few other publishers; his narrative was reprinted that same year in the *Long Island Star* and *Connecticut Courant*.[54]

Back in Coventry, beginning in the 1830s, three would-be biographers of Hale scrambled to collect information from family and friends. One of them solicited testimony from eighty-two-year-old Asher Wright, who, "besides the infirmities of advanced age, has been affected in his mind, ever since the melancholy death of his young master, Captain Nathan Hale." They approached younger family members, even the cousin of the man alleged to have betrayed Hale to the British. They wrote to relatives of Gilbert Saltonstall, Hale's New London friend. They tracked down the "aged" Betsey Adams Poole. They searched for possible eyewitnesses to Hale's execution. Oddly enough, the only group these prospective biographers seem to have neglected—other than by consulting Hull's and Tallmadge's memoirs—consisted of Hale's Yale classmates. In the end, just one of the writers, I. W. Stuart, saw his book appear in print. *Life of Captain Nathan Hale, the Martyr-Spy of the American Revolution*, published in 1856, opened with an epigraph from Dwight's *Conquest of Canaan*.[55]

By this point, the American public welcomed the literary productions of chroniclers, historians, and biographers as tools for shaping a national identity. Such works instructed readers in the achievements of the Revolutionary generation, thereby inculcating solid republican values. But these same citizens were slower to abandon their concern that physical monuments to Revolutionary heroes—especially grand statues—smacked of aristocratic presumption and ought to be discouraged. Even when they came to accept the idea of erecting simple memorials in the form of obelisks or columns, Americans generally frowned on proposals to pay for them with public money. These notions hampered, but did not halt, the campaign to erect a monument to Hale.[56]

Nearly sixty years after their kinsman's death, family members joined with Coventry residents to push for a public memorial to Hale in town. In 1833, Joseph Rose, son of Nathan's oldest sister, cautiously sought his uncle Enoch's approval for such a project. Enoch, who professed to be "glad that you have thought of the subject," hoped "that you and other friends at Coventry will pursue it." Everyone seemed to think that Congress would happily appropriate the necessary funds, although Enoch advised that the request for money should come from one of Connecticut's representatives and not family members or friends. This approach would promote Hale as a national, and not merely a local, hero. Dr. Nathan Howard, husband of Nathan's youngest sister Joanna, recruited Congressman Ebenezer Young in 1835 to present Coventry's request. Although Young's petition yet again summoned up the shameful disparity between the public memories of Hale and André and other representatives agreed that Hale deserved commemoration, Congress refused to foot the bill.[57]

Not until September 1846—seventy years after Hale's death—did a forty-five-foot-tall memorial obelisk finally rise into the sky in Coventry. Hale's siblings all lay in their graves by this point, but a younger generation was there to celebrate an achievement that owed much to the dogged persistence of the Hale Monument Association. Founded in 1836, this organization solicited donations from the Hale family, Yale professors, local businessmen—anyone its members could convince of the worthiness of their cause. In May 1844, a group of Coventry women sponsored a fair where they sold "useful and fancy articles" to raise $268 for the monument fund. After a decade of such efforts, however, the Association still fell short of its goal. It took a last-minute appropriation of $1,200—about a third of the total cost—from the state legislature to complete the project.[58]

The granite monument, located on elevated ground near South Coventry's Congregational church, represented more than a long-overdue tribute to a native son. Its supporters hoped that, like the Bunker Hill Monument and similar sites, the Hale memorial would become a place of pilgrimage for ordinary Americans interested in their Revolutionary heritage. This would at once strengthen Hale's national reputation and acquaint visitors with Coventry's many charms. The authors of gazetteers already promoted this felicitous mingling of the politics of remembrance and commercial opportunity by featuring Hale's story prominently in their descriptions of the town and, in one instance, including an engraved illustration of the Hale homestead. Local boosters anticipated that people coming to Coventry to see the monument would also be suitably impressed by the town's thriving dairy industry, its cotton and glass factories, and its paper mill. At the very least, any money they spent on food and lodging would end up in local pockets.[59]

Coventry probably reaped little in the way of economic benefits from the occasional trickle of tourists into town, but Hale's star continued to rise. From the end of the Civil War until well into the twentieth century, commemorative statues of Hale, no longer deemed unsuitable for a republic, proliferated. Most stood in Connecticut: three in Hartford, two in New Haven—including a statue at Yale designed by Bela Pratt and later much copied—and one each in New London and Coventry. But others appeared as far away as New York City, Washington DC, Chicago, St. Paul, and at the Central Intelligence Agency headquarters in Langley, Virginia. In every case, the physical representation of the martyr-spy sprang from an artist's imagination, for no known contemporary likenesses of Hale have survived. A handsome young man clad in eighteenth-century garb, in some instances with arms pinioned behind his back and in others not, gazes out at a world the actual Hale could never have envisioned.[60]

Had he somehow been able to foresee how posterity would remember him, Hale might well have reacted with a mixture of pleasure and embarrassment. He would doubtless have been grateful that the circumstances of his death had not expunged his memory, but he had never sought fame purely for its own sake. During his brief life, he aimed instead to cultivate a sense of honor, to achieve a measure of distinction that impressed others but also encouraged a spirit of emulation in them. Sharing the predilections of his place, time, and Congregationalist upbringing, he would have rejected statues on pedestals as invitations to adulation rather than admiration. Hale would have been far more pleased to know that at their centennial anniversary gala in 1853—eighty years after his Yale graduation—members of the Linonia Society still celebrated him in verse as one of their own.[61]

The farther away the Revolution is from the present, the easier it has become for Americans to ignore its complexities and regard it as the unproblematic birth of a nation and shared national tradition.[62] In similar fashion, the passage of years has transformed the flesh-and-blood Hale, whose life trajectory tracked the ferment of his times, into a bronze emblem of patriotic sacrifice. It no longer matters that Hale once aspired to act the English gentleman or that he failed in a spy mission that many contemporaries regarded as dishonorable. What counts is that in his final moments, this youthful farmer's son retained his poise under immense pressure, summoning up eloquent words that have floated free of their historical mooring to enter American memory as a reminder of the better angels of our nature.

Nowhere in America is there a statue of Moses Dunbar. There is no Dunbar Monument Association, nor is there ever likely to be one. No poet has struggled to compose rhymed couplets lauding his virtues or lamenting his untimely death. One contemporary chronicler—Thomas Jones, a former New York judge and unrepentant loyalist—did include Dunbar in his narrative of the Revolution. But that embittered author was settling personal scores, mentioning Dunbar (who he thought was convicted under an ex post facto law) to illustrate American hypocrisy and accuse a dissolute General William Howe of "lolling in the arms of his mistress" instead of intervening to save a loyal Englishman from the noose. Historians writing about the Revolution from the perspective of the victors saw no reason to refer to Dunbar at all.[63]

Memories of Dunbar seemed fated to disappear altogether as Americans looked toward a bright future and away from a divisive Revolutionary past. Then, on the eve of the national centenary, someone found two old documents hidden away in a house about to be demolished in Harwinton. The *Waterbury Daily American* reported in 1875 on the discovery of these "discolored" manuscripts, "nearly illegible" in places. They proved to be copies of Moses Dunbar's dying statement and his final letter to his children, and their emergence from a dusty garret into the light of day provoked an unprecedented curiosity about the life and times of an all-but-forgotten loyalist.[64]

The turn of the twentieth century witnessed a surge of interest in local history, and in Connecticut it seemed that virtually every community found an enthusiastic scribe to record its illustrious past. Most of these works paid particular attention to their town's note-worthy contributions to America's independence. Chroniclers of the places central to Dunbar's story, however, leavened their accounts with surprisingly sympathetic portraits of him. The Reverend Joseph Anderson, in his history of Waterbury, proclaimed Dunbar "a conspicuous martyr," whose story "will forever appeal to the heart of an American—be he the descendant of Whig or of Tory." Writing in 1909, E. LeRoy Pond insisted that it was "certainly time that some memorial" to the persecuted Farmington loyalists be produced and characterized Dunbar's life story as "a tragedy meet for a poet's pen." Pond went so far as to compare vengeful Sons of Liberty to the Ku Klux Klan. The rather more temperate Epaphroditus Peck, a Yale law professor and Hartford judge, offered a different if equally striking analogy in his history of Bristol, asserting that Dunbar's "career in many ways paralleled [Nathan] Hale's."[65]

What prompted these writers to portray a disgraced traitor as an honorable man, even to the point of likening him to a Revolutionary hero? Family connections account, at least in part, for Pond's provocative stance. His ancestor Jonathan Pond had strongly opposed Whig violence and once rescued his brother-in-law Chauncy Jerome from an angry mob.[66] Yet genealogy hardly suffices to explain such a profound reversal in Dunbar's historical reputation. Far more influential was the power of Dunbar's own words, rediscovered in those fragile manuscripts. Every one of the local historians inserted lengthy excerpts from Dunbar's dying statement and the letter to his children in their books, allowing the long-dead loyalist to make his case to a posterity far removed from the turmoil that cut short his life.[67]

More than a century separated these historians from the Revolution, but far less time had passed since the end of another civil conflict. Only Judge Peck drew an explicit parallel between loyalists and Confederates, but all the writers crafted their revisionist portraits of Dunbar during a prolonged national effort at North-South reconciliation—at least among white citizens.[68] Yet the recovery of Dunbar's personal testimony served as the real catalyst initiating a commemorative reaction, for it allowed local historians to elevate religious principles over political differences. Joseph Anderson emphasized Dunbar's devotion to the Church of England and described his "Cause" as "sacred." Judge Peck argued that Connecticut authorities deliberately chose "a shining mark," a "man of high character" to impress Tories with the power of the law. Dunbar died "for the faith which he had deliberately adopted and the King to whom he believed that his loyalty was due." This praise, moreover, came not from Episcopalians, but from staunch Congregationalists.[69] Without the Dunbar manuscripts, the only source materials available to these authors would have been the sparse legal records pronouncing him a dangerous traitor.

The Dunbar family took no part in encouraging the positive image of Moses that emerged in local, if not national, memories of the Revolution. His brothers preferred to forget him altogether. Some of them prospered; others did not, and none bestowed the name of the infamous traitor on a son. Aaron, Jonathan, and David Dunbar all remained in Plymouth, with the eldest, Aaron, achieving a level of local distinction that his striving father might have envied. Elected selectman at Plymouth's first town meeting after its incorporation in 1795, he owned enough land at the time of his death in 1820 to make modest bequests to each of his five sons and two daughters. Jonathan, who inherited his father's home farm to share with his twin David, died at age seventy-three in 1843 with about 160 acres of real property. How the brothers acquired substantially more land than their father ever possessed is unclear. Perhaps they purchased it from neighbors who emigrated to what became the town of Plymouth, Ohio, around the time of the War of 1812.[70]

The fortunes of the two brothers who risked their lives in the Continental Army were far less bright. First Joel and then Miles left Connecticut for upstate New York early in the nineteenth century, taking up land grants offered to army veterans on property seized from the Iroquois after the war. Neither man could make a go of it and both ended up destitute, forced to seek military pensions. In his 1820 application, sixty-seven-year-old Joel admitted to having no property "except my clothes of which I have two suits worth about

$15." Disabled by smallpox-induced blindness linked to his army ser-
vice, Joel survived only "by the assistance of friends." "My wife is
dead, and my family scattered," he pleaded, forcing him to "look to
my country for support." Miles's circumstances were slightly less dire;
he claimed ownership of about five acres of land and a hundred dollars' worth of personal property. Yet he too had "lost the sight of one
of his eyes" and could see "but dimly with the other." His wife was
"feeble & infirm," and the only other members of the household were
"two orphan and portionless grandchildren." Choosing to fight on the
victorious side in the Revolutionary War had not done either brother
much good in the long run.[71]

Moses Dunbar's children made no deliberate effort to reshape public opinion, but the shift in perspective about their father would never
have occurred had not two daughters preserved those crucial documents as private memorials to him. The Harwinton house in which
the manuscripts were found most likely belonged at one time to
Bede Dunbar and her husband Sylvanus Cook. Although it is impossible to know for sure, several local historians claimed that the copies
were in Cook's hand.[72] An additional version was preserved in a small
pamphlet inscribed by another daughter: "Sene Dunbar Her Book
Harwinton 15 Day of August, 1788."[73]

Trying to reconstruct the postwar lives of Moses Dunbar's children
is like chasing shadows at twilight. Bede's name is barely visible in
surviving records. In May 1784, at age nineteen, she married Sylvanus
Cook, a cousin on her mother's side and a Harwinton farmer of modest means. She probably bore two sons before Sylvanus died around
1795. She was counted in the federal censuses of 1800 and 1810 as a
widow. Then she disappears. There is no way to know if she moved,
remarried, or died.[74] Sene Dunbar's historical presence is even more
ephemeral, with no trace except the inscription on "Her Book" placing her in Harwinton in 1788. For Phoebe Dunbar, there is nothing
beyond a record of her baptism in 1774.[75]

Actions taken by Chauncy and Esther Jerome perhaps fostered this
invisibility. Once their own children began to arrive, the couple may
have placed some of the Dunbars as servants in other households,
making it harder to track their subsequent movements.[76] This dispersal may have anticipated the next. With no property, weak family ties,
and the burden of their father's infamy, there was little incentive for

Moses's children to stay in the area. Like Bede, other daughters might have found spouses who tied them to Connecticut, but the sons had every reason to leave. One of them may have been the elusive Dana Dunbar. New Cambridge baptismal records mention only three of Moses's seven children with Phoebe; Dana was likely one of the unrecorded ones. If so, he married Esther Blakeslee of Watertown in 1794 and was living in Plymouth in 1800. Then he probably moved first to Genesee County, New York, and later to Detroit, Michigan, where he died in 1842.[77] Zina Dunbar left a more distinct imprint in the records beginning with his 1773 baptism. Once grown, he joined the postwar exodus of Connecticut inhabitants to Pennsylvania. By 1820, he was living as a farmer in Bradford County, in an area once claimed by the same Susquehannah Company that had aroused the speculative ambitions of his grandfather Zerubbabel Jerome more than a half-century earlier. There Zina remained until his death in 1852.[78]

And what of Moses, born after his father's death and marked for life with a traitor's name? Esther Jerome prevailed upon her husband to let this child—her own son—grow up in their Bristol household. In April 1792, when Moses was not quite fifteen, Chauncy formally became his guardian. The legal bond confirming this relationship noted that Moses had no property at all—not even, evidently, a dungfork.[79] What happened when he reached adulthood? Here the documentary trail all but vanishes.

The 1800 federal census lists a young man named Moses Dunbar living in New London. If this was the son of Moses and Esther, he was at age twenty-three already married and the father of two boys, replicating a familial pattern of early marriage and parenthood. It is easy to understand why he would have left Bristol, where he lacked property and good prospects, and would always bear the stigma of his father's infamy. Perhaps he was drawn to New London by a notion of going to sea. But if this is the right Moses, his destiny was to remain on land, probably toiling for wages on other men's farms. When Britain and America again went to war, he briefly served with the New London militia in the summer of 1813. Any sum earned for his service would have helped to support his growing family. And did that family include a son named Moses? The 1840 census places a Moses Dunbar—too young to be the traitor's son but the right age for a grandson—in nearby East Lyme. This Moses did try his luck at seafaring, leaving a wife and children to await his safe return from distant and dangerous voyages. Was one of his little boys also named Moses?[80]

The fate of Moses Dunbar's posthumous son remains shrouded in mystery. Wherever he ended up, perhaps he spared a thought now and then for the father he never knew. Perhaps his mother told him stories and Bede shared their father's eloquent words, making him proud to bear the name of a man whom others reviled and then tried to forget. Perhaps he told his own children about the grandfather who did what he thought was right even at the cost of his life. The younger Moses, like his father before him, probably found his path through life strewn with obstacles, and good fortune always beyond reach. We can nevertheless hope he remembered that worldly things are but shadows and vapors, nowhere near as precious as a good conscience.

NOTES

ABBREVIATIONS

Conn. Arch.	Connecticut Archives, Connecticut State Library, Hartford, CT.
CSL	Connecticut State Library, Hartford, CT.
Ct. Colony Recs.	J. Hammond Trumbull and C. J. Hoadly, eds., *The Public Records of the Colony of Connecticut*, 15 vols., Hartford: Brown & Parsons, 1850–1885.
Ct. State Recs.	Charles J. Hoadly and Leonard Woods Labaree, eds., *The Public Records of the State of Connecticut*, 7 vols., Hartford: Case, Lockwood & Brainard, 1894–1948.
Dexter, *Bio. Sketches*	Franklin B. Dexter, *Biographical Sketches of the Graduates of Yale College, with Annals of the College History*, 6 vols. New York: Henry Holt and Co., 1885–1912.
EH Diary	Enoch Hale Diary, Enoch Hale Papers, Record Group No. 66, Box 2, Ser. II, III, Special Collections, Yale University Divinity School Library, New Haven, CT.
"Last Speech"	"The last Speech & Dying Wordes of Moses Dunbar," contemporary manuscript copy, MA 896, The Morgan Library & Museum, New York.
Seymour, *Doc. Life*	George Dudley Seymour, *Documentary Life of Nathan Hale, Comprising All Available Official and Private Documents Bearing on the Life of The Patriot,* ... New Haven, CT: Tuttle, Morehouse, and Taylor, 1941.
SPG Recs.	Records of the Society for the Propagation of the Gospel in Foreign Parts, London; microfilm copies at the Firestone Library, Princeton University.
WMQ	*William and Mary Quarterly*.

PROLOGUE

1. Stuart Banner, *The Death Penalty: An American History* (Cambridge, MA: Harvard University Press, 2002), 10–23, 45–47; Douglas Hay et al., *Albion's Fatal Tree: Crime and Society in Eighteenth-Century England* (New York: Pantheon, 1975), 66; V. A. C. Gatrell, *The Hanging Tree: Execution and the English People, 1770–1868* (Oxford: Oxford University Press, 1994), 39, 46.

2. Dominick J. DiMaio and Vincent J. M. DiMaio, *Forensic Pathology* (New York: Elsevier, 1989), 222–24. The rope compressed the jugular veins, preventing an outflow of blood from the brain, while the more deeply positioned carotid arteries usually remained open, carrying more blood in. If the noose was not tight enough or the knot slipped to the back of the neck, the victim might remain conscious

longer; see Gatrell, *Hanging Tree*, 48. By the end of the eighteenth century, the gallows gave way to taller and more elaborate scaffolds with hinged platforms on which the condemned stood. See Banner, *Death Penalty*, 45–47; Gatrell, *Hanging Tree*, 52–54; Irene Quenzler Brown and Richard D. Brown, *The Hanging of Ephraim Wheeler: A Story of Rape, Incest, and Justice in Early America* (Cambridge, MA: Harvard University Press, 2003), 254–55.

3. Thirty-two of the 48 people were executed before 1700. Half of the women who were executed (9 of 18) had been convicted of witchcraft during the seventeenth century. Lawrence B. Goodheart, *The Solemn Sentence of Death: Capital Punishment in Connecticut* (Amherst: University of Massachusetts Press, 2011), 17, 22, 33, 50, 57, 61, 66. For the relative rarity of capital crimes in colonial New England legal codes, see Banner, *Death Penalty*, 6–8, and 48–52 on the availability of published accounts of executions.

4. Banner, *Death Penalty*, 20–21, 39–40.

5. For a succinct overview of main themes in Revolutionary historiography, see the introduction to Edward G. Gray and Jane Kamensky, eds., *The Oxford Handbook of the American Revolution* (New York: Oxford University Press, 2013), 1–11. For a small sample of the growing body of scholarship exploring the Revolution from new perspectives, see Claudio Saunt, *West of the Revolution: An Uncommon History of 1776* (New York: Norton, 2014); Kathleen DuVal, *Independence Lost: Lives on the Edge of the American Revolution* (New York: Random House, 2015); Maya Jasanoff, *Liberty's Exiles: American Loyalists in the Revolutionary World* (New York: Knopf, 2011); J. H. Elliott, *Empires of the Atlantic World: Britain and Spain in America, 1492–1830* (New Haven, CT: Yale University Press, 2006); David Armitage, *The Declaration of Independence: A Global History* (Cambridge, MA: Harvard University Press, 2007); P. J. Marshall, *The Making and Unmaking of Empires: Britain, India, and America c. 1750–1783* (Oxford: Oxford University Press, 2005); Andrew Jackson O'Shaughnessy, *An Empire Divided: The American Revolution and the British Caribbean* (Philadelphia: University of Pennsylvania Press, 2000).

6. For a somewhat different, yet related, consideration of this topic, see Allan Kulikoff, "Revolutionary Violence and the Origins of American Democracy," *Journal of the Historical Society* 2 (2002): 229–60.

7. See, for instance, Colin G. Calloway, *The American Revolution in Indian Country: Crisis and Diversity in Native American Communities* (New York: Cambridge University Press, 1995); Sylvia R. Frey, *Water from the Rock: Black Resistance in a Revolutionary Age* (Princeton, NJ: Princeton University Press, 1991); DuVal, *Independence Lost*.

8. Ronald Hoffman, Thad W. Tate, and Peter J. Albert, eds., *An Uncivil War: The Southern Backcountry during the American Revolution* (Charlottesville: published for the US Capitol Historical Society by the University Press of Virginia, 1985); Adrian C. Leiby, *The Revolutionary War in the Hackensack Valley: The Jersey Dutch and the Neutral Ground, 1775–1783* (New Brunswick, NJ: Rutgers University Press, 1962); Joseph S. Tiedemann, "A Revolution Foiled: Queens County, New York, 1775–1776," *Journal of American History* 75 (1988): 417–44.

9. The most comprehensive collection of sources about Hale can be found in George Dudley Seymour, ed., *Documentary Life of Nathan Hale* (New Haven, CT: Tuttle, Morehouse and Taylor, 1941).

10. The earliest surviving bound manuscript copy of "The last Speech & Dying Words of Moses Dunbar," by an unknown copyist, is at the Morgan Library and Museum, New York, MA 896. The manuscript appears to date from the late eighteenth century. Several slightly varying versions of this speech, and a letter Dunbar wrote to his children, were printed beginning in the nineteenth century, but no original manuscripts are known to exist. The oldest printed copy, without a date but probably from the early nineteenth century, can be found in the Malcolm Harris Papers, Hamden Historical Society, Hamden, CT. Another version appeared in a Connecticut Episcopalian publication, *The Calendar* 2 (August 22, 1846), p. 136. An article in the *Waterbury Daily American* for February 6, 1875, announced the discovery of manuscripts of Dunbar's speech and letter to his children in a house being demolished in Harwinton, CT. The article summarizes the documents but does not say where the manuscripts ended up. The Mattatuck Historical Society in Waterbury, Connecticut, has what appears to be a late-nineteenth- or early-twentieth-century handwritten copy of the speech and letter (document ID no. M-12), as well as a letter from the local historian Epaphroditus Peck, who compares the version to a printed one that appears in Joseph Anderson, ed., *The Town and City of Waterbury, Connecticut, from the Aboriginal Period to the Year Eighteen Hundred and Ninety-Five*, 3 vols. (New Haven, CT: Price and Lee, 1896), 1: 434–36. Because the Morgan Library copy appears to be the one made closest to Dunbar's death, it is the version used throughout this book.

11. For the most recent work on the loyalist diaspora, see Jasanoff, *Liberty's Exiles*.

CHAPTER 1

1. For the kinds of tasks performed on Connecticut farms in July, see Sidney H. Miner and George D. Stanton Jr., eds., *The Diary of Thomas Minor, Stonington, Connecticut, 1653 to 1684* (New London, CT: Day Publishing, 1899) and Frank Denison Miner, ed., *The Diary of Manasseh Minor, Stonington, Conn., 1696–1720* (n. p., 1915), passim. See also Daniel Vickers, *Farmers & Fishermen: Two Centuries of Work in Essex County, Massachusetts, 1630–1850* (Chapel Hill: University of North Carolina Press, 1994), 64–66. Fitch's proclamation appeared in *New-London Summary*, June 24, 1763.

2. Harold E. Selesky, *War & Society in Colonial Connecticut* (New Haven, CT: Yale University Press, 1990), 139–40, 169–70, 190. For a complete account of the war, see Fred Anderson, *Crucible of War: The Seven Years' War and the Fate of Empire in British North America, 1754–1766* (New York: Alfred A. Knopf, 2000).

3. James Lockwood, *A Sermon Preached at Weathersfield, July 6, 1763, Being the Day appointed by Authority for a Public Thanksgiving, on Account of the Peace, Concluded with France and Spain* (New Haven, CT: James Parker, 1763); quotations on pp. 19–20. For a discussion of ministers' interpretations of the meaning of Britain's victory over France, see Nathan O. Hatch, *The Sacred Cause of Liberty: Republican Thought and the Millennium in Revolutionary New England* (New Haven, CT: Yale University Press, 1977), 36–51.

4. For John Dunbar's military service, see Albert C. Bates, ed., "Rolls of Connecticut Men in the French and Indian War, 1755–1762," *Collections of the Connecticut Historical Society*, vol. 9 (1903): 26. On the presence of teenaged soldiers

in provincial armies, see Selesky, *War & Society*, 172–73; Fred Anderson, *A People's Army: Massachusetts Soldiers and Society in the Seven Years' War* (Chapel Hill: University of North Carolina Press, 1984), 53, 231. Some youths as young as age fourteen served, but most were eighteen or older. There is a brief physical description of Dunbar in the *Connecticut Courant*, March 3, 1777.

5. On the Northbury church and Reverend Todd, see Henry Bronson, *The History of Waterbury, Connecticut; . . .* (Waterbury, CT: Bronson Brothers, 1858), 264–67. For an overview of the thematic focus of postwar sermons, see Harry S. Stout, *The New England Soul: Preaching and Religious Culture in Colonial New England* (New York: Oxford University Press, 1986), 250–55.

6. Seymour, *Doc. Life*, 334, 365; Dexter, *Bio. Sketches*, 2: 750–55.

7. For the postwar recession, see Anderson, *Crucible of War*, 588–92.

8. *Historical Statistics of the United States, Colonial Times to 1970*, 2 vols. (Washington, DC: US Bureau of the Census, 1975), 2: 1169; Jackson Turner Main, *Society and Economy in Colonial Connecticut* (Princeton, NJ: Princeton University Press, 1985); Christopher Collier, *Roger Sherman's Connecticut: Yankee Politics and the American Revolution* (Middletown, CT: Wesleyan University Press, 1971), 24–28. For a discussion of Connecticut's experience during the Dominion of New England episode, see David S. Lovejoy, *The Glorious Revolution in America* (New York: Harper & Row, 1972), 203–8, 248–50.

9. For the influence of royal and proprietary governors on colonial politics, see Bernard Bailyn, *The Origins of American Politics* (New York: Vintage, 1967), 66–95. Richard Bushman also describes the shift in Massachusetts political culture after the new charter of 1691 instituted a royal governor there; see his *King and People in Provincial Massachusetts* (Chapel Hill: University of North Carolina Press, 1992).

10. Richard L. Bushman, *From Puritan to Yankee: Character and the Social Order in Connecticut, 1690–1765* (Cambridge, MA: Harvard University Press, 1967), 183–266. Recent general studies of the Great Awakening include Thomas S. Kidd, *The Great Awakening: The Roots of Evangelical Christianity in Colonial America* (New Haven, CT: Yale University Press, 2009); Frank Lambert, *Inventing the "Great Awakening"* (Princeton, NJ: Princeton University Press, 1999).

11. Bushman, *From Puritan to Yankee*, 73–134, 256–58; Anderson, *Crucible of War*, 529–34; Oscar Zeichner, *Connecticut's Years of Controversy, 1750–1776* (Chapel Hill: University of North Carolina Press, 1949), 29–42; Eric Hinderaker and Peter C. Mancall, *At the Edge of Empire: The Backcountry in British North America* (Baltimore: Johns Hopkins University Press, 2003), 129–31; Paul B. Moyer, *Wild Yankees: The Struggle for Independence along Pennsylvania's Revolutionary Frontier* (Ithaca, NY: Cornell University Press, 2007), 3, 14–18.

12. Donald Lines Jacobus, comp., "Families of Ancient New Haven," *New Haven Genealogical Magazine* 3 (July 1925): 583–85.

13. Lois Kimball Mathews Rosenberry, *Migrations from Connecticut Prior to 1800* (*Publications of the Tercentenary Commission of the State of Connecticut* [no. 28]) (New Haven, CT: Yale University Press, 1934), 6–13.

14. For Edward Dunbar's early land purchases in Waterbury, see Waterbury Land Records, vol. 5, p. 575; vol. 6, pp. 253, 311; vol. 7, p. 56; microfilmed copies at

CSL. Edward Dunbar's daughter Mary was born in Waterbury in September 1754, but his land transactions suggest that he may have moved there as early as 1750; for family information, see Jacobus, comp., "Families of Ancient New Haven," 584.

15. Selesky, *War & Society*, 145–51. On financial incentives for enlistment, see Anderson, *A People's Army*, 38–39. For John Dunbar's gun, see the will of John Dunbar Sr., 1746, Wallingford Probate Records, reel 836, no. 3688 at CSL.

16. Bates, ed., "Rolls of Connecticut Men in the French and Indian War, 1755–1762," *Collections of the Connecticut Historical Society*, 9: 26; Anderson, *A People's Army*, 10.

17. Anderson, *Crucible of War*, 115–23; Selesky, *War & Society*, 103–4. Quotation from Louis Effingham DeForest, ed., *Journals and Papers of Seth Pomeroy, Sometime General in the Colonial Service* (New Haven, CT: Tuttle, Morehouse & Taylor, 1926), 114.

18. DeForest, ed., *Journals and Papers of Seth Pomeroy*, 115–16; Selesky, *War & Society*, 104, 169, 198; Bates, ed., "Rolls of Connecticut Men in the French and Indian War, 1755–1762," *Collections of the Connecticut Historical Society*, 9: 26.

19. Selesky, *War & Society*, 128–29, 168; *Ct. Colony Recs.*, 10: 478.

20. Wallingford Land Records, vol. 9, 384; vol. 11, pp. 506, 509, 533; vol. 12, p. 399; vol. 14, p. 183; Waterbury Land Records, vol. 9, pp. 386–87, 391, 410, 526 at CSL. For "lawful money" and bills of credit, see John J. McCusker, *Money & Exchange in Europe & America 1600–1775: A Handbook* (Chapel Hill: University of North Carolina Press, 1978), 135–36; Charles M. Andrews, "Current Lawful Money of New England," *American Historical Review* 24 (1918): 73–77; Selesky, *War & Society*, 129–30. On land prices in eighteenth-century Connecticut, see Main, *Society and Economy*, 119–20, 206. Dunbar's landholdings approximated the median acreage owned by a sample of young farmers (aged 30–39) in two Connecticut counties; see Main, *Society and Economy*, 201. Edward Dunbar apparently used the proceeds of the sale to his brother to purchase another house lot in Waterbury in early 1759; see Waterbury Land Records, vol. 9, pp. 386, 419, at CSL.

21. In a colony census from 1756, Wallingford ranked sixth and Waterbury twenty-ninth out of sixty-two towns in terms of population. In a listing of taxable wealth in Connecticut towns compiled in October 1755, Wallingford ranked tenth and Waterbury twenty-seventh. See *Ct. Colony Recs.*, 10: 440–41, 617–18. For a comparison between population densities in these two towns, see Bruce C. Daniels, *The Connecticut Town: Growth and Development, 1635–1790* (Middletown, CT: Wesleyan University Press, 1979), 58.

22. Main, *Society and Economy*, 131–32, 134–35; Albert Laverne Olson, *Agricultural Economy and the Population in Eighteenth-Century Connecticut (Publications of the Tercentenary Commission of the State of Connecticut* [no. 40]) (New Haven, CT: Yale University Press, 1935), 5–7; Daniels, *Connecticut Town*, 55–56; John Warner Barber, *Connecticut Historical Collections*, 2nd ed. (New Haven, CT: Durrie & Peck and J. W. Barber, 1836), 254, 257; Bronson, *History of Waterbury*, 98–101. A census taken in 1756 listed Waterbury's population at 1,829; see Bronson, *History of Waterbury*, 248.

23. Bronson, *History of Waterbury*, 261–62; Bushman, *From Puritan to Yankee*, 57–58.

24. Bronson, *History of Waterbury*, 237–42. It is not clear when Northbury got its own school, but it was probably in the late 1730s, about when the adjoining parish of

Westbury got one. A portion of school funding came from renting out lands that had been allocated expressly for the support of education. Inhabitants in the town center were reluctant to share the proceeds with outlying districts such as Northbury. On the grievances of outliers in general, see Bushman, *From Puritan to Yankee*, ch. 4.

25. Bronson, *History of Waterbury*, 264–68, 270–72, 310–11; Dexter, *Bio. Sketches*, 1: 516–18; C. C. Goen, *Revivalism and Separatism in New England, 1740–1800* (New Haven, CT: Yale University Press, 1962), 61, 112; Plymouth, Connecticut, First Congregational Church Records, 1739–1897 [formerly Northbury Society], vol. 4 (Society Records, 1739–1785): 21–22, 28, microfilm reel no. 594 at CSL.

26. Bushman, *From Puritan to Yankee*, 216–19.

27. Donald Lines Jacobus and Edgar Francis Waterman, *Hale, House and Related Families Mainly of the Connecticut River Valley* (Hartford: Connecticut Historical Society, 1952), 290–91; Robert Charles Anderson, *The Great Migration Begins: Immigrants to New England 1620–1633*, 3 vols. (Boston: New England Historic Genealogical Society, 1995), 2: 834–38.

28. Jacobus and Waterman, *Hale, House and Related Families*, 291–92; John J. Currier, *History of Newbury, Massachusetts, 1635–1902* (Boston: Damrell & Upham, 1902), 264–65; Olson, *Agricultural Economy and the Population in Eighteenth-Century Connecticut*, 12.

29. Coventry ranked thirty-third among sixty-two Connecticut towns in terms of population in 1756 (compared to a rank of 29 for Waterbury) and thirty-fifth out of sixty-two towns in terms of taxable property in 1755 (compared to a rank of 27 for Waterbury). See *Ct. Colony Recs.*, 10: 440–41, 617–18.

30. Barber, *Connecticut Historical Collections*, 545; Toby L. Ditz, *Property and Kinship: Inheritance in Early Connecticut, 1750–1820* (Princeton, NJ: Princeton University Press, 1986), 16–17, 19; Daniels, *Connecticut Town*, 56; Anthony N. B. Garvan, *Architecture and Town Planning in Colonial Connecticut* (New Haven, CT: Yale University Press, 1951), 66–67; *Ct. Colony Recs.*, 10: 618.

31. Bushman, *From Puritan to Yankee*, 98; *Ct. Colony Recs.*, 8: 67–68.

32. In 1743, another group of Coventry residents petitioned the Assembly to be joined with worshippers from the towns of Hebron and Lebanon in yet another new ecclesiastical society. For these church disputes, see *Ct. Colony Recs.*, 8: 66–67, 303, 337–38, 476, 504, 536; 9: 70, 200, 301–2. On the geographical extent of Coventry, see Garvan, *Architecture and Town Planning*, 67.

33. Coventry Land Records, vol. 3, p. 418; microfilm at CSL. For the conversion ratio for Old Tenor to Lawful Money, see McCusker, *Money & Exchange*, 133–35. On the landholdings of farmers in their twenties, see Main, *Society and Economy*, 201.

34. Jacobus and Waterman, *Hale, House and Related Families*, 292; Henry Phelps Johnston, *Nathan Hale, 1776: Biography and Memorials* (New Haven, CT: Yale University Press, 1914), 8–9; Anne S. Lombard, *Making Manhood: Growing Up Male in Colonial New England* (Cambridge, MA: Harvard University Press, 2003), 88–89, 98–100; Lisa Wilson, *Ye Heart of a Man: The Domestic Life of Men in Colonial New England* (New Haven, CT: Yale University Press, 1999), 75–82, 209–10 n. 98.

35. Jacobus and Waterman, *Hale, House and Related Families*, 292–95; Gloria L. Main, *Peoples of a Spacious Land: Families and Cultures in Colonial New England*

(Cambridge, MA: Harvard University Press, 2001), 104, 109; Daniel Scott Smith, "Continuity and Discontinuity in Puritan Naming: Massachusetts 1771," *WMQ*, 3rd ser., 51 (1994): 68.

36. Jacobus, comp., "Families of Ancient New Haven," 584–85; Jacobus and Waterman, *Hale, House and Related Families*, 292–95; Main, *Peoples of a Spacious Land*, 110–11. Temperance Dunbar bore a total of fourteen children. About one out of seven children in eighteenth-century New England died before reaching adulthood. Average completed family size for a sample of Hingham, Massachusetts, families married between 1741 and 1760 was 7.16 children; see Daniel Scott Smith, "The Demographic History of Colonial New England," in Michael Gordon, ed., *The American Family in Social-Historical Perspective* (New York: St. Martin's Press, 1973), 406. On the importance of family labor, see Vickers, *Farmers & Fishermen*, 220–21.

37. I. W. Stuart, *Life of Captain Nathan Hale, the Martyr-Spy of the American Revolution* (Hartford, CT: F. A. Brown, 1856), 211–12. Stuart's book is hagiographic, but he did interview people with personal memories of the Hale family. For genealogical information, see Jacobus and Waterman, *Hale, House and Related Families*, 290–91. Richard's brother Samuel attended Harvard as a scholarship student; see John Langdon Sibley et al., *Biographical Sketches of Graduates of Harvard University, in Cambridge, Massachusetts*, 18 vols. to date (Cambridge, MA and Boston: Charles William Sever, 1873–), 10: 497–501.

38. On rising land prices in the mid-eighteenth century, see Main, *Society and Economy*, 119–20.

39. For average age at marriage for eighteenth-century New England men, see Smith, "The Demographic History of Colonial New England," 406; Main, *Peoples of a Spacious Land*, 80.

40. During the 1740s and 1750s, Hale regularly purchased land to augment his farm; see Coventry Land Recs., vol. 3, pp. 430–31; vol. 4, pp. 27–28, 255, 369, 494 at CSL. For Huntington's role in the Coventry church, see Dexter, *Bio. Sketches*, 2: 750. For Hale as deacon, see Johnston, *Nathan Hale, 1776*, p. 11; for Hale in the legislature, see *Ct. Colony Recs.*, 12: 546; 13: 93, 124, 284. For the political role of deacons, see Edward M. Cook Jr., *The Fathers of the Towns: Leadership and Community Structure in Eighteenth-Century New England* (Baltimore: Johns Hopkins University Press, 1976), 131–32.

41. Jacobus, comp., "Families of Ancient New Haven," 583–84; Richard Godbeer, *Sexual Revolution in Early America* (Baltimore: Johns Hopkins University Press, 2002), 228–30; Cornelia Hughes Dayton, *Women before the Bar: Gender, Law, & Society in Connecticut, 1639–1789* (Chapel Hill: University of North Carolina Press, 1995), 157–93; Daniel Scott Smith and Michael S. Hindus, "Premarital Pregnancy in America 1640–1971: An Overview and Interpretation," *Journal of Interdisciplinary History* 5 (Spring 1975): 537–70. Dayton describes a sharp rise in civil litigation at the same time that prosecutions for fornication diminished.

42. Cornelia Hughes Dayton, "Taking the Trade: Abortion and Gender Relations in an Eighteenth-Century New England Village," *WMQ*, 3rd ser., 48 (1991): 31; Laurel Thatcher Ulrich, *A Midwife's Tale: The Life of Martha Ballard, Based on Her Diary, 1785–1812* (New York: Alfred A. Knopf, 1990), 147–60.

43. Vickers, *Farmers & Fishermen*, 220–29; Philip J. Greven Jr., *Four Generations: Population, Land, and Family in Colonial Andover, Massachusetts* (Ithaca, NY: Cornell University Press, 1970), 206–7; Smith, "The Demographic History of Colonial New England," 406–7. Smith calculates the average age at first marriage in mid-eighteenth-century Hingham, Massachusetts, as 26 for men and 22.8 for women.

44. Jacobus, comp., "Families of Ancient New Haven," 583; Smith and Hindus, "Premarital Pregnancy in America 1640–1971," 542; Greven, *Four Generations*, 207.

45. For John Dunbar Sr.'s 1746 will, see microfilmed probate records for Wallingford, District of New Haven, reel 836, no. 3688 at CSL. His inventory includes a "Tayler's goose" and "tailer sheers." His father (another John Dunbar) is described as a tailor in a New Haven deed; see New Haven Land Records and Deeds, vol. 4, p. 218 at CSL. For the deeds of gift, see Wallingford Land Records, vol. 9, p. 384 (John) and vol. 10, p. 124 (Edward) at CSL. On the use of deeds of gift to transfer property to sons, see Greven, *Four Generations*, 131–33. Toby Ditz discovered that sons were more often named as executors in upland towns; see *Property and Kinship*, 146–47.

46. Lombard, *Making Manhood*, 18–45; E. Anthony Rotundo, *American Manhood: Transformations in Masculinity from the Revolution to the Modern Era* (New York: Basic Books, 1993), 2; Wilson, *Ye Heart of a Man*, 115–39; John Demos, *Past, Present, and Personal: The Family and The Life Course in American History* (New York: Oxford University Press, 1986), 41–48.

47. Johnston, *Nathan Hale, 1776*, 7–10; Seymour, *Doc. Life*, 80.

48. For Dunbar's committee service, see Plymouth, Connecticut, First Congregational Church Records, 1739–1897 [formerly Northbury Society], 4: 26–27, microfilm reel no. 594, at CSL.

49. Moses Dunbar mentions his different relationships with his mother and father in "Last Speech."

CHAPTER 2

1. Toby L. Ditz, *Property and Kinship: Inheritance in Early Connecticut, 1750–1820* (Princeton, NJ: Princeton University Press, 1986), 111–15; Gloria L. Main, *Peoples of a Spacious Land: Families and Cultures in Colonial New England* (Cambridge, MA: Harvard University Press, 2001), 79; Laurel Thatcher Ulrich, *A Midwife's Tale: The Life of Martha Ballard, Based on Her Diary, 1785–1812* (New York: Alfred A. Knopf, 1990), 138–44; Ellen K. Rothman, *Hands and Hearts: A History of Courtship in America* (Cambridge, MA: Harvard University Press, 1987), 76.

2. *Ct. Colony Recs.*, 4: 136; Main, *Peoples of a Spacious Land*, 79–80; Rothman, *Hands and Hearts*, 78–80; Ulrich, *Midwife's Tale*, 140–42.

3. Oscar Zeichner, *Connecticut's Years of Controversy, 1750–1776* (Chapel Hill: University of North Carolina Press, 1949), 46–48; *Connecticut Courant*, December 3, 1764, p. 1.

4. Donald Lines Jacobus, comp., "Families of Ancient New Haven," *New Haven Genealogical Magazine* 3 (1925): 584; 4 (1927): 942. Although Bede Dunbar was baptized on July 28, 1765, fourteen months after her parents' wedding, she was almost certainly the product of a premarital pregnancy. Little else could explain the marriage of two teenagers in colonial New England.

5. Jacobus, "Families of Ancient New Haven," 3: 583–84.

6. For Jerome's land in Northbury, see Waterbury Land Records, vol. 12, p. 198, at CSL.

7. Cornelia Hughes Dayton, "Taking the Trade: Abortion and Gender Relations in an Eighteenth-Century New England Village," *WMQ*, 3rd ser., 48 (1991): 34; Laurel Thatcher Ulrich, *The Age of Homespun: Objects and Stories in the Creation of an American Myth* (New York: Alfred A. Knopf, 2001), 212–14, 219.

8. Harry C. Durston, comp., "Preprints from compiler's forthcoming 'Genealogy of the Jerome Family,'" typescript at the CSL, p. 1; will and inventory for Timothy Jerome (1750), Probate Records of Wallingford, vol. 7, 588–60, at CSL. The inventory includes four slaves worth a total of £1,040 (probably Old Tenor money); Jerome's slaveholding is also mentioned in Charles Henry Stanley Davis, *History of Wallingford, Conn.* (Meriden, CT: privately published, 1870), 342.

9. For the deed of gift, see Farmington Land Records, vol. 7, p. 374; for Jerome's marriages, see Durston, pp. 1–2, both at CSL. A daughter named Mary died in May 1737 at about the same time as Sarah Cook Jerome, suggesting that the mother died in, or shortly after, childbirth.

10. Founded in 1645, Farmington grew to 3,700 inhabitants by the time of the 1756 census, ranking seventh of sixty-two towns in terms of population. It ranked fifth in taxable wealth as of October 1755; see *Ct. Colony Recs.*, 10: 440–41, 617–18. See also Christopher P. Bickford, *Farmington in Connecticut* (Canaan, NH: Phoenix, 1982), 94, 95, 130–33, 142; John C. Pease and John M. Niles, *A Gazetteer of the States of Connecticut and Rhode-Island* (Hartford, CT: William S. Marsh, 1819), 71–72.

11. According to Jackson Turner Main, about 18 percent of Connecticut farmers in their thirties owned 100 acres or more; see *Society and Economy in Colonial Connecticut* (Princeton, NJ: Princeton University Press, 1985), 201. For Jerome's land transactions, see Farmington Land Records, vol. 9, p. 559; vol. 10, p. 44; vol. 12, p. 329; vol. 14, pp. 34, 215, 359, 460; vol. 15, p. 157; vol. 16, p. 73; vol. 17, pp. 70–71, at CSL.

12. Paul B. Moyer, *Wild Yankees: The Struggle for Independence along Pennsylvania's Revolutionary Frontier* (Ithaca, NY: Cornell University Press, 2007), 17; Julian P. Boyd, ed., *The Susquehannah Company Papers*, 11 vols. (Ithaca, NY: Cornell University Press, 1930–1971), 1: 13–15.

13. Boyd, ed., *Susquehannah Company Papers*, 2: 130–33, 135, 139, 142–45, 204–7 (quote on p. 206); Moyer, *Wild Yankees*, 18–22.

14. Boyd, ed., *Susquehannah Company Papers*, 2: xvii–xxxix, 241–47, 254–57, 277–78; Fred Anderson, *Crucible of War: The Seven Years' War and the Fate of Empire in British North America, 1754–1766* (New York: Alfred A. Knopf, 2000), 529–34.

15. Boyd, ed., *Susquehannah Company Papers*, 3: xx–xxxiii, 91–93, 130–35.

16. Moyer, *Wild Yankees*, 27; Eric Hinderaker and Peter C. Mancall, *At the Edge of Empire: The Backcountry in British North America* (Baltimore: Johns Hopkins University Press, 2003), 135–37.

17. Moyer, *Wild Yankees*, 28–31; Boyd, ed., *Susquehannah Company Papers*, 4: 97; 5: 41–44. In December 1772, Jerome appeared before witnesses in Farmington to register a sale of land; see Bristol Land Records, vol. 2, p. 264, in the CSL.

18. The 1785 inventory of Jerome's estate lists £11 and 6 shillings "advanced" to Phoebe, presumably as her marriage portion, since by this date she had been dead

for nearly a decade; see Farmington Probate Records, #1601, microfilm reel no. 376; for the land sale, see Waterbury Land Records, vol. 12, p. 198, at CSL.

19. Waterbury Land Records, vol. 13, p. 259, at CSL.

20. Nearly two-thirds of a sample of Connecticut farmers aged twenty-one to twenty-nine possessed estates of twenty acres or more; see Main, *Society and Economy in Colonial Connecticut*, 201.

21. "Last Speech."

22. "Last Speech."

23. I am grateful to Bruce Steiner for help in sorting out the religious leanings of the Dunbar and Hall families, which he shared in a personal communication. For the religious controversy in Wallingford, see Benjamin Trumbull, *A Complete History of Connecticut, Civil and Ecclesiastical*, . . . , 2 vols. (New London, CT: H. D. Utley, 1898), 2: 408–49. Moses Dunbar referred to his mother's affection in his "Last Speech."

24. Brooks Mather Kelley, *Yale: A History* (New Haven, CT: Yale University Press, 1974), 31–33; Bruce E. Steiner, *Connecticut Anglicans in the Revolutionary Era: A Study in Communal Tensions* (Hartford: American Revolution Bicentennial Commission of Connecticut, 1978), 9.

25. Steiner, *Connecticut Anglicans*, 9–10; Kenneth Walter Cameron, ed., *Connecticut Churchmanship: Records and Historical Papers Concerning the Anglican Church in Connecticut in the Eighteenth and Early Nineteenth Centuries* (Hartford, CT: Transcendental Books, 1969), 17; E. LeRoy Pond, *The Tories of Chippeny Hill, Connecticut* (New York: Grafton Press, 1909), 11–12. The quote is from a 1759 letter from Francis Allison to Ezra Stiles, reprinted in Franklin Bowditch Dexter, ed., *Extracts from the Itineraries and Other Miscellanies of Ezra Stiles, D.D., LL.D. 1755–1794, with a Selection from his Correspondence* (New Haven, CT: Yale University Press, 1916), 424.

26. Steiner, *Connecticut Anglicans*, 11–12. The New Cambridge sacramental vessels are described in Plymouth, Connecticut, Records of St. Matthew's Episcopal Church (formerly the Episcopal Church in New Cambridge or Bristol), Records, 1744–1829, p. 21, copied by X. Alanson Welton, on microfilm reel no. 595 at CSL. For Congregationalist vessels, see Philip D. Zimmerman, "The Lord's Supper in Early New England: The Setting and the Service," in Peter Benes, ed., *New England Meeting House and Church: 1630–1850* (Boston: Boston University, 1979), 128–33.

27. James B. Bell, *A War of Religion: Dissenters, Anglicans, and the American Revolution* (Basingstoke: Palgrave Macmillan, 2008), 241; Dexter, *Bio. Sketches*, 2: 492–94.

28. Dexter, *Bio. Sketches*, 2: 493.

29. Sheldon S. Cohen, *Connecticut's Loyalist Gadfly: The Reverend Samuel Andrew Peters* (Hartford, CT: American Revolution Bicentennial Commission of Connecticut, 1976), 8; Charles Mampoteng, "The Reverend Samuel Peters, M.A., Missionary at Hebron, Connecticut, 1760–1774," *Historical Magazine of the Protestant Episcopal Church* 5 (1936): 76–77. For a nearly contemporaneous account of another voyage by a candidate for ordination, see *The Rev. John Tyler's Journal* (San Francisco: C. A. Murdock & Co., 1894), 8. Julie Flavell describes the experiences of colonial visitors to Georgian London in *When London Was Capital of America* (New Haven, CT: Yale University Press, 2010).

30. This paragraph draws on the experiences of John Tyler, a Wallingford native who traveled to London for ordination in 1768; see *Rev. John Tyler's Journal*, passim. See also Flavell, *When London Was Capital of America*, 9, 125.

31. Mampoteng, "Reverend Samuel Peters, M.A.," 77–78; H. P. Thompson, *Into All Lands: The History of the Society for the Propagation of the Gospel in Foreign Parts, 1701–1950* (London: S. P. C. K., 1951), 84–91; Bell, *War of Religion*, 27–29; *Rev. John Tyler's Journal*, 9–10; Dexter, *Bio. Sketches*, 2: 493.

32. Francis Hawks and William Perry, *Documentary History of the Protestant Episcopal Church in the United States of America*, 2 vols. (New York: James Pott, 1863–64), 1: 308–9, 2:17; SPG Recs., Letter Series B (1701–1786), vol. 23, p. 337.

33. SPG Recs., Letter Series B (1701–1786), vol. 23, pp. 338–41. For Scovil's marriage, see Dexter, *Bio. Sketches*, 2: 494.

34. The figures for Scovil's congregations date from 1765. See SPG Recs., Letter Series B (1701–1786), vol. 23, pp. 339, 341; Plymouth, Connecticut, Congregational Church (formerly Northbury Society) Records, 1765–1810, in two volumes; 1: 1 (microfilm reel #328 at CSL).

35. SPG Recs., Letter Series B (1701–1786), vol. 13, pp. 341–43, Pond, *Tories of Chippeny Hill*, 84–85.

36. Dunbar referred to Scovil as a "Missionary" in his "Last Speech," a designation linked to Anglican ministers' duty as SPG-funded clergy to recruit new church members.

37. Bruce E. Steiner notes that many rural (though not urban) Anglicans in Connecticut tended to be poor; see "New England Anglicanism: A Genteel Faith?" *WMQ*, 3d ser., 27 (1970): 122–35. For the size of New Cambridge parish, see SPG Recs., Letter Series B (1701–1786), vol. 23, p. 341. For Bede's baptism, see Plymouth, Connecticut, St. Matthew's Episcopal Church (formerly the Episcopal Church in New Cambridge or Bristol), Records, 1744–1829, [copy by X. Alanson Welton on microfilm reel #329 at CSL], Record of Baptisms, p. 32.

38. *Connecticut Courant*, June 24, 1765, pp. 6–7.

39. Anderson, *Crucible of War*, 562, 574–80; Edmund Morgan and Helen Morgan, *The Stamp Act Crisis: Prologue to Revolution*, 2nd ed. (New York: Collier Books, 1962), 36–46.

40. Morgan and Morgan, *Stamp Act Crisis*, 96–262, quotation on p. 139; *Ct. Colony Recs.*, 12: 410.

41. Steiner, *Connecticut Anglicans*, 16–17; Morgan and Morgan, *Stamp Act Crisis*, 163–64, 256, 258, 297; Zeichner, *Connecticut's Years of Controversy*, 51–52, 60–65; Lawrence Henry Gipson, *American Loyalist: Jared Ingersoll* (New Haven, CT: Yale University Press, 1920), 168–73; *Connecticut Courant*, September 2, 1765, p. 2.

42. Steiner, *Connecticut Anglicans*, 17; Morgan and Morgan, *Stamp Act Crisis*, 297; Richard Bushman, *From Puritan to Yankee: Character and the Social Order in Connecticut, 1690–1765* (Cambridge, MA: Harvard University Press, 1967), 262–63; Zeichner, *Connecticut's Years of Controversy*, 50–77.

43. Hawks and Perry, *Documentary Hist. of the Protestant Episcopal Church*, 2: 81, 92; Steiner, *Connecticut Anglicans*, 17–18 (Beach quotation on p. 18). For additional examples of similar ministerial reports, see Kenneth Walter Cameron, ed., *The Church of England in Pre-Revolutionary Connecticut: New Documents and Letters*

Concerning the Loyalist Clergy and the Plight of Their Surviving Church (Hartford, CT: Transcendental Books, 1976), 136, 138; SPG Recs., Letter Series B (1701–1786), vol. 23, p. 377.

44. *Connecticut Courant*, May 26, 1766, p. 4; *New-London Gazette*, May 23, 1766, p. 3; Zeichner, *Connecticut's Years of Controversy*, 75–76; Morgan and Morgan, *Stamp Act Crisis*, 327–52.

45. Cameron, ed., *Church of England in Pre-Revolutionary Connecticut*, 132–33, 135, 141–42, 144–45, 163; Hawks and Perry, *Documentary Hist. of the Protestant Episcopal Church*, 2: 103–4, 176–77; SPG Recs., Letter Series B (1701–1786), vol. 23, pp. 342, 343, 377; Steiner, *Connecticut Anglicans*, 24–25.

46. Steiner, *Connecticut Anglicans*, 24–26; Bell, *War of Religion*, 67–80; Nancy L. Rhoden, *Revolutionary Anglicanism: The Colonial Church of England Clergy during the American Revolution* (New York: New York University Press, 1999), 46–63.

47. Harold E. Selesky, ed., *Encyclopedia of the American Revolution*, 2nd ed., 2 vols. (Detroit: Charles Scribner's Sons, 2006), 2: 1158–59.

48. Steiner, *Connecticut Anglicans*, 22–23; Zeichner, *Connecticut's Years of Controversy*, 83–87; Cameron, ed., *Church of England in Pre-Revolutionary Connecticut*, 154–57 (quotations on pp. 154, 155).

49. Steiner, *Connecticut Anglicans*, 24; Zeichner, *Connecticut's Years of Controversy*, 87–89; Selesky, ed., *Encyclopedia of the American Revolution*, 2: 846.

50. *Connecticut Courant*, March 19, 1770, p. 1; Zeichner, *Connecticut's Years of Controversy*, 92–95. For the Boston Massacre, see Hiller B. Zobel, *The Boston Massacre* (New York: Norton, 1970). For the Whig ideology that framed many colonists' understanding of the imperial crisis, see Bernard Bailyn, *The Ideological Origins of the American Revolution* (Cambridge, MA: Harvard University Press, 1967).

51. T. H. Breen, *The Marketplace of Revolution: How Consumer Politics Shaped American Independence* (New York: Oxford University Press, 2004), 289–93; for advertisements, see, for instance, *Connecticut Courant*, June 1, 1773, pp. 2, 5.

52. On the efforts of Boston radicals to keep colonists everywhere vigilant during the so-called quiet period of 1770–1773, see Richard D. Brown, *Revolutionary Politics in Massachusetts: The Boston Committee of Correspondence and the Towns, 1772–1774* (Cambridge, MA: Harvard University Press, 1970), esp. chs. 3–6; Elizabeth P. McCaughey, *From Loyalist to Founding Father: The Political Odyssey of William Samuel Johnson* (New York: Columbia University Press, 1980), 152–53; *Connecticut Journal*, February 12, 1773, p. 1 (quotation); *Connecticut Courant*, June 1, 1773. Zeichner suggests that the author of the *Connecticut Journal* essay was John Trumbull; see *Connecticut's Years of Controversy*, 137, 310, n 46.

53. Conn. Arch., Militia Records, series II, vol. 6, no. 1338.

54. Jacobus, "Families of Ancient New Haven," 3: 583–85; quotations from "Last Speech." On mothers' roles as sources of emotional support in families, see Anne S. Lombard, *Making Manhood: Growing Up Male in Colonial New England* (Cambridge, MA: Harvard University Press, 2003), 20–21, 43. For widowers' propensity to remarry, see Main, *Peoples of a Spacious Land*, 85.

55. In his last speech, Dunbar stated that he and Phoebe had seven children, five of whom were alive in March 1777. The New Cambridge church records, however, record the baptisms of only three: Bede on July 28, 1765, a son Zina on May 30,

1773, and a daughter Phoebe on December 4, 1774. Some of the "missing" children almost certainly were born in the eight-year span between the baptisms of Bede and Zina. See Plymouth, Connecticut, St. Matthew's Episcopal Church (formerly the Episcopal church in New Cambridge or Bristol), Records, 1744–1829; Baptisms, 1747–99, pp. 32, 34, 35; copy by X. Alanson Welton, microfilm reel no. 329 at the CSL. For Dunbar's land sale, see Waterbury Land Records, vol. 15, p. 224 at the CSL. For Ebenezer Cook, see Jacobus, "Families of Ancient New Haven," 1:443. For 40 acres as a viable farm, see Main, *Society and Economy in Colonial Connecticut*, 200–201.

56. J. William Frost, *Connecticut Education in the Revolutionary Era* (Chester, CT: Pequot Press, 1974), 14; Plymouth, Connecticut, First Congregational Church Records, 1739–1897, vol. 4, p. 39, microfilm reel #594 at the CSL.

CHAPTER 3

1. Seymour, *Doc. Life*, 493.
2. Dexter, *Bio. Sketches*, 3: 357–58.
3. Conrad Edick Wright, *Revolutionary Generation: Harvard Men and the Consequences of Independence* (Amherst: University of Massachusetts Press, 2005), 18; Dexter, *Bio. Sketches*, 3: 357; Donald Lines Jacobus and Edgar Francis Waterman, *Hale, House and Related Families, Mainly of the Connecticut River Valley* (Hartford: Connecticut Historical Society, 1952), 290–92; Seymour, *Doc. Life*, 334.
4. Wright, *Revolutionary Generation*, 44–46, 229; Lawrence A. Cremin, *American Education: The Colonial Experience, 1607–1783* (New York: Harper & Row, 1970), 554.
5. J. William Frost, *Connecticut Education in the Revolutionary Era* (Chester, CT: Pequot Press, 1974), 14.
6. Dexter, *Bio. Sketches*, 2: 750–55; Seymour, *Doc. Life*, 80.
7. Dexter, *Bio. Sketches*, 2: 750–55; *The Laws of Yale-College, in New-Haven, in Connecticut, Enacted by the President and Fellows* (New Haven, CT: Thomas and Samuel Green, 1774), 3; Robert Middlekauff, *Ancients and Axioms: Secondary Education in Eighteenth-Century New England* (New Haven, CT: Yale University Press, 1963), 71–102.
8. Seymour, *Doc. Life*, 95–107; *Laws of Yale College*, 3–4. Another son, David, went to Yale, graduating in 1785, while Billy Hale trained as a blacksmith. See Jacobus and Waterman, *Hale, House and Related Families*, 294; Seymour, *Doc. Life*, 17. Gloria Main calculated the daily wage for male New England farm laborers at 21.8 pence; at that rate, it would take a laborer 275 days to earn £25. See Gloria L. Main, "Gender, Work, and Wages in Colonial New England," *WMQ*, 3rd ser., 51 (1994): 48.
9. Rollin G. Osterweis, *Three Centuries of New Haven, 1638–1938* (New Haven, CT: Yale University Press, 1953), 38, 75; Samuel Davis, "Journal of a Tour to Connecticut [1789]," *Proceedings of the Massachusetts Historical Society*, 11 (1869–70): 15–16; Franklin Bowditch Dexter, ed., *Extracts from the Itineraries and Other Miscellanies of Ezra Stiles, D.D., LL.D., 1755–1794, with a Selection from his Correspondence* (New Haven, CT: Yale University Press, 1916), 28, 42–49, 157; Edmund S. Morgan, *The Gentle Puritan: A Life of Ezra Stiles* (Chapel Hill: University of North Carolina Press, 1962), 311–12.

10. Brooks Mather Kelley, *Yale: A History* (New Haven, CT: Yale University Press, 1974), 59–60; Seymour, *Doc. Life*, 430.

11. Dexter, *Bio. Sketches*, 3: 365, 466–512. The age profile of Harvard students was quite similar; see Wright, *Revolutionary Generation*, 228.

12. Seymour, *Doc. Life*, 109; Dexter, *Bio Sketches*, 3: 466–512; for a Harvard comparison, see Wright, *Revolutionary Generation*, 229.

13. Kelley, *Yale*, 75–77; Dexter, *Bio. Sketches*, 3: 466–512.

14. Kelley, *Yale*, 77; Dexter, *Bio. Sketches*, 3: 264.

15. Franklin Bowditch Dexter, *Sketch of the History of Yale University* (New York: Henry Holt, 1887), 27–38; Kelley, *Yale*, 60–72; Alexander Cowie, *Educational Problems at Yale College in the Eighteenth Century*, Tercentenary Commission of the State of Connecticut, Committee on Historical Publications, vol. 55 (New Haven, CT: Yale University Press, 1936), 10–25; Louis Leonard Tucker, *Puritan Protagonist: President Thomas Clap of Yale College* (Chapel Hill: University of North Carolina Press, 1962).

16. Kelley, *Yale*, 73–74; Yale Manuscripts and Archives, Student Life & Discipline, RU 811, Box 1, Folder 1, at the Sterling Memorial Library, Yale University; *Providence Gazette*, July 13–20, 1771.

17. Kelley, *Yale*, 42–43, 80; Morgan, *Gentle Puritan*, 43; Cowie, *Educational Problems at Yale*, 6–7; *Laws of Yale College*, 6–7; Yale Manuscripts and Archives, Student Life & Discipline, RU 811, Box 1, Folder 1.

18. Cowie, *Educational Problems at Yale*, 7; Dexter, *Bio. Sketches*, 3: 467.

19. Dexter, *Bio. Sketches*, 3: 264, 305–10.

20. *Laws of Yale College*, 7; Cowie, *Educational Problems at Yale*, 11–14.

21. Dexter, *Bio. Sketches*, 3: 251–52.

22. Kenneth Silverman, *A Cultural History of the American Revolution: Painting, Music, Literature, and the Theatre in the Colonies and the United States from the Treaty of Paris to the Inauguration of George Washington, 1763–1789* (New York: Columbia University Press, 1987), 221–24; Christopher Grasso, *A Speaking Aristocracy: Transforming Public Discourse in Eighteenth-Century Connecticut* (Chapel Hill: University of North Carolina Press, 1999), 288–99; John Trumbull, *An Essay on the Use and Advantages of the Fine Arts* (New Haven, CT: T. and S. Green, 1770), quotation on p. 4; John Trumbull, *The Progress of Dulness* (New Haven, CT: Thomas and Samuel Green, 1772), quotations on pp. 12, 26. Parts two and three of Trumbull's satire ridiculed Dick Hairbrain, whose nouveau-riche parents send him to college to compensate for his rural origins, and the insufferable coquette Harriet Simper, who ends up as Tom Brainless's wife. Thus one target of Trumbull's ridicule was the egalitarian impulse that was so important to students like David Avery.

23. Silverman, *Cultural History of the American Revolution*, 221–23.

24. Kelley, *Yale*, 81–82; Silverman, *Cultural History of the American Revolution*, 222.

25. Richard L. Bushman, *The Refinement of America: Persons, Houses, Cities* (New York: Alfred A. Knopf, 1992), 3–138; David S. Shields, *Civil Tongues & Polite Letters in British America* (Chapel Hill: University of North Carolina Press, 1997), xxvii–xxix.

26. William L. Kingsley, ed., *Yale College: A Sketch of Its History*, 2 vols. (New York: Henry Holt, 1879), 1: 78–79, 95, 308, 315; Kelley, *Yale*, 107. The names of Linonia

members can be gleaned from the Society's minutes, some of which are reprinted in Seymour, *Doc. Life*, 110–44. On exclusivity in student organizations, see Nicholas L. Syrett, *The Company He Keeps: A History of White College Fraternities* (Chapel Hill: University of North Carolina Press, 2009), 4. It has been suggested that the name "Linonia" was meant to invoke the goddess of flax; see Kingsley, ed., *Yale College*, 1: 309. Timothy Dwight was also a member. David Avery, former carpenter's apprentice, and James Nichols, college rebel, both joined the Brothers in Unity; see *A Catalogue of the Society of Brothers in Unity, Yale College, Founded 1768* (New Haven, CT: Hitchcock and Stafford, 1841), 14, 16.

27. Shields, *Civil Tongues & Polite Letters*, xviii, 211–14; Catherine O'Donnell Kaplan, *Men of Letters in the Early Republic: Cultivating Forums of Citizenship* (Chapel Hill: University of North Carolina Press, 2008), 14–19; Lawrence E. Klein, *Shaftesbury and the Culture of Politeness: Moral Discourse and Cultural Politics in Early Eighteenth-Century England* (New York: Cambridge University Press, 1994), 3–4.

28. J. David Hoeveler, *Creating the American Mind: Intellect and Politics in the Colonial Colleges* (Lanham, MD: Rowman & Littlefield, 2002), 62–63; *A Catalogue of the Library of Yale-College in New Haven* (New London, CT: T. Green, 1743); for borrowing privileges, see *Laws of Yale College*, 22–23. Underclassmen, on occasion, could receive special permission to borrow a book from the college library. On the significance of reading for would-be gentlemen, see Shields, *Civil Tongues & Polite Letters*, 298; Bushman, *Refinement of America*, 88.

29. Seymour, *Doc. Life*, 121, 128, 151; Dexter, *Bio. Sketches*, 3: 193–94, 395–96. The full title of Jonas Hanway's work is *An Historic Account of the British Trade over the Caspian Sea, with a Journal of Travels from London through Russia into Persia.*

30. Seymour, *Doc. Life*, 151–53; Catalogue of Books Belonging to the Linonian Society, 1796, at Sterling Memorial Library, Yale University; Kathy M. Umbricht Straka, "The Linonian Society Library of Yale College: The First Years, 1768–1790," *Yale University Library Gazette* 54 (March 1980): 183–92.

31. Seymour, *Doc. Life*, 110–50.

32. Seymour, *Doc. Life*, 128, 130, 131.

33. On the importance of oratory in America during this period, see Sandra M. Gustafson, *Eloquence Is Power: Oratory & Performance in Early America* (Chapel Hill: University of North Carolina Press, 2000), 140–70.

34. Dexter, *Bio. Sketches*, 3: 483; Seymour, *Doc. Life*, 124–26, 129, 131–32, 134, 141.

35. Enoch performed just nine times during the same period. Seymour, *Doc. Life*, 121, 124, 128–30, 132–38, 140–42, 144. Enoch was usually identified as Hale 1[mus] and Nathan as Hale 2[dus] to reflect their birth order.

36. Seymour, *Doc. Life*, 124, 127, 494. Only three letters from Richard to his sons at Yale survive.

37. Seymour, *Doc. Life*, 505; Dexter, *Bio. Sketches*, 3: 469–70, 486–90, 494–95, 511–12; for Wyllys, see also *Catalogue of the Society of Brothers in Unity*, 17.

38. For discussions of the changing meaning of friendship, especially among males, in this period, see Richard Godbeer, *The Overflowing of Friendship: Love between Men and the Creation of the American Republic* (Baltimore: Johns Hopkins University Press, 2009); Alan Bray, *The Friend* (Chicago: University of Chicago Press, 2003); Naomi Tadmor, *Family and Friends in Eighteenth-Century England: Household, Kinship, and Patronage* (New York: Cambridge University Press, 2001).

39. Godbeer, *Overflowing of Friendship*, 51–54.

40. Seymour, *Doc. Life*, 124, 126–27, 134–35, 142–44; Arthur W. Bloom, "The Emergence of Theatrical Entertainment in New Haven, Connecticut, during the Eighteenth Century," *New Haven Colony Historical Society*, 17 (1968): 123–39, esp. pp. 126, 127.

41. Records of the Linonian Society, 1753–1870, RU 206, Ser. II, Box 2, Folder 1, at Sterling Memorial Library, Yale University. Roger Alden's speech in this folder is missing some pages; a more complete version of the speech appears in a photostat copy in Oliver Lewis's commonplace book in Box 8, Folder 31.

42. Seymour, *Doc. Life*, 124, 126–27, 134–35, 142–44; in 1771, Linonians planned also to perform Richard Steele's *The Conscious Lovers*, but did not in the end do so. See also Bloom, "Emergence of Theatrical Entertainment," 126–29; Jason Shaffer, *Performing Patriotism: National Identity in the Colonial and Revolutionary American Theater* (Philadelphia: University of Pennsylvania Press, 2007), 131–43; Silverman, *Cultural History of the American Revolution*, 63, 220.

43. Bloom, "Emergence of Theatrical Entertainment," 124–25, 134; Cowie, *Educational Problems at Yale*, 8, 28–29; *Laws of Yale College*, 11; Kelley, *Yale*, 107–8. Kelley suggests that plays were informally allowed so long as there were no women in the audience.

44. For examples of commencement speeches, see *A Valedictory Oration, Pronounced at the Commencement, held in Nassau-Hall, in New-Jersey; September 26, 1759, By one of the Bachelors: a youth of eighteen* (New York, 1759); Samuel Davies, *Religion and Public Spirit; A Valedictory Address to the Senior Class . . .* (New York, 1761); Timothy Dwight, *A Valedictory Address to the Young Gentlemen, who Commenced Bachelors of Arts, at Yale-College, July 25th* (New Haven, CT., 1776). See also the description of Yale's 1769 commencement, when "Mr. Ingersoll" (probably Jared Ingersoll) delivered the valedictory oration; *Connecticut Courant*, September 25, 1769, p. 1.

45. Records of the Linonian Society, 1753–1870, RU 206, Ser. II, Box 2, Folder 1. The speeches by Billings and Hale are reprinted in Seymour, *Doc. Life*, 145–50.

46. Records of the Linonian Society, 1753–1870, RU 206, Ser. II, Box 2, Folder 1.

47. Records of the Linonian Society, 1753–1870, RU 206, Ser. II, Box 2, Folder 1; Nicole Eustace, *Passion Is the Gale: Emotion, Power, and the Coming of the American Revolution* (Chapel Hill: University of North Carolina Press, 2008), 64–69, 76–82; Godbeer, *Overflowing of Friendship*, 10–13; Sarah Knott, *Sensibility and the American Revolution* (Chapel Hill: University of North Carolina Press, 2009), 23–24, 112–22.

48. *Ct. Colony Recs.*, 13: 236; Oscar Zeichner, *Connecticut's Years of Controversy, 1750–1776* (Chapel Hill: University of North Carolina Press, 1969), 128–42. Richard Hale typically served at the spring legislative session, which convened in Hartford.

49. John Roche, *The Colonial Colleges in the War for American Independence* (Millwood, NY: Associated Faculty Press, 1986), 11–12, 20, 57; Louis Leonard Tucker, *Connecticut's Seminary of Sedition: Yale College* (Chester, CT: Pequot Press, 1974), 41–42; Dexter, *Bio. Sketches*, 3: 170; *Connecticut Courant*, January 16, 1769, p. 3.

50. Lawrence Henry Gipson suggests that Daggett held a long-standing grudge against Ingersoll for opposing his appointment as Yale's professor of divinity; see his *American Loyalist: Jared Ingersoll* (New Haven, CT: Yale University Press, 1971), 158–60; Tucker, *Connecticut's Seminary of Sedition*, 29–31; David W. Robson,

Educating Republicans: The College in the Era of the American Revolution, 1750–1800
(Westport, CT: Greenwood Press, 1985), 48; Roche, *Colonial Colleges*, 20; Hoeveler,
Creating the American Mind, 260, 269.

51. Tucker, *Connecticut's Seminary of Sedition*, 26–27; Kelley, *Yale*, 80–81.
52. Trumbull, *Essay on the Use and Advantages of the Fine Arts*, quotations on pp. 6, 8,
11, 12, 16. See also Silverman, *Cultural History of the American Revolution*, 161–62;
Grasso, *A Speaking Aristocracy*, 289–92; Joseph J. Ellis, *After the Revolution: Profiles of
Early American Culture* (New York: Norton, 1979), 8–9.
53. *Connecticut Journal*, September 21, 1770, p. 1; Ellis, *After the Revolution*, 24–26.
54. Robson, *Educating Republicans*, 14–18, 73–74, 81–83, 90; Cremin, *American
Education*, 460. For the influence of Commonwealth and Whig writers on
Revolutionary ideology, see Bernard Bailyn, *Ideological Origins of the American
Revolution* (Cambridge, MA: Harvard University Press, 1967), 34–54. For Yale
commencement theses, see Viro præstantissimo, ingenuis artibus ac sublimi
virtute omnique fœlicissimè gubernandi ratione ornatissimo, Jonathani
Trumbull . . . (New Haven, CT, 1770); Viro præstantissimo, ingenuis artibus ac
sublimi virtute omnique fœlicissimè gubernandi ratione ornatissimo, Jonathani
Trumbull . . . (New Haven, 1771); Viro præstantissimo, ingenuis artibus ac
sublimi virtute omnique fœlicissimè gubernandi ratione ornatissimo, Jonathani
Trumbull . . . (New Haven, 1772); these and a sampling of quaestiones topics
are available in the Early American Imprints database. Thanks to Jen Starkey
for help translating these titles. For Harvard commencement theses, see
Samuel Eliot Morison, *Three Centuries of Harvard, 1636–1936* (Cambridge,
MA: Harvard University Press, 1936), 90–91. Louis Tucker has argued that
colonial colleges fostered Whig political sympathies, though this seems to have
been less so at Yale than other colleges; see Louis Leonard Tucker, "Centers
of Sedition: Colonial Colleges and the American Revolution," *Proceedings of the
Massachusetts Historical Society*, 91 (1979): 16–34.
55. Seymour, *Doc. Life*, 151–53; Benjamin Franklin, *The Autobiography and other Writings
on Politics, Economics, and Virtue*, ed. Alan Houston (Cambridge: Cambridge
University Press, 2004), 12; Shaffer, *Performing Patriotism*, 131–33.
56. *Connecticut Journal*, September 10, 1773, p. 3; Dexter, *Bio. Sketches*, 3: 467.
57. Linda K. Kerber, *Women of the Republic: Intellect & Ideology in Revolutionary America*
(Chapel Hill: University of North Carolina Press, 1980), 24–27; Middlekauff,
Ancients and Axioms, 103–9; Kaplan, *Men of Letters*, 39–41; G. J. Barker-
Benfield, *The Culture of Sensibility: Sex and Society in Eighteenth-Century Britain*
(Chicago: University of Chicago Press, 1992), 237–38, 319–21.
58. The timing of these exams is somewhat confusing. Enoch Hale noted in his diary
that May 3 was the day for the "Seniors Examination," and he and Nathan were
back in Coventry by early June. He mentions that Nathan went back to New
Haven on June 2, but it is unclear if Enoch went along as well. On July 9, Benjamin
Tallmadge addressed a letter to Nathan at Yale College, asking therein for Nathan
to let him "know the Day of our Examination." The College Laws stipulated that
senior examinations would occur around July 20 each year. According to Enoch's
diary, both brothers appear to have been back in Coventry by July 27. See EH
Diary, entry for May 3, 1773; Seymour, *Doc. Life*, 3–4; *Laws of Yale College*, 8.

59. Dexter, *Bio. Sketches*, 3: 481.
60. Hale's ambition resembled that of many rural youths who came of age in the 1770s, especially those who had some college experience. See, for instance, Edward G. Gray, *The Making of John Ledyard: Empire and Ambition in the Life of an Early American Traveler* (New Haven, CT: Yale University Press, 2007); J. M. Opal, *Beyond the Farm: National Ambitions in Rural New England* (Philadelphia: University of Pennsylvania Press, 2008); John Fea, *The Way of Improvement Leads Home: Philip Vickers Fithian and the Rural Enlightenment in Early America* (Philadelphia: University of Pennsylvania Press, 2008).
61. Grasso, *A Speaking Aristocracy*, 431–41.

CHAPTER 4

1. *Connecticut Courant*, December 21, 1773, p. 3.
2. For two recent accounts of the Tea Party, see Benjamin L. Carp, *Defiance of the Patriots: The Boston Tea Party & the Making of America* (New Haven, CT: Yale University Press, 2010), and Alfred F. Young, *The Shoemaker and the Tea Party: Memory and the American Revolution* (Boston: Beacon Press, 1999).
3. Oscar Zeichner, *Connecticut's Years of Controversy, 1750–1776* (Chapel Hill: University of North Carolina Press, 1949), 143–60.
4. SPG Recs., Letter Series B (1701–1786), vol. 23, pp. 339, 348 (quote), 349. The doubling of Waterbury's Anglican population slightly outpaced the town's overall population growth. Between 1756 and 1774, colonial censuses record the number of white inhabitants in Waterbury growing from 1802 to 3498, about a 94 percent increase. Scovil's ministry, however, did not begin until 1759. For census information, see *Ct. Colony Recs.*, 14: 486, 492.
5. SPG Recs., Letter Series B, vol. 23, p. 349.
6. SPG Recs., Letter Series B, vol. 23, pp. 350–51; Dexter, *Bio. Sketches*, 3: 425–27.
7. SPG Recs., Letter Series B, vol. 23, p. 352; Dexter, *Bio. Sketches*, 3: 425.
8. SPG Recs., Letter Series B, vol. 23, pp. 340–44, 346–48.
9. Claremont's population in late 1773 was 423. SPG Recs., Letter Series B, vol. 23, pp. 343, 419, 420; Otis F. R. Waite, *History of the Town of Claremont, New Hampshire, . . .* (Manchester, NH: John B. Clarke, 1895), 26–30, 33.
10. For the numbers of New Cambridge families in 1765 and 1767, see SPG Recs., Letter Series B, vol. 23, pp. 341, 343.
11. Waterbury Land Records, vol. 15, p. 502 at CSL.
12. SPG Recs., Letter Series B, vol. 23, pp. 419; Jere R. Daniell, *Experiment in Republicanism: New Hampshire Politics and the American Revolution, 1741–1794* (Cambridge, MA: Harvard University Press, 1970), 16. By February 1774, Moses and Phoebe Dunbar probably had four children, although the baptismal records for New Cambridge list only two up to that point. Colonial New England families tended to produce a new child every two years or so, which suggests that at least two or possibly three Dunbar children arrived in the eight years between Bede's baptism in 1765 and Zina's in 1773.
13. The Dunbars' daughter Phoebe was baptized in New Cambridge church on December 4, 1774. If the baby was born in late November, and Moses did not leave for Claremont until a few weeks after selling his land to his father, Phoebe senior

would have been in the early stage of pregnancy at the time of his departure. For infant Phoebe's baptismal date, see Donald Lines Jacobus, comp., "Families of Ancient New Haven," *New Haven Genealogical Magazine* 3 (1925): 584. Other men who moved to Claremont arrived on their own, and then sent for their families; see Waite, *History of the Town of Claremont*, 39.

14. There is no record of Dunbar purchasing land in Claremont. The September 7, 1774, deed with Judd, however, describes him as "Moses Dunbar of Claremont aforesaid lately of Waterbury." Waterbury Land Records, vol. 18, p. 344 at CSL; Henry Bronson, *The History of Waterbury, Connecticut*, ... (Waterbury, CT: Bronson Brothers, 1858), 296; Waite, *History of the Town of Claremont*, 225. Forty acres was about the minimum for a viable farm in Connecticut; see Jackson Turner Main, *Society and Economy in Colonial Connecticut* (Princeton, NJ: Princeton University Press, 1985): 201.

15. Carp, *Defiance of the Patriots*, 185–94 (quote on p. 187); Robert Middlekauff, *The Glorious Cause: The American Revolution, 1763–1789* (rev. ed., New York: Oxford University Press, 2005), 233–37.

16. *Connecticut Courant*, May 17, 1774, p. 2; June 21, 1774, p. 1.

17. *Connecticut Courant*, May 24, 1774, p. 3; Mabel S. Hurlburt, *Farmington Town Clerks and Their Times (1645–1940)* (Hartford, CT: Finlay Brothers, 1943), 78; Christopher P. Bickford, *Farmington in Connecticut* (Canaan, NH: Phoenix, 1982), 169–70.

18. *Connecticut Courant*, June 7, 1774, p. 3; June 14, 1774, p. 3; June 21, 1774, p. 2; July 5, 1774, p. 4; Bickford, *Farmington in Connecticut*, 170; T. H. Breen, *American Insurgents, American Patriots: The Revolution of the People* (New York: Hill and Wang, 2010), 77–78, 116–27; David Ammerman, *In the Common Cause: American Response to the Coercive Acts of 1774* (Charlottesville: University Press of Virginia, 1974), 21–22.

19. K. G. Davies, ed., *Documents of the American Revolution 1770–1783 (Colonial Office Series)*, 21 vols. (Dublin: Irish University Press, 1972–81) 8: 165–66, 180–81; Ammerman, *In the Common Cause*, 15–16.

20. *By the Honorable Jonathan Trumbull ... A Proclamation* (Hartford, CT: Thomas and Samuel Green, 1774).

21. Sheldon S. Cohen, *Connecticut's Loyalist Gadfly: The Reverend Samuel Andrew Peters* (Hartford, CT: American Revolution Bicentennial Commission of Connecticut, 1977), 15–19; *Connecticut Courant*, September 12, 1774, p. 4; Zeichner, *Connecticut's Years of Controversy*, 175–76.

22. *Connecticut Courant*, September 19, 1774, p. 2; Bruce E. Steiner, *Connecticut Anglicans in the Revolutionary Era: A Study in Communal Tensions* (Hartford, CT: American Revolution Bicentennial Commission of Connecticut, 1978), 35–36.

23. David Henry Villers, "Loyalism in Connecticut, 1763–1783" (Ph.D. dissertation, University of Connecticut, 1975), 49–51; *Connecticut Courant*, October 17, 1774, pp. 1, 2.

24. Villers, "Loyalism in Connecticut," 48–49, 51–52; James B. Bell, *A War of Religion: Dissenters, Anglicans, and the American Revolution* (Basingstoke: Palgrave Macmillan, 2008), 125–38.

25. *Norwich Packet*, October 13, 1774, p. 3; *New-London Gazette*, October 24, 1774, p. 7; Cohen, *Connecticut's Loyalist Gadfly*, 20–22; Zeichner, *Connecticut's Years of Controversy*, 327; Villers, "Loyalism in Connecticut," 52–53.

26. Steiner, *Connecticut Anglicans*, 38–39; Zeichner, *Connecticut's Years of Controversy*, ch. 10; Villers, "Loyalism in Connecticut," 166–69. On crowd actions during the Revolution, see Gordon S. Wood, "A Note on Mobs in the American Revolution," *WMQ*, 3d ser., 23 (1966): 635–42.

27. Jack N. Rakove, *The Beginnings of National Politics: An Interpretive History of the Continental Congress* (New York: Knopf, 1979), 42–63; Ammerman, *In the Common Cause*, chs. 5–6.

28. Zeichner, *Connecticut's Years of Controversy*, 181–82; Ammerman, *In the Common Cause*, 107; *Ct. Colony Recs.*, 14: 485, 491 (about one in 25 Farmington men served on their town's committee); *Connecticut Journal*, December 2, 1774, p. 2; Farmington Town Meeting Records, pp. 430–31, microfilm reel 83896, the Connecticut Historical Society, Hartford. Towns other than Waterbury included Anglicans on committees of inspection, though their influence quickly waned; see Steiner, *Connecticut Anglicans*, 40–41.

29. Farmington Town Meeting Records, p. 430; Hurlburt, *Farmington Town Clerks*, 80–87. Royce's name appears in the New Cambridge Church Records. Leaming, whose brother was an Anglican minister, was almost certainly Anglican as well; see Epaphroditus Peck, *The Loyalists of Connecticut* (New Haven, CT: Yale University Press, 1934), 21.

30. Hurlburt, *Farmington Town Clerks*, 85–87; *Connecticut Courant*, April 3, 1775, p. 3; April 24, 1775, p. 1; for tea substitutes, see Carp, *Defiance of the Patriots*, 169.

31. Bronson, *History of Waterbury*, 331; SPG Recs., Letter Series B, vol. 23, p. 349; Hurlburt, *Farmington Town Clerks*, 84.

32. Waterbury Land Records, vol. 18, p. 6 at CSL. For the role of taverns in the political culture of Revolutionary New England, see David W. Conroy, *In Public Houses: Drink and the Revolution of Authority in Colonial Massachusetts* (Chapel Hill: University of North Carolina Press, 1995); for drink and training days, see *Ct. Colony Recs.*, 13: 580. Dunbar admitted in his "Last Speech" that he spoke freely about his political views.

33. Steiner, *Connecticut Anglicans*, 38; Robert McCluer Calhoon, *The Loyalists in Revolutionary America, 1760–1781* (New York: Harcourt Brace Jovanovich, 1965), 281–83; Breen, *American Insurgents, American Patriots*, 132–44; Davies, ed., *Documents of the American Revolution*, 8: 198, 211; Hurlburt, *Farmington Town Clerks*, 80.

34. Davies, ed., *Documents of the American Revolution*, 9: 102–3; David Hackett Fischer, *Paul Revere's Ride* (New York: Oxford University Press, 1994), 184–232.

35. Zeichner, *Connecticut's Years of Controversy*, 189–91; *Ct. Colony Recs.*, 14: 415–20, 434–35; *Connecticut Courant*, May 1 and May 8, 1775.

36. Bronson, *History of Waterbury*, 351–52; Conn. Arch., Militia Records, Series II, vol. 11: 2070a, b. As a resident of Northbury, Moses Dunbar would have served in the local militia, but surviving records do not indicate if he was a member of this particular company.

37. Bronson, *History of Waterbury*, 351–52; Steiner, *Connecticut Anglicans*, 46–47; *Ct. Colony Recs.*, 14: 439; Conn. Arch., Revolutionary Series I, vol. 1: 413a, 413b, 414–19. A similar militia controversy emerged in New Haven; see Zeichner, *Connecticut's Years of Controversy*, 196. Amos Bronson was a vestryman in Northbury's Anglican church; see SPG Recs., Letter Series B, vol. 23, p. 350.

38. Davies, ed., *Documents of the American Revolution*, 9: 143; Zeichner, *Connecticut's Years of Controversy*, 199–200; *New-London Gazette*, September 29, 1775.

39. *Connecticut Courant*, July 17, 1775, p. 3; July 31, 1775, p. 3; September 18, 1775, p. 3; *Connecticut Journal*, October 18, 1775, p. 4; Hurlburt, *Farmington Town Clerks*, 87–88; Zeichner, *Connecticut's Years of Controversy*, 200–202; Calhoon, *Loyalists in Revolutionary America*, 261–62.

40. Zeichner, *Connecticut's Years of Controversy*, 198–201; *Connecticut Courant*, September 18, 1775, p. 3; David H. Villers, "'King Mob' and the Rule of Law: Revolutionary Justice and the Suppression of Loyalism in Connecticut, 1774–1783," in Robert M. Calhoon, Timothy M. Barnes, and George A Rawlyk, eds., *Loyalists and Community in North America* (Westport, CT: Greenwood Press, 1994), 17–30; esp. 18–20.

41. Zeichner, *Connecticut's Years of Controversy*, 203–7; Steiner, *Connecticut Anglicans*, 49–50; *Connecticut Courant*, September 25, 1775, p. 3; William H. Nelson, *The American Tory* (Boston: Beacon Press, 1961), 97–98.

42. Richard Buel Jr., *Dear Liberty: Connecticut's Mobilization for the Revolutionary War* (Middletown, CT: Wesleyan University Press, 1980), 47–51; Zeichner, *Connecticut's Years of Controversy*, 204–5. For a description of the Quebec expedition, see Middlekauff, *Glorious Cause*, 309–14.

43. Villers, "'King Mob' and the Rule of Law," 17–30.

44. For Dunbar, see "Last Speech." Mary Beth Norton offers a succinct summary of loyalist views in "The Loyalist Critique of the Revolution," in *The Development of a Revolutionary Mentality* (Washington, DC: Library of Congress, 1972): 127–48. For the spectrum of loyalist beliefs in the colonies as a whole, see Calhoon, *Loyalists in Revolutionary America*, passim.

45. "Last Speech"; E. LeRoy Pond, *The Tories of Chippeny Hill, Connecticut: A Brief Account of the Loyalists of Bristol, Plymouth and Harwinton, who Founded St. Matthew's Church in East Plymouth in 1791* (New York: Grafton Press, 1909), 19, 42–43, 52.

46. Pond, *The Tories of Chippeny Hill*, 40–44, 53. Allan Kulikoff has drawn attention to, and called for further study of, violence in the Revolution; see "Revolutionary Violence and the Origins of American Democracy," *Journal of the Historical Society* 2 (2002): 229–60.

47. Pond, *The Tories of Chippeny Hill*, 43. On the predicament of Tory women, see Linda K. Kerber, *Women of the Republic: Intellect & Ideology in Revolutionary America* (Chapel Hill: University of North Carolina Press, 1980), 9, 36, 46–53; Mary Beth Norton, "Eighteenth-Century American Women in Peace and War: The Case of the Loyalists," *WMQ*, 3d ser., 33 (1976): 386–409; Sarah C. Chambers and Lisa Norling, "Choosing to Be a Subject: Loyalist Women in the Revolutionary Atlantic World," *Journal of Women's History* 20 (2008): 39–62.

48. Paul H. Smith, "The American Loyalists: Notes on Their Organization and Numerical Strength," *WMQ*, 3d ser., 25 (1968): 259–77; see especially p. 269. Smith's figure derives from enrollments in loyalist regiments. John Adams suggested that one in three colonists remained loyal to Britain; see John Adams to James Lloyd, January 1815 in Charles Francis Adams, ed., *The Works of John Adams*, 10 vols. (Boston: Little, Brown, 1856), 10: 110.

49. On the components of British national identity, see Linda Colley, *Britons: Forging the Nation 1707–1837* (New Haven, CT: Yale University Press, 1992). For discussions of Loyalist ideology, see Janice Potter, *The Liberty We Seek: Loyalist Ideology in Colonial New York and Massachusetts* (Cambridge, MA: Harvard University Press, 1983); Calhoon, *Loyalists in Revolutionary America*, esp. pp. 257–65, 502; Wallace Brown, *The Good Americans: The Loyalists in the American Revolution* (New York: William Morrow, 1969), 44–81. On the ubiquity of conspiratorial thinking in this period, see Gordon Wood, "Conspiracy and the Paranoid Style: Causality and Deceit in the Eighteenth Century," *WMQ*, 3d ser., 39 (1982): 402–41.

50. Calhoon, *Loyalists in Revolutionary America*, 210–12, 281–83; Nancy L. Rhoden, *Revolutionary Anglicanism: The Colonial Church of England Clergy during the American Revolution* (New York: New York University Press, 1999), 89. The only other places where all Anglican clergy were loyalists were Maine and New Hampshire, with two ministers each.

51. Samuel Andrews, *A Discourse, Shewing the Necessity of Joining Internal Repentance, with the External Profession of It* (New Haven, CT: Thomas and Samuel Green, 1775), 18 and passim. Manuscript sermon by Roger Viets, 252 V6791se, at CSL. This box contains numerous bound sermons and loose pages. The sermon quoted here was delivered at least four times between July 1773 and February 1775, as recorded in Viets's headnotes. For the connection between religion and politics among Whigs, see Nathan O. Hatch, *The Sacred Cause of Liberty: Republican Thought and the Millennium in Revolutionary New England* (New Haven, CT: Yale University Press, 1977).

52. *Ct. Colony Recs.*, 15: 192–95.

53. Philander D. Chase, et al., eds., *The Papers of George Washington, Revolutionary War Series*, 24 vols. (Charlottesville: University Press of Virginia, 1985–), 3: 7–9, 13–14, 19–20, 44, 51; Middlekauff, *Glorious Cause*, 309–14; Villers, "Loyalism in Connecticut," 219–20.

54. Claude Halstead Van Tyne, *The Loyalists in the American Revolution* (New York: Macmillan, 1902), 327–28.

55. Rakove, *Beginnings of National Politics*, 79–81.

56. *Acts and Laws of His Majesties Colony of Connecticut in New-England* (Boston: Bartholomew Green and John Allen, 1702), 13–14. See also Bradley Chapin, "Colonial and Revolutionary Origins of the American Law of Treason," *WMQ*, 3rd ser., 17 (1960): 3–7.

CHAPTER 5

1. EH Diary, entry for November 8, 1773; Seymour, *Doc. Life*, 514–15.

2. Dexter, *Bio. Sketches*, 3: 469, 476, 479, 481, 484, 493, 499, 506.

3. EH Diary, entry for September 28, 1773; Seymour, *Doc. Life*, 25–26; John L. Sibley and Clifford K. Shipton, *Biographical Sketches of Those Who Attended Harvard College*, ... 18 vols. (Cambridge, MA: Harvard University Press, 1873–), 10: 497–501. Samuel Hale was commissioned major in October 1745 when he agreed to remain at Louisbourg as part of the regular garrison.

4. Benjamin Trumbull, *A Complete History of Connecticut, Civil and Ecclesiastical, From the Emigration of its First Planters*, ..., 2 vols. (first published Hartford, 1797; reprinted New London, CT: H. D. Utley, 1898) 2: 65–67; Richard Cullen Rath, *How*

Early America Sounded (Ithaca, NY: Cornell University Press, 2003), 27–29. The sounds continue to the present day; geologists attribute them to seismic activity.

5. *Ct. Colony Recs.*, 14: 204–5, 485, 489; John Warner Barber, *Connecticut Historical Collections*, 2nd ed. (New Haven, CT: Durrie & Peck and J. W. Barber, 1836), 524–28; David D. Field, *A History of the Towns of Haddam and East-Haddam* (Middletown, CT: Loomis & Richards, 1814), 8–13; Bruce C. Daniels, *The Connecticut Town: Growth and Development, 1635–1790* (Middletown, CT: Wesleyan University Press, 1979), 153, 187–90.

6. I. W. Stuart, *Life of Captain Nathan Hale, the Martyr-Spy of the American Revolution* (Hartford, CT: F. A. Brown, 1856), 30–31; Seymour, *Doc. Life*, 7, 15–16.

7. Robert Middlekauff, *Ancients and Axioms: Secondary Education in Eighteenth-Century New England* (New Haven, CT: Yale University Press, 1963), 138–39; Lisa Wilson, *Ye Heart of a Man: The Domestic Life of Men in Colonial New England* (New Haven, CT: Yale University Press, 1999), 31; Letter from Ebenezer Williams to Nathan Hale, May 1774, and Letter from Elihu Marvin to Nathan Hale, May 24, 1774, Nathan Hale Collection, Beinecke Rare Book and Manuscript Library, Yale University; Seymour, *Doc. Life*, 34.

8. J. M. Opal, *Beyond the Farm: National Ambitions in Rural New England* (Philadelphia: University of Pennsylvania Press, 2008), 27; J. William Frost, *Connecticut Education in the Revolutionary Era* (Chester, CT: Pequot Press, 1974), 35–37.

9. Seymour, *Doc. Life*, 14–15, 23–24; Letters from Ebenezer Williams to Nathan Hale, January 24, 1774; Elihu Marvin to Nathan Hale, May 24, 1774; Elihu Marvin to Nathan Hale, August 14, 1774, all in Nathan Hale Collection, Beinecke Library. Patricia Cline Cohen describes colonial students using tables of equivalence—for example, for different measures of volume or area—for arithmetical computations; these may have been the "tables" Marvin mentioned; see *A Calculating People: The Spread of Numeracy in Early America* (Chicago: University of Chicago Press, 1982), 121.

10. Letter from Elihu Marvin to Nathan Hale, August 7, 1773, in Nathan Hale Collection, Beinecke Library; Seymour, *Doc. Life*, 5, 8, 158, 160, 161. Though six years older than Hale, William Little graduated with Yale's class of 1777; how he came to know Hale is unclear. See Dexter, *Bio. Sketches*, 3: 689.

11. *New-London Gazette*, December 3, 1773, p. 2; Middlekauff, *Ancients and Axioms*, 68; *Ct. Colony Recs.*, 14: 382–84.

12. Seymour, *Doc. Life*, 7, 12–14.

13. According to the 1774 census, black residents comprised nearly 10 percent of New London's population—552 of 5,888 inhabitants; see *Ct. Colony Recs.*, 14: 487. On the importance of black sailors in the colonies, see W. Jeffrey Bolster, *Black Jacks: African American Seamen in the Age of Sail* (Cambridge, MA: Harvard University Press, 1997). For New London's economy, see Barber, *Connecticut Historical Collections*, 285; Frances Manwaring Caulkins, *History of New London, Connecticut* (New London, CT: published by the author, 1852), 483–85.

14. Seymour, *Doc. Life*, 25–27; quotation on p. 26.

15. Seymour, *Doc. Life*, 26 (quotation), 160. For the leading New London families, see Caulkins, *History of New London*, 316, 358, 531; for Saltonstall, see Sibley and Shipton, *Biographical Sketches of Those Who Graduated from Harvard*, 17: 426–28.

16. Seymour, *Doc. Life*, 10–11, 15–16; Letter from Ebenezer Williams to Nathan Hale, January 24, 1774, Nathan Hale Collection, Beinecke Library. Hale did in fact receive letters in East Haddam.

17. Konstantin Dierks, *In My Power: Letter Writing and Communications in Early America* (Philadelphia: University of Pennsylvania Press, 2009), 131–32, 197; Frank H. Norton, ed., *Journal Kept by Hugh Finlay, Surveyor of the Post Roads on the Continent of North America, . . .* (Brooklyn: F. H. Norton, 1867), 34–35, 38; Lester J. Cappon, ed., *Atlas of Early American History: The Revolutionary Era 1760–1790* (Princeton, NJ: Princeton University Press, 1976), 32, 108.

18. Seymour, *Doc. Life*, 16; Richard Godbeer, *The Overflowing of Friendship: Love between Men and the Creation of the American Republic* (Baltimore: Johns Hopkins University Press, 2009), 52–61.

19. This and the following paragraphs are based on close examination of seventeen surviving letters—one written by Hale and the others received from friends—from the period between their Yale graduation and the outbreak of the Revolutionary War in April 1775. The letters can be found in Seymour, *Doc. Life*, 5–35, and in the Nathan Hale Collection, Beinecke Library.

20. For an account of the materials used in letter writing, see Dierks, *In My Power*, 177–88.

21. Seymour, *Doc. Life*, 11, 21–22, and 90–91 for examples of poems by Hale; Letter from Ebenezer Williams to Nathan Hale, May 1774, in Nathan Hale Collection, Beinecke Library.

22. Dierks, *In My Power*, ch. 4; Godbeer, *Overflowing of Friendship*, 10–14, 70–73; Lawrence E. Klein, *Shaftesbury and the Culture of Politeness* (Cambridge: Cambridge University Press, 1994), 115.

23. Quotations from Seymour, *Doc. Life*, 11, 16, 21. For the importance of sincerity as an emotional marker of elite status, see Nicole Eustace, *Passion Is the Gale: Emotion, Power, and the Coming of the American Revolution* (Chapel Hill: University of North Carolina Press, 2008), 82–89.

24. Seymour, *Doc. Life*, 28, 33–35; Eustace, *Passion Is the Gale*, 75–89.

25. Seymour, *Doc. Life*, 14.

26. The following works helped to shape the interpretation of this and the following paragraphs: Eustace, *Passion Is the Gale*, 111–33, 145–50; Godbeer, *Overflowing of Friendship*, 77–81; Anne S. Lombard, *Making Manhood: Growing Up Male in Colonial New England* (Cambridge, MA: Harvard University Press, 2003), 96–97; John Gilbert McCurdy, *Citizen Bachelors: Manhood and the Creation of the United States* (Ithaca, NY: Cornell University Press, 2009), 121–59. For Hale's comment about "weaning," a reference included in a letter from Ebenezer Williams, see Seymour, *Doc. Life*, 23.

27. The average age at first marriage was about twenty-five; see Daniel Scott Smith, "The Demographic History of Colonial New England," in Michael Gordon, ed., *The American Family in Social-Historical Perspective* (New York: St. Martin's Press, 1973), 406. The average age of Hale's classmates just after graduation was about twenty.

28. Dexter, *Bio. Sketches*, 3: 475; Seymour, *Doc. Life*, 11; Letter from Ebenezer Williams to Nathan Hale, May 1774, in Nathan Hale Collection, Beinecke Library.

29. There has been considerable speculation about the identity of the woman who captured Hale's affections. I. W. Stuart asserted that she was Alice Adams of Canterbury, who became Hale's stepsister when the widowed Richard Hale married Alice's mother. Stuart goes so far as to declare that the two were engaged to be wed. Henry Phelps Johnson included this version in his biography of Hale. George Dudley Seymour, however, offers a more plausible case for Betsey Adams and casts doubt on the idea of any official Hale engagement. Seymour also alleges that Hale carried on a romance with an East Haddam girl, but his evidentiary basis is thin—a poem by Hale that mentions an "intimate" friendship with someone from town. Seymour, not Hale, titled this poem "The Tryst of Haddam Landing." See Stuart, *Life of Captain Nathan Hale*, 36–38; Henry Phelps Johnson, *Nathan Hale, 1776: Biography and Memorials* (New Haven, CT: Yale University Press, 1914), 55–60; Seymour, *Doc. Life*, 90, 568–76, 583–88. For Tallmadge, see Letter from Tallmadge to Hale, May 5, 1774, in Nathan Hale Collection, Beinecke Library; Seymour, *Doc. Life*, 20.

30. Seymour, *Doc. Life*, 18–19, 22–23, 27–29.

31. Seymour, *Doc. Life*, 45, 177.

32. Royal R. Hinman, *A Historical Collection From Official Records, Files, Etc., Of The Part Sustained By Connecticut During The War Of The Revolution* (Hartford, CT: E. Gleason, 1842), 54–58.

33. Oscar Zeichner, *Connecticut's Years of Controversy, 1750–1776* (Chapel Hill: University of North Carolina Press, 1949), 164; *The New-London Gazette*, June 10, 1774, p. 3; Letter from Elihu Marvin to Nathan Hale, May 24, 1774, Nathan Hale Collection, Beinecke Library.

34. Seymour, *Doc. Life*, 21.

35. Seymour, *Doc. Life*, 24–25. For the rumored attack on Boston, see T. H. Breen, *American Insurgents, American Patriots: The Revolution of the People* (New York: Hill and Wang, 2010), ch. 5.

36. *The New-London Gazette*, September 30, 1774, p. 3; December 30, 1774, p. 3; February 3, 1775, p. 3; March 10, 1775, p. 3; *Ct. Colony Recs.*, 14: 346.

37. Bernard Bailyn, *The Ideological Origins of the American Revolution* (Cambridge, MA: Harvard University Press, 1967), ch. 2; Louis Leonard Tucker, *Connecticut's Seminary of Sedition: Yale College* (Chester, CT: Pequot Press, 1974), 23–25; Lawrence A. Cremin, *American Education: The Colonial Experience, 1607–1783* (New York: Harper and Row, 1970), 459–68; David W. Robson, *Educating Republicans: The College in the Era of the American Revolution, 1750–1800* (Westport, CT: Greenwood Press, 1985), 57–93.

38. For the offer of a permanent teaching position and the quotation, see Seymour, *Doc. Life*, 26; a list of the Union School proprietors is on p. 29. For the members of the committee of correspondence, see Caulkins, *History of New London*, 502–3; for the legislative representatives, see *The New-London Gazette*, October 21, 1774, p. 3.

39. Records of the Independent Artillery Company of New London, 1762–1777, at the New London County Historical Society; quotations from pp. 1, 2; Hale's election is on p. 25 and his sergeant's position on p. 28. The initial uniform, with blue coat and sword, was altered at the meeting when Hale was elected; see pp. 2, 25. Thanks to Rachel Smith for providing scanned images of this material.

40. The vast majority of Yale students in this period sided with the Whigs. Hale's class of 1773 included just one loyalist (William Chandler), and only four or five others attended at the same time as Hale did. These included Daniel Lyman (class of 1770); Thomas Cutler, Sylvester Muirson, and James Nichols (1771), and possibly John Chandler (1772). See Dexter, *Bio. Sketches*, 3: 387, 411, 424–27, 441, 474–75; also Tucker, *Connecticut's Seminary of Sedition*, 21.

41. Elihu Marvin to Nathan Hale, May 24, 1774, Nathan Hale Collection, Beinecke Library; Jay Fliegelman, *Prodigals & Pilgrims: The American Revolution against Patriarchal Authority, 1750–1800* (New York: Cambridge University Press, 1982); Gordon S. Wood, *The Radicalism of the American Revolution* (New York: Knopf, 1992), 95–225; Eustace, *Passion Is the Gale*, 385–88, 427–37; Catherine O'Donnell Kaplan, *Men of Letters in the Early Republic: Cultivating Forms of Citizenship* (Chapel Hill: University of North Carolina Press, 2008), 13–39.

42. Seymour, *Doc. Life*, 30–31, 35; John F. Roche, *The Colonial Colleges in the War for American Independence* (Millwood, NY: Associated Faculty Press, 1986), 76.

43. David Hackett Fischer, *Paul Revere's Ride* (New York: Oxford University Press, 1994), 202–62; Richard Buel Jr., *Dear Liberty: Connecticut's Mobilization for the Revolutionary War* (Middletown, CT: Wesleyan University Press, 1980), 35–36; Harold E. Selesky, *War & Society in Colonial Connecticut* (New Haven, CT: Yale University Press, 1990), 228–29; Henry Phelps Johnston, *Record of Service of Connecticut Men in the War of the Revolution*, 2 parts (Hartford: Case, Lockwood, and Brainard, 1889), 1: 7–8.

44. Benjamin Tallmadge to Nathan Hale, May 9, 1775, Nathan Hale Collection, Beinecke Library.

45. Charles Royster, *A Revolutionary People at War: The Continental Army and American Character, 1775–1783* (Chapel Hill: University of North Carolina Press, 1979), ch. 1; John A. Ruddiman, *Becoming Men of Some Consequence: Youth and Military Service in the Revolutionary War* (Charlottesville: University Press of Virginia, 2014), 26–35; Caroline Cox, *A Proper Sense of Honor: Service and Sacrifice in George Washington's Army* (Chapel Hill: University of North Carolina Press, 2004), 21–22, 25–28.

46. Henry P. Johnston lists eleven members of the class of 1773 who served in the military; see *Yale: Her Honor-Roll In The American Revolution* (New York: privately printed, 1888), 282–300. Dexter, however, shows fourteen members doing so; see *Bio. Sketches*, 3: 469–512.

47. Royster, *A Revolutionary People at War*, 48; Buel, *Dear Liberty*, 45. More than fifty years after the battle of Lexington, Richard Law—a young student of Hale's in 1775, and son of the school proprietor of the same name—recalled that Hale announced his support of independence in April 1775 and promptly marched off with Captain Coit's company to Massachusetts. I. W. Stuart included a version of the story in his *Life of Captain Nathan Hale*, 44–45. There is, however, no corroborating evidence; New London's local historian, Frances Caulkins, doubted its accuracy. See Seymour, *Doc. Life*, 347; Caulkins, *History of New London*, 515.

48. Seymour, *Doc. Life*, 36–37.

49. *Ct. Colony Recs.*, 15: 93–94. Hull graduated with Yale's class of 1772.

50. Seymour, *Doc. Life*, 40, 162.

51. Henry Phelps Johnston, ed., *Memoir of Colonel Benjamin Tallmadge* (New York: Gilliss Press, 1904), 6–7.
52. Seymour, *Doc. Life*, 37–39; Johnston, *Yale*, 295.
53. *Ct. Colony Recs.*, 15: 92–93; Selesky, *War & Society*, 236–37; Philander D. Chase et al., eds., *The Papers of George Washington, Revolutionary War Series*, 24 vols. (Charlottesville: University Press of Virginia, 1985–) 1: 152–53; Seymour, *Doc. Life*, 40–41.
54. Chase, et al., eds., *Papers of George Washington*, 1: 204, 267, 276; Buel, *Dear Liberty*, 46–47.
55. Don Higginbotham, *The War of American Independence: Military Attitudes, Policies, and Practice, 1763–1789* (New York: Macmillan, 1971), 81–95.
56. *Ct. Colony Recs.*, 15: 94. John Belcher rose to rank of first lieutenant at the same time.
57. Seymour, *Doc. Life*, 174–75.
58. Johnston, *Yale*, 263, 265–66, 278, 291, 292, 293, 297, 298, 301, 303–4, 308–9, 314, 315, 317; Dexter, *Bio. Sketches*, 3: 393, 518, 529, 533, 537.
59. Several more Yale graduates from the time when Hale attended college, including these four friends, entered the army in succeeding years; see Johnston, *Yale*, 262–320.
60. Robert Middlekauff, *The Glorious Cause: The American Revolution, 1763–1789*, rev. ed. (New York: Oxford University Press, 2005), 279, 298, 319–20.
61. Middlekauff, *The Glorious Cause*, 321–22.
62. Seymour, *Doc. Life*, 173–99.
63. Seymour, *Doc. Life*, 174; William M. Fowler Jr., *Rebels under Sail: The American Navy during the Revolution* (New York: Scribner, 1976), 51; Norman M. Isham and Albert F. Brown, *Early Rhode Island Houses: Historical and Architectural Study* (Providence: Preston and Rounds, 1895), 49–51, 177–83.

CHAPTER 6
1. Letters from William Tudor to John Adams, September 30 and October 25, 1775, in Robert J. Taylor et al., eds., *Papers of John Adams*, 11 vols. (Cambridge, MA: Harvard University Press, 1977–), 3: 173–73, 251; Philander D. Chase et al., eds., *The Papers of George Washington, Revolutionary War Series*, 24 vols. (Charlottesville: University Press of Virginia, 1985–), 2: 72, 76, 95, 112; Hale's Army Diary in Seymour, *Doc. Life*, 175–78. For smallpox in the British and American armies early in the war, see Elizabeth A. Fenn, *Pox Americana: The Great Smallpox Epidemic of 1775–82* (New York: Hill and Wang, 2001), chs. 2–3.
2. Seymour, *Doc. Life*, 46.
3. Seymour, *Doc. Life*, 179, 182; Chase et al., eds., *Papers of George Washington*, 2: 55. In Massachusetts's provincial army during the French and Indian War, captains were typically in their early thirties; see Fred Anderson, *A People's Army: Massachusetts Soldiers and Society in the Seven Years' War* (Chapel Hill: University of North Carolina Press, 1984), Table 22, p. 237.
4. Seymour, *Doc. Life*, 46; *Ct. Colony Recs.*, 15: 93.
5. Seymour, *Doc. Life*, 181 (quote), 183–88, 194, 200–278; Reminiscences of Elisha Bostwick, photostat of original document in US Army Miscellaneous file, box 1, New York Public Library. Bostwick's account is reprinted in the Seymour collection,

and further citations will refer to that published version; see Seymour, *Doc. Life,* 319–25. See also Caroline Cox, *A Proper Sense of Honor: Service and Sacrifice in George Washington's Army* (Chapel Hill: University of North Carolina Press, 2004), 151; John A. Ruddiman, *Becoming Men of Some Consequence: Youth and Military Service in the Revolutionary War* (Charlottesville: University Press of Virginia, 2014), 62.

6. Cox, *Proper Sense of Honor,* chs. 1–2; Seymour, *Doc. Life,* 178–79, 181, 193, 325; in his December 1, 1775, diary entry, Hale mentioned that most soldiers remained in his unit "by means of General Lee" (p. 193). Connecticut soldiers who joined the army in late June and early July were to serve only five months; see Richard Buel Jr., *Dear Liberty: Connecticut's Mobilization for the Revolutionary War* (Middletown, CT: Wesleyan University Press, 1980), 44.

7. Seymour, *Doc. Life,* 325; the poem is reprinted on pp. 92–94, with the original in the Nathan Hale Collection, Beinecke Rare Book and Manuscript Library, Yale University. Caroline Cox notes that literacy was a distinguishing characteristic of officers; see *Proper Sense of Honor,* 33. For techniques of pen-making in this period, see Konstantin Dierks, *In My Power: Letter Writing and Communications in Early America* (Philadelphia: University of Pennsylvania Press, 2009), 78.

8. Seymour, *Doc. Life,* 41–66, 89; quote from p. 62; see also letter to Hale from Betsy Hallam, October 29, 1775, in the Nathan Hale Collection, Beinecke Library. Saltonstall eventually served at sea; see John Langdon Sibley and Clifford K. Shipton, eds., *Biographical Sketches of Graduates of Harvard University,* 18 vols. (Cambridge, MA: Charles William Sever, 1873–), 17: 426–28.

9. Seymour, *Doc. Life,* 52–53, 59–60, 70–71; for other letters from Yale classmates, see pp. 68–70, 71–73, 74–75, 82–83. Roger Alden received his desired commission in January 1777. Elihu Marvin enlisted as a lieutenant in early 1777. See Dexter, *Bio. Sketches,* 3: 469, 493.

10. Seymour, *Doc. Life,* 176, 178, 179, 180, 181, 190, 191, 195; Dexter, *Bio. Sketches,* 3: 477, 510.

11. Seymour, *Doc. Life,* 175, 179, 180, 191. For brief sketches of Lee, Putnam, and Spencer, see Harold Selesky, ed., *Encyclopedia of the American Revolution,* 2nd ed., 2 vols. (Detroit: Charles Scribner's Sons, 2006), 1: 611–13; 2: 948–50, 1098–99. On learning from senior officers, see Ruddiman, *Becoming Men of Some Consequence,* 62–64.

12. On the decision to change to one-year enlistments, see Charles Royster, *A Revolutionary People at War: The Continental Army and American Character, 1775–1783* (Chapel Hill: University of North Carolina Press, 1979), 48–49. For the reorganization of Hale's regiment, see Robert K. Wright Jr., *The Continental Army* (Washington, DC: Center of Military History, 1983), 239. Hale's request for a new commission and his December activities are discussed in his army diary; see Seymour, *Doc. Life,* 181, 191, 193–94.

13. Seymour, *Doc. Life,* 196–97, 213.

14. Royster, *Revolutionary People at War,* 48–53; Seymour, *Doc. Life,* 66–67.

15. In 1836, the eighty-one-year-old Asher Wright was asked for his reminiscences of Hale, and this testimony was recorded by local historians; see Seymour, *Doc. Life,* 315–17; Hale mentions Wright in a letter home on pp. 80–81. For information on waiters, see Cox, *Proper Sense of Honor,* 50–51.

16. Seymour, *Doc. Life*, 197–98.

17. Seymour, *Doc. Life*, 198–99; Henry P. Johnston, *Yale: Her Honor-Roll In The American Revolution* (New York: G. P. Putnam's Sons, 1888), 263, 266, 278, 291, 292–93, 298.

18. Seymour, *Doc. Life*, 68–69, 71–73. This unknown female might have been "P.H." of Norwich, an otherwise unidentified correspondent of Hale's; she would, however, have been a neighbor of Marvin (who was teaching school in Norwich) and not Hale.

19. Letter from Gilbert Saltonstall to Nathan Hale, March 18, 1776, Nathan Hale Collection, Beinecke Library. George Washington described the Nook Hill engagement in a letter to John Hancock; see Chase et al., eds., *Papers of George Washington*, 3: 420–26.

20. Robert Middlekauff, *The Glorious Cause: The American Revolution, 1763–1789* (New York: Oxford University Press, 1982), 315–16.

21. Ira D. Gruber, *The Howe Brothers and the American Revolution* (Chapel Hill: University of North Carolina Press, 1972), 67–71, 77–78; EH Diary, entry for March 2, 1776; Robinson comment in Seymour, *Doc. Life*, 69. On growing support for independence, see Middlekauff, *Glorious Cause*, ch. 14.

22. Middlekauff, *Glorious Cause*, 316–17, 345; Chase et al., eds., *Papers of George Washington*, 3: 458, 461–63; Fenn, *Pox Americana*, 51–52; Don Higginbotham, *The War of American Independence: Military Attitudes, Policies, and Practice, 1763–1789* (New York: Macmillan, 1971), 150.

23. Chase et al., eds., *Papers of George Washington*, 3: 466, 491, 540; Seymour, *Doc. Life*, 75–76; EH Diary, entry for March 29, 1776.

24. Hale's arrival in New York was noted in Colonel Charles Webb's orderly book, extracts of which are reprinted in Seymour, *Doc. Life*, 168; Higginbotham, *War of American Independence*, 152–53; Middlekauff, *Glorious Cause*, 347; Chase et al., eds., *Papers of George Washington*, 4: 384, 414.

25. Seymour, *Doc. Life*, 76–82. For conditions in New York during the war, see Judith L. Van Buskirk, *Generous Enemies: Patriots and Loyalists in Revolutionary New York* (Philadelphia: University of Pennsylvania Press, 2002).

26. Asher Wright's reminiscences regarding Hale's military career suggest that Hale led this expedition, although there is no corroborating evidence. See I. W. Stuart, *Life of Captain Nathan Hale, the Martyr-Spy of the American Revolution* (Hartford, CT: F. A. Brown, 1856), 70–72. In a letter to Washington, Israel Putnam mentioned the incident without naming Hale or any other participants; see Chase et al., eds., *Papers of George Washington*, 4: 408–9. Letters to Hale from "P.H." and Elihu Marvin refer to Hale's account of the incident, which appeared in letters that have not survived; see Seymour, *Doc. Life*, 81–82.

27. For Yale classmates in New York, see Johnston, *Yale*, 37–39; Henry Phelps Johnston, *Memoir of Colonel Benjamin Tallmadge* (New York: Gilliss Press, 1904), 7–8. Hale mentioned his pleasure at Tallmadge's arrival in a fragment of a letter that apparently was never completed; see Seymour, *Doc. Life*, 82.

28. Middlekauff, *Glorious Cause*, 347.

29. Chase et al., eds., *Papers of George Washington*, 5: 246; Worthington Chauncey Ford, ed., *Correspondence and Journals of Samuel Blachley Webb*, 3 vols. (New York

and Lancaster, PA: Wickersham Press, 1893–94), 1: 153; David C. Hendrickson, *Peace Pact: The Lost World of the American Founding* (Lawrence: University Press of Kansas, 2003), 125–26.

30. See, for instance, Gregory T. Knouff, *The Soldiers' Revolution: Pennsylvanians in Arms and the Forging of Early American Identity* (University Park: Pennsylvania State University Press, 2004), esp. ch. 2.

31. Seymour, *Doc. Life*, 83–84. For an English civilian's account of this attempt to burn British ships, see Edward H. Tatum Jr., *The American Journal of Ambrose Serle* (New York: New York Times, 1969), 68.

32. Seymour, *Doc. Life*, 199; Major Abner Benedict's account (doc. 15) in Thomas W. Field, *The Battle of Long Island, with Connected Preceding Events, and the Subsequent American Retreat* (Brooklyn: Long Island Historical Society, 1869), 349–51.

33. Middlekauff, *Glorious Cause*, 348–50; Higginbotham, *War of American Independence*, 151–59; see also Barnet Schecter, *The Battle for New York: The City at the Heart of the American Revolution* (New York: Penguin, 2002), ch. 8.

34. Johnston, *Memoir of Tallmadge*, 11; John C. Dann, ed., *The Revolution Remembered: Eyewitness Accounts of the War for Independence* (Chicago: University of Chicago Press, 1980), 50; Michael Stephenson, *Patriot Battles: How the War of Independence Was Fought* (New York: HarperCollins, 2007), 141; *Diary of Frederick Mackenzie*, 2 vols. (Cambridge, MA: Harvard University Press, 1930), 1: 45; Higginbotham, *War of American Independence*, 158 [Washington quote]; Selesky, ed., *Encyclopedia*, 1: 655.

35. Tatum, ed., *Journal of Ambrose Serle*, 92, 96; Middlekauff, *Glorious Cause*, 353; Chase et al., eds., *Papers of George Washington*, 6: 153, 156, 199–200.

36. Middlekauff, *Glorious Cause*, 354; Higginbotham, *War of American Independence*, 159–60; Chase et al., eds., *Papers of George Washington*, 6: 207, 223; EH Diary, entry for September 4, 1776.

37. Gruber, *Howe Brothers and the American Revolution*, 118–20.

38. Middlekauff, *Glorious Cause*, 355; Chase et al., eds., *Papers of George Washington*, 6: 251, 273, 286, 290.

39. Higginbotham, *War of American Independence*, 160; Tatum, ed., *Journal of Ambrose Serle*, 104; Chase et al., eds., *Papers of George Washington*, 6: 313; *Diary of Frederick Mackenzie*, 1: 51. For an account of the battle, see Selesky, ed., *Encyclopedia*, 1: 490–92.

40. Chase et al., eds., *Papers of George Washington*, 6: 357; Ashbel Woodward, *Memoir of Col. Thomas Knowlton, of Ashford, Connecticut* (Boston: H. W. Dutton and Son, 1861), 3–13.

41. Wright, *Continental Army*, 90; Woodward, *Memoir of Col. Thomas Knowlton*, 13. Robert Rogers, who organized a well-known ranger unit during the French and Indian War, composed a set of rules for rangers, emphasizing that they should "preserve a firmness and presence of mind on every occasion." See Franklin B. Hough, ed., *Journals of Major Robert Rogers*, ... (Albany, NY: Munsell, 1883), 82–86, quotation on 86.

42. Woodward, *Memoir of Col. Thomas Knowlton*, 15.

43. Chase et al., eds., *Papers of George Washington*, 6: 195, 224 (quotation); Alexander Rose, *Washington's Spies: The Story of America's First Spy Ring* (New York: Bantam, 2006), 14–16.

44. Colonel Webb's orderly book listed Hale as ill in July and present in camp through August. He was absent on September 6, most likely one of the three captains listed as "on command," in his case under Knowlton. Webb specified on September 13 that one of his unit's captains, without naming Hale, was with Knowlton. See extracts from Webb's orderly book in Seymour, *Doc. Life*, 168–69.

45. Information in this paragraph comes from William Hull's memoir, an extract of which appears in Seymour, *Doc. Life*, 307–10. The quoted remarks reflect Hull's memory of his conversation with Hale. The memoir was published, along with other manuscript material, as *Revolutionary Services and Civil Life of General William Hull* (New York: D. Appleton and Co., 1848) by Hull's daughter, Maria Campbell, twenty-three years after Hull's death. Hull's reminiscence about Hale, however, dates from the late eighteenth century. It informs Hannah Adams's treatment of the spy incident in her *A Summary History of New-England*, ... (Dedham, MA: H. Mann and J. H. Adams, 1799); Adams cites Hull in a footnote on p. 361.

46. Stephen Hempstead mentioned the brown suit in his memoirs; Asher Wright noted the Latin descriptions during his reminiscences of Hale. See Seymour, *Doc. Life*, 309, 312, 317. Catherine O'Donnell Kaplan discusses how behaviors nurtured in college literary societies and similar venues prior to the Revolution were put to nationalist purposes after Independence; see *Men of Letters in the Early Republic: Cultivating Forums of Citizenship* (Chapel Hill: University of North Carolina Press, 2008).

47. Seymour, *Doc. Life*, 312, 316.

48. Joseph S. Tiedemann, "Queens County," in Joseph S. Tiedemann and Eugene R. Fingerhut, eds., *The Other New York: The American Revolution beyond New York City, 1763–1787* (Albany: State University of New York Press, 2005), 46–50; W. H. Siebert, "The Refugee Loyalists of Connecticut," *Transactions of the Royal Society of Canada*, 3rd series, 10 (1916): 75–92.

49. "The Diary of William Bamford," *Maryland Historical Magazine* 28 (1933): 9; *Diary of Frederick Mackenzie*, 1: 56–57; Tatum, ed., *Journal of Ambrose Serle*, 109. Asher Wright recalled that Hale hid his information in his shoes; see Seymour, *Doc. Life*, 317.

50. *Diary of Frederick Mackenzie*, 1: 58–61; "Diary of William Bamford," 9; Loftus Cliffe to Bartholomew Cliffe, September 21–23, 1776, in the Loftus Cliffe Papers, 1769–1784, William L. Clements Library, University of Michigan; *Journal of Ambrose Serle*, 110–11; Governor William Tryon to Lord George Germain, September 24, 1776, in K. G. Davies, ed., *Docs. of the American Revolution 1770–1783 (Colonial Office Series)*, 21 vols. (Dublin: Irish University Press, 1972–1981), 12: 230–31.

51. *Diary of Frederick Mackenzie*, 1: 59–60; "Diary of William Bamford," 9; Loftus Cliffe to Bartholomew Cliffe, September 21, 1776, Loftus Cliffe Papers; *Journal of Ambrose Serle*, 111; Governor Tryon to Lord Germain, September 24, 1776, in Davies, ed., *Docs. of the American Revolution*, 12: 231; Chase et al., eds., *Papers of George Washington*, 6: 495. Benjamin L. Carp argues that American revolutionaries most likely set the blaze but never admitted their complicity; see "The Night the Yankees Burned Broadway," *Early American Studies*, 4 (2006), 471–511.

52. See the profile of Rogers in Selesky, ed., *Encyclopedia of the American Revolution*, 2: 1001. For Rogers's presence in Flushing in September 1776, see Chase et al., eds.,

Papers of George Washington, 6:254. I thank John Grenier for sharing insights from his forthcoming book about Rogers.

53. Davies, ed., *Docs. of the American Revolution*, 11: 194; Chase et al., eds., *Papers of George Washington*, 2: 549–51, 567–68; 5: 114–15, 122–23, 167. In his letter to Washington, Sullivan noted that he "waited on" Rogers, which may mean that the brigadier general went to the Medford tavern where Rogers was staying, rather than having Rogers come to Winter Hill.

54. Davies, ed., *Docs. of the American Revolution*, 12: 35, 179; Seymour, *Doc. Life*, 316, 324.

55. It seems most likely that initial contact with Hale was made by one of the loyalist officers Rogers had commissioned for his ranger unit. Rogers was later reprimanded by British authorities for following the colonial practice of commissioning men who were able to enlist a certain number of recruits. British officers scorned such commissioned loyalists as lacking the necessary gentility for officer rank. Rogers also claimed to have enlisted more men than he actually did. See Paul H. Smith, *Loyalists and Redcoats: A Study in British Revolutionary Policy* (Chapel Hill: University of North Carolina Press, 1964), 70–71; John R. Cuneo, *Robert Rogers of the Rangers* (New York: Oxford University Press, 1959), 266–68.

56. This version of Hale's capture appeared in a manuscript history of the Revolution written by Consider Tiffany, a Connecticut loyalist from the town of Barkhamsted. Now owned by the Library of Congress, the manuscript has been tentatively dated ca. 1778–1796. For an analysis of the plausibility of Tiffany's account, see James Hutson, "Nathan Hale Revisited: A Tory's Account of the Arrest of the First American Spy," *Library of Congress Information Bulletin*, 62 (July/August 2003). Rogers's role in Hale's capture is corroborated by another contemporary document. The British officer William Bamford's diary entry for September 22, 1776, identified Hale as "a spy [who] was taken by Majr Rogers"; see "Diary of William Bamford," 10. Consider Tiffany, an outspoken Anglican of loyalist views, was confined to his farm for more than a year during the war; see Ella F. Wright, *Genealogical Sketch of the Tiffany Family* (Waterbury, CT: Mattatuck Press, 1904), 7.

57. The allegation and this quotation are from the Tiffany manuscript as cited in Hutson, "Nathan Hale Revisited."

58. Hale's army accounts for June to August 1776 noted purchases of such items as "Scr. Drivers" and butter, along with sums for meals, washing, and "board at Mrs. Spicers." Enoch Hale later heard that deserters confirmed his brother's identity. See Seymour, *Doc. Life*, 239–41, 297. For ranger recruits from Connecticut, see Governor Jonathan Trumbull's letter to Washington, dated October 13, 1776, in Chase et al., eds., *Papers of George Washington*, 6: 559–61.

59. For a biographical sketch of Samuel Hale, see Sibley and Shipton, eds., *Biographical Sketches of Graduates of Harvard University*, 16: 368–71. For various references to the rumor of the cousin's betrayal, see Seymour, ed., *Doc. Life*, 296, 303, 305–6, 317, 345, 449.

60. "William Bamford's Diary," 10, mentions that Hale "had several Papers w[i]t[h] accts of our Force &c."

61. *Diary of Frederick Mackenzie*, 1: 61–62.

62. *Rivington's New York Gazetteer*, March 9, 1775, p. 3; Schecter, *Battle for New York*, 213. In his memoirs, William Hull recounted his meeting with the British officer,

John Montresor, who brought the news of Hale's execution to the American camp. According to Hull, Montresor offered the details about the provost marshal's "inhuman" behavior toward Hale. See Seymour, *Doc. Life*, 310.

63. Quotation from Hull's version of Montresor's report of Hale's last day; see Seymour, *Doc. Life*, 310.

64. Seymour, *Doc. Life*, 310. Enoch Hale mentioned in a diary entry for January 25, 1777, that he met with college friend John Palsgrave Wyllys, who was a prisoner of the British in New York at the time of Hale's capture. Wyllys told Enoch that the provost marshal had showed him Hale's diploma and these two letters; see Seymour, *Doc. Life*, 298. For a brief biography of Montresor, see G. D. Scull, ed., "The Montresor Journals," *Collections of the New-York Historical Society* (1881), 4–8.

65. *Diary of Frederick Mackenzie*, 62; Montresor's words as noted in Hull's memoirs, extracted in Seymour, ed., *Doc. Life*, 310.

66. Joseph Addison, *Cato: A Tragedy, and Selected Essays*, ed. Christine Dunn Henderson (Indianapolis: Liberty Fund, 2004), 84 (Act IV, scene iv).

67. Jason Shaffer, *Performing Patriotism: National Identity in the Colonial and Revolutionary American Theater* (Philadelphia: University of Pennsylvania Press, 2007), ch. 2; Fredric M. Litto, "Addison's Cato in the Colonies," *WMQ*, 3rd ser., 23 (1966): 431–49; Garry Wills, *Cincinnatus: George Washington & the Enlightenment* (Garden City, NY: Doubleday, 1984): 134–37. For Hale's familiarity with *Cato*, see the letter to him from Betsy Hallam, October 29, 1775, Nathan Hale Collection, Beinecke Library. The account of Hale's death in the *Essex Journal* on February 13, 1777, reported that Hale's "sensible and spirited speech" included his assertion that "if he had ten thousand lives, he would lay them all down, if called to it, in defence of his injured, bleeding Country." Though this version differs from other accounts of Hale's final words, it echoes the line from *Cato*, further suggesting that Hale made some sort of allusion to the play; see Seymour, *Doc. Life*, 303. American as well as British officers saw familiarity with the play as a marker of gentility; see Mark Evans Bryan, "'Slideing into Monarchical extravagance': *Cato* at Valley Forge and the Testimony of William Bradford Jr.," *WMQ*, 3rd ser., 67 (2010): 123–44.

68. Loftus Cliffe to Bartholomew Cliffe, September 21–23, 1776, Loftus Cliffe Papers. On clothing and personal appearance as indicators of gentility, see Richard L. Bushman, *The Refinement of America: Persons, Houses, Cities* (New York: Knopf, 1992), 63–74.

69. EH Diary, entry for September 22, 1776.

CHAPTER 7

1. The information in the above paragraphs is from "Last Speech."

2. Fairfield Committee of Inspection to George Washington, May 14, 1776, in Philander D. Chase et al., eds., *The Papers of George Washington, Revolutionary War Series*, 24 vols. (Charlottesville: University Press of Virginia, 1985–), 4: 298–99.

3. Bruce E. Steiner, *Connecticut Anglicans in the Revolutionary Era: A Study in Communal Tensions* (Hartford: American Revolution Bicentennial Commission of Connecticut, 1978), 52–53, 56; Kenneth Walter Cameron, ed., *The Church of England in Pre-Revolutionary Connecticut* (Hartford, CT: Transcendental Books, 1976), 199–200.

4. Cameron, ed., *Church of England in Pre-Revolutionary Connecticut*, 200.

5. Cameron, ed., *Church of England in Pre-Revolutionary Connecticut*, 200.

6. Steiner, *Connecticut Anglicans*, 56.

7. *Ct. Colony Recs.*, 15: 192–95, 281–83; Oscar Zeichner, *Connecticut's Years of Controversy, 1750–1776* (Chapel Hill: University of North Carolina Press, 1949), 207–13.

8. Worthington C. Ford, ed., *Journals of the Continental Congress, 1774–1789*, 34 vols. (Washington, DC: US Government Printing Office, 1904–1937), 5: 475; Bradley Chapin, "Colonial and Revolutionary Origins of the American Law of Treason," *WMQ*, 3rd series, 17 (1960): 4–21; James H. Kettner, *The Development of American Citizenship 1608–1870* (Chapel Hill: University of North Carolina Press, 1978), 174–83.

9. Zeichner, *Connecticut's Years of Controversy*, 213.

10. *Connecticut Courant*, July 22, 1776, p. 3; August 5, 1776, p. 4; August 12, 1776, p. 1; *Connecticut Journal*, July 10, 1776, p. 2. For Newgate prison, see Richard H. Phelps, *Newgate of Connecticut: Its Origin and Early History* (Hartford, CT: E. Greer, 1876), 26–41.

11. "Last Speech."

12. Quotation from "Last Speech"; for the heat wave, see *Connecticut Journal*, June 26, 1776, p. 3. For the two land transfers, see Waterbury Land Records, vol. 17, pp. 110, 141, at CSL. Ebenezer Cook belonged to Northbury's Congregationalist Church; see Donald Lines Jacobus, comp., *Families of Ancient New Haven*, 3 vols. (Rome, NY: C. Smith, 1923), 1: 443. For David Shelton's Anglicanism, see Henry Bronson, *The History of Waterbury, Connecticut*, . . . (Waterbury, CT: Bronson Brothers, 1858), 575.

13. Jacobus, comp., *Families of Ancient New Haven*, 1:382; E. LeRoy Pond, *The Tories of Chippeny Hill, Connecticut: A Brief Account of the Loyalists of Bristol, Plymouth and Harwinton, who Founded St. Matthew's Church in East Plymouth in 1791* (New York: Grafton Press, 1909), 42; for baptisms of Carrington children, see Plymouth, Connecticut, St. Matthew's Episcopal Church (formerly the Episcopal Church in New Cambridge or Bristol), Records 1744–1829, copy by X. Alanson Welton, p. 34, microfilm reel no. 329 at CSL; James Shepard, "A History of the Colonial Episcopal Parish of New Cambridge (Bristol) Conn," MS 34189, Box 1, Folder 1, pp. 79–3 [pagination includes interpolated notes], at the Connecticut Historical Society.

14. Lisa Wilson, *Ye Heart of a Man: The Domestic Life of Men in Colonial New England* (New Haven, CT: Yale University Press, 1999), 154–64.

15. Donald Lines Jacobus, comp., "Families of Ancient New Haven," *New Haven Genealogical Magazine* 1 (1922): 11; 3 (1925): 584. For John Adams's toryism, see *Connecticut Courant*, November 11, 1776, p. 3.

16. "Last Speech."

17. Judith L. Van Buskirk, *Generous Enemies: Patriots and Loyalists in Revolutionary New York* (Philadelphia: University of Pennsylvania Press, 2002), 22, 129–30; Ruma Chopra, *Unnatural Rebellion: Loyalists in New York City during the Revolution* (Charlottesville: University Press of Virginia, 2011), 46; David H. Villers, "The British Army and the Connecticut Loyalists during the War of Independence,

1775–1783," *Connecticut Historical Society Bulletin* 43 (July 1978): 76; John G. Staudt, "Suffolk County," in Joseph S. Tiedemann and Eugene R. Fingerhut, eds., *The Other New York: The American Revolution beyond New York City, 1763–1787* (Albany: State University of New York Press, 2005), 67, 69; Frederic Gregory Mather, *The Refugees of 1776 from Long Island to Connecticut* (Albany, NY: J. B. Lyon, 1913), 166–70.

18. Mather, *Refugees of 1776*, 209–24; Van Buskirk, *Generous Enemies*, 22, 118, 121; W. H. Siebert, "The Refugee Loyalists of Connecticut," *Transactions of the Royal Society of Canada*, ser. III, vol. 10 (1916): 75; Robert A. East, *Connecticut's Loyalists* (Chester, CT: Pequot Press, 1974), 24; David H. Villers, "British Army and the Connecticut Loyalists," 69–70. For Dunbar's September visit to New York, see his confession in the Superior Court Records, Hartford County, Papers by Subject, 1711–1886, Box 128, at CSL.

19. Chopra, *Unnatural Rebellion*, 52–53, 66; Edwin G. Burrows, "Kings County," in Tiedemann and Fingerhut, eds., *The Other New York*, 30. The Howes issued another proclamation in November 1776 with more insistent language about American submission and the text of an oath of allegiance. For the two proclamations, see British Headquarters Papers, Box 2, Items 269 and 334 (photostats of originals), at the New York Public Library. For Clinton's letter, see Henry Clinton Papers, vol. 18, no. 21, at the William L. Clements Library, University of Michigan. Long Islanders' opinion of the redcoats soured once the troops began seizing provisions and plundering; see, for instance, Burrows and Tiedemann essays in Tiedemann and Fingerhut, eds., *The Other New York*, 30–31, 50.

20. Perhaps as many as 19,000 loyalists fought on Britain's behalf during the war; for this figure as well as estimates of the likely sizes of different units, see Paul H. Smith, "The American Loyalists: Notes on Their Organization and Numerical Strength," *WMQ*, 3rd ser., 25 (1968): 259–77.

21. Paul H. Smith, *Loyalists and Redcoats: A Study in British Revolutionary Policy* (Chapel Hill: University of North Carolina Press, 1964), 36–49; Ira D. Gruber, *The Howe Brothers and the American Revolution* (Chapel Hill: University of North Carolina Press, 1972), 115–16; Chase et al., eds., *Papers of George Washington*, 6: 440.

22. Dexter, *Bio. Sketches*, 2: 458–62; Lorenzo Sabine, *Biographical Sketches of Loyalists of the American Revolution, with an Historical Essay*, 2 vols. (Boston: Little, Brown and Co., 1864), 1: 415–17. For Fanning's activities in North Carolina, see Marjoleine Kars, *Breaking Loose Together: The Regulator Rebellion in Pre-Revolutionary North Carolina* (Chapel Hill: University of North Carolina Press, 2002).

23. Smith, *Loyalists and Redcoats*, 34–35, 48–49, 63, 66; Sabine, *Biographical Sketches*, 1: 416.

24. Quote from "Last Speech."

25. Quoted material comes from a document labeled "Dunbars Confesion" and dated January 18, 1777; see the Superior Court Records, Hartford County, Papers by Subject, 1711–1886, Box 128 in CSL. For the Howes' brief sojourn in Eastchester, see Barnet Schecter, *The Battle for New York: The City at the Heart of the American Revolution* (New York: Penguin, 2002), 231, and *Connecticut Journal*, November 6, 1776, p. 2.

26. David H. Villers, "British Army and the Connecticut Loyalists," 65.

27. Fanning was Anglican, and Samuel Seabury (Yale, 1748) served as chaplain of the King's American Regiment. Dexter, *Bio. Sketches*, 2: 179–84, 446–49, 458–61, 492–94, 537–39, 557–59, 568–69, 701–5, 707–8; Henry P. Johnston, *Yale: Her Honor-Roll In The American Revolution* (New York: G. P. Putnam's Sons, 1888), 109.

28. For Dunbar's wages, see his "Confession" in the Superior Court Records, Hartford County, Papers by Subject, 1711–1886, Box 128 at CSL. Although the value fluctuated somewhat in different colonies, a dollar was generally worth about five shillings; see John J. McCusker, *Money & Exchange in Europe & America, 1600–1775: A Handbook* (Chapel Hill: University of North Carolina Press, 1978), 8, 118. In November 1776, the Connecticut Assembly set farm laborers' summertime wages at no more than three shillings a day; see *Ct. State Recs.*, 1: 62.

29. "Last Speech." On the importance of "family feeling" during times of crisis, see Sarah M. S. Pearsall, *Atlantic Families: Lives and letters in the Later Eighteenth Century* (New York: Oxford University Press, 2008), 11–12.

30. *Ct. State Recs.*, 1: 4. The *Connecticut Journal* of New Haven printed a copy of the law on November 13, 1776, and it appeared in the *Connecticut Courant* of Hartford on November 18.

31. In his "Last Speech," Dunbar stated that his wedding to Esther Adams occurred between his first and second trips to Long Island; the precise date is unknown. For average ages of captains in provincial armies, see Fred Anderson, *A People's Army: Massachusetts Soldiers and Society in the Seven Years' War* (Chapel Hill: University of North Carolina Press, 1984), Table 22, p. 237. For the recruitment quota for captains in the King's American Regiment, see the King's American Regiment orderly book, December 1776–November 1777, p. 12, in the Orderly Book Collection, 1764–1815, at the William L. Clements Library, University of Michigan.

32. The list of recruits appeared on a scrap of paper found in Dunbar's pocket at the time of his arrest; see Hartford County Superior Court Records, Papers by Subject 1711–1886, Box 128, at CSL. John Adams is described in a newspaper notice calling for his arrest; see *Connecticut Courant*, November 11, 1776, p. 3. For the other men, see Shepard, "A History of the Colonial Episcopal Parish of New Cambridge (Bristol), Conn.," and Bronson, *History of Waterbury*, pp. 354–56. For the Blakeslees' kin ties to Dunbar, see Donald Lines Jacobus, comp. "Families of Ancient New Haven," *New Haven Genealogical Magazine* 1 (1923): 216–17, 3 (July 1925): 585. Daniel Tuttle's farm was indeed confiscated; see Conn. Arch., Hartford County, County Court, Papers by Subject 1715–1855, Confiscated Estates & Loyalists, RG3, Box 555.

33. Conn. Arch., Revolutionary War, Series I, vol. 4: 162a. For a brief description of the Ticonderoga expedition, see Harold E. Selesky, ed., *Encyclopedia of the American Revolution*, 2nd ed., 2 vols. (Detroit: Charles Scribner's Sons, 2006), 2: 1151–52.

34. Bronson, *History of Waterbury*, 353–57.

35. An Ensign Tuttle was appointed to Dunbar's company in April 1777; see the King's American Regiment orderly book, p. 7. In 1780, Edmund Fanning supplied Daniel Tuttle, "a refugee from Connecticut," with a receipt testifying that he had recruited

seven men when he joined the regiment; see Christopher P. Bickford, *Farmington in Connecticut*, rev. ed. (Canaan, NH: Phoenix, 1988), 179.

36. Dunbar mentioned in his "confession" that he had taken his clothes to Long Island; see Superior Court, Hartford County, Papers by Subject, 1711–1886, Box 128 at CSL.

37. The speculations about Dunbar's travel are based on another loyalist's account of his flight from Connecticut to New York; see Charles M. Jarvis, ed., "An American's Experience in the British Army," *Connecticut Magazine*, 2 (1907), 191–215, 477–90; esp. 194–97.

38. The indictment of Dunbar, dated January 13, 1777, accused him of going from Farmington to New York "on or about the 10th day of November" 1776 and also "on or about the 1st day of January" 1777. This suggests two separate trips, but in his "Last Speech," Dunbar mentions only two trips in all, with the second one, just after his marriage, devoted to preparing to move his family and acquiring his captain's warrant. A more plausible version of events would suggest that these dates are rough approximations of the beginning and end of his second trip, though as noted, the November date has to be pushed back to October if Dunbar indeed met up with the Howes in Eastchester. Dunbar's "confession" specifies that he was in New York in December. See Superior Court, Hartford County, Papers by Subject 1711–1886, Box 128, at CSL, and "Last Speech."

39. Schecter, *Battle for New York*, 231.

40. Schecter, *Battle for New York*, 232–41. Washington, of course, was not captured, but slipped away with his army once again.

41. King's American Regiment orderly book, p. 2.

42. *Connecticut Courant*, November 11, 18, and 25, 1776. The advertisement notes that Adams was "suspected to travel towards the Nine Partners," part of Dutchess County in eastern New York bordering on Connecticut. The date of the ad was November 7, suggesting that Adams's escape occurred the first week of that month. The timing of the departures of Dunbar's other recruits is unknown. The only other scrap of evidence is the proceedings to confiscate Daniel Tuttle's estate, which claim only that he left "some time in the year 1776." See Conn. Arch., Hartford County Court, Papers by Subject, 1715–1855, Confiscated Estates & Loyalists, RG 3, Box 555.

43. King's American Regiment orderly book, pp. 2–5.

44. King's American Regiment orderly book, p. 2.

45. Dunbar's confession and paper found in his pocket, Superior Court, Hartford County, Papers by Subject, 1711–1886, Box 128 at CSL.

46. Superior Court, Hartford County, Papers by Subject, 1711–1886, Box 128 at CSL. The phrases "Forcys Kings" and "A Papper found in Dunbar's Pocket" appear to have been written in two different hands.

47. "Last Speech"; Superior Court, Hartford County, Papers by Subject, 1711–1886, Box 128 at CSL. For Whitman's and Strong's appointments as justices, see *Ct. Colony Recs.*, 15: 276. For the justices' local prominence, see Mabel S. Hurlburt, *Farmington Town Clerks and Their Times* (Hartford, CT: Finlay Brothers, 1943), 70–71, 75, 78.

48. Superior Court, Hartford County, Papers by Subject, 1711–1886, Box 128; Connecticut Superior Court Records, vol. 21, 1772–1777, pp. 383–84, at CSL. Dunbar mentioned the date of the trial and sentencing in "Last Speech."

49. For an account of these victories, see David Hackett Fischer, *Washington's Crossing* (New York: Oxford University Press, 2004).

50. *Connecticut Courant*, January 20, 1777, p. 1.

51. Bradley Chapin, *The American Law of Treason: Revolutionary and Early National Origins* (Seattle: University of Washington Press, 1964), chs. 1–3; *Ct. State Recs.*, 1: 4.

52. *Ct. State Recs.*, 1: 132–33.

53. The description of jail conditions is based on the journal of Major Christopher French, a British prisoner of war confined there shortly before Dunbar's arrival. See Sheldon S. Cohen, "The Connecticut Captivity of Major Christopher French," *Connecticut Historical Society Bulletin*, 55 (Summer/Fall 1990): 157, 181, 185, 189, 203, 221.

54. For Bill, Wadsworth, and Whitmore as Dunbar's roommates, see Conn. Arch., Revolutionary War, Series 1, vol. 29, fol. 69. Dunbar referred to Viets as his fellow prisoner in "Last Speech."

55. Conn. Arch., Revolutionary War, Series 1, vol. 29, fol. 68.

56. Conn. Arch., Revolutionary War, Series 1, vol. 8, fol. 220a.

57. *Connecticut Courant*, November 11, 1776, p. 3; Cohen, "Captivity of Major Christopher French," 211; Connecticut Superior Court Records, vol. 21 (1772–1777), pp. 381–82; Conn. Arch., Revolutionary War, Series 1, vol. 7, p. 187; *Ct. State Recs.*, 1: 495–96.

58. Dexter, *Bio. Sketches*, 2: 557–59; Cohen, "Captivity of Major Christopher French," 190, 205, 210, 216; Hartford Superior Court files, January Term 1777, Drawer 9 (December 1775–March 1778) at CSL; Connecticut Superior Court Records, vol. 21 (1772–1777), pp. 384–85 at CSL; *Connecticut Courant*, January 27, 1777; *Ct. State Recs.*, 1: 310.

59. *Connecticut Courant*, May 6, 1776, December 30, 1776; Hartford County Superior Court Files 1764–1849, Drawer 9 (December 1775–March 1778) at CSL; Cohen, "Captivity of Major Christopher French," 144; Conn. Arch., Revolutionary War, Series 1, vol. 13, 209a.

60. Conn. Arch., Revolutionary War, Series 1, vol. 13, 209a. For a brief biographical sketch of Skene, see Selesky, ed., *Encyclopedia of the American Revolution*, 2: 1062.

61. French did not specifically mention that Whitmore participated in this escape attempt, but a newspaper notice about the men's second try in December implies that Whitmore was involved. See Cohen, "Captivity of Major Christopher French," 204–10; *Connecticut Courant*, December 30, 1776.

62. Hartford County Superior Court Files 1764–1849, Drawer 9 (December 1775– March 1778) at CSL; Cohen, "Captivity of Major Christopher French," 219. There is no direct evidence that Whitmore joined a loyalist regiment, although the accusations of recruitment suggest that he might have done so.

63. Cohen, "Captivity of Major Christopher French," 223, 225–28.

64. Hartford County Superior Court Files 1764–1849, Drawer 9 (December 1775– March 1778) at CSL; Conn. Arch., Revolutionary War Series 1, vol. 13, 209a; *Connecticut Courant*, March 17, 1777. For the December 1775 statute, see *Ct. Colony Recs.*, 15: 192–95. I thank Bruce Mann for help in interpreting the legal issues in this

case. The record lists no first name for Ellsworth. It is possible that he was Oliver Ellsworth, who was admitted to the Connecticut bar in 1771, and subsequently went on to an illustrious career as a Federalist delegate to Congress and chief justice of the Supreme Court. For a brief sketch of his life, see John A. Garraty and Mark C. Carnes, gen. eds., *American National Biography*, 24 vols. (New York: Oxford University Press, 1999), 7: 456–58.

65. Conn. Arch., Revolutionary War, Series 1, vol. 8, fol. 228a, 228b. Whitmore's petition suggests that he had already been remanded to his father's custody but hoped to make that status permanent.

66. Conn. Arch., Revolutionary War Series 1, vol. 13, fol. 210, 211a, 211b; vol. 8, fol. 228c. One copy of the neighbors' endorsement of Daniel Whitmore contained forty-two signatures and another had seventy-one.

67. Hartford County Superior Court, Papers by Subject 1711–1886, Box 128 at CSL. The November date may be linked to John Adams's escape, and the January one to Moses Dunbar's capture—neither of which can be definitively connected to Dunbar's trips to New York, as charged.

68. Pond, *The Tories of Chippeny Hill*, 57. Dunbar's first father-in-law, Zerubbabel Jerome, sided with the Americans and thus would not come to his aid either; see Epaphroditus Peck, *A History of Bristol, Connecticut* (Hartford, CT: Lewis Street Bookshop, 1932), 83.

69. Hartford Superior Court Files, January Term 1777, Drawer 9 (December 1775– March 1778) at CSL; *Connecticut Courant*, January 27, 1777.

70. In "Last Speech," Dunbar stated that "I was betrayed by Jos. Smith." For the Smiths' Anglican affiliation, see Plymouth, Connecticut, Records of St. Matthew's Episcopal Church, microfilm reel #329, p. 29, at CSL, which notes David's baptism on July 9, 1758. Surviving court records of the case do not reveal whether the elder Smith gave testimony during the trial.

71. Hartford Superior Court Files, March Term 1777, Drawer 9 at CSL; Conn. Arch., Revolutionary War, Series 1, vol. 29, fol. 67; vol. 8, fol. 219a. Wadsworth was ultimately sentenced to a year in jail and fined £40. In a series of petitions to the Assembly, Wadsworth begged for clemency, but the case dragged on, in part because he could not afford the fine or jail costs. As late as 1780, Gurdon Whitmore and Solomon Bill both testified that Wadsworth played no role in the escape, leaving open the question of how Dunbar removed his irons. See Conn. Arch., Revolutionary War Series 1, vol. 8, fol. 219a, 220a; vol. 29, fol. 67, 69.

72. *Connecticut Journal*, March 5, 1777.

73. In "Last Speech," Dunbar mentions June 3, not June 14, as his birth date. The difference stems from Britain's switch from the Julian to the Gregorian calendar in 1752, which required an eleven-day adjustment. Only printed versions of this letter to the children survive. See, for instance, Peck, *History of Bristol*, 92–93; Pond, *Tories of Chippeny Hill*, 65; Joseph Anderson, ed., *The Town and City of Waterbury, Connecticut, from the Aboriginal Period to the Year Eighteen Hundred and Ninety-Five* (New Haven, CT: Price and Lee Co., 1896), 434. None of these versions contains the statement about Phoebe's dying words, but it does appear in the version printed in a Hartford diocese Episcopalian publication, the *Calendar*, vol. 2, no. 34 (August 22, 1846), p. 136.

74. Louis P. Masur, *Rites of Execution: Capital Punishment and the Transformation of American Culture, 1776–1865* (New York: Oxford University Press, 1989), 33–35; Scott D. Seay, *Hanging between Heaven and Earth: Capital Crime, Execution Preaching, and Theology in Early New England* (DeKalb: Northern Illinois University Press, 2009), 33–34.

75. "Last Speech." For a more conventional such statement, see Barnett Davenport, *A Brief Narrative of the Life and Confession of Barnett Davenport* ([Hartford?], 1780).

76. EH Diary, entry for March 19, 1777; "Revolutionary Diary Kept by George Norton of Ipswich, 1777–1778," *Essex Institute Historical Collections*, 74 (October 1938), 340.

77. Shepard, "A History of the Colonial Episcopal Parish of New Cambridge (Bristol) Conn.," p. 109a; "Revolutionary Diary Kept by George Norton," 340. The costs of keeping Dunbar in jail from January 24 to March 19 amounted to just over £3; see Hartford Superior Court Records, Papers by Subject 1711–1886, Drawer 113, Costs 1753–1849, at CSL.

78. *Connecticut Courant*, March 17 and 24, 1777; Nathan Strong, *The Reasons and Design of Public Punishments; A Sermon Delivered Before the People Who Were Collected to the Execution of Moses Dunbar* . . . (Hartford, CT: Eben. Watson, 1777), 5. The March 17 *Connecticut Courant* announcement indicated that Strong delivered the sermon in the North Meeting House. For the 1743 executions, see Lawrence B. Goodheart, *The Solemn Sentence of Death: Capital Punishment in Connecticut* (Amherst: University of Massachusetts Press, 2011), 57, 61.

79. Strong, *Reasons and Design of Public Punishments*, 5–18; quotations on pp. 16, 17, italics in the original. See also Mazur, *Rites of Execution*, 28–29; Seay, *Hanging between Heaven and Earth*, 65, 131–33.

80. "Revolutionary Diary Kept by George Norton," 340.

81. Kenneth Walter Cameron, ed., *Connecticut Churchmanship: Records and Historical Papers Concerning the Anglican Church in Connecticut in the Eighteenth and Early Nineteenth Centuries* (Hartford, CT: Transcendental Books, 1969), 36–37; Mary K. Talcott, ed., "List of Burials, or 'Sexton's List,' of the Center Church Burying Ground, Hartford," *Connecticut Quarterly* 4 (1898): 271.

82. *Ct. State Recs.*, 1: 198.

83. Henry Phelps Johnston, *Record of Service of Connecticut Men in the I. War of the Revolution, II. War of 1812, III. Mexican War,* 2 parts (Hartford, CT: Case, Lockwood & Brainard, 1889), part 1: 43, 117, 231.

84. Katharine A. Prichard, ed., *Extracts from the First Book of Town Meetings of Waterbury Relating to the Revolutionary War*, [1895], pp. 4–6, in the CSL.

85. Jacobus, comp., *Families of Ancient New Haven*, 1: 584.

CHAPTER 8

1. The information for this and the next paragraph can be found in EH Diary, entries for September 30–October 26, 1776; Seymour, *Doc. Life*, 295–97, 541.

2. George Washington to Major General William Howe, September 23, 1776, in Philander D. Chase et al., eds., *The Papers of George Washington, Revolutionary War Series*, 24 vols. (Charlottesville: University Press of Virginia, 1985–), 6: 377–79; Seymour, *Doc. Life*, 310; Sheldon S. Cohen, "The Connecticut Captivity of Major Christopher French," *Connecticut Historical Society Bulletin* 55 (Summer/Fall 1990): 180; EH Diary, entry for October 21–26, 1776.

3. EH Diary, entry for January 25, 1777; George Dudley Seymour, *Captain Nathan Hale, Major John Palsgrave Wyllys: A Digressive History* (New Haven, CT, privately printed, 1933), 55–61; Henry P. Johnston, *Yale: Her Honor-Roll In The American Revolution* (New York: G. P. Putnam's Sons, 1888), 298.

4. Seymour, *Doc. Life*, 448–49 (Richard Hale letter), 303 (excerpt from the *Essex Journal* of Newburyport, February 13, 1777). The account was reprinted in the *New London Gazette*, March 14, 1777. An estimated 25,000 American servicemen died during the war—about 6,800 in combat; 8,500 in British prisons; and 10,000 in hospitals and camps; see Richard L. Blanco, ed., *The American Revolution 1775– 1783: An Encyclopedia*, 2 vols. (New York: Garland, 1993), 1: 272.

5. Seymour, *Doc. Life*, 299, 556, 560–61; on June 28, 1777, Enoch made "in part a distribution" of Nathan's clothing; see p. 299; also see EH Diary, entries for January 25, June 3 and 6, 1777.

6. Donald Lines Jacobus and Edgar Francis Waterman, *Hale, House and Related Families Mainly of the Connecticut River Valley* (Hartford: Connecticut Historical Society, 1952), 293. Joseph Hale's wife Rebecca also gave birth to a fifth stillborn daughter.

7. Dexter, *Bio. Sketches*, 3: 481–82; Joseph Huntington, *A Discourse at the Ordination of the Reverend Mr. Enoch Hale, ...* (Hartford, CT: Hudson and Goodwin, 1780), 26–7.

8. Thomas Mead died in April 1775 at age twenty while studying theology at college. For brief biographies of class of 1773 members, see Dexter, *Bio. Sketches*, 3: 469–512.

9. Johnston, *Yale: Her Honor-Roll In The American Revolution*, 278–80; Chase et al., eds., *Papers of George Washington*, 23: 237, 541–43, 594 (quotation); Maria Campbell, *Revolutionary Services and Civil Life of General William Hull* (New York: D. Appleton and Co., 1848), 171–75, 176 (quotation). Hull's army service during the War of 1812 ended in disgrace when he was court-martialed for surrendering Detroit to the British; see Dexter, *Bio. Sketches*, 3: 446–47.

10. Johnston, *Yale: Her Honor-Roll In The American Revolution*, 295–97; Henry Phelps Johnston, ed., *Memoir of Colonel Benjamin Tallmadge* (New York: Gilliss Press, 1904), 7–98, quotation from p. 42. For a general discussion of the secret service, see Alexander Rose, *Washington's Spies: The Story of America's First Spy Ring* (New York: Bantam, 2006).

11. Judith L. Van Buskirk, *Generous Enemies: Patriots and Loyalists in Revolutionary New York* (Philadelphia: University of Pennsylvania Press, 2002), 90–103; Sarah Knott, *Sensibility and the American Revolution* (Chapel Hill: University of North Carolina Press, 2009), 154–60, 168, 174, 184; Johnston, *Memoir of Colonel Benjamin Tallmadge*, 52–57, 132–34, quotation on p. 133. On American officers' identification with André's gentility, see also Robert E. Cray Jr., "Major John André and the Three Captors: Class Dynamics and Revolutionary Memory Wars in the Early Republic, 1780–1831," *Journal of the Early Republic*, 17 (Autumn 1997), 371–97.

12. Seymour, *Doc. Life*, 300, 545.

13. Henry Phelps Johnston, *Record of Service of Connecticut Men in the I. War of the Revolution, II. War of 1812, III. Mexican War* (Hartford, CT: Case, Lockwood, and Brainard, 1889), 1: 231; Robert K. Wright, Jr., *The Continental Army* (Washington, DC: Center of Military History, 1983), 237–38.

14. Johnston, *Record of Service of Connecticut Men*, 1: 117, and his pension record in Revolutionary War Pension Application Files, microfilm reel 862 in the New York

Public Library. Malnourished victims of smallpox, such as many Revolutionary soldiers, were at particular risk of blindness as a consequence of their infection; see Elizabeth A. Fenn, *Pox Americana: The Great Smallpox Epidemic of 1775–1782* (New York: Hill and Wang, 2001), 22.

15. "Extracts from the 1st Book of Town Meetings of Waterbury Relating to the Revolutionary War," copied by Katharine A. Prichard, [1895], pp. 4–8, 15, 45, 53, 55; at CSL. Aaron Dunbar served on militia expeditions, but not in the Continental Army; see Francis Atwater, *History of the Town of Plymouth, Connecticut* (Meriden, CT: Journal Publishing Co., 1895), 93. The remaining three Dunbar sons were too young for military or public service.

16. Harold E. Selesky, ed., *Encyclopedia of the American Revolution*, 2nd ed., 2 vols. (Detroit: Charles Scribner's Sons, 2006) 1: 298–99; Richard Buel Jr., *Dear Liberty: Connecticut's Mobilization for the Revolutionary War* (Middletown, CT: Wesleyan University Press, 1980), 111–14; John Warner Barber, *Connecticut Historical Collections*, 2nd ed. (New Haven, CT: Durrie and Peck and J. W. Barber, 1836), 364–67.

17. The list included George Beckwith, Lemuel and Riverus Carrington, Ezra Dorman, Abel and Levi Frisbie, Chauncy Jerome, Zerubbabel Jerome Jr., Nathaniel Jones, John and Nathaniel Matthews, Jared Peck, Abel and Nehemiah Royce, Joel and Simon Tuttle, and Abraham Waters. The names appear frequently in the minutes of society meetings and list of baptisms in Plymouth, Connecticut, Records of St. Matthew's Episcopal Church (formerly New Cambridge or Bristol), copy by X. Alanson Welton, microfilm reel #329 at CSL; see also Bruce Clouette and Matthew Roth, *Bristol, Connecticut: A Bicentennial History, 1785–1985* (Canaan, NH: Phoenix Publishing, 1984), 13, 29–30.

18. Conn. Arch., Revolutionary War Series I, vol. 8, fol. 152a.

19. The members included James Church, Samuel Comstock, "Mr. Edwards," Jesse Root, and Samuel Wadsworth. Comstock was a representative from New Milford; "Mr. Edwards" may have been Pierpont Edwards, representative from New Haven. Root was a Hartford County justice of the peace, and Church and Wadsworth were active in Hartford's town affairs. For the member list, see Conn. Arch., Revolutionary War Series I, vol. 8, fol. 152b.

20. Conn. Arch., Revolutionary War, Series I, vol. 8, fols. 153, 155a.

21. Conn. Arch., Revolutionary War, Series I, vol. 8, fol. 153; *Ct. State Recs.*, 1: 259–60. For Levi Frisbie's enlistment, see "Lists and Returns of Connecticut Men in the Revolution," *Collections of the Connecticut Historical Society*, 12 (1909), p. 49. For Connecticut Tories involved in the Danbury attack, see W. H. Siebert, "The Refugee Loyalists of Connecticut," *Transactions of the Royal Society of Canada*, 3rd ser., 10 (1916), 78.

22. See John Shy's discussion of the war as a "political education conducted by military means" in *A People Numerous and Armed: Reflections on the Military Struggle for American Independence* (New York: Oxford University Press, 1976), ch. 9, quotation from p. 216.

23. See, for instance, *Ct. State Recs.*, 1: 283, 284, 296, 298–99, 373, 479, 496, 551.

24. *Ct. State Recs.*, 2: 279–80.

25. *Ct. State Recs.*, 2: 386–87; Buel, *Dear Liberty*, 190–96, 263–65, 272–75, 287–88.

26. Dexter, *Bio. Sketches*, 3: 426; Record of Baptisms in the Records of the Episcopal Church in New Cambridge, microfilm reel #329, p. 36, CSL. There is no record of the date of the Jeromes' marriage, but it probably did not occur before early 1778. It is thus likely that there was at least one set of twins among the four children brought for baptism in August 1780. E. LeRoy Pond, among others, suggests that Chauncy and Esther Jerome moved to Nova Scotia until after the war, but there is no evidence that they went there at all, and the church records show them in Farmington in 1780; see *The Tories of Chippeny Hill, Connecticut* (New York: Grafton Press, 1909), 68.

27. Jonathan Trumbull, *A Proclamation For a Day of Public Thanksgiving* (New Haven, CT: Thomas and Samuel Green, 1783); *Ct. State Recs.*, 5: 210.

28. John Marsh, *A Discourse Delivered at Wethersfield, December 11th, 1783* (Hartford, CT: Hudson and Goodwin, 1784), 19, 20; Benjamin Trumbull, *A Sermon, Delivered at North-Haven, December 11, 1783* (New Haven, CT: Thomas and Samuel Green, 1784), 11. On the mingling of religion and Whig politics, see Nathan O. Hatch, *The Sacred Cause of Liberty: Republican Thought and the Millennium in Revolutionary New England* (New Haven, CT: Yale University Press, 1977).

29. Thomas Brockway, *America saved, or Divine Glory displayed, in the late War with Great-Britain* (Hartford, CT: Hudson and Goodwin, 1784), 20–21; Trumbull, *Sermon*, 14; Marsh, *Discourse*, 15. See also Sarah J. Purcell, *Sealed with Blood: War, Sacrifice, and Memory in Revolutionary America* (Philadelphia: University of Pennsylvania Press, 2002), 62–63.

30. Robert McCluer Calhoon, *The Loyalists in Revolutionary America, 1760–1781* (New York: Harcourt Brace Jovanovich, Inc., 1965), 281–82.

31. Mary Beth Norton, *The British Americans: The Loyalist Exiles in England, 1774–1789* (Boston: Little, Brown, 1972), 37; North Callahan, *Flight from the Republic: The Tories of the American Revolution* (Indianapolis: Bobbs-Merrill, 1967), 125, 142–43; Oscar Zeichner, "The Rehabilitation of Loyalists in Connecticut," *New England Quarterly* 11 (1938): 309. On the loyalist diaspora, see Maya Jasanoff, *Liberty's Exiles: American Loyalists in the Revolutionary World* (New York: Knopf, 2011).

32. Buel, *Dear Liberty*, 297; Zeichner, "Rehabilitation of Loyalists," 315–23.

33. Bruce C. Daniels, *The Connecticut Town: Growth and Development, 1635–1790* (Middletown, CT: Wesleyan University Press, 1979), 34–33.

34. *Ct. State Recs.*, 6: 84–85; Christopher P. Bickford, *Farmington in Connecticut*, 2nd ed. (Canaan, NH: Phoenix Publishing, 1988), 101, 202 (quotation); Clouette and Roth, *Bristol, Connecticut*, 9, 34–36.

35. Zeichner, "Rehabilitation of Loyalists," 320–21; Bruce E. Steiner, *Connecticut Anglicans in the Revolutionary Era: A Study in Communal Tensions* (Hartford: American Revolution Bicentennial Commission of Connecticut, 1978), 67–71.

36. Nancy L. Rhoden, *Revolutionary Anglicanism: The Colonial Church of England Clergy during the American Revolution* (New York: New York University Press, 1999), 118; SPG Recs., Correspondence relating to the North American Colonies (1701–1786), Series C, vol. 3, pp. 91–92.

37. E. Edwards Beardsley, *The History of the Episcopal Church in Connecticut, from the Settlement of the Colony to the Death of Bishop Seabury*, 4th ed., 2 vols. (Boston: Houghton, Mifflin, 1883), 1: 353–55; SPG Recs., Correspondence relating to the

North American Colonies (1701–1786), Series C, vol. 3, pp. 57–59; Ross N. Hebb, *The Church of England in Loyalist New Brunswick, 1783–1825* (Cranbury, NJ: Fairleigh Dickinson University Press, 2004), 29–31, 54, 57, 131, 184.

38. Dexter, *Bio. Sketches*, 3: 426; *Acts and Laws of the State of Connecticut* (New London, CT: Timothy Green, 1784), 21–22; James Shepard, *The Episcopal Church and Early Ecclesiastical Laws of Connecticut* (New Britain, CT: n. p., 1908), 127–28; Records of St. Matthew's Church, Plymouth, Connecticut, 1747–1877, microfilm reel no. 329, p. 11, at CSL; Eddy N. Smith, George Benton Smith, and Allena J. Dates, *Bristol, Connecticut ("In the Olden Time New Cambridge") Which Includes Forestville* (Hartford, CT: City Print Co., 1907), 34–35.

39. Beardsley, *History of the Episcopal Church in Connecticut*, 1: 347–51; 358–404; Rhoden, *Revolutionary Anglicanism*, 118–20. The Scots bishops willing to consecrate Seabury were successors to the non-juring bishops who had refused to take the Oath of Allegiance to William and Mary after the Glorious Revolution. The best study of Seabury is Bruce E. Steiner, *Samuel Seabury, 1729–1796: A Study in the High Church Tradition* (Athens: Ohio University Press, 1971). Connecticut's Congregationalist Church was finally disestablished in 1818.

40. See John Dunbar Jr.'s will, Waterbury District Probate Records, no. 2444, at the CSL. John Dunbar Sr.'s will is no. 2445, and contains several anomalous features. He named his twin sons, Jonathan and David, as his executors even though they were just sixteen years old when he wrote his will (and when he died); county officials replaced them with their older brother Aaron. Also, it is unclear why John Dunbar named only Moses Jr. and not any of the grandchildren that Phoebe Dunbar bore.

41. The distribution of property is included in probate documents for John Dunbar, Waterbury District Probate Records, no. 2445.

42. Pond, *Tories of Chippeny Hill*, 69; Purcell, *Sealed with Blood*, 70–71. Michael Kammen notes that "amnesia is more likely to be induced by the desire for reconciliation"; see *Mystic Chords of Memory: The Transformation of Tradition in American Culture* (New York: Knopf, 1991), 13.

43. Dexter, *Bio. Sketches*, 3: 481; Henry Phelps Johnston, *Nathan Hale, 1776: Biography and Memorials* (New Haven, CT: Yale University Press, 1914), 9–10.

44. On the emergence of Revolutionary-era heroes, see Purcell, *Sealed with Blood*, 18–38.

45. Knott, *Sensibility and the American Revolution*, 180; Benson J. Lossing, *The Two Spies: Nathan Hale and John André* (New York: D. Appleton and Co., 1886), 106–8; *The Independent Chronicle and the Universal Advertiser* (Boston, Massachusetts), May 17, 1781, p. 1. On the appeal of André, see also Michael Kammen, *A Season of Youth: The American Revolution and the Historical Imagination* (New York: Knopf, 1978), 105–6, 118, 131.

46. George Dudley Seymour attributes the poem to Munson; others have suggested it was the work of Timothy Dwight; see *Doc. Life*, 357–63. Seward's poem is reprinted in Lossing, *Two Spies*, 131–51; see also Kenneth Silverman, *A Cultural History of the American Revolution* (New York: Columbia University Press, 1987), 380.

47. Timothy Dwight, *The Conquest of Canaan; A Poem, in Eleven Books* (Hartford, CT: Elisha Babcock, 1785), pp. 3–4; Seymour, *Doc. Life*, 70–71; Silverman, *Cultural*

History of the American Revolution, 500–3. For a brief biographical portrait of Dwight, see Dexter, *Bio. Sketches*, 3: 321–26.

48. Hannah Adams, *A Summary History of New England, From the First Settlement at Plymouth, to the Acceptance of the Federal Constitution* (Dedham, MA: H. Mann and J. H. Adams, 1799), 358–61 (quotations from unpaginated introduction and p. 361); Campbell, *Revolutionary Services and Civil Life Of General William Hull*, 49–51. For biographical information about Adams, s. v. "Hannah Adams" in John A. Garraty and Mark C. Carnes, gen. eds., *American National Biography* 24 vols. (New York: Oxford University Press, 1999). On the limited success of efforts to memorialize Hale right after the war, see also Robert E. Cray Jr., "The Revolutionary Spy as Hero: Nathan Hale in the Public Memory, 1776–1846," *Connecticut History*, 38 (Fall 1999), 91–93; Mary Beth Baker, "Nathan Hale: Icon of Innocence," *Connecticut History*, 45 (Spring 2006), 8.

49. Alfred F. Young, *The Shoemaker and the Tea Party: Memory and the American Revolution* (Boston: Beacon Press, 1999), 108–17; Kammen, *Mystic Chords of Memory*, 54–55; Purcell, *Sealed with Blood*, 18–48; John Resch, *Suffering Soldiers: Revolutionary War Veterans, Moral Sentiment, and Political Culture in the Early Republic* (Amherst: University of Massachusetts Press, 1999), 2–5, 65.

50. On the class dimensions of the André episode, see Cray, "Major John André and the Three Captors," 371–97. When a controversy erupted in 1817 over giving pensions to André's captors, Benjamin Tallmadge—then a state representative—vigorously opposed rewarding men he saw as ruffians. For the cenotaph, see Seymour, *Doc. Life*, 548–49. On the political uses of sensibility in this period, see David Waldstreicher, *In the Midst of Perpetual Fetes: The Making of American Nationalism, 1776–1820* (Chapel Hill: University of North Carolina Press, 1997), 74–77.

51. Young, *Shoemaker and the Tea Party*; Alfred F. Young, *Masquerade: The Life and Times of Deborah Sampson, Continental Soldier* (New York: Knopf, 2004); Resch, *Suffering Soldiers*; Purcell, *Sealed with Blood*.

52. Resch, *Suffering Soldiers*, 118; Seymour, *Doc. Life*, 319–25 (quotations on 368, 324, 325), 367–75, 412–14. Bostwick's reminiscence dates from 1826. See also William S. Powell, "A Connecticut Soldier under Washington: Elisha Bostwick's Memoirs of the First Years of the Revolution," *WMQ*, 3rd ser., 6 (January 1949): 94–107.

53. Young, *Shoemaker and the Tea Party*, 132–42; Kammen, *Season of Youth*, 26, 41–49; Purcell, *Sealed with Blood*, 171–80, 187–209.

54. Seymour, *Doc. Life*, 311–14 (quotation on 314). Hempstead noted that Mercy Otis Warren mentioned Hale in the context of the André episode in her history of the Revolution; see Mercy Warren, *History of the Rise, Progress and Termination of the American Revolution*, 3 vols. (Boston: Manning and Loring, 1805), 2: 264–65.

55. In addition to Stuart, I. Holbrook of Norwich, Connecticut, and Cyrus P. Bradley of Hanover, New Hampshire, planned to produce Hale biographies. See Seymour, *Doc. Life*, 315–18, 333–54; quote from 315. Stuart described his search for biographical material in his book's preface; see *Life of Captain Nathan Hale, the Martyr-Spy of the American Revolution* (Hartford, CT: F. A. Brown, 1856), i–vii. On the effort to preserve testimony of Revolutionary survivors, see Kammen, *Season of Youth*, 43–49.

56. Purcell, *Sealed with Blood*, 96, 103–6, 125–26, 145–49, 194–201; Kammen, *Mystic Chords of Memory*, 11, 54–55; Kammen, *Season of Youth*, 106–9.

57. Seymour, *Doc. Life*, 331; Cray, "Revolutionary Spy as Hero," 95–96; *Connecticut Courant*, January 19, 1835, p. 2.

58. For a thorough account of this fund-raising effort, see Cray, "Revolutionary Spy as Hero," 96–98; see also Johnston, *Nathan Hale, 1776*, 143. A detailed description of the monument, including an engraved illustration, appears in Stuart, *Life of Captain Nathan Hale*, 155–59.

59. Waldstreicher, *In the Midst of Perpetual Fetes*, ch. 5; Cray, "Revolutionary Spy as Hero," 99; John C. Pease and John M. Niles, *A Gazetteer of the States of Connecticut and Rhode Island* (Hartford, CT: William S. Marsh, 1819), 291–95; Barber, *Connecticut Historical Collections*, 545–47. On the role of print in promoting democratic culture and commercial opportunity in New England, see David Jaffee, "The Village Enlightenment in New England, 1760–1820," *WMQ*, 3rd ser., 47 (1990): 327–46.

60. Cray, "Revolutionary Spy as Hero," 98; Seymour, *Doc. Life*, 562–63; Kammen, *Season of Youth*, 87.

61. Johnston, *Nathan Hale, 1776*, 143–46. For a discussion of eighteenth-century understandings of fame and honor, see Trevor Colbourn, ed., *Fame and the Founding Fathers: Essays by Douglass Adair* (New York: Norton, 1974), 4–26.

62. Kammen, *Mystic Chords of Memory*, 12–13; Kammen, *Season of Youth*, 15–21, 108, 133.

63. Jones's history remained unpublished for nearly a century; see Thomas Jones, *History of New York During the Revolutionary War, and of the Leading Events in the Other Colonies at that Period*, ed. Edward Floyd deLancey, 2 vols. (New York: New York Historical Society, 1879), 1: 175–77.

64. *Waterbury Daily American*, February 6, 1875. Epaphroditus Peck reported that the papers were taken to Joseph Anderson, a Waterbury Congregationalist minister and president of the Mattatuck Historical Society; see Peck's *A History of Bristol, Connecticut* (Hartford, CT: Lewis Street Bookshop, 1932), 84. A slightly different version of these documents appeared nearly thirty years earlier, in a Connecticut Episcopalian publication, *The Calendar*, vol. 2, no. 34 (August 22, 1846), p. 136. This version notes that Dunbar's statement was printed "at the request of his son," but there is no information about the whereabouts of the original manuscript.

65. Kammen, *Season of Youth*, 63; Joseph Anderson, ed., *The Town and City of Waterbury, Connecticut, from the Aboriginal Period to the Year Eighteen Hundred and Ninety-Five*, 3 vols. (New Haven, CT: Price and Lee, 1896) 1: 434; Pond, *Tories of Chippeny Hill*, 9, 46, 56; Peck, *History of Bristol*, 82. Peck produced several versions of his Bristol history, always including Dunbar. See his "Loyal to the Crown," *Connecticut Magazine* 8 (1903–4): 129–36, 297–300; "Moses Dunbar, Loyalist" in Smith et al., eds., *Bristol, Connecticut*, 141–57; *The Loyalists of Connecticut* (New Haven: Tercentenary Commission of the State of Connecticut, 1934). For a briefer mention of Dunbar, see also Atwater, *History of the Town of Plymouth*, 92.

66. James Shepard mentions LeRoy Pond's ancestry, which included a connection to the loyalist Stephen Graves as well, in a June 12, 1908, letter to George Dudley Seymour; see James Shepard Correspondence and Research, 1897–1919, MS 83889, Connecticut Historical Society.

67. Anderson, ed., *Town and City of Waterbury*, 434–36; Pond, *Tories of Chippeny Hill*, 56–59, 61–62, 65; Peck, *History of Bristol*, 85–86, 92–94.

68. See Peck's chapter in Smith et al., eds., *Bristol, Connecticut*, 155–57. For an account of how this search for national reconciliation led to a retreat from racial equality, see David W. Blight, *Race and Reunion: The Civil War in American Memory* (Cambridge, MA: Harvard University Press, 2001).

69. Anderson, ed., *Town and City of Waterbury*, 434; Peck, *History of Bristol*, 90, 95. For Peck's religious affiliation, see his obituary in the *New York Times*, October 30, 1938, p. L41. James Shepard portrayed Dunbar as an Anglican victim in his unpublished work, "A History of the Colonial Episcopal Parish of New Cambridge (Bristol), Conn.," MS 34189, Box 1, Folder 1 at the Connecticut Historical Society. Shepard was a descendant of James Nichols; see his letter of February 25, 1913, to George Dudley Seymour, James Shepard Correspondence and Research, 1897–1919, MS 83889, at the Connecticut Historical Society.

70. Atwater, *History of the Town of Plymouth*, 14, 47, 429–30; for Aaron Dunbar's will and inventory, see Waterbury Probate District records, no. 2440; and for Jonathan Dunbar, Plymouth Probate District, no. 264, both at CSL. Jonathan's twin brother, David, died in 1847, but no probate materials survive. For death dates for the brothers, see Donald Lines Jacobus, comp. "Families of Ancient New Haven," *New Haven Genealogical Magazine* 3, no. 2 (July 1925): 584–85.

71. Revolutionary War Pension Application Files, *R-USLHG, Reel 862, microfilm at the New York Public Library. On the poverty and health problems of many veterans, see Resch, *Suffering Soldiers*. For the New York land grants, see W. W. Clayton, *History of Onondaga County, New York* (Syracuse, NY: D. Mason and Co., 1878), 7–10, and p. 395 for a mention of Pompey, where Miles lived, as township #10 of the Military Tract. For Joel, see Mrs. E. T. Pike et al., *Pioneer History of Camden, Oneida County, New York* (Utica, NY: T. J. Griffith, 1897), 169, 387, 390.

72. Anderson believed that the letter to the children was in Dunbar's hand, but the dying statement had been copied by Cook; see *Town and City of Waterbury*, pp. 434, 436. For other mentions of Cook as the copyist, see the letter by Epaphroditus Peck, September 8, 1934, MS. M-12 in the Collections of the Mattatuck Museum Arts & History Center, Waterbury, CT; and the letter from James Shepard to George Dudley Seymour, April 16, 1914, James Shepard Correspondence and Research, 1897–1919, MS 83889 at the Connecticut Historical Society.

73. *Waterbury Daily American*, February 6, 1875.

74. Donald Lines Jacobus, comp., *Families of Ancient New Haven*, 3 vols. (Rome, NY: C. Smith, 1923), 1:443; Connecticut Marriage Records, Barbour Collection, Harwinton Vital Records, p. 62, at the CSL. A land record dated April 27, 1795, lists Sylvanus Cook as deceased; see Harwinton Land Records, Book 5, p. 668, at the CSL. US Federal Census Records for 1790, 1800, and 1810, are available online at Ancestry.com.

75. Phoebe's birth was listed in the New Cambridge church records, but there is no mention of a Sene Dunbar.

76. This supposition is supported by the entry in the 1790 federal census for Chauncy (misspelled as "Canuy") Jerome of Bristol, which lists just seven members in his household.

77. The marriage of Dana Dunbar and Esther Blakeslee is listed in the Watertown Vital Records, Connecticut Marriage Records, pre-1870 (Barbour Collection) at CSL and the possible New York residences can be tracked in the US Federal Census Records for 1800 (Plymouth, CT), 1820 and 1830 (Sheldon, Genesee County, NY). The ages match for a son born around 1770. These materials are available online at Ancestry.com. The Dana Dunbar who died in Detroit had a son named Chauncy, which suggests the link to Moses; for a record of the administration of his intestate estate, see Probate Orders, Letters, Bonds, 1841–1969, Surrogate's Court (Wyoming County, NY) at Ancestry.com.

78. Zina Dunbar is recorded as living in the town of Troy, Bradford County, Pennsylvania, in the 1820, 1830, 1840, and 1850 federal censuses; these records are available at Ancestry.com. See also H. C. Bradsby, *History of Bradford County, Pennsylvania, with Biographical Selections* (Chicago: S. B. Nelson, 1891), 353, 433; Paul B. Moyer, *Wild Yankees: The Struggle for Independence along Pennsylvania's Revolutionary Frontier* (Ithaca, NY: Cornell University Press, 2007), 194–95.

79. Guardianship bond, 1792, Farmington Probate District, no. 935, at CSL.

80. According to census records, a Moses Dunbar of the right age as the traitor's son appears in New London in 1800 and Waterford (which split off from New London in 1801) in 1810 and 1820; the latter census notes that the household head worked in agriculture. A younger Moses, who might possibly be a grandson of the traitor, is listed in the 1830 census for Waterford and the 1840 census for East Lyme (which split off from Waterford in 1839), where he is described as employed in the "navigation of the ocean." See these census materials at Ancestry.com. For the Moses Dunbar who served briefly as a militia private in the War of 1812, see Johnston, *Record of Service of Connecticut Men*, pt. 2, p. 48.

INDEX

A

Adams, Betsey, 108–9, 118, 124, 203, 237n29

Adams, Hannah, 200, 243n45, 257n48

Adams, John (Dunbar's brother-in-law), 156, 162–65, 246n15, 248n32, 249n42, 251n67

Adams, John (national leader), 137, 202, 233n48

Adams, Samuel, 156

African Americans, 2–3, 102, 164, 235n13

Alden, Roger, 64–65, 67, 73, 97, 100–1, 105–6, 118, 124, 228n41, 240n9

American Duties Act of 1764 (Sugar Act), 42, 70

Anderson, Joseph, 207, 215n10, 258n64

Anderson, Samuel, 8, 22, 87

André, John, 186–87, 198–201, 203–4, 257n50

Andrews, Samuel, 83, 90, 95, 160

Anglicans: American Protestant Episcopal Church and, 196; attacked or threatened, 44, 83–84, 87, 92, 142, 150–53, 188, 191, 194–95; bishops or clergy, 37–39, 45, 111, 151–52, 160, 170, 194–96, 256n39; in Claremont (NH), 78–79; Congregationalists and (*see under* Congregationalists); Dunbars as (*see under* Dunbar, Moses; Dunbar, Phoebe); in Hartford (CT), 179; loyalist (or not), 5, 44, 83–84, 87–90, 94–95, 110, 152, 160, 170, 174, 188; in New Cambridge (CT), (*see under* New Cambridge); New Lights vs., 16, 36–37; in Northbury or Waterbury (CT), 36, 38–41, 77–80, 155, 160, 232n37; protests by, 43, 46–47. *See also* Church of England

Arnold, Benedict, 186, 192

Ashford (CT), 19, 21, 129, 139

Avery, David, 59, 226n22, 227n26

B

Barns, Asahel, 163, 165

Belcher, John, 116

Bible, 40, 60–61, 65, 146–47, 152, 175, 179

Bill, Solomon, 170, 250n54, 251n71

Billings, Elisha, 68–69

Boston: British soldiers evacuate, 131–32, 139, 151; British soldiers in or siege of, 90, 114–15, 121–22, 125–26, 130–31, 135, 144, 146; Dorchester Heights, 131, 135; Hale in or near, 117–26; Harvard and, 72; map, 126–27; news or rumors about, 87–88, 110–11, 237n35; newspapers, 45, 198; port closure, 82, 85, 109; protests, radicals, or mobs in, 43, 45–48 (*see also* Boston Massacre; Boston Tea Party)

Boston Massacre, 47

Boston Port Act, 81–82

Boston Tea Party, 75–76, 80–83, 89, 109

Bostwick, Elisha, 202, 239n5, 257n52

boycotts, 43, 45–47, 87, 91

Bristol (CT), 194, 207, 210

British army, 131–34, 142–43, 161, 163, 168; Hessians in, 133, 136, 142, 157; King's American Regiment, 158–59, 248n27, 248n31; loyalists join or support, 131, 151, 153, 156–64, 233n48, 244n55, 247n20; officers, 138, 143, 148, 170–71; provincial troops, 8, 13–15, 23–25, 88, 117, 138, 161, 182, 216n4, 239n3, 248n31; training, 136, 164

British Empire, 4, 8, 10, 28, 42, 94, 96, 109–10, 153; colonies, 10, 28, 39, 94, 96, 116. *See also* Great Britain

British navy. *See* Great Britain: navy

Brothers in Unity, 62, 64, 227n26

Bunker Hill, 90, 115, 118, 139, 205

C

Cambridge (MA), 95, 116, 118, 124–25, 139, 144

Canada, 8, 13, 193, 195; Halifax, 131–32, 151; Montreal, 125; New Brunswick, 195; Quebec, 91, 95

Carrington, Lemuel, 155–56, 188

Cato, 70, 111

Cato (play), 148, 245n67

Charles II, King, 10

Charleston, 46, 76

Christophers, Betsey, 122, 124

Church of England, 16, 35–41, 45, 79, 87, 177, 194, 208, 234n50. *See also* Anglicans

Civil War, 205, 207

Clap, Thomas, 56–57, 59, 70

Claremont (NH), 78–80, 150, 230n9, 230–31n13, 231n14

class, social or economic, 3, 55, 70, 103. *See also* gentility

Cliffe, Loftus, 148–49

Clinton, Henry, 157–58

Clinton, James, 139–40

Coercive Acts, 80–81, 84, 109

committees of correspondence, 48, 82, 109–11

committees of inspection or observation, 86, 90, 151, 165, 173–74, 189, 232n28

Concord (MA), 88, 113, 118, 126

Congregational Church, 10, 16, 18, 49, 57, 178, 184, 205

Congregationalists, 9, 20, 49, 78, 84, 89, 115, 177, 179, 192, 194, 196, 206, 208, 256n39; Anglicans and, 16, 36–41, 43–44, 49, 85, 194

Connecticut: British attacks on, 187–90; charter of, 10–12, 33, 44, 47, 77, 82, 91; clergy or religion in, 36–37, 44, 46, 78–79, 83, 85, 94, 193–94; as colony vs. state, 153–54, 168–69; committees of inspection in, 85–86, 90–91, 111, 151, 232n28; courts, 2–3, 165; factions or divisions in, 3, 5, 11–12, 18, 36, 89, 91, 94; French and Indian War's impact on, 7–8, 10, 28; government, 10–11, 46, 96, 109, 153, 178–79 (*see also* Connecticut General Assembly); governors, 10, 44, 46, 56, 77, 103, 112, 153 (*see also* Fitch, Thomas; Trumbull, Jonathan); Hale memorials in, 204–6; history or economy of, 10–11, 30, 46–47, 102–3, 194, 206–8; landowners in, 20, 22,

30, 32, 35; loyalists in, 6, 93–96, 141, 145, 151, 153, 157, 160, 168, 189–90, 193, 197; militia or regiments from, 13–14, 88–91, 110, 112, 114–17, 125, 128, 135, 138–39, 163, 179–81, 187–89, 191, 202; newspapers in, 70–71, 90, 102, 154, 161, 203 (*see also Connecticut Courant*; *Waterbury Daily American*); northeastern, 19; officials, 47, 56, 88, 170, 190, 193, 204, 208; postal service in, 104; postwar, 191–97, 202–5; protests or mobs in, 43, 82, 85, 90; western, 16, 94, 160, 188

Connecticut Council of Safety, 180, 190

Connecticut Courant, 30, 42–43, 47, 75–76, 83, 163, 203

Connecticut General Assembly, 43, 44, 48, 112, 162, 188–89; charters and, 10, 77, 102; Hale commissioned by, 115–16; legislation, 95–96, 153–54, 161, 169, 172, 193, 195; R. Hale as member of, 23, 69, 228n48; reacts to British acts, 44, 48, 69, 81; reacts to start of war, 88–91; Wyoming Valley settlement and, 32, 77; Yale and, 57

Connecticut River, 15, 19, 55, 78, 97, 98, 170

Continental Army, 128, 140, 122–25, 128, 136, 157, 164, 180, 185–90, 208, 254n15

Continental Association, 85–86, 95, 111

Continental Congress, 80, 91, 94–96, 137–38, 191; Declaration of Independence by, 132–33, 152–54, 202; Declaration of Rights and Resolves by, 85; disagreements in, 96, 117, 119; opposition to or treason against, 86, 89–90, 92, 94–95, 153–54, 169; Robert Rogers and, 144–45; trade embargo by, 85–86, 110; Washington and, 117, 132, 136, 143–44

Cook, Ebenezer, 49, 155, 246n12, 259n72

Cook, Sylvanus, 209

Cooley, Daniel, 105, 107–8

Coventry (CT), 19, 218n29; churches in, 10, 20, 205, 219n40; disputes in, 19–20, 218n32; Hale's legacy in, 203–5; Hales in, 9, 19, 22–23, 25–26, 28, 51–54, 69, 73–74, 97, 128–29, 133, 137, 149, 181, 183, 201, 229n58

criminals, 2, 154, 170, 176, 214n3

Cunningham, William, 146, 182

currency, 11, 15, 20, 30, 47, 61, 185, 218n33

Cutler, Timothy, 36

D

Daggett, Naphtali, 56–57, 61, 67–68, 70, 228n50

Danbury (CT), 55, 187–90

Declaration of Independence, 132–33, 152–54, 202

Declaratory Act, 45–46

Dorchester (MA), 129

Dunbar, Aaron, 187, 196–97, 208, 254n15, 256n40

Dunbar, Bede, 42, 79, 150, 176, 209–211, 220n4, 224–25n55, 230n12

Dunbar, Dana, 210, 260n77

Dunbar, Edward, 13, 15, 18, 24–25, 48, 216–17n14, 217n20, 220n45

Dunbar, Esther Adams, 156, 161, 163, 165, 179–80, 191, 209–10, 248n31, 255n26

Dunbar, Joel, 180, 187, 208–9

Dunbar, John (father of Moses), 9, 12–15, 18, 21–27, 48–49, 196, 220n45, 256n40; in military, 13–14, 27; Moses and, 26–27, 30–31, 35–36, 48, 79, 173–74, 176, 196–97, 220n49; move to Waterbury of, 12–13, 15, 26

Dunbar, John (grandfather of Moses), 24–25

Dunbar, Miles, 180, 187, 196–97, 208–9
Dunbar, Moses: as Anglican, 5, 35–36,
    40–42, 49, 87, 110, 153, 159, 174,
    178, 208; arrested, 165; brothers
    of, in Continental Army, 180,
    187, 208–9; childhood and youth
    of, 9–10, 12, 26–27; children of, 42,
    48–49, 79, 87, 150–51, 161, 163, 165,
    175–76, 196–97, 209–10, 224–25n55,
    230n12, 230–31n13, 258n64, 260n77,
    260n78 (*see also* Dunbar, Bede;
    Dunbar, Dana; Dunbar, Moses [son];
    Dunbar, Zina); "confession," of 165,
    168, 173, 249n36, 249n38; described,
    9, 175, 216n4; documents about,
    5, 159; enlists, 159–60; escape
    attempt, 174–75, 251n71; executed,
    168, 177–80; family and friends after
    execution, 180, 183, 187, 191–92,
    196–97, 206–11; in Farmington
    (CT), 156, 161, 165; father of (*see*
    Dunbar, John [father]); finances,
    49, 79, 155, 160; Hale compared
    to, 2, 4–6, 21–22, 157, 183–84, 183;
    Howe and, 159, 163, 206; in jail, 4–5,
    169–70, 172–77, 192, 252n77; "Last
    Speech" of, 5, 176–77, 206, 215n10,
    220n49, 223n36, 224–25n55, 232n32,
    251n70, 251n73; letter from, 175–76,
    207, 215n10, 251n73, 259n72; on
    Long Island, 156–57, 159–61, 163,
    248n31, 249n36; marries Esther
    Adams, 156, 161; marries Phoebe
    Jerome, 30–32, 48, 107, 248n31;
    mob attacks, 92, 110, 150, 155, 176;
    outspokenness of, 5, 9, 87, 176,
    232n32; recruits others, 161–67,
    248n32; sentenced, 168–69, 173–74;
    siblings, 180, 187, 196–97, 208–9;
    sympathetic accounts of, 206–8;
    as traitor, 2, 4, 165, 167, 197; trial
    of, 165, 172, 181; on "Unhappy
    Misunderstanding," 91–92; in
    Waterbury (CT), 79–80, 85, 151,
    154–56, 165; Whitmore compared
    to, 172–74

Dunbar, Moses (son of Moses and
    Esther), 180, 197, 210–11, 260n80
Dunbar, Phoebe (wife of Moses), 80,
    153, 155–56, 175–76, 188, 210; as
    Anglican, 35–37, 40–42, 79; children
    of, 42, 48–49, 79, 87, 150–51,
    176, 209–10, 224–25n55, 230n12,
    230–31n13, 256n40; death of,
    150–51, 153, 155; marriage of, 30–32,
    35, 107
Dunbar, Phoebe (daughter of Moses),
    87, 209
Dunbar, Sene, 209
Dunbar, Temperance, 36, 48–49,
    162, 197; children of, 12, 21, 23–24,
    26–27, 30, 219n36, 254n15; Moses
    and, 36, 48, 176, 220n49, 222n23
Dunbar, Zina, 49, 210, 260n78
Dwight, Samuel, 55, 97
Dwight, Timothy, 61, 63, 70, 124,
    199–200, 202–3, 227n26, 256n46

E
Eastchester (NY), 159, 163
East Haddam (CT), 74, 84, 97–99,
    102–4, 120
East India Company, 75–76, 80, 87
East River, 132–33, 136, 138, 142
Episcopalians, 195, 208
executions, 1–2, 39, 176, 182, 187, 190,
    198, 202–3, 213–14n2, 214n3;
    Dunbar's, 168–69, 177–79; Hale's, 2,
    4, 146–48, 186

F
Fanning, Edmund, 158–61, 163–64,
    248n27, 248n35
farmers, 4, 20, 24–25, 28, 50, 52, 56,
    210, 225n8; Connecticut, 5, 7, 10, 21,
    27, 32, 162, 188, 209, 221n11, 222n20;
    difficulties facing, 13, 19, 30, 54,
    60, 77, 99, 158; troops provisioned
    by, 14–15
Farmington (CT), 32, 88, 221n10;
    churches or parishes of, 37, 39,
    83–84, 92, 194; Dunbars in, 15,

92, 110, 156, 159, 161–65, 173–74;
Jeromes in, 30–35, 92, 188; loyalists
vs. radicals in, 81–84, 86, 92, 110,
180, 187, 207; officials or militia in,
159, 163–65, 173–74, 188–91
Fitch, Thomas, 7, 33, 44, 191
Flatbush (NY), 163–64
Fort Saint Frédéric, 13–14
Franklin, Benjamin, 72, 137
French, 3, 27, 98
French, Christopher, 170–71, 182,
250n53, 250n61
French and Indian War, 7–10, 23, 28,
33, 112, 191, 239n3; costs of, 8, 42;
Crown Point campaign, 13–14, 27;
veterans of, 43, 125, 138, 143, 147,
171, 242n41

G
Gage, Thomas, 81–82, 88–90, 121, 131,
144, 146
gentility, 52, 61–62, 72–73, 106–7,
124, 140, 147–49, 186, 201,
244n55, 245n67
George III, King, 80–81, 109, 119, 146,
155, 196, 198
Great Awakening, 11, 16, 41
Great Britain: André honored in, 198, 200;
army (*see* British army) art, literature,
or culture of, 67, 71, 118, 148; calendar,
251n73; colonists from, 27–28;
economy or trade, 42–43, 45–47, 75,
85, 102, 109; loyalists move to, 193;
navy, 88, 117, 120, 131, 133–34,
137–38, 156, 171; negotiations with,
131, 134, 137; Parliament, 42–48,
69–70, 76, 80, 82, 92, 96, 109–10,
119, 194, 198; predicted to win war,
134, 141, 153, 157; religion in, 11, 39,
46, 194; Scovil visits, 38–39; treason
against, 96; Whigs in, 71. *See also*
British Empire
Greek, 53, 59, 73, 101
Green, Timothy, 102, 112
Greene, Nathanael, 137
Gridley, Isaac, 55, 97

H
Hale, Elizabeth, 20–22, 52
Hale, Enoch, 105, 131, 182–84, 197, 204,
244n58, 253n5; as clergyman, 53,
74, 97, 184; diary of, 132, 137, 149,
181, 183, 229n58, 245n64; letters to
or from Nathan, 111, 124, 133–34,
147, 149; at Yale, 51–54, 56, 62–63,
65, 69, 73–74, 97, 227n35, 229n58
Hale, James, 19, 21
Hale, Joseph, 183–84
Hale, Nathan: André compared to,
186–87, 198–201, 203–4; British
vs. American identity of, 5, 140; as
captain, 117, 122–26, 128–35, 202;
as captain in Boston area, 117–21; as
captain in New York, 132–33, 145;
captured, 145–46, 244n56; childhood
of, 9–12, 21, 25–26, 28, 52; described,
9, 145, 202; diary of, 4, 119–20, 123,
128, 132, 135, 183, 240n6, 240n12;
Dunbar compared to, 2, 4–6, 21–22,
157, 184; enlists, 115–16; executed,
2, 4, 146–49, 202; family learns of
death of, 181–82; final speech of, 5,
147–48; furlough in Connecticut of,
128–29; letters to or from, 4, 53, 147;
letters to or from family, 51, 65, 111,
124, 133–34, 147, 227n36; letters
to or from friends, 73, 101, 103–6,
108–12, 115–16, 122, 124, 130–31,
133, 183, 236n19; as martyr or hero,
2, 5, 197–99, 203–5; memory or
memorialization of, 197–205, 257n48;
romantic connections of, 108–9,
237n29; as schoolmaster, 97–103,
112, 115–16, 123; siblings of, 21, 114,
128, 183–84 (*see also* Hale, Enoch);
spy, 139–43, 145–47; at Yale, 51–56,
58, 60, 62–63, 65, 67–69, 72–74, 97,
103, 206
Hale, Richard, 9–10, 18–23, 25–26,
51–54, 65, 128, 182–83, 201, 219n40,
227n36, 228n48
Hale, Samuel (Nathan's cousin), 145–46,
181, 183, 187, 244n59

Hale, Samuel (Nathan's uncle), 98, 182, 219n37

Hale Monument Association, 204

Hall, Temperance. *See* Dunbar, Temperance

Hallams (Betsy, John, et al.), 103, 124

Hamilton, Alexander, 182, 186

Hancock, John, 136

Harlem Heights, 138–39, 141, 182

Harlem River, 138–39

Hartford (CT), 19, 28, 46–47, 54, 177–79, 189, 205, 207; jail, 169–72, 174–75, 182, 188; reaction to Stamp Act in, 43–44; reaction to Townshend Acts in, 46–47; Superior Court, 19, 165–66, 170

Harvard College, 22, 52, 54, 72, 98, 103

Harwinton (CT), 196, 206, 209

Havana, 125, 139

Heath, William, 139–40

Hebron (CT), 83, 111

Hempstead, Stephen, 141, 203, 243n46

Hillhouse, James, 56, 65, 105–6, 110, 112, 118

Howe, Richard, 131, 137, 157, 159, 163, 247n19

Howe, William, 131, 133, 135–37, 142, 144, 148, 157–59, 163–64, 186, 206, 247n19; Hale and, 145–46

Hubbard, Bela, 152, 160

Hudson River, 132, 185

Hull, William, 115, 122, 125, 128–29, 238n49; memoir by, 200, 203, 243n45, 244–45n62; military career of, 184–85, 253n9; misgivings of, 140–41, 145, 147, 182, 243n45; told of Hale's death, 148, 182

Huntington (NY), 141, 143

Huntington, Joseph, 9, 23, 53, 74, 102, 128, 184, 219n40

Huntington Bay, 157

Hutchinson, Thomas, 43, 76, 81

I

identity, 5, 16, 94, 140, 146, 186, 203–4

Independent Artillery Company, 112, 122, 237n39

Indians. *See* Native Americans

Ingersoll, Jared, 43, 70, 228n44, 228n50

Intolerable Acts, 80–81, 84, 109

J

James II, King, 10

Jarvis, Abraham, 45, 160, 178

Jefferson, Thomas, 202

Jerome, Chauncy, 92, 188, 191, 207, 209–10, 254n17, 255n26, 259n76

Jerome, Esther, 191, 209–10, 255n26. *See also* Dunbar, Esther Adams

Jerome, Phoebe (wife of Moses). *See* Dunbar, Phoebe

Jerome, Phoebe (wife of Zerubbabel), 32

Jerome, Timothy, 31–32, 221n8

Jerome, Zerubbabel, 30–34, 41, 49, 188, 210, 221–22n18, 251n68

Johnson, Samuel, 36, 38, 43, 45

Johnson, William Samuel, 43, 46–47

Jones, Thomas, 206, 258n63

Judd, Ebenezer, 80, 150, 155

K

Keyes, Stephen, 73, 115, 118, 129

King George's War, 25, 98

Knowlton, Thomas, 138–41, 147

L

Lake Champlain, 13, 171

Lake George, 13–14, 125

Latin, 51, 53, 59–60, 98, 100, 102–3, 108, 111, 141

Law, Richard, 112, 115, 238n47

Lebanon (CT), 43, 73, 82, 117, 192

Lee, Charles, 125, 132, 240n6

Lexington (MA), 88, 94, 113–14, 118

Linonia Society, 62–69, 72–73, 100, 104, 107, 115, 118, 181, 199, 227n26; Hales join, 62, 65; library of, 62–63, 72; meetings of, 63–64, 66–69, 105, 112, 140, 206, 228n42

Litchfield (CT), 191, 195

Little, William, 101, 235n10

Lockwood, James, 8–9, 57, 63

Long Island, 3, 54, 55, 151, 158–59, 247n19; Battle of, 135–37, 139, 145;

Dunbar in, 156–57, 159–61, 163, 248n31, 249n36; Hale in, 141–43, 145, 157, 203; people fleeing from or to, 141, 156–57, 159; recruits sought in, 144–45, 158–59, 164
Long Island Sound, 111, 157, 161, 163
Louisbourg, 25, 98
loyalists, 5–6, 197, 206–7; amnesty for, 190, 193; Anglicans as (*see under* Anglicans); anxiety about, 90, 164, 168, 187, 190, 193; attacks on, 93, 140, 153, 156, 187; in British army (*see under* British army); in Connecticut (*see under* Connecticut); emigration of, 5, 131, 193; Hale's cousin as, 146; in New York or Long Island, 141, 144–46, 157, 159, 168; numbers of, 94, 193, 233n48, 238n40, 247n20; prosecuted or laws against, 2, 95, 153–54, 161, 168, 193; rewarded, 160; as traitors, 2, 96, 161, 168, 178; views of, 92–94, 137. *See also* Tories
Lyman, Gershom, 73, 105, 108, 181
Lyman, Joseph, 70

M
Mackenzie, Frederick, 143, 147
Marsh, John, 177, 192
Marvin, Elihu, 73, 97, 100–1, 107, 110, 113, 118, 124, 130, 240n9
Massachusetts, 47, 85, 88, 114; Coercive/Intolerable Act and, 80–82; Hale family's links to, 18, 21, 53, 184; Hingham, 219n36, 220n43; legislature, 185; militia or soldiers, 95, 136, 201, 239n3; Northampton, 170, 172; Salem, 31; southeastern, 117; western, 12, 27
Massachusetts Government Act, 81
Mead, Thomas, 65, 106
Middletown (CT), 45, 97, 160, 170, 173, 178
Moland, Joseph, 171
Montresor, John, 147–48, 182, 186, 245n62
Munson, Aeneas, 198, 202, 256n46

N
Native Americans, 2–3, 19, 98, 144; Algonquian, 98; converted to Christianity, 8, 34, 61; Delaware, 33; in French and Indian War, 8, 13–14, 27; Iroquois, 33, 208; settlers vs., 12, 33–34
New Cambridge (CT): Anglicans in, 37, 39–41, 48, 77–79, 83, 86–87, 92–93, 152, 155, 162, 174, 188, 191, 194–95, 210, 222n26; Congregationalists in, 37, 41; Jeromes in, 31
New England, 7–8, 14, 214n3; education in, 60, 73, 99–100; families or marriage in, 20–25, 27, 29–30, 107, 156, 219n36, 220n43, 230n12; histories of, 200; land ownership in, 32; religion in, 36, 45, 94, 168; wages in, 53, 225n8
New Hampshire, 70, 79, 85, 94, 97–98, 182, 234n50. *See also* Claremont
New Haven (CT), 54, 63, 90–91, 110, 130, 160, 198, 205, 220n45, 232n37, 254n19; Alden in, 97, 100–1, 105, 124; Assembly meets in, 69, 161; British attack, 117, 160, 190; churches or clergy in, 16, 57, 151–52; Dunbar jailed in, 154–55; Yale in, 51, 53–55, 57, 67–69, 73, 160, 229n58
New Jersey, 3, 157, 160, 183
New Lights, 11, 36–37, 41, 44, 46
New London (CT), 43, 82, 89, 102–3, 129, 203, 205, 210, 235n13, 260n80; British attack on, 117, 190; committee of correspondence in, 109–10, 112; Hale in, 102–4, 106, 108–13, 115–18, 128, 132, 134; Hale writes to friends in, 122, 124; town meetings in, 109
New York, 3, 46, 104, 157, 160–61, 210; French and Indian War battles in, 13, 138; governors of, 187; upstate, 208; Westchester County, 163

New York City, 38, 43, 45, 76, 144, 146, 205; Americans retreat from, 138, 182; battles over or British in, 132–33, 136–39, 143–44, 148–49, 151, 156, 158–59, 168, 171, 185; Brooklyn Heights, 132, 135; Dunbar in, 156, 165, 173; fire in, 142–43, 146, 243n51; Hale in, 132, 142, 146, 181–82, 184 (*see also* Long Island: Hale in); Long Island (*see* Long Island); Manhattan, 132–33, 135–36, 138–39, 142–43, 145, 157; Sandy Hook, 133; Staten Island, 133, 137, 159; Stony Point, 185

Newbury (MA), 18–19

Newgate Prison, 154, 170

Nichols, James: as clergyman, 77–78, 83, 152, 191; Dunbar's children baptized by, 87, 180; as loyalist, 92, 174, 189, 191, 195, 238n40; at Yale, 57–58, 77, 227n26

Nook Hill, 130–31, 241n19

Northbury (CT), 28, 32, 150, 217n24; churches or parishes in, 9, 15–16, 18, 37, 39–41, 49, 77–79, 87, 196, 232n37; Dunbars in, 9, 15, 30, 35, 49, 87, 155; map, 17; militia, 89; Waterbury and, 15–16, 32, 37

North Carolina, 158

Norwalk (CT), 141, 157, 190

Norwich (CT), 43, 97, 102, 107, 110, 124, 132–33

O

Old Lights, 11, 37, 40–41, 44–46

Olive Branch Petition, 118–19

P

Paine, Thomas, 131

Peck, Epaphroditus, 207, 215n10, 258n64, 258n65

Pennsylvania, 3, 33, 70, 105, 136, 210; Wyoming Valley in, 12, 32, 34–35, 77

Peters, Samuel, 38–39, 83, 111

Philadelphia, 34, 45–46, 76, 80, 85, 137, 144, 187

Pond, Charles, 141–43

Pond, E. LeRoy, 207, 258n66

Pond, Jonathan, 92, 207

Poole, Betsey Adams, 108–9, 118, 124, 203, 237n29

Poole, Thomas, 109, 124

Portsmouth (NH), 78, 97–98, 182

power, 2, 11, 169, 179, 190

Pratt, Bela, 205

Princeton (college), 72

Princeton, battle of, 168, 185

Protestants, 8, 10 (*see also* Anglicans; Church of England; Congregationalists; Episcopalians)

Putnam, Israel, 125, 133, 135, 139, 143, 241n26

Q

Quartering Act, 81

R

rangers, 138–40, 143–45, 158

Revolutionary War, 2–6; British views of, 168; casualties in, 88, 118, 136, 253n4; as civil vs. imperial conflict, 3, 88, 91; heroes of, 197, 200–1, 204–7; as moral issue, 95; narratives about, 3, 200, 206–8; neutrality in, 3, 86, 89, 94, 96, 142, 189, 193, 197; nostalgia for, 202, 205–6; veterans of, 200–2, 208; Whig ideology and, 178

Revolutionary War battles: Bunker Hill, 90, 115, 118, 139, 205; Germantown and Monmouth, 185, 187; Harlem Heights, 138–39; Lexington and Concord, 88, 94, 113–14, 118; Long Island, 135–37, 139, 145; Saratoga, 185; Trenton and Princeton, 168, 185. *See also* Boston; New York City

Rhode Island, 10, 46, 82, 88, 90, 96, 104, 117, 120

Richards, Guy, 112

Richards, John, 103, 108, 116

rights, 34, 71, 84, 194; charter, 10, 91; colonists', 47, 72, 81, 84–85, 89, 93–94; freedom of speech, 90;

liberties and, 3, 81; property, 19; universal, 3

Robinson, William, 73, 97, 105, 130–31

Rogers, Robert, 143–45, 158, 242n41, 243n52, 244n53, 244nn55–56

Roman Catholics, 8

Roxbury (MA), 115, 117–18, 120, 129

Royce, Nehemiah, 86, 189

Rutledge, Edward, 137

S

Saltonstall, Gilbert, 103, 112, 118, 124, 130–32, 203, 240n8

Saltonstall, Gurdon, 103, 112

Sampson, Deborah, 201

Sampson, Ezra, 73, 115, 118, 129, 201

schools, 16, 26, 30, 49, 52, 86, 87, 97–103, 217–18n24

Scovil, James, 44–45, 49, 77–79, 83–84, 89, 151–52, 158, 160, 195, 230n4; Dunbars and, 37, 40–42, 48, 223n36; education and ordination, 37–39

Seabury, Samuel, 196, 248n27, 256n39

Selden, Ezra, 114–15, 118, 129

sermons, 7–10, 16, 53, 74, 83, 90, 151–52, 178, 184, 192

Simsbury (CT), 95, 154, 160, 170

Skene, Philip, 171

slavery, 3, 31, 221n8

smallpox, 39, 121, 131, 187, 209, 254n14

Smith, David, 162, 174, 176, 251n70

Smith, Joseph, 162, 174, 176–77, 251n70

Society for the Propagation of the Gospel in Foreign Parts (SPG), 39–40, 44, 46, 77–78, 94, 194–95, 223n36

Sons of Liberty, 43, 81, 83–84, 94–95, 111, 207

Spanish, 3, 7, 144

Spectator, The, 60, 62–63, 72

Spencer, Joseph, 125, 129

Stamp Act, 42–46, 69–70, 72, 76

Strong, Elizabeth. *See* Hale, Elizabeth

Strong, Elnathan, 181

Strong, Joseph, 20, 23, 181

Strong, Nathan, 51, 177–78, 252n78

Strong family, 23, 26, 28, 51–52, 56, 128, 181

Stuart, I. W., 203, 219n37, 238n47, 257n55

Sugar Act, 42, 70

Sullivan, John, 144

Superior Court (Hartford), 19, 47, 165–66, 170

Susquehannah Company, 12, 32–34, 44, 77, 210

T

Tallmadge, Benjamin, 73, 97, 101, 108, 114, 116, 118, 203, 229n58, 241n27, 257n50; military service of, 133, 135, 184–86

taxation, 8, 16, 69–70, 76, 81, 84, 91, 119, 158, 194; protests against, 42–43, 45–48; on tea, 46–47

tea, 46–47, 69, 75–77, 80, 83, 87, 89, 107, 109, 232n30. *See also* Boston Tea Party

Tea Act, 76, 83

Ticonderoga, 139, 162

Tiffany, Consider, 244n56, 244n57

Todd, Samuel, 9, 16, 18, 37, 41

Tories, 86–93, 95–96, 146, 193, 207; "confessions" by, 83, 87, 90, 92; legislation against, 95–96, 153–54, 161. *See also* loyalists

Townshend Acts, 46–47, 69–70, 76, 105

trade, 19, 42, 47, 102–3, 109–10, 120, 154

traitors, 4, 83, 96, 119, 153, 161, 169–70, 197, 207–8, 210

treason, 2, 144, 152–54, 165, 168–69, 172–75, 177, 190

Trumbull, Benjamin, 192

Trumbull, John, 60–61, 70–72, 224n52, 226n22

Trumbull, Jonathan, 77, 82–83, 91, 95, 117, 154, 168, 180, 190–91

Tryon, William, 158, 160, 187–88

Tuttle, Daniel, 162, 188, 248n32, 248n35, 249n42

Tuttle, Joel, 92, 162, 188, 254n17

U

U.S. Congress, 202, 204

Union School, 102–3, 112, 115, 123

United States of America, 3, 6, 117, 134, 154, 169–70, 173, 189, 194

V

Vermont, 195

Viets, Roger, 95, 160, 170–71, 176–77, 250n54

W

Wadsworth, Elisha, 169, 174–75, 250n54, 251n71

Waldo, John, 181

Wallingford (CT), 12–13, 15, 18, 27, 31, 36, 43, 83, 90, 95, 217n21

War of 1812, 201, 208

warships, 133, 134, 138. *See also* Great Britain: navy

Washington, George, 95–96, 125, 147, 152, 182, 192, 199–200; in Boston, 117–19, 122, 131; Continental Congress and, 117, 132, 136, 143–44; Hull and, 184–85; in New Jersey, 168; in New York, 132–44, 148, 157–58, 163, 249n40; subordinates and, 122–23; Tallmadge and, 185; troops needed by, 116–17, 123, 132, 180

Waterbury (CT), 15, 19, 32, 92, 207, 217n21, 217n22, 230n4; churches, clergy, or parishes in, 16, 18, 36–40, 49, 77–78, 84, 151–52, 160, 195–96, 230n4; committee of inspection in, 86–87, 90, 151, 154–56; Dunbars in, 9, 12–13, 15, 18, 26–27, 36, 48, 80, 151, 154–55, 165, 176, 180, 187, 216–17n14; loyalists in, 160, 162; map, 17; militia, 180, 187; Northbury and (*see under* Northbury)

Waterbury Daily American, 206, 215n10

Webb, Charles, 115, 117, 122, 128, 132, 182, 184, 202, 241n24, 243n44

West Indian, The, 67, 72

West Indies, 19, 32, 42, 102

Wethersfield (CT), 8–9, 97, 101, 104, 177, 182, 192

Whigs, 116, 180, 190, 207; in Connecticut, 83–85, 87, 89–94, 96, 110–11, 151–58, 162, 165; in Great Britain, 71–72; harassment by, 83–85, 87, 90–94, 110, 141, 152–56, 162, 174, 176, 188; ideology of, 71–72, 113, 119, 178, 224n50, 229n54; in Massachusetts, 81, 88; in New England, 87–88, 114

White Plains (NY), 163

Whitmore, Daniel, 172–73

Whitmore, Gurdon, 170–73, 250n54, 250nn61–62, 251n71

Williams, Ebenezer, 73, 97, 100–1, 106, 108, 113, 160

Williams, Ezekiel, 176–78

Windham (CT), 43, 82, 202

Windsor (CT), 74, 97, 104

Winter Hill, 118, 121, 124–26, 144, 147, 244n53

women, 2, 10, 29, 73, 92–93, 106–7, 214n3

Woodbridge, Joshua, 115, 118, 125

Wright, Asher, 129, 141, 183, 203, 240n15, 241n26, 243n46, 243n49

Wyllys, John Palsgrave, 65, 105, 118, 129, 182, 245n64

Y

Yale College, 77, 100, 228n44, 229n54; alumni, 9, 16, 38, 53, 70, 97–98, 103, 105, 107–10, 114–15, 118, 125, 128, 129, 158, 160, 181, 184, 203, 238n40, 238n46, 239n59; campus, 54, 160, 205; clubs (*see* Brothers in Unity; Linonia Society); cost of, 53; curriculum, 59–61; diploma carried by Hale, 141, 182; Hale at (*see under* Hale); loyalists from, 160, 238n40; military training of students, 110, 113; professors, tutors, or rectors, 36, 51–53, 56–58, 61, 63, 68, 70–72, 204, 207; protests at, 57, 69–70